Living in Britain

Results from the 2001 General Household Survey

Alison Walker
Maureen O'Brien
Joe Traynor
Kate Fox
Eileen Goddard
Kate Foster

London: TSO

ISBN 0 11 621574 7
ISSN 1469-2759

Contact points

For enquiries about this publication, contact Lesley Sanders:
Tel: 020 7533 5444
E-mail: **lesley.sanders@ons.gov.uk**

To order this publication, call TSO on **0870 600 5522**. See also back cover.

For general enquiries, contact the National Statistics Customer Enquiry Centre on **0845 601 3034**
(minicom: 01633 812399)
E-mail: **info@statistics.gov.uk**
Fax: 01633 652747
Letters: Room D115, Government Buildings, Cardiff Road, Newport NP10 8XG

You can also find National Statistics on the internet – go to **www.statistics.gov.uk**.

This report is available on the National Statistics website
www.statistics.gov.uk/lib

For further information about access to GHS data deposited at The Data Archive contact:

The Data Archive
University of Essex
Wivenhoe Park
Colchester
Essex CO4 3SQ

Tel: 01206 872001
Fax: 01206 872003
E-mail: **archive@essex.ac.uk**
Website: **www.data-archive.ac.uk**

About the Office for National Statistics

The Office for National Statistics (ONS) is the government agency responsible for compiling, analysing and disseminating many of the United Kingdom's economic, social and demographic statistics, including the retail prices index, trade figures and labour market data, as well as the periodic census of the population and health statistics. The Director of ONS is also the National Statistician and the Registrar General for England and Wales, and the agency administers the registration of births, marriages and deaths there.

A National Statistics publication

National Statistics are produced to high professional standards set out in the National Statistics Code of Practice. They undergo regular quality assurance reviews to ensure that they meet customer needs. They are produced free from any political interference.

Contents

Acknowledgements

We would like to thank everybody who contributed to the Survey and the production of this report. We were supported by our specialist colleagues in ONS who were responsible for sampling, fieldwork, coding and editing.

Our thanks also go to colleagues who supported us with administrative duties and during publication. Particular thanks are due to the interviewers who worked on the 2001 survey, and to all those members of the public who gave their time and co-operation.

1. **Harmonised outputs:** where appropriate, tables including marital status, living arrangements, ethnic groups, tenure, economic activity, accommodation type, length of residence and general health have adopted the harmonised output categories . However, where long established time series are shown, harmonised outputs may not have been used.

2. **Classification variables:** variables such as age and income, are not presented in a standard form throughout the report partly because the groupings of interest depend on the subject matter of the chapter, and partly because many of the trend series were started when the results used in the report had to be extracted from tabulations prepared to meet different departmental requirements.

3. **Nonresponse and missing information:** the information from a household which co-operates in the survey may be incomplete, either because of a partial refusal (eg to income), or because information was collected by proxy and certain questions omitted because considered inappropriate for proxy interviews (eg marriage and income data), or because a particular item was missed because of lack of understanding or an error.

Households who did not co-operate at all are omitted from all the analyses; those who omitted whole sections (eg marriages) because they were partial refusals or interviewed by proxy are omitted from the analyses of that section. The 'no answers' arising from omission of particular items have been excluded from the base numbers shown in the tables and from the bases used in percentaging. The number of 'no answers' is generally less than 0.5% of the total and at the level of precision used on GHS the percentages for valid answers are not materially affected by the treatment of 'no answers'.

Socio-economic group and income variables are the most common variables which have too many missing answers to ignore.

4. **Base numbers:** Very small bases have been avoided wherever possible because of the relatively high sampling errors that attach to small numbers. In general, percentage distributions are shown if the base is 50 or more. Where the base is 20-49, the percentages are shown in square brackets. For some analysis several years data have been combined to increase the sample size to enable appropriate analysis.

5. **Percentages:** A percentage may be quoted in the text for a single category that is identifiable in the tables only by summing two or more component percentages. In order to avoid rounding errors, the percentage has been recalculated for the single category and therefore may differ by one percentage point from the sum of the percentages derived from the tables.

The row or column percentages may add to 99% or 101% because of rounding.

6. **Conventions:** The following conventions have been used within tables:

.. data not available

- category not applicable

0 less than 0.5% or no observations

[] the numbers in square brackets are percentages on a base of 20-49. See note 4.

7. **Statistical significance:** Unless otherwise stated, changes and differences mentioned in the text have been found to be statistically significant at the 95% confidence level.

8. **Mean:** Throughout the report the arithmetic term 'mean' is used rather than 'average'. The mean is a measure of the central tendency for continuous variables, calculated as the sum of all scores in a distribution, divided by the total number of scores.

9. **Weighting:** All percentages and means presented in the tables in the substantive chapters are based on data weighted to compensate for differential nonresponse. Both the unweighted and weighted bases are given. The unweighted base represents the number of people/households interviewed in the specified group. The weighted base gives a grossed up population estimate in thousands. Trend tables show unweighted and weighted figures for 1998 to give an indication of the effect of the weighting. For the weighted data (1998, 2000 and 2001) the weighted base (000's) is the base for percentages. Unweighted data (up to 1998) are based on the unweighted sample.

Missing answers are excluded from the tables and in some cases this is reflected in the weighted bases, ie these numbers vary between tables. For this reason, the bases themselves are not recommended as a source for population estimates. Recommended data sources for population estimates for most socio-demographic groups are: ONS mid-year estimates, the Labour Force Survey, or Housing Statistics from the Office of the Deputy Prime Minister. See Appendix D for details regarding the revision of the 2001 mid-year estimates.

Chapter 1

Introduction

The General Household Survey (GHS) is a multi-purpose continuous survey carried out by the Social Survey Division of the Office for National Statistics (ONS) which collects information on a range of topics from people living in private households in Great Britain. The survey started in 1971 and has been carried out continuously since then, except for breaks in 1997/98 (when the survey was reviewed) and 1999/2000 when the survey was re-developed.

An overview of the General Household Survey

The main aim of the survey is to collect data on a range of core topics, comprising: household and family information; housing tenure and household accommodation; consumer durables including vehicle ownership; employment; education; health and use of health services; smoking and drinking; family information including marriage, cohabitation and fertility; income; and demographic information about household members including migration. The information is used by government departments and other organisations for planning, policy and monitoring purposes, and to present a picture of households, families and people in Great Britain.

The GHS has documented the major changes in households, families and people which have occurred over the last 30 years. These include the decline in average household size and the growth in the proportion of the population who live alone, the increase in the proportion of families headed by a lone parent and in the percentage of people who are cohabiting. It has also recorded changes in housing, such as the growth of home ownership, and the increasing proportion of homes with household facilities and goods such as central heating, washing machines, and, more recently, home computers and access to the internet. The survey also monitors trends in the prevalence of smoking and drinking.

Fieldwork for the GHS is conducted on a financial year basis[1], with interviewing taking place continuously throughout the year. A sample of approximately 13,000 addresses is selected each year from the Postcode Address File. All adults aged 16 and over are interviewed in each responding household. Demographic and health information is also collected about children in the household. For 2001/2, the survey response rate was 72%, with an achieved sample size of 8989 households and 21180 people of all ages (see Appendix B).

The survey is sponsored by ONS, the Department of Health, the Office of the Deputy Prime Minister and the Department of Transport (formerly DTLR), the Department of Culture, Media and Sport, the Department for Work and Pensions, the Inland Revenue, the Department for Education and Skills, the Scottish Executive, the Government Actuary's Department, and a public sector organisation, the Health Development Agency.

The 2001/2 survey

The General Household Survey was 30 years old in 2001. To mark this occasion a 'birthday' leaflet was produced for respondents telling them about the survey and the policy changes it had affected and asking them to join more than half a million others who had already taken part. The 2001/2 survey was the second year of fieldwork following the introduction of the recommendations of the 1997 review.

Content of the interview

Following the 1997 review, the survey was re-launched from April 2000 with a different design. The relevant development work and the changes made are described in the report of the 2000 survey.[2]

The GHS now consists of two elements: the Continuous Survey and Trailers. The Continuous Survey is to remain unchanged for the five-year period April 2000-March 2005, apart from essential changes to take account of, for example, changes in benefits and pensions. It consists of a household questionnaire, to be answered by the Household Reference Person (see Appendix A) or spouse, and an individual questionnaire to be completed by all adults aged 16 and over resident in the household. The household questionnaire covers the following topics:

- demographic information about household members
- household and family information
- household accommodation
- housing tenure

- consumer durables including vehicle ownership
- migration.

The individual questionnaire includes sections on:

- employment
- pensions
- education
- health and use of health services
- smoking
- drinking in the last seven days
- family information including marriage, cohabitation and fertility history
- income.

The GHS has retained its modular structure, which allows a number of trailers to be included each year to a plan agreed by sponsoring Departments.Trailers included in 2001/2 survey were:

- people aged 65 and over
- mobility aids
- usual alcohol consumption in the last 12 months.

People aged 65 and over

Questions specifically designed to cover aspects of the lives of older people have been included in the survey in 1980, 1985, 1991, 1994 and 1998.[3] The module of questions asks people aged 65 and over about their living circumstances, their health, their ability to perform a range of domestic and other tasks, and the use they make of health and social services. The information collected has enabled the GHS to present regular snapshots of older people's lives and to examine how they have changed over the years. The results are presented in a separate report to be published in 2003.

Mobility aids

Questions about difficulties with mobility and the possession of mobility aids were first asked on the GHS in 1993 and were repeated in 1996. The aim was to provide estimates of the proportion of people who need aids to get about, and also the proportion of aids that people have but do not use. The results are presented in Chapter 10.

Usual alcohol consumption in the last 12 months

The continuous element of the GHS includes questions about alcohol consumption on the heaviest day during the week prior to interview. These questions were introduced in 1998 following the publication, in 1995, of an inter-departmental review of drinking (see Chapter 9). Also included in 1998 was the measure which had been in use since 1984 based on average weekly consumption over the past year. During the review of the GHS it was agreed that because of the need to control the length of the interview, the data required to continue this trend series would continue to be collected every two years in the form of a trailer starting in 2000/1. However, capacity was available in the 2001/2 interview and so this trailer was retained.

Changes to classification variables

In line with National Statistics guidelines and to maintain a harmonised approach to data collection and outputs, in particular with respect to the census, the GHS, along with other major Government surveys, introduced the new socio-economic and ethnic classification questions and their associated outputs for the 2001 survey. This has had major implications for the analysis and presentation of these data.

The new socio-economic classification: NS-SEC

From 2001 the National Statistics Socio-economic Classification (NS-SEC) is being used for all official statistics and surveys. It replaces Social Class based on occupation and Socio-economic Groups (SEG).

This change has been agreed by the National Statistician following a major review of government social classifications commissioned in 1994 by the Office of Population Censuses and Surveys (now the Office for National Statistics) and carried out by the Economic and Social Research Council.

NS-SEC is an occupationally based classification but has rules to provide coverage of the whole adult population. The information required to create NS-SEC is occupation coded to the unit groups (OUG) of the Standard Occupational Classification 2000 (SOC2000) and details of employment status (whether an employer, self-employed or employee; whether a supervisor; number of employees at the workplace). Similar information was previously required for Social Class and SEG. The full classification comprises 17 classes. There are three harmonised reduced versions, with eight, five and three classes (for the eight class version, the first class can be subdivided). A major change from SEG is that there is no longer a manual/non-maunal split. See Appendix E for more details.

The report presents the new categories of NS-SEC in all tables where previously SEG was used. In general we have used the eight category version and where tables were previously presented for the manual /non-manual groups we have used the three category version of NS-SEC. This clearly is not appropriate for the time series tables. Figures for the current year data are presented classified by NS-SEC. A supplement will be published soon after the completion of this report containing analyses investigating the effect of this change on time series data. This supplement will focus on smoking and drinking for which the GHS is an important source of socio-economic time series data.

Classification of ethnic groups

In order to improve the relevance of the ethnicity classification to the changing nature of the ethnic composition of the population, the new classification has introduced a separate category for people from mixed ethnic backgrounds. In the previous system, people with these backgrounds had to select a specific ethnic group or categorise themselves as 'other'. Analysis conducted on the Labour Force Survey (see Appendix E) showed that it is not possible to map from the old to the new classification.

In terms of analysis by ethnic group, the GHS sample has always been too small to analyse single year data. Previously the data have been added across three years to produce large enough sample sizes, but with the change in classification it is no longer possible to do this. The Labour Force Survey, with its considerably larger sample size, has, for some time, been the recommended source for minority ethnic group data, much of which is published in Social Trends each year.[4] For these reasons, the 2001 report of the GHS does not present analyses by ethnic group. In 2002, when two years of data are available using the new classification, ethnic analyses will be re-considered.

National identity

There has been interest in UK national identities to inform servece and policy needs. In recognition of these requirements ONS recommended a second dimension of national group information based on the following categories: English, Scottish, Welsh, Irish, British and Other. The GHS adopted this proposal and included this question in the 2001/2 questionnaire. Respondents were able to choose more than one category. The results are presented in Chapter 3.

Weighting and grossing

A major methodological change introduced for the new survey in 2000 was the introduction of weighting and grossing. A full description of this can be found in the 2000 report with additional technical papers on the website.

A dual weighting scheme was introduced. First, weighting to compensate for non-response in the sample based on known under-coverage in the Census-linked study of non-response[5] (Foster, 1994). Second, the (weighted) sample has been weighted (grossed) up to match known population distributions (as used in the Labour Force Survey). The substantive chapters of the report present data for 2001/2 in weighted form only. For further details of the weighting see Appendix D. Details of presentation of the data in report tables can be found in 'Notes to tables'.

The results from the 2001 Census, published on 30 September 2002, showed that previous estimates of the total UK population were around one million too high, with disparities being most apparent among men aged 25 to 39. These disparities were larger than expected and thus have two implications for figures presented in this report:

- some of the percentages may need revision as they are based on old population figures
- the weighted bases will all change to some degree because of the reduction in estimated population size.

Thus, for this 2001 report the general caution regarding the use of weighted bases is reiterated. Weighted bases should primarily be considered as bases for the percentages shown rather than estimates of population size.

Revised GHS data will be released in Spring 2003, focussing on results where percentage estimates have been affected. For more details about the revised census-based estimates see www.statistics.gov.uk/census2001.

Inclusion of extra households

Each year on the GHS there are a small proportion of responding households where one or more members do not complete the individual questionnaire. For these households there is a complete set of data at household level and a full individual interview for at least one adult in the household. Prior to 2001, these households were excluded from the analysis which resulted in the loss of some data each year. From 2001, these households are included in the analysis. This serves to increase both the household sample size and the individual sample size. The effect on the non-response weighting, which was calculated based on a responding sample which excluded these households, was judged to be negligible since the numbers involved are small (around 240 households).

It should be noted that the response rate quoted for 2001/2 excluded these households to provide direct comparison with previous years. See Appendix B for full details.

Disseminating the results

Following the successful publication of the GHS 2000 'Living in Britain' report as the first major ONS report to be published as a web designed publication, we have continued to use this format for the 2001 report. As was the case for the 2000 report, a hard copy is also available.

Content of the report

The report is based on the data collected by the GHS in 2001/2 and provides information across a wide range of topics. Also included are a number of tables presenting data on trends and changes measured by the GHS since it began.
The main analysis is presented in Chapters 2-10.

- Chapter 2 presents an overview of change
- Chapters 3 to 10 cover information relating to the different topics included in the GHS.

Technical information is provided in the appendices. These include:

- a glossary of definitions and terms used throughout the report and notes on how these have changed over time (A)
- information about the sample design and response (B)
- sampling errors (C)
- weighting and grossing (D)
- a description of the changes to social classifications (E)
- the household and individual questionnaires used in 2001, excluding self-completion forms and prompt cards (F)
- a list of the main topics covered by the survey since 1971 (G)
- a list of tables in the report (H).

The availability of unpublished data

Unpublished GHS data can be made available to researchers, for a charge, if resources are available, and provided that confidentiality of informants is preserved. Any work based on the GHS data is the responsibility of the individuals concerned, but ONS should be given the opportunity to comment in advance on any report or paper using GHS data, whether prepared for publication or for a lecture, conference or seminar.

In addition, copies of GHS datasets are available for specific research projects, subject to similar conditions, through the Data Archive at the University of Essex.[6]

Notes and references

1 Prior to 1988 fieldwork was conducted on a calendar year basis.
2 Walker A et al *Living in Britain Results from the 2000 General Household Survey* TSO London 2002 also available on the web: www.statistics.gov.uk/lib
3 Results for the 1980 and 1985 surveys were reported in the GHS 1980 and 1986 (not 1985) Reports respectively, for the 1991 survey in *People aged 65 and over: Series GHS no.22 Supplement A*, and for the 1994 survey in *Living in Britain: Results from the 1994 General Household Survey.* Some of the questions from the elderly module were included in the 1996 GHS questionnaire, and reported on in the health chapter of *Living in Britain: Results from the 1996 General Household Survey.*
4 Matheson J and Babb P (eds) *Social Trends 2002.* 32nd edition. TSO London 2002.
5 Foster, K (1994) *The General Household Survey report of the 1991 census-linked study of survey non-respondents.* OPCS (*unpublished paper*).
6 For further information, contact:
Data Archive
University of Essex
Wivenhoe Park
Colchester
Essex
CO4 3SQ
Tel: 01206 872 001
Fax: 01206 872 003
e-mail: archive@essex.ac.uk

Chapter 2

A summary of changes over time

The GHS was 30 years old in 2001. Over the past 30 years it has monitored changes in the demographic, social and economic characteristics of households, families and people in Great Britain. Among the key changes which have been measured by the survey during this time are:

- a decline in household size and changes in household composition
- a growth in the proportion of lone-parent families
- an increase in the proportion of people living alone
- an increase in the proportion of people who are cohabiting
- an increase in home ownership and a decline in the proportion of households living in social housing
- an increase in the household availability of consumer durables
- an increase in the prevalence of self-reported longstanding illness or disability
- a decline in the prevalence of smoking
- changes in the proportion of respondents belonging to occupational pension schemes.

This chapter presents an overview of some of the main changes which the GHS has measured between 1971 and 2001. More detailed analyses of life in Britain in 2001 are given in subsequent chapters. Changes and additions to question wording mean that the time period for which information is available varies between topics. The introduction of weighting for non-response in 2000 had a small effect on some of the trend data. Details can be found in Appendix D. The introduction of the new National Statistics Socio-economic Classification (NS-SEC) in 2001 has also affected the presentation of time series data. Details can be found in Appendix E.

Households

Over the last 30 years, household size has declined from an average of 2.91 persons in 1971 to 2.48 in 1991. It continued to decline, though at a slower rate, throughout the nineties, to 2.33 in 2001, representing no statistically significant change since 2000.

There have also been marked changes in household composition, with increases in the proportion of one-person households, and of households headed by a lone parent. Between 1971 and 2001, the proportion of one-person households overall has almost doubled, from 17% to 31%, and the proportion consisting of one person aged 16-59 has tripled, from 5% to 15%. The proportion of people aged 65 and over living alone has remained stable since the mid 80s but, among those aged 25 to 44, the proportion increased from 5% in 1985 to 12% in 2001.

The proportion of households containing a married or cohabiting couple with dependent children declined from 31% of all households in 1979 to 25% in 1991 and then decreased more gradually to 22% in 2001. Households with dependent children headed by a lone parent showed the reverse trend, rising from 4% of all households in 1979, to 7% in 1993 and remaining at this level thereafter.

Families with dependent children

Changes in *family* composition show the same pattern as those in *household* composition, Thus, there has been a steady decline in the proportion of families with dependent children headed by a married or cohabiting couple and a corresponding increase in the proportion headed by a lone parent. Whereas couple families accounted for 92% of all families in 1971, they comprised 78% of families in 1993 and 75% in 2001. Most of the growth in lone-parent families has been among lone mothers, lone-father families accounting for 1-3% of all families throughout the lifetime of the GHS. The proportion of families headed by a lone mother rose from 7% in 1971 to 22% in 2001. The proportion headed by a single (never-married) mother increased from 1% in 1971 to 10% in 2001 while the proportion headed by a divorced, separated or widowed mother rose from 6% to 12%, during the same period.

People

Over the last 30 years, the proportion of people aged 75 and over[1] almost doubled from 4% in 1971 to 7% in 1991 but has shown no change since then, while the proportion of those aged less than 16 declined from 25% to 20%.

National identity

In most of its 30 years the GHS has introduced new measures to reflect changes in society. In 2001, a new question on national identity was introduced. People were able to choose one or more categories

from the following list: English, Scottish, Welsh, Irish, British, Other. For more details see Appendix E. Forty nine per cent of people described themselves as one of: English, Scottish, Welsh or Irish; 31% described themselves as British only; and 15% described themselves as British and English, Scottish, Welsh or Irish. Five per cent gave an 'other' identity and 1% gave other combinations. Future surveys will be able to measure the changing trends in people's assessment of their national identity.
Chapter 3

Housing tenure

There has been a marked increased in home ownership over the last 30 years. About a half of all households were owner occupiers in 1971. This proportion increased to about two thirds by the late 1980s since when the increase has levelled off and, in 2001, 68% of households were owner occupiers. There was a corresponding decline in the 1980s in the proportion of households living in social housing, from about a third to about a quarter of all households. These opposing trends are partly attributable to the 'Right to buy' legislation in the early 1980s. The downward trend in the number of council tenants continued during the 1990s as council properties in some areas were transferred to housing associations (now more correctly described as 'Registered Social Landlords' or 'RSLs'). Thus, between 1989 and 2001, the proportion of council tenants decreased from 24% to 15% while the proportion renting from a housing association rose from 2% to 6% .

Cars

Car ownership has risen over the lifetime of the GHS with the greatest rate of increase in the 1970s and 1980s. The proportion of households with access to a car or van rose from 52% in 1972 to 59% in 1981 rising to 68% in 1991 and then to 72% in 2001. The proportion of households with two or more cars tripled, from 9% in 1972 to 28% in 2001.

Consumer durables

The availability of some consumer goods, such as televisions, has always been high, and is now almost universal. Others started at relatively high levels in 1972, and quickly became even more widespread; for example, 73% of households had a refrigerator in 1972, a proportion which had risen to 92% by the end of the 1970s. Other household amenities and items were available to only a minority of households when the GHS first asked about them, but are now widespread. For example, whereas only 37% of households had central heating and 42% a telephone in 1972, the proportions had risen to 92% and 98% respectively by 2001. The proportion of households with access to more recently introduced items, such as microwave ovens, tumble driers and dishwashers is still growing.

Household access to some entertainment items has been particularly rapid. In 1983, 18% of households had a video recorder, a proportion which had risen to 88% in 2001. The availability of CD players rose more than five-fold from 15% of households in 1989 to 80% in 2001. More recently, between 1998 and 2001 there were sharp increases in the availability of home computers, from 34% to 50%, and satellite, cable and digital television receivers, from 29% to 42%. Internet access at home was measured for the first time in the GHS in 2000, when a third (33%) of all households where found to have such access. This had risen to two fifths (40%) by 2001.
Chapter 4

Marriage and cohabitation

Much of the longer term trend data about marriage and cohabitation in the GHS refers to women aged 18 to 49. Between 1979 and 2001, the proportion of women aged 18 to 49 who were married declined from nearly three quarters (74%) to a half (50%). In contrast, over the same period, the proportion of single women in this age group doubled from 18% to 36%.

Among single women aged 18 to 49, the proportion who were cohabiting at the time of interview had more than quadrupled, from less than one in ten (8%) in 1979 to over a third (35%) in 2001. The proportion of divorced women who were cohabiting rose from one in five (20%) in 1979 to a third (33%) in 2001.
Chapter 5

Pensions[2]

Between 1989 and 2001 the proportion of full-time male employees belonging to their employer's scheme decreased from 64% to 54% reflecting to some extent the decline in the proportion of employees who were offered a pension by their employer. Over the same period, participation in employer schemes among full-time female employees rose slightly from 55% to 58% and among female part-time employees the level more than doubled from 15% to 33%. This upward trend among female employees is partly the result of an increase in the proportion of women joining a scheme provided by their employer and, particulary for part-time employees, partly due to an increase in the proportion of employers providing such a scheme.
Chapter 6

Self-reported illness

The prevalence of self-reported longstanding illness has increased over the lifetime of the GHS rising from 21% of adults and children in 1972 to 32% in 2001. The proportion reporting a longstanding illness increased steadily during the 1970s but has since fluctuated between 29% and 35%, with no clear pattern over time. The prevalence of limiting longstanding illness has shown a similar trend although the overall increase has been smaller: the proportion reporting a condition which limited their activities rose from 15% in 1975 to 19% in 2001. Reports of chronic sickness are based on respondents' own assessments; increases in prevalence may reflect increased expectations which people have about their health as well as changes in the actual prevalence of sickness.

The proportions reporting an acute sickness in the 14 days before interview also increased in the 1970s, from 8% of adults and children in 1972 to 12% in 1981. Prevalence remained fairly stable during the 1980s but then increased slightly in the early 1990s to 16% in 1996 and has since shown a slight decline to 14% in 2001.

Use of health services

The upward trends in the prevalence of chronic and acute conditions have been accompanied by an increase in the use of some health services. The proportion of adults and children who had seen a GP in the 14 days prior to interview rose from 12% in 1972 to a peak of 17% in 1993. It fell to 14% in 1998 and has remained at around that level. Similar patterns were seen for trends in hospital outpatient and day-patient rates. Thus, the proportion of people visiting an outpatient or casualty department at least once in the three months prior to interview rose from 10% in 1972 to 16% in 1998 and then declined slightly to 14% in 2001, while the proportion attending as a day-patient in the 12 months prior to interview increased from 4% in 1992 to 7% in 1998 and then remained at that level. The proportion reporting an inpatient stay in the 12 months prior to interview has fluctuated between 8% and 10% since 1982 when it was first monitored.

Chapter 7

Mobility

In 2001, 8% of adults reported having difficulties with getting around their home and/or going out of doors and walking down the road without assistance. This was the same proportion as in 1993 and 1996 when the questions were last asked.

Chapter 10

Smoking

The prevalence of cigarette smoking fell substantially in the 1970s and the early 1980s - from 45% in 1974 to 35% in 1982. The rate of decline then continued more slowly until the early 1990s since when it has levelled out at 27-28%. In 2001, 27% of people aged 16 and over were smokers.

In the 1970s, men were much more likely than women to be smokers - in 1974, for example, 51% of men, compared with 41% of women, smoked cigarettes. Since then, the difference in smoking prevalence between men and women has reduced, although it has not disappeared completely. In 2001, 28% of men and 26% of women were cigarette smokers.

Throughout the 1990s, the prevalence of cigarette smoking was highest among people aged 20 to 24. Since 2000, however, there has been no statistically significant difference between prevalence levels among this age group and those aged 25 to 34.

The GHS has consistently shown that cigarette smoking is considerably more prevalent among people in manual groups than among those in non-manual groups. In the 1970s and 1980s, the prevalence of cigarette smoking fell more sharply among those in non-manual than in manual groups. In the 1990s there was little further change in the relative proportions smoking cigarettes until 2000, when, compared with 1998, there was a fall of two percentage points in the prevalence of smoking among those in manual socio-economic groups. The new NS-SEC (see Appendix E) does not allow categories to be collapsed into broad non-manual and manual groupings. However, as was the case with the groupings used previously, prevalence was lowest among those in the managerial and professional households (19%) and highest, at 33%, among those in routine or manual households.

Chapter 8

Drinking

Two measures of alcohol consumption are used in this report (one daily-based and the other weekly-based) reflecting the move from weekly to daily-based guidelines from the Department of Health in 1995. Thus, long term trend data is currently available only for the weekly-based measures. However, 2001 was the third year in which the questions relating to maximum daily amount were asked.

Maximum daily amount drunk last week

There were no significant changes between 1998 and 2001 in the proportions of men and women who had exceeded the recommended number of daily units on at least one day in the week prior to interview. However, there was an increase in heavy drinking among women: the proportion of women who had drunk more than 6 units on at least one day in the previous week rose from 8% in 1998 to 10% in 2000 and remained at that level in 2001.

Weekly alcohol consumption level

During the 1990s there was a slight increase in overall alcohol consumption among men and a much more marked one among women, but in 2001, there was evidence of a slight decline in terms of the proportion of men drinking more than 21 units a week and of women drinking more than 14 units a week. Thus, for men there was no difference between the proportions drinking more than 21 units a week in 1992 and 2001 (26% and 27%) but there was still a marked increase in the proportion of women drinking more than 14 units per week; from 11% in 1992 to 15% in 2001. Among women aged 16 to 24, the proportion drinking more than 14 units rose from 17% in 1992 to 31% in 2001 and their average weekly consumption nearly doubled (7.3 to 14.0 units) over the same period. **Chapter 9**

Notes and references

1 The GHS interviews all people aged 16 and over in private households. This means that the population figures presented here do not include those living in institutions and residential homes.
2 The GHS has included questions on pensions from time to time since 1971. A change in July 1988 in the rules governing personal pension arrangements means, however, that a strictly comparable time series on occupational pensions can only be presented from 1988.

Chapter 3

Households, families and people

The GHS has provided data about households, families and people for thirty years. This chapter looks at how the composition of households and families has changed during this time and describes the socio-economic groups, ethnic origin and national identity of the people within these households.

Tables in this chapter look at three different levels of data: households and the families and the people who comprise households.

Household size and composition

- During the 30 years since the GHS began in 1971, there has been a clear downward trend in mean household size. Between 1971 and 1981 household size declined steadily from 2.91 in 1971 to 2.70 in 1981. The decline continued throughout the next decade, falling to 2.48 by 1991. Since then household size has continued to fall, though at a slower rate, to 2.33 in 2001, representing no statistically significant change since 2000.
- Just over three in ten households contained one person only[1] (31%), while a little over a third contained two people (34%) and 35% consisted of three or more people.
- Just over a quarter of households (27%) included children aged under 16, which was similar to the 26% found in 2000 but considerably less than 30 years ago, when households containing children were almost two fifths (39%) of the total.
- In 2001 30% of households comprised one or two adults aged 60 or over.

Tables 3.1-3.2, Figures 3A-3B

Figure 3A **Mean household size: Great Britain, 1971-2001**
(data not available for 1997 and 1999)

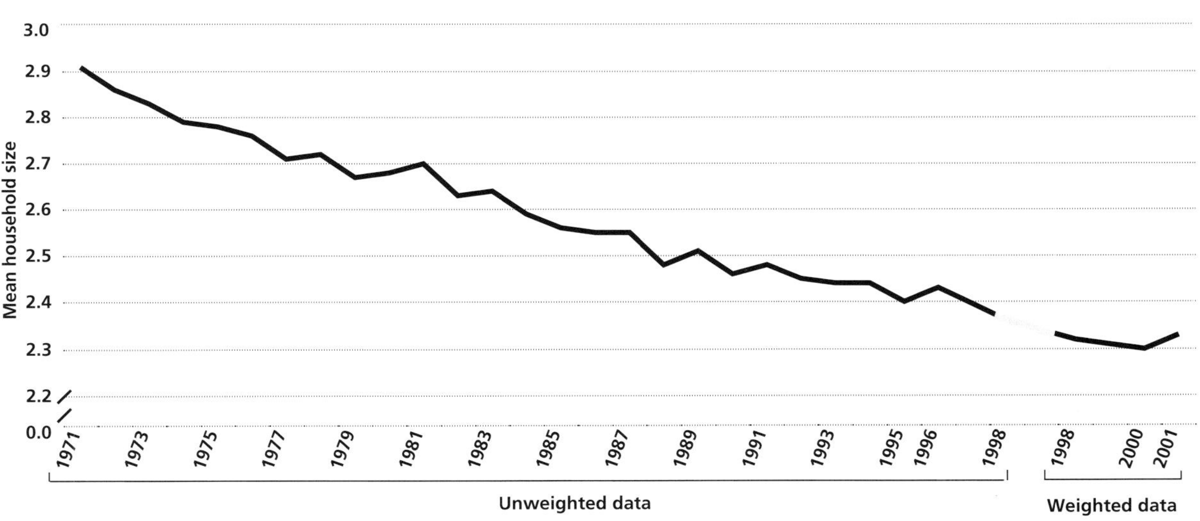

Figure 3B **Households by type of household: Great Britain, 1979 and 2001**

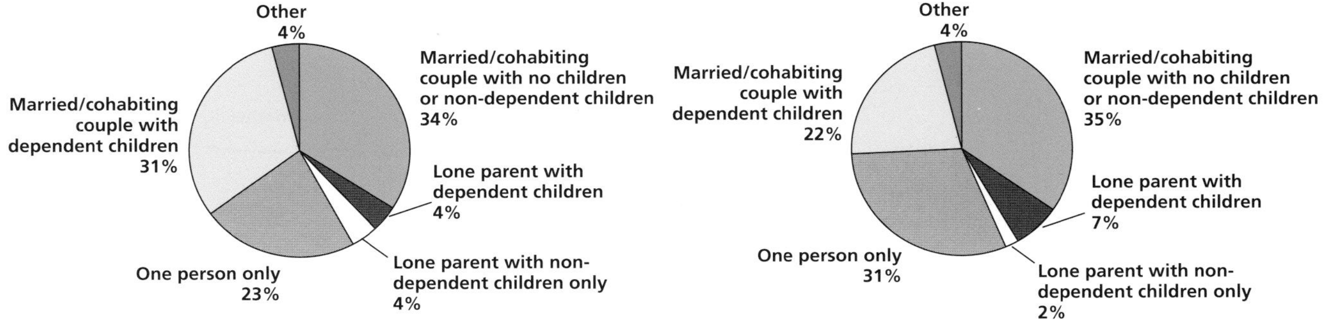

One person households

The proportion of one person households has almost doubled since 1971 from 17% in that year to 31% in 2001. This increase has played an important part in reducing the overall average household size. The proportion of households containing one adult aged 16 to 59 was 15%, which was no different from 2000 but represents a threefold increase since the GHS began, from 5% in 1971.

Tables 3.1-3.2, Figures 3A-3B

Among adults aged 16 and over, 16% lived alone in 2001, not statistically significantly different from the proportion in 2000. During the 1970s and 1980s, there was a continuing upward trend in the proportion of adults living alone, but there has been little change over the past decade, other than a small increase in the late 1990s.

The likelihood of living alone increased with age, with 49% of people aged 75 and over[2] living alone compared with 12% of those aged 25 to 44. Among people under 45, men were more likely than women to live alone; 15% did so compared with 5% of women. The situation was reversed for those aged 75 and over. Among women in this age group, 59% lived alone compared with 32% of men. The proportion of people aged 65 and over living alone has remained relatively stable since the mid 1980s. Among people aged 25 to 44, the proportion living alone has increased from 2% in 1971 to 12% in 2001, although there has been no change since 1998.

Tables 3.3-3.4

Households containing two or more adults without dependent children

There has been little change since the late 1970s in the proportion of households containing two or more adults without dependent children.

- In 2001, 37% of households comprised two or more adults without dependent children. The same proportion was found in 1979.
- The proportion of households consisting of a married or cohabiting couple with no children of any age has remained stable from the late 1970s to 2001 at around 28%.
- The proportion of households containing two or more unrelated adults has also remained stable (3% in both 1979 and 2001).
- The proportion of households consisting of a married or cohabiting couple with non-dependent (adult) children only has varied slightly since the late 1970s but has remained consistently at 6% since the mid 1990s.
- Only 2% of households comprised lone parents with non-dependent (adult) children, which represents a slow decline from 4% in 1979.

Table 3.5

Households and families with dependent[3] children

The proportion of households containing a married or cohabiting couple and dependent children has shown considerable change over the last three decades. At the beginning of the 1980s around 30% of households consisted of a married or cohabiting couple and dependent children. This had declined to 25% by 1991. In 2001, 22% of households in Britain contained a married or cohabiting couple and dependent children representing no statistically significant change from 21% in 2000. The proportion of households comprising a cohabiting couple with dependent children has remained steady at 3% since 1996, while the proportion of married couples with dependent children has declined from 23% to 18% over this period. **Table 3.5**

Figure 3C **Families with dependent children by family type: Great Britain, 1971-2001**
(data is not available for 1972, 1974, 1976, 1980, 1982, 1997 and 1999)

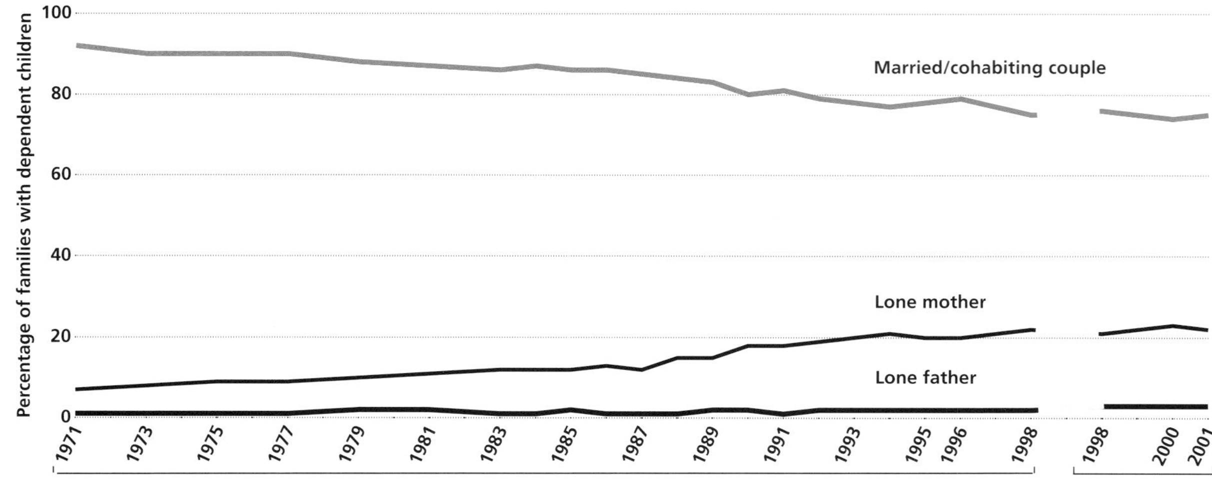

Seven per cent of households contained a lone parent and dependent children in 2001, as in 2000. In 1979 this group represented 4% of households. It increased slowly to 7% in 1993 since when there has been no change. **Table 3.5**

Table 3.5 showed that lone parents with dependent children formed 7% of the total household population. Table 3.6 looks just at families with dependent children. It shows that a quarter of all families with dependent children was headed by a lone parent, 22% being lone mothers and 3% lone fathers. There has been a substantial increase in the proportion of families headed by a lone parent over the thirty years since the survey began. In 1971 they were 8% of all families with dependent children. This proportion had risen to 24% by 1998, and has remained around that level.

In 1971, previously married lone mothers headed 6% of families with dependent children, compared with 1% of lone mothers who had never married. By 2001 both groups of lone mothers had increased, but there was less difference between the proportions who were single and those who were previously married; 12% of families with dependent children were headed by previously married lone mothers, compared with 10% who had not been married. **Table 3.6, Figure 3C**

Dependent children

Table 3.7 examines the variation in the proportion of dependent children living in different types of family. In 2001, 77% of dependent children lived in a married or cohabiting couple family and 23% in a lone parent family compared with 88% and 12% respectively in 1981.

Twenty four percent of dependent children were the only dependent child in their family in 2001 compared with 18% in 1972. **Table 3.7**

Among families with dependent children, the average number of dependent children has remained relatively stable since 1981. In 2001, the average numbers of children in married couple families, at 1.9, was a little higher than those in cohabiting couple families and lone parent families (1.6 and 1.7 respectively). Overall, the mean number of children in households containing dependent children has fallen from 2.0 in 1971 to 1.8 in 2001. **Table 3.8**

Age of youngest child

Families headed by a lone parent were less likely to have a child under five than married or cohabiting couple families (35% compared with 41%).[4]

The dependent children of lone fathers were more likely to be older than those of lone mothers or married and cohabiting couples:

- in almost three-fifths (59%) of families headed by a lone father the youngest dependent child was aged 10 or over, compared with 31% of lone mother families and 32% of the families of couples;
- in 18% of families headed by a lone father the youngest child was under five, compared with 36% of families headed by lone mothers, and 41% of two-parent families. **Table 3.9**

Step-families

People aged 16 to 59 were asked whether they had any stepchildren living with them. As in previous years, the great majority of stepfamilies consisted of those with one or more children from the woman's previous relationship:

- 83% consisted of a couple with a child or children from the woman's previous relationship;
- 9% were a couple with at least one child from the man's previous relationship;
- 8% were families containing children from previous relationships of both partners.

Table 3.10

Household income

There were substantial differences in gross weekly household income between different types of families with dependent children.

- Married couples with children had the highest incomes. Six out of ten of these families (61%) had household incomes of over £500, compared with four out of ten (39%) cohabiting couples with dependent children, and one in ten lone parents.
- Among lone mothers, 9% had household incomes of over £500 compared with 21% of lone fathers.

Lone parents had markedly lower gross weekly household incomes than married or cohabiting couples with dependent children:

- over a third (36%) of lone parent families had gross weekly household incomes of £150 or less, compared with 10% of married couples and 15% of cohabiting couples with dependent children;
- there was no statistically significant difference between lone mothers and lone fathers in the proportion with incomes of £150 or less.

Single (never married) lone mothers were particularly likely to have low gross weekly household incomes:

- over half of single mothers (51%) had incomes of £150 or less compared with 28% of divorced lone mothers and 26% of separated lone mothers. **Table 3.11**

People

The gradual ageing of the British population has been reflected in the GHS sample since 1971. In that year, 12% of people were aged 65 or over compared with 15% in 2001. There has been a corresponding fall in the proportion of the population aged under 16, from 25% in 1971 to 20% in 2001. Figure 3D shows the change between 1971 and 2001 in the proportions of the population aged under 16 and 65 and over.

The greater life span of women is illustrated in Table 3.13. While for most age groups the male/female distribution is relatively even, there are more women than men among people aged 65 and over. Women represent over three fifths (62%) of people aged 75 and over.

Tables 3.12-3.13, Figure 3D

Socio-economic classification

As discussed in the introduction to this report, 2001 saw the introduction of the new National Statistics Socio-economic Classification (NS-SEC). It has replaced Social Class based on occupation and Socio-economic Groups (SEG). Like social class and SEG, the new classification is based on occupation and employment status. The version of the new classification, which will be used for most analyses has eight classes (see Appendix E for a more detailed description).

One of the major differences from SEG is that there is no longer a manual/non-manual split. However, the categories of NS-SEC can be aggregated to produce an approximation of Social Class and SEG. When this is done the level of continuity between these approximations and the old classification is 87%. Because of the differences between the two classification systems, this report does not present time series data on socio-economic group.

Table 3.14 shows the new classification. It should be noted that the recommended source for data on NS-SEC and SEG is the Labour Force Survey because of its considerably larger sample. Appendix E includes a comparison of LFS and GHS distributions on NS-SEC.

Overall, 10% of people were in the higher professional and managerial group. Men were much more likely than women to be classified in the higher professional and managerial group, 16% and 5% for men and women respectively in 2001. Just over a fifth (21%) of people were in the lower managerial and professional group, with similar proportions for both men and women. Thirteen percent were classified in the intermediate occupation group (which included clerical workers, secretaries, nursery nurses and nursing auxiliaries, call centre workers). Women were more likely to be classified into this group, 19% compared with only 6% of men.

Eight percent of people were in the small employers and own-account workers group, and 11% in the lower supervisory and technical group (including occupations such as train drivers, plumbers, fitters, inspectors, printers). Men were twice as likely as women to be in the small employers and own-account workers group (11% compared with 5%). They were also more likely than women to be in the lower supervisory and technical group, 15%

Figure 3D **Children and older people - the proportion of the population aged under 16 or 65 and over in 1971 and 2001**

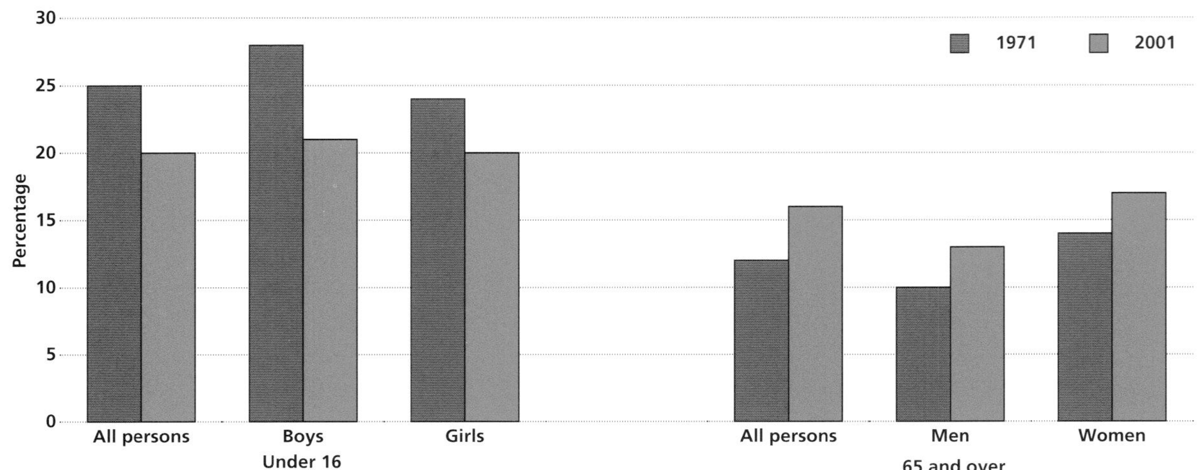

compared with 6%. Almost a quarter (23%) of women were in the semi-routine occupation group compared with 12% of men. Fifteen percent of people were in the routine occupation group (which included occupations such as machine operators, packers, cleaners, labourers, sales assistants, HGV drivers and bar staff). This proportion was the same for men and women.

The proportion of people in the higher managerial and professional group peaked between the ages of 25 and 44, and thereafter began to decline. Only 3% of those aged 16 to 24 were in this group, rising to 13% of people aged 25 to 34 and 14% of people aged 35 to 44. The pattern was similar for men and women. A similar distribution was found for the lower managerial and professional group. The proportion of people in the semi-routine and routine group was highest among the youngest and oldest groups. A little over two-fifths of people aged 16 to 24 (42%) were in the routine or semi-routine group compared with less than a quarter (24%) of people aged 25 to 34. **Table 3.14**

Ethnic group

As well as the introduction of NS-SEC, a new classification of ethnicity was introduced in 2001. This classification separately identifies people of mixed ethnic background, which means that is not comparable with the old classification. The GHS sample has always been too small to analyse single year data on ethnicity, and, until this year, data have been added across three years to produce large enough sample sizes for analysis. The change in classification means it is no longer possible to do this. Consequently, this report includes only the overall distribution in terms of the new ethnic classification[5] (see Appendix E).

Table 3.15 shows the ethnic distribution of the sample using the new classification.

- Eighty nine percent of people described themselves as White British and 3% as 'Other White', a total of 92% who described themselves as White.
- Two percent described themselves as Indian and 3% as Pakistani, Bangladeshi or other Asian, giving a total of 4% of the sample describing themselves as Asian.
- Two percent gave their ethnic origin as Black, comprising 1% each as Caribbean and African, with a very small number describing themselves as of 'other Black' ethnic origin.
- One percent described themselves as of mixed race and 1% were from some other ethnic origin. **Table 3.15**

National identity

In addition to the ethnic classification, the 2001 survey introduced a new question on national identity. This question was used on the 2001 Census and added to a number of government surveys, including the Labour Force Survey and the GHS (see Appendix E). People were able to choose between English, Scottish, Welsh, Irish, British and other, and could choose as many or as few of the categories as they wished. This question was asked in the household section of the questionnaire and was asked separately for each member of the household. This section shows how people described their national identity, and how they combined national identities when they categorised themselves as belonging to more than one group.

Overall, 46% of people described themselves as British, 51% of people considered themselves to be English, 9% Scottish, 4% Welsh and 2% Irish.

- 31% described themselves as British only;
- 15% described themselves as British and also English, Welsh, Scottish or Irish;
- 49% described themselves as English, Welsh, Scottish or Irish only;
- 5% gave a non-British national identity and 1% gave other combinations of national identity. **Tables 3.16-3.17**

Comparison across age groups showed that people most likely to identify themselves as British were those aged between 35 and 44:

- over half of people aged 35 to 44 (52%) identified themselves as British compared with 48% of younger adults aged 16 to 34 and just over a third (36%) of those aged 65 and over.

Older adults were most likely to identify themselves as English.

- Among people aged less than 55, under half of adults described themselves as English, compared with, for example, 58% of those aged 75 and over.

Younger people were more likely than older people to describe themselves as having an 'other' national identity:

- 7% of 16 to 24 year olds and 10% of those aged 25 to 34 did so, compared with between 2% and 5% of older adults. **Table 3.16**

People aged less than 55 were more likely than older people to describe themselves as British only.

- Among those aged less than 55, between 26% and 33% described themselves as British only compared with 23% of those aged 65 and over.

Older people were more likely to describe themselves as English, Welsh, Scottish or Irish only - 54% of people aged 55 to 64 and 62% of those aged 65 and over described themselves in this way compared with between 43% and 48% of people aged less than 55. **Table 3.17**

People living in Wales and Scotland were less likely to describe themselves as British than people living in England.

- Almost a half (48%) of people in England considered themselves to be British, compared with around a third (35%) of those living in Wales and a quarter (27%) of those living in Scotland.

In each of the regions of England, people were slightly more likely to describe themselves as English than British, with two exceptions. People in the North East and in London were equally likely to describe themselves as British and as English. However, in the case of the North East, this was because the proportion choosing British was high in comparison with other regions while in London the proportion choosing English was low. People living in London were considerably more likely than people in other regions to describe themselves as having a national identity other than those of the UK nations.

- 19% of people in London described their national identity as 'other' compared with between 2% and 5% in other areas of England, Scotland and Wales. **Table 3.18**

People from minority ethnic groups were more likely to consider themselves British than were those of White ethnic origin - almost three fifths (57%) did so compared with less than half (45%) of those in the White group. Conversely, people from minority ethnic groups were less likely to consider themselves as English, Scottish, Welsh or Irish:

- 11% of people from minority ethnic groups described themselves as English compared with 54% of people of White ethnic origin.

As Table 3.20 shows, people from minority ethic groups were also considerably less likely to describe themselves as having more than one national identity than were those of White ethnic origin.

- Over half (51%) of people from minority ethic groups described themselves as British only, compared with 29% from those who said their ethnic origin was White. **Tables 3.19-3.20**

Notes and references

1 The introduction of weighting for nonresponse has had an important effect on the proportion of one-person households. This effect suggests that the increase seen over time has been slightly underestimated in the past.

2 As the GHS interviews all people aged 16 and over in private households, the figures presented for those living alone aged 75 and over does not take account of the proportion of people in this age group who live in institutions and residential homes.

3 Dependent children are persons aged under 16 or single persons aged 16 but under 19, in full-time education, in the family unit and living as part of the household.

4 This finding is based on aggregated data from 2000 and 2001 to improve statistical reliability.

5 The Labour Force Survey, with its considerably larger sample, is the recommended source for data on ethnic origin and nationality. A comparison of LFS and GHS distributions on these two variables is shown in Appendix E.

Table 3.1 **Household size: 1971 to 2001**

(a) Households and (b) Persons — *Great Britain*

Number of persons in household (all ages)	Unweighted									Weighted		
	1971	1975	1981	1985	1991	1993	1995	1996	1998	1998	2000	2001
	Percentage of households of each size											
(a) Households	%	%	%	%	%	%	%	%	%	%	%	%
1	17	20	22	24	26	27	28	27	29	31	32	31
2	31	32	31	33	34	35	35	34	36	34	34	34
3	19	18	17	17	17	16	16	16	15	16	15	16
4	18	17	18	17	16	15	15	15	14	14	13	13
5	8	8	7	6	6	5	5	5	5	4	5	4
6 or more	6	5	4	2	2	2	2	2	2	2	2	2
*Weighted base (000's) = 100%**										*24,450*	*24,845*	*24,592*
*Unweighted sample**	*11988*	*12097*	*12006*	*9993*	*9955*	*9852*	*9758*	*9158*	*8636*		*8221*	*8989*
Average (mean) household size	2.91	2.78	2.70	2.56	2.48	2.44	2.40	2.43	2.36	2.32	2.30	2.33
	Percentage of persons in households of each size											
(b) Persons	%	%	%	%	%	%	%	%	%	%	%	%
1	6	7	8	10	11	11	12	11	12	13	14	13
2	22	23	23	26	27	28	29	28	30	30	30	29
3	20	19	19	20	20	19	20	20	19	20	20	20
4	25	25	27	27	25	25	24	25	24	23	22	23
5	15	14	14	12	11	10	10	10	10	9	10	9
6 or more	13	11	9	6	5	6	5	6	5	4	5	5
*Weighted base (000's) = 100%**										*56,751*	*57,106*	*57,260*
*Unweighted sample**	*34849*	*33579*	*32410*	*25555*	*24657*	*24079*	*23385*	*22274*	*20396*		*19266*	*21180*

* Trend tables show unweighted and weighted figures for 1998 to give an indication of the effect of the weighting. For weighted data (1998, 2000 and 2001) the weighted base (000's) is the base for percentages. Unweighted data (up to 1998) are based on the unweighted sample.

Weighting to be revised in Spring 2003 following the 2001 census revisions of population estimates. See Appendix D.

Table 3.2 **Household type: 1971 to 2001**

(a) Households and (b) Persons *Great Britain*

Household type	Unweighted									Weighted		
	1971	1975	1981	1985	1991	1993	1995	1996	1998	1998	2000	2001
	Percentage of households of each type											
(a) Households	%	%	%	%	%	%	%	%	%	%	%	%
1 adult aged 16-59	5	6	7	8	10	10	12	11	13	15	16	15
2 adults aged 16-59	14	14	13	15	16	16	17	15	16	16	17	17
Youngest person aged 0-4	18	15	13	13	14	14	13	13	13	12	11	11
Youngest person aged 5-15	21	22	22	18	16	16	16	17	16	16	15	16
3 or more adults	13	11	13	12	12	11	10	11	9	10	10	11
2 adults, 1 or both aged 60 or over	17	17	17	17	16	17	16	16	17	15	15	15
1 adult aged 60 or over	12	15	15	16	16	17	15	16	16	15	16	15
*Weighted base (000's) = 100%**										*24,450*	*24,845*	*24,592*
*Unweighted sample**	*11934*	*12090*	*12006*	*9993*	*9955*	*9852*	*9758*	*9158*	*8636*		*8221*	*8989*
	Percentage of persons in each type of household											
(b) Persons	%	%	%	%	%	%	%	%	%	%	%	%
1 adult aged 16-59	2	2	3	3	4	4	5	5	5	7	7	7
2 adults aged 16-59	10	10	10	12	13	13	14	13	14	14	14	14
Youngest person aged 0-4	27	23	21	21	22	22	20	21	21	19	19	18
Youngest person aged 5-15	31	34	33	28	25	25	26	27	25	26	25	25
3 or more adults	15	13	16	17	16	15	15	15	13	15	15	16
2 adults, 1 or both aged 60 or over	11	12	12	13	13	14	14	13	14	13	13	13
1 adult aged 60 or over	4	5	6	6	7	7	6	7	7	7	7	7
*Weighted base (000's) = 100%**										*56,751*	*57,106*	*57,260*
*Unweighted sample**	*34720*	*33561*	*32410*	*25555*	*24657*	*24079*	*23385*	*22274*	*20396*		*19266*	*21180*

* See the footnote to Table 3.1.

Weighting to be revised in Spring 2003 following the 2001 census revisions of population estimates. See Appendix D.

Table 3.3 **Percentage living alone, by age: 1973 to 2001**

All persons aged 16 and over *Great Britain*

	Percentage who lived alone										
	Unweighted								Weighted†		
	1973	1983	1987	1991	1993	1995	1996	1998	1998	2000	2001
16-24	2	2	3	3	4	5	4	4	4	5	5
25-44	2	4	6	7	8	9	8	10	12	12	12
45-64	8	9	10	11	11	12	11	14	15	16	15
65-74	26	28	28	29	28	27	31	27	28	29	27
75 and over	40	47	50	50	50	51	47	48	48	50	49
All aged 16 and over	9	11	12	14	14	15	14	16	17	17	16
*Unweighted sample**											
16-24	*3811*	*3498*	*3558*	*2819*	*2574*	*2318*	*2233*	*1885*		*1870*	*2064*
25-44	*8169*	*7017*	*7418*	*7118*	*6875*	*6761*	*6489*	*5861*		*5393*	*6118*
45-64	*7949*	*5947*	*5802*	*5493*	*5360*	*5615*	*5114*	*4892*		*4803*	*5147*
65-74	*2847*	*2494*	*2389*	*2196*	*2303*	*2129*	*1943*	*1862*		*1672*	*1882*
75 and over	*1432*	*1490*	*1596*	*1603*	*1581*	*1451*	*1485*	*1374*		*1344*	*1474*
All aged 16 and over	*24208*	*20446*	*20763*	*19229*	*18693*	*18274*	*17264*	*15874*		*15082*	*16685*

* See the footnote to Table 3.1.
† Weighted bases are shown in Table 3.21.

Weighting to be revised in Spring 2003 following the 2001 census revisions of population estimates. See Appendix D.

Table 3.4 **Percentage living alone, by age and sex**

All persons aged 16 and over *Great Britain: 2001*

	Percentage who lived alone		
	Men	Women	Total
16-24	7	3	5
25-44	17	6	12
45-64	15	14	15
65-74	19	35	27
75 and over	32	59	49
All aged 16 and over	16	17	16
All persons*	13	13	13
Weighted base (000's) = 100%			
16-24	*3,169*	*3,023*	*6,192*
25-44	*8,793*	*8,482*	*17,275*
45-64	*6,711*	*6,829*	*13,540*
65-74	*2,203*	*2,524*	*4,727*
75 and over	*1,467*	*2,431*	*3,898*
All aged 16 and over	*22,342*	*23,290*	*45,632*
All persons*	*28,212*	*29,048*	*57,260*
Unweighted sample			
16-24	*987*	*1077*	*2064*
25-44	*2934*	*3184*	*6118*
45-64	*2508*	*2639*	*5147*
65-74	*905*	*977*	*1882*
75 and over	*569*	*905*	*1474*
All aged 16 and over	*7903*	*8782*	*16685*
All persons*	*10166*	*11014*	*21180*

* Including children.

Weighting to be revised in Spring 2003 following the 2001 census revisions of population estimates. See Appendix D.

Table 3.5 **Type of household: 1979 to 2001**

(a) Households and (b) Persons — *Great Britain*

Household type	Unweighted							Weighted		
	1979	1985	1991	1993	1995	1996	1998	1998	2000	2001
	Percentage of households of each type									
(a) Households	%	%	%	%	%	%	%	%	%	%
1 person only	23	24	26	27	28	27	29	31	32	31
2 or more unrelated adults	3	4	3	3	2	3	2	3	3	3
Married/cohabiting couple										
with dependent children	31	28	25	24	24	25	23	22	21	22
with non-dependent children only	7	8	8	7	6	6	6	6	6	6
no children	27	27	28	28	29	28	30	28	28	29
Married couple										
with dependent children	..	..	..	..	..	23	20	19	18	18
with non-dependent children	..	..	..	..	..	6	5	6	6	6
no children	..	..	..	..	..	25	26	24	24	23
Cohabiting couple										
with dependent children	..	..	..	..	..	3	3	3	3	3
with non-dependent children	..	..	..	..	..	0	0	0	0	0
no children	..	..	..	..	..	4	4	5	5	5
Lone parent										
with dependent children	4	4	6	7	7	7	7	7	7	7
with non-dependent children only	4	4	4	3	3	3	3	3	2	2
Two or more families	1	1	1	1	1	1	1	1	1	1
*Weighted base (000's) = 100%**								*24,389*	*24,787*	*24,493*
*Unweighted sample**	*11454*	*9993*	*9955*	*9852*	*9738*	*9138*	*8617*		*8204*	*8955*
	Percentage of persons in each type of household									
(b) Persons	%	%	%	%	%	%	%	%	%	%
1 person only	9	10	11	11	12	11	12	13	14	13
2 or more unrelated adults	2	3	2	3	2	3	2	3	3	3
Married/cohabiting couple										
with dependent children	49	45	41	41	40	42	39	38	36	37
with non-dependent children only	9	11	11	9	9	9	8	9	9	9
no children	20	21	23	23	25	24	26	25	25	25
Married couple										
with dependent children	..	..	..	..	..	37	34	33	32	32
with non-dependent children	..	..	..	..	..	9	8	8	9	9
no children	..	..	..	..	..	21	22	21	21	20
Cohabiting couple										
with dependent children	..	..	..	..	..	4	5	5	5	5
with non-dependent children	..	..	..	..	..	0	0	0	0	0
no children	..	..	..	..	..	3	4	4	4	5
Lone parent										
with dependent children	5	5	7	8	8	8	9	8	9	8
with non-dependent children only	3	4	3	3	3	3	3	3	2	2
Two or more families	2	1	2	2	1	1	2	2	2	2
*Weighted base (000's) = 100%**								*56,605*	*56,955*	*56,921*
*Unweighted sample**	*30546*	*25454*	*24657*	*24079*	*23325*	*22190*	*20350*		*19220*	*21065*

* See the footnote to Table 3.1.
See Appendix A for the definition of a household.

Weighting to be revised in Spring 2003 following the 2001 census revisions of population estimates. See Appendix D.

Table 3.6 Family type, and marital status of lone mothers: 1971 to 2001

*Families with dependent children** — *Great Britain*

Family type	Unweighted									Weighted		
	1971	1975	1981	1985	1991	1993	1995	1996	1998	1998	2000	2001
	%	%	%	%	%	%	%	%	%	%	%	%
Married/cohabiting couple†	92	90	87	86	81	78	78	79	75	76	74	75
Lone mother	7	9	11	12	18	20	20	20	22	21	23	22
single	1	1	2	3	6	8	8	7	9	8	11	10
widowed	2	2	2	1	1	1	1	1	1	1	1	1
divorced	2	3	4	5	6	7	7	6	8	7	7	7
separated	2	2	2	3	4	4	5	5	5	5	5	4
Lone father	1	1	2	2	1	2	2	2	2	3	3	3
All lone parents	8	10	13	14	19	22	22	21	25	24	26	25
*Weighted base (000's) = 100%***										*7,182*	*7,105*	*7,146*
*Unweighted sample***	*4864*	*4776*	*4445*	*3348*	*3143*	*3145*	*3022*	*2975*	*2659*		*2464*	*2700*

* Dependent children are persons under 16, or aged 16-18 and in full-time education, in the family unit, and living in the household.
† Including married women whose husbands were not defined as resident in the household.
** See the footnote to Table 3.1.

Weighting to be revised in Spring 2003 following the 2001 census revisions of population estimates. See Appendix D.

Table 3.7 Family type and number of dependent children: 1972 to 2001

*Dependent children** — *Great Britain*

	Percentage of all dependent children in each family type											
	Unweighted									Weighted		
	1972	1975	1981	1985	1991	1993	1995	1996	1998	1998	2000	2001
	%	%	%	%	%	%	%	%	%	%	%	%
Married/cohabiting couple with												
1 dependent child	16	17	18	19	17	15	16	17	15	17	17	17
2 or more dependent children	76	74	70	69	66	65	64	63	62	61	58	60
Lone mother with												
1 dependent child	2	3	3	4	5	6	5	5	6	6	7	6
2 or more dependent children	5	6	7	7	12	12	14	13	15	13	15	15
Lone father with												
1 dependent child	0	0	1	1	0	1	1	0	1	1	1	1
2 or more dependent children	1	1	1	1	1	1	1	1	1	1	2	1
Weighted base (000's) = 100%†										*12,799*	*12,641*	*12,606*
Unweighted sample†	*9474*	*9293*	*8216*	*5966*	*5799*	*5794*	*5559*	*5431*	*4897*		*4499*	*4846*

* Dependent children are persons under 16, or aged 16-18 and in full-time education, in the family unit, and living in the household.
† See footnote to Table 3.1.

Weighting to be revised in Spring 2003 following the 2001 census revisions of population estimates. See Appendix D.

Table 3.8 **Average (mean) number of dependent children by family type: 1971 to 2001**

*Families with dependent children** *Great Britain*

Family type	Average (mean) number of children											
	Unweighted									Weighted††		
	1971	1975	1981	1985	1991	1993	1995	1996	1998	1998	2000	2001
Married/cohabiting couple†	2.0	2.0	1.9	1.8	1.9	1.9	1.9	1.9	1.9	1.8	1.8	1.8
Married couple	..	..	..	..	..	..	..	1.9	1.9	1.8	1.8	1.9
Cohabiting couple	..	..	..	..	..	..	..	1.7	1.7	1.7	1.7	1.6
Lone parent	1.8	1.7	1.6	1.6	1.7	1.7	1.7	1.7	1.7	1.6	1.7	1.7
Total: all families with dependent children	2.0	1.9	1.8	1.8	1.8	1.8	1.8	1.8	1.8	1.8	1.8	1.8
*Unweighted sample***												
Married/cohabiting couple	*4482*	*4299*	*3887*	*2890*	*2541*	*2453*	*2358*	*2329*	*2004*		*1804*	*2004*
Married couple	..	..	..	..	..	..	..	*2086*	*1753*		*1558*	*1720*
Cohabiting couple	..	..	..	..	..	..	..	*243*	*251*		*246*	*284*
Lone parent	*382*	*477*	*558*	*458*	*595*	*682*	*658*	*635*	*652*		*660*	*682*
Total	*4864*	*4776*	*4445*	*3348*	*3136*	*3135*	*3016*	*2964*	*2656*		*2464*	*2686*

* Dependent children are persons aged under 16, or aged 16-18 and in full-time education, in the family unit, and living in the household.
† Including married women whose husbands were not defined as resident in the household.
** See footnote to Table 3.1.
†† Weighted bases are shown in Table 3.21.

Weighting to be revised in Spring 2003 following the 2001 census revisions of population estimates. See Appendix D.

Table 3.9 **Age of youngest dependent child by family type**

*Families with dependent children** *Great Britain: 2000 and 2001 combined*

Family type		Age of youngest dependent child					
		0-4	5-9	10-15	16 and over	*Unweighted sample***	Total
							%
Married/cohabiting couple†	%	41	26	25	7	*3817*	75
Lone mother	%	36	32	26	5	*1228*	23
Lone father	%	18	23	48	11	*120*	2
All lone parents	%	35	31	28	6	*1348*	25
Total	%	40	27	26	7	*5165*	100

* Dependent children are persons aged under 16, or aged 16-18 and in full-time education, in the family unit, and living in the household.
† Including married women whose husbands were not defined as resident in the household.
** Weighted base not shown for combined data sets.

Table 3.10 **Stepfamilies by family type**

*Stepfamilies with dependent children**
(Family head aged 16-59) *Great Britain: 2001*

Type of stepfamily	
	%
Couple with child(ren) from the woman's previous marriage/ cohabitation	88
Couple with child(ren) from the man's previous marriage/ cohabitation	9
Couple with child(ren) from both partners' previous marriage/ cohabitation	8
Weighted base (000's) = 100%	*369*
Unweighted sample	*136*

* Dependent children are persons under 16, or aged 16-18 and in full-time education, in the family unit, and living in the household.

Weighting to be revised in Spring 2003 following the 2001 census revisions of population estimates. See Appendix D.

Table 3.11 **Usual gross weekly household income by family type**

*Families with dependent children**

Great Britain: 2001

Family type		Usual gross weekly household income										*Weighted base (000's) = 100%†*	*Unweighted sample*
		£0.01- £100.00	£100.01 - £150.00	£150.01 - £200.00	£200.01 - £250.00	£250.01 - £300.00	£300.01 - £350.00	£350.01 - £400.00	£400.01 - £450.00	£450.01 - £500.00	£500.01 and over		
Married couple	%	7	3	3	3	3	4	5	5	6	61	*4,208*	*1579*
Cohabiting couple	%	9	6	8	4	6	8	7	5	7	39	*741*	*268*
Lone mother**	%	15	23	15	10	9	7	5	4	3	9	*1,507*	*604*
Single	%	24	27	15	7	7	4	4	3	2	7	*670*	*267*
Divorced	%	7	21	14	11	12	10	6	5	4	10	*501*	*199*
Separated	%	7	19	16	14	12	11	6	6	4	5	*273*	*114*
Lone father	%	12	18	14	11	9	2	6	1	7	21	*170*	*55*
All lone parents**	%	14	22	15	10	9	7	5	4	3	10	*1,679*	*659*

* Dependent children are persons aged under 16, or aged 16-18 and in full-time education, in the family unit, and living in the household.
† Bases exclude cases where income is not known.
** Includes twenty four widowed lone mothers.

Weighting to be revised in Spring 2003 following the 2001 census revisions of population estimates. See Appendix D.

Table 3.12 **Age by sex: 1971 to 2001**

All persons

Great Britain

Age	Unweighted									Weighted		
	1971	1975	1981	1985	1991	1993	1995	1996	1998	1998	2000	2001
	%	%	%	%	%	%	%	%	%	%	%	%
Males												
0- 4	9	8	7	7	8	8	7	7	8	6	6	6
5-15*	19	18	18	16	15	16	16	16	16	15	15	15
16-44*	39	40	41	42	41	40	39	39	38	42	42	42
45-64	24	23	22	22	22	23	24	23	24	23	24	24
65-74	7	8	8	9	8	9	9	8	9	8	8	8
75 and over	3	3	4	4	5	5	5	6	5	5	5	5
Weighted base (000's) = 100%†										*27,921*	*28,134*	*28,212*
Unweighted sample†	*16908*	*16242*	*15735*	*12551*	*11913*	*11514*	*11376*	*10781*	*9831*		*9322*	*10166*
	%	%	%	%	%	%	%	%	%	%	%	%
Females												
0- 4	8	6	6	6	7	7	6	7	7	6	6	6
5-15*	16	17	16	15	14	14	14	15	14	14	14	14
16-44*	37	38	39	41	39	38	39	39	38	40	40	40
45-64	24	24	22	21	22	22	24	23	24	23	24	24
65-74	9	10	10	10	10	10	9	9	9	9	9	9
75 and over	5	6	7	8	8	8	8	7	8	8	8	8
Weighted base (000's) = 100%†										*28,828*	*28,973*	*29,048*
Unweighted sample†	*17871*	*17328*	*16675*	*13522*	*12744*	*12565*	*12009*	*11493*	*10564*		*9944*	*11014*
	%	%	%	%	%	%	%	%	%	%	%	%
Total												
0- 4	8	7	6	6	7	7	7	7	7	6	6	6
5-15*	17	17	17	15	15	15	15	15	15	14	14	14
16-44*	38	39	40	42	40	39	39	39	38	41	41	41
45-64	24	23	22	21	22	22	24	23	24	23	24	24
65-74	8	9	9	9	9	10	9	9	9	8	8	8
75 and over	4	4	5	6	7	7	6	7	7	7	7	7
Weighted base (000's) = 100%†										*56,749*	*57,106*	*57,260*
Unweighted sample†	*34779*	*33570*	*32410*	*26073*	*24657*	*24079*	*23385*	*22274*	*20395*		*19266*	*21180*

* 5-14 and 15-44 in 1971 and 1975.
† See the footnote to Table 3.1.

Weighting to be revised in Spring 2003 following the 2001 census revisions of population estimates. See Appendix D.

Table 3.13 **Sex by age**

All persons — *Great Britain: 2001*

Age		Males	Females	*Weighted base (000's) = 100%*	*Unweighted sample*
0- 4	%	51	49	*3,441*	*1348*
5-15	%	50	50	*8,186*	*3147*
16-19	%	50	50	*2,755*	*947*
20-24	%	52	48	*3,437*	*1117*
25-29	%	51	49	*3,677*	*1270*
30-34	%	51	49	*4,668*	*1629*
35-39	%	52	48	*4,751*	*1713*
40-44	%	50	50	*4,180*	*1506*
45-49	%	49	51	*3,375*	*1261*
50-54	%	49	51	*4,080*	*1516*
55-59	%	49	51	*3,302*	*1264*
60-64	%	52	48	*2,783*	*1106*
65-69	%	47	53	*2,418*	*976*
70-74	%	46	54	*2,309*	*906*
75 and over	%	38	62	*3,898*	*1474*
Total	%	49	51	*57,260*	*21180*

Weighting to be revised in Spring 2003 following the 2001 census revisions of population estimates. See Appendix D.

Table 3.14 **Socio-economic classification based on own current or last job by age and sex**

All persons aged 16 and over — *Great Britain: 2001*

Socio-economic classification*	Age group						
	16-24	25-34	35-44	45-54	55-64	65 and over	All
	%	%	%	%	%	%	%
Males							
Higher managerial and professional	4	18	20	17	16	14	16
Lower managerial and professional	13	23	22	22	18	17	20
Intermediate	10	8	7	5	4	5	6
Small employers and own account	3	10	12	13	14	11	11
Lower supervisory and technical	12	15	14	15	15	19	15
Semi-routine	20	10	10	11	13	14	12
Routine	22	12	13	14	17	18	15
Never worked and long-term unemployed	16	5	2	2	2	1	4
Weighted base (000's) = 100%	*2,103*	*4,014*	*4,452*	*3,558*	*3,029*	*3,645*	*20,801*
Unweighted sample	*654*	*1306*	*1528*	*1328*	*1138*	*1466*	*7420*
	%	%	%	%	%	%	%
Females							
Higher managerial and professional	3	9	8	5	3	2	5
Lower managerial and professional	14	27	25	25	20	14	21
Intermediate	20	21	19	20	20	18	19
Small employers and own account	2	4	5	5	6	4	5
Lower supervisory and technical	6	6	6	6	6	7	6
Semi-routine	25	17	21	24	25	25	23
Routine	17	9	11	12	17	22	15
Never worked and long-term unemployed	14	7	5	4	4	7	6
Weighted base (000's) = 100%	*1,964*	*3,955*	*4,282*	*3,740*	*2,994*	*4,935*	*21,870*
Unweighted sample	*694*	*1468*	*1626*	*1394*	*1208*	*1874*	*8264*
	%	%	%	%	%	%	%
Total							
Higher managerial and professional	3	13	14	11	9	7	10
Lower managerial and professional	13	25	23	23	19	16	21
Intermediate	15	14	13	13	12	12	13
Small employers and own account	3	7	9	9	10	7	8
Lower supervisory and technical	9	10	10	11	11	12	11
Semi-routine	22	14	15	18	19	21	18
Routine	20	10	12	13	17	21	15
Never worked and long-term unemployed	15	6	3	3	3	4	5
Weighted base (000's) = 100%	*4,067*	*7,968*	*8,734*	*7,299*	*6,023*	*8,582*	*42,673*
Unweighted sample	*1348*	*2774*	*3154*	*2722*	*2346*	*3340*	*15684*

* From April 2001 the National Statistics Social-economic Classification (NS-SEC) was introduced for all official statistics and surveys. It has replaced Social Class based on Occupation and Socio-economic Groups (SEG). Full-time students and persons in inadequately described occupations are excluded (see Appendix A).

Weighting to be revised in Spring 2003 following the 2001 census revisions of population estimates. See Appendix D.

Table 3.15 **Ethnic group**

All persons *Great Britain: 2001*

Ethnic group		
	%	
White British	89	92
Other white	3	
Mixed background	1	
Indian	2	4
Other Asian background	3	
Black Caribbean	1	2*
Black African	1	
Other ethnic group	1	
Weighted base (000's) = 100%	*57,034*	
Unweighted sample	*21102*	

* Including other Black groups not shown separately.

Weighting to be revised in Spring 2003 following the 2001 census revisions of population estimates. See Appendix D.

Table 3.16 **National identity and age**

Persons aged 16 and over *Great Britain: 2001*

National identity*	16-24	25-34	35-44	45-54	55-64	65-74	75 and over	Total
	%	%	%	%	%	%	%	%
British	48	48	52	47	43	36	36	46
English	48	47	47	49	53	60	58	51
Scottish	9	9	8	10	10	9	8	9
Welsh	4	4	4	4	5	5	4	4
Irish	1	2	2	2	2	2	1	2
Other	7	10	5	5	3	2	2	5
Weighted bases (000's) = 100%	*6,142*	*8,298*	*8,922*	*7,435*	*6,069*	*4,721*	*3,896*	*45,482*
Unweighted sample	*2048*	*2883*	*3216*	*2770*	*2364*	*1880*	*1473*	*16634*

* Percentages sum to more than 100% because some respondents gave more than one answer.

Weighting to be revised in Spring 2003 following the 2001 census revisions of population estimates. See Appendix D.

Table 3.17 **Combined national identities and age**

All persons aged 16 and over *Great Britain: 2001*

National identity combinations	Age group							
	16-24	25-34	35-44	45-54	55-64	65-74	75 and over	Total
	%	%	%	%	%	%	%	%
British only	33	31	36	32	28	23	26	31
English/Scottish/Welsh/Irish only	45	43	43	48	54	62	62	49
Other national identity only	6	9	4	4	3	2	2	5
English/Scottish/Welsh/Irish and British	15	16	16	15	14	13	10	15
Other combinations	1	1	1	1	1	0	0	1
Weighted base (000's) = 100%	*6,093*	*8,187*	*8,833*	*7,365*	*6,029*	*4,702*	*3,877*	*45,086*
Unweighted sample	*2032*	*2346*	*3184*	*2744*	*2350*	*1872*	*1466*	*16494*

Weighting to be revised in Spring 2003 following the 2001 census revisions of population estimates. See Appendix D.

Table 3.18 **National identity and Government Office Region**

Persons aged 16 and over *Great Britain: 2001*

National identity*	Government Office Region									Country			
	North East	North West	Yorkshire and the Humber	East Midlands	West Midlands	East of England	London	South East	South West	England	Wales	Scotland	Great Britain
	%	%	%	%	%	%	%	%	%	%	%	%	%
British	56	48	52	45	48	49	46	49	47	48	35	27	46
English	56	63	59	57	61	58	45	59	60	57	19	4	51
Scottish	3	2	1	2	1	1	2	2	1	2	1	80	9
Welsh	1	1	0	1	2	1	1	2	2	1	62	0	4
Irish	1	2	1	1	2	1	4	2	1	2	0	1	2
Other	2	3	3	4	5	3	19	5	4	6	3	2	5
Weighted base (000's) = 100%	*2,061*	*5,228*	*3,676*	*3,570*	*3,871*	*4,113*	*5,711*	*6,534*	*4,275*	*39,038*	*2,262*	*4,181*	*45,482*
Unweighted sample	*762*	*2071*	*1480*	*1236*	*1507*	*1607*	*1823*	*2353*	*1521*	*14360*	*828*	*1446*	*16634*

* Percentages sum to more than 100% because some respondents gave more than one answer.

Weighting to be revised in Spring 2003 following the 2001 census revisions of population estimates. See Appendix D.

Table 3.19 **National identity and ethnic group**

Persons aged 16 and over *Great Britain: 2001*

National identity*	Ethnic group	
	White	Minority ethnic groups
	%	%
British	45	57
English	54	11
Scottish	10	1
Welsh	4	1
Irish	2	1
Other	3	37
Weighted base (000's) = 100%	*42,019*	*3,418*
Unweighted sample	*15432*	*1188*

* Percentages sum to more than 100% because respondents gave more than one answer.

Weighting to be revised in Spring 2003 following the 2001 census revisions of population estimates. See Appendix D.

Table 3.20 **Combined national identities and ethnic origin**

Persons aged 16 and over *Great Britain: 2001*

National identity combinations	Ethnic origin		
	White	Minority ethnic groups	Total
	%	%	%
British only	29	51	31
English/Scottish/Welsh/Irish only	52	11	49
Other national identity only	2	32	5
English/Scottish/Welsh/Irish and British	16	2	15
Other combinations	0	5	1
Weighted base (000's) = 100%	*41,644*	*3,397*	*45,041*
Unweighted sample	*15299*	*1181*	*16480*

Weighting to be revised in Spring 2003 following the 2001 census revisions of population estimates. See Appendix D.

Table 3.21 **Weighted bases for tables 3.3 and 3.8**

(a) Persons aged 16 and over *Great Britain*

	1998	2000	2001	Table Reference
16-24	6,139	6,191	6,192	3.3
25-44	17,117	17,130	17,275	3.3
45-64	13,226	13,519	13,540	3.3
65-74	4,767	4,719	4,727	3.3
75 and over	3,836	3,888	3,898	3.3
All aged 16 and over	45,085	45,447	45,632	3.3

*(b) Families with dependent children** *Great Britain*

	1998	2000	2001	Table Reference
Married/cohabiting couple†	5,465	5,232	5,366	3.8
Married couple	4,765	4,496	4,580	3.8
Cohabiting couple	700	736	785	3.8
Lone parent	1,717	1,861	1,739	3.8
Total	7,182	7,093	7,105	3.8

* Dependent children are persons aged under 16, or aged 16-18 and in full-time education, in the family unit, and living in the household.
† Including married women whose husbands were not defined as resident in the household.

Weighting to be revised in Spring 2003 following the 2001 census revisions of population estimates. See Appendix D.

Chapter 4

Housing and consumer durables

Over the last thirty years the General Household Survey has included questions on housing and the availability of consumer durables including cars and vans. This chapter looks at trends as well as data from the 2001 General Household Survey.

Tenure - trends over time

Sixty nine percent of all households owned their own home in 2001, compared with 49% in 1971.

- Over the last thirty years increases in home ownership were recorded in every decade with the largest increase coinciding with the right to buy council properties during the 1980s (from 54% in 1981 to 67% in 1991). Within the last five years home ownership has remained relatively constant (between 67% and 69%).

Over the same period (1971-2001):

- The proportion renting council housing increased from 31% in 1971 to 34% in 1981.This was followed by a gradual decline to 24% in 1991 and 15% in 2001.
- The proportion renting from a housing association[1] increased from 1% in 1971 to 6% in 2001. Most of the increase occurred in the last ten years with 3% of households renting from housing associations in 1991 compared with 6% in 2001. Since 1996, an increasing number of local authorities have transferred ownership of their housing to Registered Social Landlords (RSLs). This explains, to some extent, the decrease in the proportion of people renting LA (council) housing and the increase in the proportion of people renting from housing associations.
- The proportion of private renters declined sharply during the period 1971 to 1991 (from 20% in 1971 to 7% in 1991). This was followed by a gradual increase to 10% in 1995 and remained constant thereafter. In 2001, 10% of all households were private renters - 7% renting unfurnished accommodation and 3% renting furnished. **Table 4.1, Figure 4A**

Accommodation

The proportion of households living in various types of accommodation has changed little over the past three decades. The greatest change occurred in the number of households living in detached houses. In 1971 the proportion of households living in a detached house was 16% compared with 21% in 2001, although there has been no change since 1998. **Table 4.2**

Characteristics of tenure groups

The following profiles show that in 2001, as in previous years, there was considerable variation between the characteristics of the households in each tenure group and the type of accommodation in which they lived.

Figure 4A **Tenure: Great Britain, 1971 to 2001**

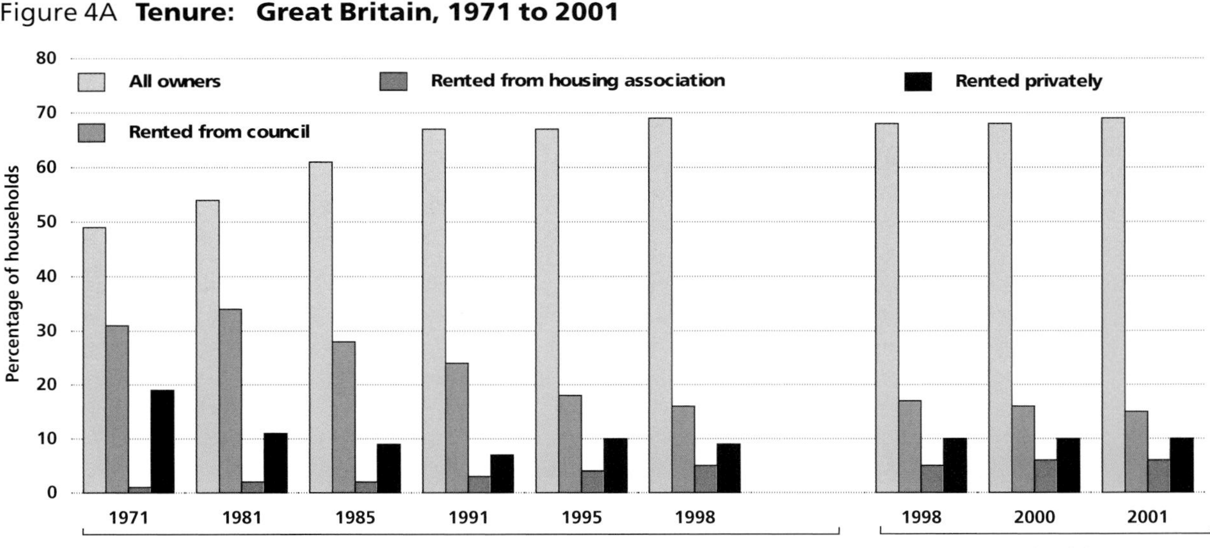

Owner occupiers

- The majority of owner occupiers lived in a house (90%). Almost two-thirds (64%) lived in a detached or semi-detached house and 26% lived in terraced houses. Of the remaining 10% who lived in a flat or room, 8% lived in a purpose built flat or maisonette while 2% lived in a converted flat/maisonette or room.
- About a third (34%) of outright owners lived in a detached house compared with a quarter (25%) of those buying their home on a mortgage. This latter group were more likely than outright owner occupiers to be living in a terraced house (29% compared with 22%).
- Unlike other tenure groups owner occupiers' accommodation was fairly evenly spread between properties of all ages.
- Among outright owners the median age of the household reference person was 65 to 69 compared with 30 to 44 for households who were buying with a mortgage.
- Lone parent families with dependent children were less than half as likely to be owner occupiers with a mortgage compared with other families with dependent children (29% of lone parent families were owner occupiers with a mortgage compared with 71% of other families with dependent children).
- Of all households, those buying with a mortgage had on average the highest household income (£713 gross per week).

Tables 4.4-4.5,4.7,4.9,4.10

Social renters

Social renters include households renting either from the council or a housing association.

- Of all social renters, 55% lived in houses, with around a quarter living in semi-detached houses (24%) and just under a third living in terraced houses (30%).
- A higher proportion of social sector tenants lived in purpose built flats and maisonettes than any other tenure group (42% compared with 17% of private renters and 8% of owner occupiers).
- Social sector tenants were more likely to live in houses built between 1945 and 1964 than any other group (35% compared with 20% of owner occupiers and 12% of private renters). In addition council tenants were more than twice as likely as housing association tenants to be housed in properties of this period (41% and 20% respectively) .This reflects the fact that local authority housing construction was at its peak in this period. A further 32% of council tenants lived in accommodation built between 1965 and 1984.
- Almost a third of housing association tenants (31%) lived in properties built in 1985 or later, while 14% of owner occupiers and 9% of private renters lived in properties built in this period. These figures reflect the fact that from around 1988, housing associations became responsible for the majority of 'new starts' i.e. building of new social rented accommodation.
- Over a quarter of all social sector accommodation consisted of households comprising one adult aged 60 or over (27%).
- Half of lone parent families with dependent children (50%) lived in social rented accommodation compared with 15% of other families with dependent children.
- Those living in social rented housing had on average the lowest income of all households (housing association tenants - £216 gross per week; council tenants - £208 gross per week).

Tables 4.4-4.7,4.9

Private renters

- Private renter households were more likely to live in converted flats, maisonettes or rooms than any other tenure group (19% compared with 3% of social sector tenants and 2% of owner occupiers).
- A higher proportion of private renters lived in accommodation built before 1919; 45% compared with 7% of social sector tenants and 23% of owner occupiers.
- Over a quarter of private renter households (27%) consisted of one adult aged 16-59. This was higher than among either social sector tenants (17%) or owner occupiers (13%).
- The household reference person in private renter households tended to be younger than those in other tenure households; 36% were aged less than 30 compared with 7% of household reference persons in owner occupied households and 13% in social renter households.
- The average household income of private renters in 2001 was £398 gross per week.

Tables 4.4-4.6,4.9-4.10

National Statistics Socio-economic Classification (NS-SEC) by tenure

From April 2001 the National Statistics Socio-economic classification (NS-SEC) was introduced for all official statistics and surveys. It has replaced Social Class based on occupation and Socio-economic Groups (SEG). See Appendix E for further information about NS-SEC. Table 4.12 shows the variation in tenure groups with respect to economic activity status and the new NS-SEC classification.

- In 64% of social sector households and 31% of both owner occupied and private rented households the household reference person was economically inactive.

Among households with an economically active household reference person;

- those headed by people in the semi-routine and routine groups were the least likely to own their property (61% each) compared with, for example, 94% of households headed by people within the large employer and higher managerial group;
- those in the routine and semi-routine groups were more likely than other households to be social sector tenants (29% and 25% respectively) compared with between 1% and 14% of other households. **Table 4.12**

Persons per room

In 2001, the mean number of persons per room was 0.46. Five percent of households had higher occupancy rates of 1 or more people per room. Higher occupancy rates were more likely among social sector households (8%) and private rented households (7%) compared with 3% of owner occupied households. Overall, 2% of households were below the bedroom standard (see Appendix A). This figure was lowest among owner occupiers (1%) with 4% of social sector tenants and 3% of private renters living in accommodation below the bedroom standard. **Tables 4.14-4.16**

Cars and vans

Nearly three quarters (72%) of households had access to a car or van in 2001, compared with 68% in 1991, 59% in 1981 and 52% in 1972. The rate of increase in car ownership, although continuing, was slower in the 1990s than in any of the previous three decades. Since 1998 no overall change occurred in the number of households without a car or van (28%).

- From 1972, the number of households with access to a single car or van varied little, with 43% of households in 1972 having access to a car or van and 44% in 2001. Over the same period the number of households with access to two cars or vans rose from 8% in 1972 to 23% in 2001 and with 3 or more cars from 1% in 1972 to 5% in 2001.
- The proportion of households headed by economically inactive individuals without access to a car or van (51%) was more than twice that of households headed by an economically active individual within other NS-SEC groups.
- Within households headed by economically active individuals, those headed by semi-routine and routine workers were least likely to have access to a car or van (25% of semi-routine worker households and 23% of routine worker households, compared with 4% of large employer/higher managerial households, 5% of higher professional worker households and 5% of small employers and own account worker households).
- Households headed by individuals in the large employer/higher managerial group and those in the small employers/own account worker group were the most likely to own two or more cars or vans (65% and 59% respectively), compared with between 48% and 20% of other economically active households.

Tables 4.17-4.19

Consumer durables - trends over time

The steady increase in the ownership and range of consumer durables has been evident since data was

Figure 4B **Households with access to a car or van: Great Britain, 1972 to 2001**

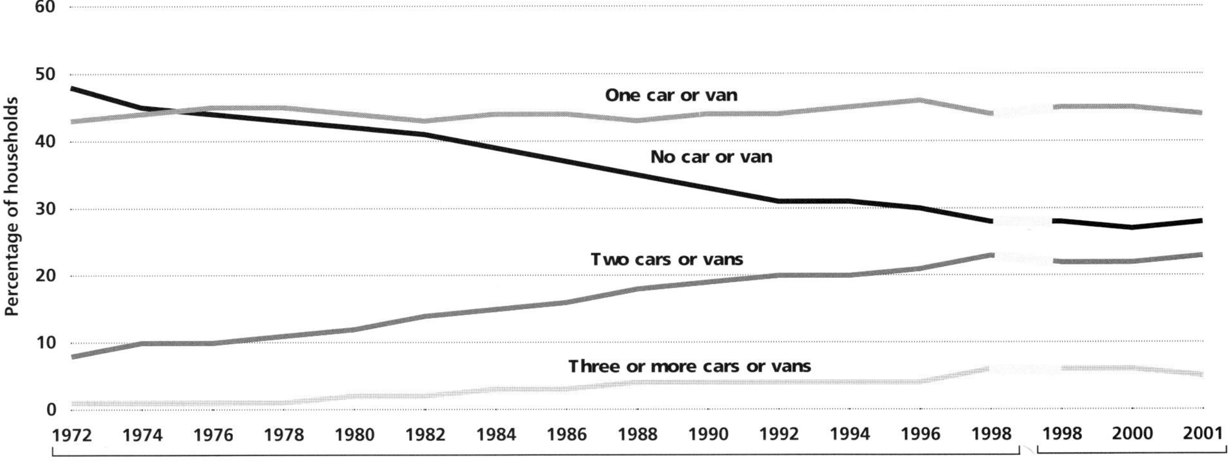

first collected by the GHS three decades ago. This has continued up to 2001 with a few exceptions. Colour, black and white televisions and washing machines were available in most households by the early 1990s. In 2001, nearly all households had central heating (92%) and a telephone (98%).

Increases in ownership of consumer durables mainly related to new technologies. The following were recorded in 2001:

- satellite, cable and digital television receivers increased from 29% in 1998 to 40% in 2000, but this increase has slowed considerably to 42% of households in 2001;
- CD players - increased from 69% in 1998 to 77% in 2000, and continued to increase to 80% in 2001;
- dishwasher - increased from 4% in 1981 to 28% in 2001;
- microwaves - increased from 55% in 1991 to 85% in 2001;
- home computers - increased from 34% in 1998 to 45% in 2000. This increase continued with 50% of households in 2001 having a computer.

In 2000, the GHS asked questions for the first time about access to the internet at home.

- In 2000, a third of all households had access to the internet at home. Nearly all of those households (31% of all households) accessed the internet from their home computer. In 2001, the number of households with access to the internet had grown to 40%, with 37% of all households having access from their home computer. Access to the internet from other sources had also grown with 6% of households in 2001 having other types of access to the internet compared with 2% in 2000.
- In 2000, the GHS identified fixed and mobile phones separately for the first time, and found 58% of households had a least one mobile phone. In 2001, the number of households with a mobile phone had increased to 70%. The increase in the number of households with mobile phones has not impacted on the number of households with fixed phones. The number of households with any type of telephone remained unchanged between 2000 and 2001 at 98%, as did the number of households with fixed phones (93%).

Table 4.19

Consumer durables and socio-economic classification (NS-SEC)

As stated earlier in the chapter the National Statistics Socio-economic Classification system (NS-SEC) has replaced Socio-economic Group (SEG) and Social Class (see Appendix E), this new classification of households showed similar variations in ownership of consumer durables to those seen previously with respect to SEG. Those households headed by individuals in higher NS-SEC groups were generally more likely to have the newer type of consumer durable than households in the lower NS-SEC groups or those headed by an economically inactive person.

- Households in the managerial and professional groups were most likely to have a home computer (82%, 86% and 76% respectively) and those in the semi-routine and routine groups were the least likely to have a home computer (48% and 43% respectively). Twenty four per cent of households headed by an economically inactive person had a home computer.

Figure 4C **Percentage of households with consumer durables: Great Britain, 1972 to 2001**

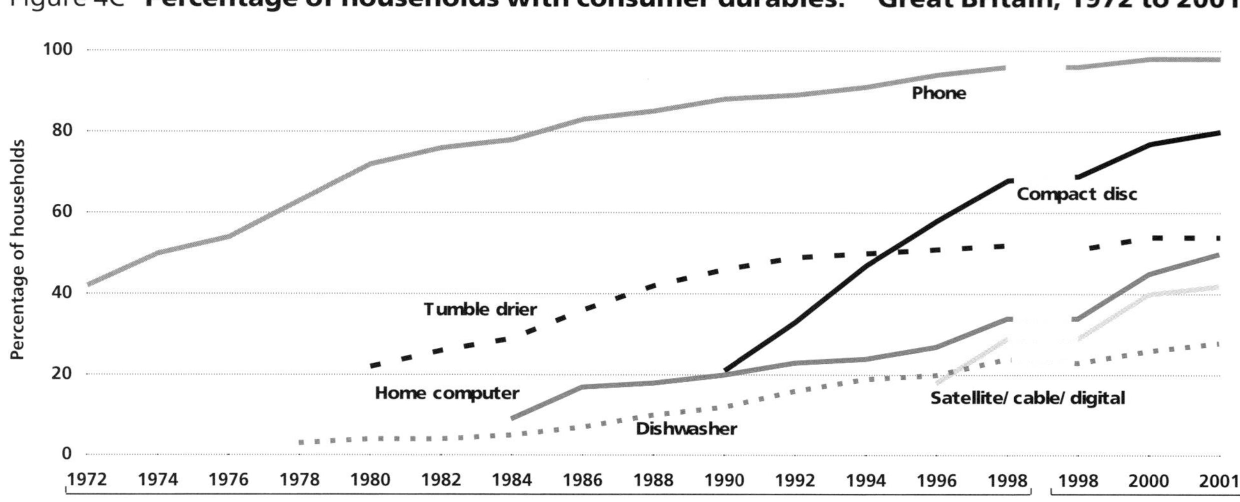

Figure 4D **New technology: Great Britain, 2000 to 2001**

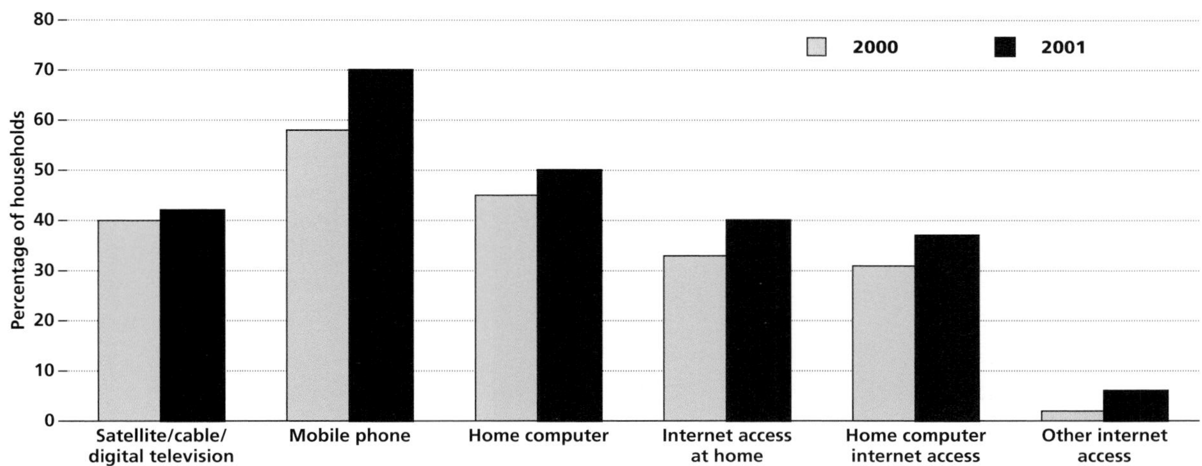

- Access to the internet from home followed the same pattern as access to home computers. Households in the managerial and professional groups being most likely to have access to the internet from home (76%, 79% and 66% respectively) and those in the semi-routine and routine groups the least likely (33% and 32% respectively). Only 17% of households headed by an economically inactive person had access to the internet from home.
- Mobile phones were most likely to be found in those households headed by people in the large employer and higher managerial group (93%) compared with 82% of intermediate households and 78% of the semi-routine group. Households headed by an economically inactive person were much less likely to have mobile phones than economically active households (45%). **Table 4.20**

Consumer durables and gross weekly income

In general, the higher the income, the more likely a household was to have consumer durables. In 2001, households with a gross weekly income of over £500 were far more likely than households with an income of £100 or less to have a:

- dishwasher (47% compared with 13%);
- home computer (75% compared with 27%);
- access to internet at home (66% compared with 20%);
- mobile phone (89% compared with 49%);
- CD player (95% compared with 59%);
- tumble drier (65% compared with 42%).

The main exception to this relationship was colour televisions with access approaching 100% for all income groups. **Table 4.21**

Consumer durables and household type

With the exception of home computers and access to the internet from home single person households were less likely than larger households to have any consumer durable listed. Pooled resources, and the increased chance of any one member of the household possessing a listed item in larger households, may go some way to explain the difference between these household types. In general terms, older households were less likely to have 'new technology' consumer durables such as computers, internet access and mobile phones.

Some of the differences between single person and other households were:

- 76% of older and 83% of younger single person households had a washing machine compared with between 96% and 99% of other households;
- 71% of older and 79% of younger single person households had a microwave oven compared with between 85% and 93% of all other households;
- 33% of older and 38% of younger single person households owned a tumble drier compared with at least half of all other households. The households most likely to own a tumble drier were large families (74%).

Differences between older and younger households were:

- households with adults aged 60 or over were the least likely to have a home computer with 30% of older two person households and 8% of older single person households having a home computer. Large family households (73%), large adult households (73%), and small family households (68%) were the most likely to have a home computer;

Figure 4E **Consumer durables: Lone parent families compared with couples with dependent children: Great Britain 2001**

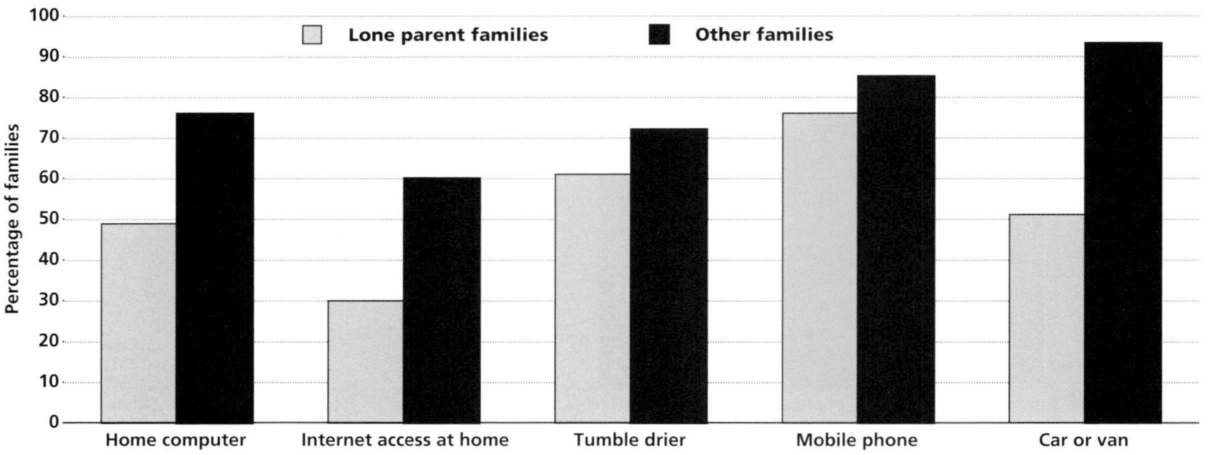

- 5% of single person households aged 60 or over had access to the internet at home as had 22% of two adult households with at least one person aged 60 or over. This compares with over half of family households, large adult households and two person households aged under 60;
- older households were the least likely to have a mobile phone (22% of older single person and 53% of older two person households compared with 72% of single person households aged under 60 and 86 to 89% of all other households);
- single person households and older two person households were less likely than other households to have satellite, cable or digital TV. For example, 16% of older single person households had satellite, cable or digital TV compared with 59% of large adult households.

Table 4.22

Consumer durables and lone parent families

Consumer durables common to most households such as televisions, video recorders, central heating and the presence of a phone showed little difference between lone parent families and other households with dependent children, while access to other facilities such as access to the internet at home, revealed greater differences. Differences between lone parent families and other families were:

- car or van (51% compared with 93%)
- home computer (49% compared with 75%)
- access to the internet (31% compared with 59%)
- tumble drier (60% compared with 72%)
- mobile phone (76% compared with 85%)
- central heating (92% compared with 95%)
- video recorder (94% compared with 98%)

Table 4.23

Notes

1 Since 1996, housing associations are more correctly described as Registered Social Landlords (RSLs). RSLs are not-for-profit organisations which include: charitable housing associations, industrial and provident societies and companies registered under the Companies Act 1985.

Table 4.1 **Tenure: 1971 to 2001**

Households *Great Britain*

Tenure	Unweighted									Weighted		
	1971	1975	1981	1985	1991	1993	1995	1996	1998	1998	2000	2001
	%	%	%	%	%	%	%	%	%			
Owner occupied, owned outright	22	22	23	24	25	26	25	26	28	26	27	27
Owner occupied, with mortgage	27	28	31	37	42	41	42	41	41	42	41	41
Rented from council*	31	33	34	28	24	22	18	19	16	17	16	15
Rented from housing association	1	1	2	2	3	3	4	5	5	5	6	6
Rented with job or business	5	3	2	2	1	1	2	**	**	**	**	**
Rented privately, unfurnished†	12	10	6	5	4	4	5	7	7	7	7	7
Rented privately, furnished	3	3	2	2	2	3	3	3	2	3	3	3
Weighted base (000's) = 100%††										*24,436*	*24,838*	*24,592*
Unweighted sample††	*11936*	*11970*	*11939*	*9933*	*9922*	*9823*	*9723*	*9155*	*8631*		*8219*	*8989*

* Council includes local authorities, New Towns and Scottish Homes from 1996.
† Unfurnished includes the answer 'partly furnished'.
** From 1996 all tenants whose accommodation goes with the job of someone in the household have been allocated to 'rented privately'. Squatters are also included in the privately rented category.
†† Trend tables show unweighted and weighted figures for 1998 to give an indication of the effect of the weighting. For the weighted data (1998, 2000 and 2001) the weighted base (000's) is the base for percentages. Unweighted data (up to 1998) are based on the unweighted sample.

Weighting to be revised in Spring 2003 following the 2001 census revisions of population estimates. See Appendix D.

Table 4.2 **Type of accommodation: 1971 to 2001**

Households *Great Britain*

Type of accommodation*	Unweighted									Weighted		
	1971	1975	1981	1985	1991	1993	1995	1996	1998	1998	2000	2001
	%	%	%	%	%	%	%	%	%			
Detached house	16	15	16	19	19	19	22	21	23	21	21	21
Semi-detached house	33	34	32	31	32	31	31	32	33	32	31	31
Terraced house	30	28	31	29	29	29	28	27	26	26	28	28
Purpose-built flat or maisonette	13	14	15	15	14	15	15	15	15	17	16	16
Converted flat or maisonette/rooms	6	8	5	5	4	5	4	5	4	4	4	4
With business premises/other	2	1	1	1	1	1	1	0	0	0	0	0
Weighted base (000's) = 100%†										*24,398*	*24,806*	*24,520*
Unweighted sample†	*11846*	*12041*	*11978*	*9890*	*9917*	*9830*	*9730*	*9128*	*8615*		*8207*	*8963*

* Tables for type of accommodation exclude households living in caravans.
† See the fourth footnote to Table 4.1.

Weighting to be revised in Spring 2003 following the 2001 census revisions of population estimates. See Appendix D.

Table 4.3 **Type of accommodation occupied by households renting from a council compared with other households: 1981 to 2001**

Households *Great Britain*

Type of accommodation	Unweighted							Weighted data		
	1981	1987	1991	1993	1995	1996	1998	1998	2000	2001
	%	%	%	%	%	%	%	%	%	%
Renting from council										
Detached house	1	1	1	1	0	1	1	1	1	1
Semi-detached house	30	28	28	26	28	28	29	27	27	26
Terraced house	34	35	34	33	33	31	28	27	31	29
Purpose-built flat or maisonette	33	34	35	37	38	38	40	43	40	42
Converted flat or maisonette	2	2	3	3	1	2	2	2	2	2
*Weighted base (000's) = 100%**								*4,021*	*3,870*	*3,695*
*Unweighted sample**	*4007*	*2600*	*2339*	*2121*	*1770*	*1748*	*1410*		*1240*	*1325*
	%	%	%	%	%	%	%	%	%	%
Other households										
Detached house	24	25	25	24	26	25	27	26	24	25
Semi-detached house	33	33	33	33	32	33	33	32	32	32
Terraced house	29	28	28	28	27	27	26	26	27	27
Purpose-built flat or maisonette	6	7	8	9	10	9	10	11	11	11
Converted flat or maisonette	7	5	5	6	4	5	4	5	5	4
*Weighted base (000's) = 100%**								*20,328*	*20,896*	*20,808*
*Unweighted sample**	*7904*	*7511*	*7578*	*7699*	*7953*	*7379*	*7189*		*6954*	*7632*
	%	%	%	%	%	%	%	%	%	%
All households										
Detached house	16	18	19	19	22	21	23	22	21	21
Semi-detached house	32	32	32	31	31	32	33	32	31	31
Terraced house	31	30	29	29	28	27	26	26	28	28
Purpose-built flat or maisonette	15	14	14	15	15	15	15	17	16	16
Converted flat or maisonette	5	5	4	5	4	5	4	4	4	4
*Weighted base (000's) = 100%**								*24,349*	*24,766*	*24,503*
*Unweighted sample**	*11911*	*10111*	*9917*	*9820*	*9723*	*9127*	*8599*		*8194*	*8957*

* See the fourth footnote to Table 4.1.

Weighting to be revised in Spring 2003 following the 2001 census revisions of population estimates. See Appendix D.

Table 4.4 (a) Type of accommodation by tenure (b) Tenure by type of accommodation

Households *Great Britain: 2001*

Tenure		Type of accommodation* Detached house	Semi-detached house	Terraced house	All houses	Purpose-built flat or maisonette	Converted flat or maisonette/ rooms	All flats/ rooms	*Weighted base (000's) = 100%*	*Unweighted sample*
(a)										
Owner occupied, owned outright	%	34	35	22	91	7	2	9	*6,612*	*2573*
Owner occupied, with mortgage	%	25	35	29	89	8	2	11	*10,171*	*3672*
All owners	%	29	35	26	90	8	2	10	*16,784*	*6245*
Rented from council†	%	1	26	29	56	42	2	44	*3,695*	*1325*
Rented from housing association	%	2	18	32	52	41	6	48	*1,532*	*555*
Social sector tenants	%	1	24	30	55	42	3	45	*5,227*	*1880*
Rented privately, unfurnished**	%	16	24	32	72	13	14	28	*1,715*	*594*
Rented privately, furnished	%	7	11	27	45	26	28	55	*777*	*238*
Private renters††	%	13	20	31	64	17	19	36	*2,493*	*832*
Total	%	21	31	28	80	16	4	20	*24,503*	*8957*
(b)										
		%	%	%	%	%	%	%	%	
Owner occupied, owned outright		43	30	22	31	12	12	12	27	
Owner occupied, with mortgage		50	47	44	47	21	24	22	42	
All owners		93	77	65	77	33	36	34	68	
Rented from council†		1	13	16	11	40	7	33	15	
Rented from housing association		0	4	7	4	16	10	15	6	
Social sector tenants		1	16	23	15	56	17	48	21	
Rented privately, unfurnished**		5	5	8	6	6	25	10	7	
Rented privately, furnished		1	1	3	2	5	22	9	3	
Private renters††		6	6	11	8	11	47	18	10	
Weighted base (000's) = 100%		*5,167*	*7,654*	*6,746*	*19,568*	*3,940*	*995*	*4,935*	*24,503*	
Unweighted sample		*1981*	*2893*	*2483*	*7357*	*1268*	*332*	*1600*	*8957*	

* Tables for type of accommodation exclude households living in caravans.
† Council includes local authorities, New Towns and Scottish Homes.
** Unfurnished includes the answer 'partly furnished'.
†† All tenants whose accommodation goes with the job of someone in the household have been allocated to 'rented privately'. Squatters are also included in the privately rented category.

Weighting to be revised in Spring 2003 following the 2001 census revisions of population estimates. See Appendix D.

Table 4.5 **Age of building by tenure**

Households *Great Britain: 2001*

Age of building* containing household's accommodation	Tenure									
	Owners			Social sector tenants			Private renters			Total
	Owned outright	With mortgage	All owners	Council†	Housing association	Social sector tenants	Unfurnished private**	Furnished private	Private Renters††	
(a)	%	%	%	%	%	%	%	%	%	%
Before 1919	23	22	23	4	16	7	43	50	45	22
1919-1944	21	19	20	18	10	15	21	18	20	19
1945-1964	23	18	20	41	20	35	14	8	12	22
1965-1984	24	23	23	32	24	30	13	15	14	24
1985 or later	9	17	14	5	31	13	9	9	9	13
Weighted base (000's) = 100%	*6,558*	*10,062*	*16,620*	*3,488*	*1,458*	*4,946*	*1,637*	*739*	*2,377*	*23,943*
Unweighted sample	*2553*	*3633*	*6186*	*1254*	*530*	*1784*	*567*	*226*	*793*	*8763*

* For an assessment of the reliability of age of building estimates, see Birch F, Age of buildings (OPCS Social Survey Division, GHS Series No.7, 1974).

† ** †† See the footnotes to Table 4.4.

Weighting to be revised in Spring 2003 following the 2001 census revisions of population estimates. See Appendix D.

Table 4.6 (a) Household type by tenure (b) Tenure by household type

Households *Great Britain: 2001*

Tenure		Household type							*Weighted base (000's) = 100%*	*Unweighted sample*
		1 adult aged 16-59	2 adults aged 16-59	Small family	Large family	Large adult household	2 adults, 1 or both aged 60 or over	1 adult aged 60 or over		
(a)										
Owner occupied, owned outright	%	8	11	4	1	11	36	29	*6,681*	*2598*
Owner occupied, with mortgage	%	16	24	27	7	19	5	2	*10,175*	*3673*
All owners	%	13	18	18	5	16	17	13	*16,856*	*6271*
Rented from council*	%	18	9	20	7	8	12	26	*3,698*	*1326*
Rented from housing association	%	16	9	21	8	9	10	27	*1,538*	*557*
Social sector tenants	%	17	9	20	7	8	11	27	*5,236*	*1883*
Rented privately, unfurnished†	%	21	23	23	6	8	8	10	*1,722*	*597*
Rented privately, furnished	%	42	22	9	1	19	1	5	*777*	*238*
Private renters**	%	27	23	19	4	11	6	9	*2,500*	*835*
Total	%	15	17	19	5	14	15	15	*24,592*	*8989*
(b)									**Total**	
		%	%	%	%	%	%	%	%	
Owner occupied, owned outright		14	17	5	7	22	66	52	27	
Owner occupied, with mortgage		44	58	61	55	56	14	5	41	
All owners		58	75	66	62	78	80	57	69	
Rented from council*		17	8	16	19	9	12	26	15	
Rented from housing association		7	3	7	10	4	4	11	6	
Social sector tenants		24	11	23	29	13	16	37	21	
Rented privately, unfurnished†		9	10	9	8	4	4	5	7	
Rented privately, furnished		9	4	2	1	4	0	1	3	
Private renters**		18	14	10	8	8	4	6	10	
Weighted base (000's) = 100%		*3,779*	*4,128*	*4,564*	*1,311*	*3,399*	*3,667*	*3,745*	*24,592*	
Unweighted sample		*1167*	*1491*	*1738*	*514*	*1172*	*1480*	*1427*	*8989*	

* † ** See the footnotes to Table 4.1.

Weighting to be revised in Spring 2003 following the 2001 census revisions of population estimates. See Appendix D.

Table 4.7 **Housing profile by family type: lone-parent families compared with other families**

*Families with dependent children** *Great Britain: 2000 and 2001 combined*

	Lone-parent families	Other families
	%	%
Tenure		
Owner occupied, owned outright	6	7
Owner occupied, with mortgage	29	71
Rented from council or from housing association	50	15
Rented privately unfurnished	12	6
Rented privately furnished	2	1
Central heating	%	%
Yes	92	95
No	8	5
Type of accommodation	%	%
Detached house	8	27
Semi-detached house	30	37
Terraced house	42	28
Purpose-built flat or maisonette	21	7
Converted flat or maisonette/rooms	0	0
Bedroom standard	%	%
2 or more below standard	1	1
1 below standard	10	4
Equals standard	54	35
1 above standard	30	44
2 or more above standard	4	16
Persons per room	%	%
Under 0.5	21	8
0.5-0.99	71	76
1.0-1.49	8	16
1.5 or above	0	0
Unweighted sample†	*1348*	*3816*

* Dependent children are persons aged under 16, or aged 16-18 and in full-time education, in the family unit, and living in the household.
† Weighted base not shown for combined data sets.

Table 4.8 **Type of accommodation by household type**

Households *Great Britain: 2001*

Household type		Type of accommodation*							*Weighted base (000's) = 100%*	*Unweighted sample*
		Detached house	Semi-detached house	Terraced house	All houses	Purpose-built flat or maisonette	Converted flat or maisonette/ rooms	All flats/ rooms		
One adult aged 16-59	%	9	20	26	55	33	12	45	*3,765*	*1163*
Two adults aged 16-59	%	22	32	27	82	13	5	18	*4,125*	*1490*
Small family	%	22	34	31	87	11	2	13	*4,560*	*1737*
Large family	%	22	39	33	94	5	1	6	*1,311*	*514*
Large adult household	%	26	36	32	94	5	1	6	*3,397*	*1171*
Two adults, one or both aged 60 or over	%	32	34	23	89	10	1	11	*3,640*	*1470*
One adult aged 60 or over	%	15	29	24	68	29	3	32	*3,705*	*1412*
Total	%	21	31	28	80	16	4	20	*24,503*	*8957*

* See the first footnote to Table 4.4.

Weighting to be revised in Spring 2003 following the 2001 census revisions of population estimates. See Appendix D.

Table 4.9 **Usual gross weekly income by tenure**

Households — *Great Britain: 2001*

Usual gross weekly income (£)	Tenure									
	Owners			Social sector tenants			Private renters			Total
	Owned outright	With mortgage	All owners	Council*	Housing association	Social sector	Unfurnished private† tenants	Furnished private	Private renters**	
Income of household reference person										
Mean	309	503	428	148	165	153	279	315	290	354
Lower quartile	116	247	156	84	85	84	99	58	92	112
Median	204	394	325	121	130	123	222	202	216	250
Upper quartile	356	577	508	200	220	204	370	381	370	441
Income of household reference person and partner										
Mean	394	675	566	186	199	190	353	361	356	462
Lower quartile	143	325	212	91	91	91	119	70	106	141
Median	255	530	420	136	146	139	261	225	249	314
Upper quartile	462	788	692	238	266	250	477	476	477	584
Total household income										
Mean	422	713	600	208	216	210	382	433	398	493
Lower quartile	156	350	232	92	92	92	126	109	120	156
Median	279	559	454	150	156	151	281	262	276	346
Upper quartile	505	843	738	273	284	275	521	546	526	628
Weighted base (000's) = 100%	*6,069*	*9,562*	*15,631*	*3,540*	*1,472*	*5,012*	*1,632*	*731*	*2,362*	*23,005*
Unweighted sample	*2354*	*3450*	*5804*	*1267*	*535*	*1802*	*566*	*224*	*790*	*8396*

* † ** See the footnotes to Table 4.1.

Weighting to be revised in Spring 2003 following the 2001 census revisions of population estimates. See Appendix D.

Table 4.10 (a) Age of household reference person by tenure (b) Tenure by age of household reference person

Household reference persons — *Great Britain: 2001*

Tenure		Age of household reference person*								Weighted base (000's) = 100%	Unweighted sample
		Under 25	25-29	30-44	45-59	60-64	65-69	70-79	80 and over		
(a)											
Owner occupied, owned outright	%	0	1	6	25	13	[15]	27	13	*6,681*	*2598*
Owner occupied, with mortgage	%	2	9	[49]	33	4	2	1	0	*10,175*	*3673*
All owners	%	2	5	32	[30]	7	7	12	5	*16,856*	*6271*
Rented from council†	%	6	7	25	[20]	7	8	16	10	*3,698*	*1326*
Rented from housing association	%	7	7	31	[18]	6	5	15	12	*1,538*	*557*
Social sector tenants	%	6	7	27	[20]	7	7	16	11	*5,236*	*1883*
Rented privately, unfurnished**	%	12	15	[37]	17	3	2	7	6	*1,722*	*597*
Rented privately, furnished	%	30	[25]	30	8	3	1	2	1	*777*	*238*
Private renters††	%	18	18	[35]	14	3	2	5	4	*2,500*	*835*
Total	%	4	7	31	[26]	7	6	12	7	*24,592*	*8989*
(b)										Total	
		%	%	%	%	%	%	%	%	%	
Owner occupied, owned outright		2	2	5	26	52	63	62	56	27	
Owner occupied, with mortgage		24	50	65	52	22	11	5	2	41	
All owners		26	52	70	78	74	74	67	58	69	
Rented from council†		22	15	12	12	16	18	21	24	15	
Rented from housing association		10	6	6	4	5	5	8	11	6	
Social sector tenants		32	21	18	16	21	23	29	36	21	
Rented privately, unfurnished**		20	15	8	5	3	2	4	7	7	
Rented privately, furnished		23	11	3	1	2	0	0	0	3	
Private renters††		43	26	11	6	5	3	5	7	10	
Weighted base (000's) = 100%		*1,033*	*1,754*	*7,694*	*6,356*	*1,671*	*1,572*	*2,910*	*1,602*	*24,592*	
Unweighted sample		*324*	*596*	*2692*	*2356*	*652*	*637*	*1132*	*600*	*8989*	

* Boxed figures indicate median age-groups.
† ** †† See the footnotes to Table 4.4.

Weighting to be revised in Spring 2003 following the 2001 census revisions of population estimates. See Appendix D.

Table 4.11 **Tenure by sex and marital status of household reference person**

Household reference persons *Great Britain: 2001*

Tenure	Males						Females						Total
	Married	Cohabiting	Single	Widowed	Divorced/ separated	All males	Married	Cohabiting	Single	Widowed	Divorced/ separated	All females	
	%	%	%	%	%	%	%	%	%	%	%	%	%
Owner occupied, owned outright	31	7	16	51	18	26	26	8	13	57	17	29	27
Owner occupied, with mortgage	53	64	38	7	34	48	53	46	27	5	35	29	41
All owners	84	71	54	58	52	74	79	55	40	62	51	58	69
Rented from council*	8	8	16	27	23	11	11	21	26	24	27	22	15
Rented from housing association	3	4	6	8	10	5	4	8	14	9	10	9	6
Social sector tenants	11	12	22	36	33	16	15	28	41	33	38	32	21
Rented privately, unfurnished†	5	13	10	5	9	7	5	11	11	4	10	8	7
Rented privately, furnished	1	4	14	1	6	3	1	6	9	1	1	3	3
Private renters**	5	17	24	7	15	10	6	17	20	5	11	11	10
Weighted base (000's) = 100%	*10,075*	*1,434*	*2,366*	*730*	*1,291*	*15,895*	*1,759*	*706*	*1,785*	*2,455*	*1,992*	*8,697*	*24,592*
Unweighted sample	*3839*	*501*	*683*	*281*	*405*	*5709*	*665*	*250*	*675*	*926*	*764*	*3280*	*8989*

* † ** See the footnotes to Table 4.1.

Weighting to be revised in Spring 2003 following the 2001 census revisions of population estimates. See Appendix D.

Table 4.12 (a) Socio-economic classification and economic activity status of household reference person by tenure (b) Tenure by socio-economic classification and economic activity status of household reference person

Household reference persons *Great Britain: 2001*

Socio-economic classification and economic activity status of household reference person*	Tenure									
	Owners			Social sector tenants			Private renters			Total
	Owned outright	With mortgage	All owners	Council†	Housing association	Social sector tenants	Unfurnished private**	Furnished private	Private Renters††	
(a)	%	%	%	%	%	%	%	%	%	%
Economically active HRP:										
Large employers and higher managerial	2	8	6	0	1	0	2	2	2	4
Higher professional	4	12	9	0	1	1	7	10	8	7
Lower managerial and professional	8	27	20	3	5	3	16	21	18	16
Intermediate	3	8	6	3	5	3	6	10	7	6
Small employers and own account	6	9	8	2	4	2	8	4	7	7
Lower supervisory and technical	3	11	8	5	6	5	8	4	7	7
Semi-routine	5	8	7	9	8	9	11	9	10	7
Routine	3	8	6	10	7	9	7	6	7	7
Never worked and long-term unemployed	0	0	0	4	3	3	3	4	3	1
Economically inactive HRP	65	8	31	65	61	64	32	30	31	38
Weighted base (000's) = 100%	*6,636*	*10,030*	*16,666*	*3,659*	*1,532*	*5,191*	*1,694*	*692*	*2,387*	*24,244*
Unweighted sample	*2582*	*3623*	*6205*	*1314*	*555*	*1869*	*587*	*213*	*800*	*8874*

(b)		Owned outright	With mortgage	All owners	Council†	Housing association	Social sector tenants	Unfurnished private**	Furnished private	Private Renters††	*Weighted base (000's) = 100%*	*Unweighted sample*
Economically active HRP:												
Large employers and higher managerial	%	15	79	94	0	1	1	4	2	5	*1,026*	*381*
Higher professional	%	14	72	87	1	1	2	7	4	12	*1,661*	*604*
Lower managerial and professional	%	14	70	85	3	2	4	7	4	11	*3,856*	*1394*
Intermediate	%	16	59	75	7	6	13	8	5	12	*1,392*	*487*
Small employers and own account	%	24	59	82	4	3	8	8	2	10	*1,590*	*572*
Lower supervisory and technical	%	12	64	79	9	5	14	8	2	9	*1,792*	*617*
Semi-routine	%	17	45	61	18	7	25	10	3	13	*1,811*	*650*
Routine	%	13	48	61	23	6	29	7	2	10	*1,646*	*577*
Never worked and long-term unemployed	%	6	7	14	47	15	62	15	10	24	*294*	*98*
Economically inactive HRP	%	47	9	56	26	10	36	6	2	8	*9,176*	*3494*
Total	%	27	41	69	15	6	21	7	3	10	*24,244*	*8874*

* From April 2001 the National Statistics Social-economic Classification (NS-SEC) was introduced for all official statistics and surveys. It has replaced Social Class based on Occupation and Socio-economic Groups (SEG). Excludes full-time students and persons in inadequately described occupations.

†, **, †† See the footnotes to Table 4.4.

Weighting to be revised in Spring 2003 following the 2001 census revisions of population estimates. See Appendix D.

Table 4.13 (a) Length of residence of household reference person by tenure (b) Tenure by length of residence of household reference person

Household reference persons — *Great Britain: 2001*

Length of residence* (years)	Tenure									
	Owners			Social sector tenants			Private renters			Total
	Owned outright	With mortgage	All owners	Council†	Housing association	Social sector tenants	Unfurnished private**	Furnished private	Private Renters††	
(a)	%	%	%	%	%	%	%	%	%	%
Less than 12 months	3	9	6	10	12	10	27	52	35	10
12 months but less than 2 years	3	8	6	6	9	7	16	17	16	7
2 years but less than 3 years	3	9	6	7	10	8	12	9	11	7
3 years but less than 5 years	6	15	11	13	18	15	12	8	10	12
5 years but less than 10 years	10	21	17	18	21	19	13	8	12	17
10 years or more	75	39	53	45	30	41	20	6	16	47
Weighted base (000's) = 100%	*6,681*	*10,175*	*16,856*	*3,698*	*1,538*	*5,236*	*1,722*	*777*	*2,500*	*24,592*
Unweighted sample	*2598*	*3673*	*6271*	*1326*	*557*	*1883*	*597*	*238*	*835*	*8989*

b)		Owned outright	With mortgage	All owners	Council†	Housing association	Social sector tenants	Unfurnished private**	Furnished private	Private Renters††	*Weighted base (000's) = 100%*	*Un-weighted sample*
Less than 12 months	%	8	36	43	14	7	22	19	16	35	*2,506*	*838*
12 months but less than 2 years	%	11	46	57	13	7	20	16	7	23	*1,771*	*616*
2 years but less than 3 years	%	12	50	61	15	9	23	11	4	15	*1,782*	*634*
3 years but less than 5 years	%	14	51	65	17	10	26	7	2	9	*2,920*	*1035*
5 years but less than 10 years	%	16	53	69	16	8	24	6	1	7	*4,120*	*1517*
10 years or more	%	44	34	78	15	4	19	3	0	3	*11,494*	*4349*
Total	%	27	41	69	15	6	21	7	3	10	*24,592*	*8989*

* Boxed figures indicate median length of residence.
† ** †† See the footnotes to Table 4.4.

Weighting to be revised in Spring 2003 following the 2001 census revisions of population estimates. See Appendix D.

Table 4.14 Persons per room: 1971 to 2001

Households — *Great Britain*

Persons per room	Unweighted									Weighted		
	1971	1975	1981	1985	1991	1993	1995	1996	1998	1998	2000	2001
	%	%	%	%	%	%	%	%	%	%	%	%
Under 0.5	37	39	42	45	50	51	52	51	55	55	57	57
0.5 to 0.65	25	25	25	26	24	24	25	24	23	23	22	22
0.66 to 0.99	24	23	23	21	19	19	18	19	18	18	16	16
1	9	8	7	6	5	5	5	5	4	4	4	4
Over 1 to 1.5	4	3	2	1	1	1	1	1	1	1	1	1
Over 1.5	1	0	0	0	0	0	0	0	0	0	0	0
*Weighted base (000's) = 100%**										*24,450*	*24,845*	*24,592*
*Unweighted sample**	*11990*	*12096*	*12002*	*9982*	*9646*	*9663*	*9754*	*9154*	*8636*		*8221*	*8989*
Mean persons per room	..	0.57	0.56	0.52	0.50	0.49	0.48	0.49	0.47	0.46	0.45	0.46

* See the fourth footnote to Table 4.1.

Weighting to be revised in Spring 2003 following the 2001 census revisions of population estimates. See Appendix D.

Table 4.15 Persons per room and mean household size by tenure

Households *Great Britain: 2001*

Persons per room*	Tenure									
	Owners			Social sector tenants			Private renters			Total
	Owned outright	With mortgage	All owners	Council†	Housing association	Social sector tenants	Unfur-nished private**	Furnished private	Private renters††	
	%	%	%	%	%	%	%	%	%	%
Under 0.5	[80]	47	[60]	[53]	47	[51]	50	46	49	[57]
0.5 to 0.65	14	[26]	22	22	[24]	23	[25]	[27]	[26]	22
0.66 to 0.99	5	22	15	17	19	18	19	20	19	16
1	1	4	3	6	7	6	6	7	6	4
Over 1	0	1	1	2	2	2	1	1	1	1
Weighted base (000's) = 100%	*6,681*	*10,175*	*16,856*	*3,698*	*1,538*	*5,236*	*1,722*	*777*	*2,500*	*24,592*
Unweighted sample	*2598*	*3673*	*6271*	*1326*	*557*	*1883*	*597*	*238*	*835*	*8989*
Mean persons per room	0.34	0.50	0.44	0.49	0.52	0.50	0.48	0.50	0.49	0.46
Mean household size	1.89	2.76	2.42	2.11	2.17	2.13	2.23	1.99	2.16	2.33

* Boxed figures indicate median density of occupation.
† ** †† See the footnotes to Table 4.4.

Weighting to be revised in Spring 2003 following the 2001 census revisions of population estimates. See Appendix D.

Table 4.16 Closeness of fit relative to the bedroom standard by tenure

Households *Great Britain: 2001*

Difference from bedroom standard (bedrooms)	Tenure									
	Owners			Social sector tenants			Private renters			Total
	Owned outright	With mortgage	All owners	Council*	Housing association	Social sector tenants	Unfur-nished private†	Furnished private	Private renters**	
	%	%	%	%	%	%	%	%	%	%
1 or more below standard	1	2	1	4	4	4	4	3	3	2
Equals standard	9	21	16	49	61	52	33	52	39	26
1 above standard	34	42	39	34	28	32	43	30	39	38
2 or more above standard	56	35	44	13	7	11	21	15	19	34
Weighted base (000's) = 100%	*6,681*	*10,175*	*16,856*	*3,698*	*1,538*	*5,236*	*1,722*	*777*	*2,500*	*24,592*
Unweighted sample	*2598*	*3673*	*6271*	*1326*	*557*	*1883*	*597*	*238*	*835*	*8989*

* Council includes local authorities, New Towns and Scottish Homes.
† Unfurnished includes the answer 'partly furnished'.
** All tenants whose accommodation goes with the job of someone in the household have been allocated to 'rented privately'. Squatters are also included in the privately rented category.

Weighting to be revised in Spring 2003 following the 2001 census revisions of population estimates. See Appendix D.

Table 4.17 Cars or vans: 1972 to 2001

Households *Great Britain*

Cars or vans	Unweighted									Weighted		
	1972	1975	1981	1985	1991	1993	1995	1996	1998	1998	2000	2001
	%	%	%	%	%	%	%	%	%	%	%	%
Households with:												
no car or van	48	44	41	38	32	32	29	30	28	28	27	28
one car or van	43	45	44	45	44	45	45	46	44	45	45	44
two cars or vans	8	10	12	14	19	20	22	21	23	22	22	23
three or more cars or vans	1	1	2	3	4	4	4	4	6	6	6	5
*Weighted base (000's) = 100%**										*24,450*	*24,845*	*24,592*
*Unweighted sample**	*11624*	*11929*	*11989*	*9963*	*9910*	*9851*	*9758*	*9158*	*8636*		*8221*	*8989*

* See the fourth footnote to Table 4.1.

Weighting to be revised in Spring 2003 following the 2001 census revisions of population estimates. See Appendix D.

Table 4.18 Availability of a car or van by socio-economic classification of household reference person

Households *Great Britain: 2001*

Socio-economic classification of household reference person*		Number of cars or vans available to household			*Weighted base (000's) = 100%*	*Unweighted sample*
		None	1	2 or more		
Economically active HRP						
Large employers and higher managerial	%	4	31	65	*1,026*	*381*
Higher professional	%	5	47	48	*1,661*	*604*
Lower managerial and professional	%	9	44	47	*3,856*	*1394*
Intermediate	%	18	56	26	*1,392*	*487*
Small employers and own account	%	5	36	59	*1,590*	*572*
Lower supervisory and technical	%	11	51	38	*1,792*	*617*
Semi-routine	%	25	56	20	*1,811*	*650*
Routine	%	23	51	26	*1,646*	*577*
Never worked and long-term unemployed	%	74	22	4	*294*	*98*
Economically inactive HRP	%	51	41	8	*9,176*	*3494*
Total	%	28	44	28	*24,244*	*8874*

* From April 2001 the National Statistics Social-economic Classification (NS-SEC) was introduced for all official statistics and surveys. It has replaced Social Class based on Occupation and Socio-economic Groups (SEG). Excludes full-time students and persons in inadequately described occupations.

Weighting to be revised in Spring 2003 following the 2001 census revisions of population estimates. See Appendix D.

Table 4.19 **Consumer durables, central heating and cars: 1972 to 2001**

Households *Great Britain*

	Unweighted									Weighted		
	1972	**1975**	**1981**	**1985**	**1991**	**1993**	**1995**	**1996**	**1998**	**1998**	**2000**	**2001**
Percentage of households with:												
Television												
colour	93	96	74 (97)	86 (98)	95 (98)	95 (98)	97 (98)	97 (99)	98 (98)	97 (98)	98 (99)	98 (99)
black and white only			23	11	4	3	2	2	1	1	1	0
satellite/cable/digital	..	..	..	..	..	..	..	18	29	29	40	42
Video recorder	..	..	..	31	68	73	79	82	85	85	88	88
CD player	..	..	..	..	27	39	52	58	68	69	77	80
Home computer	..	..	..	13	21	24	25	27	34	34	45	50
Access to internet at home	..	..	..	..	..	..	..	..	..	..	33	40
Access from home computer	..	..	..	..	..	..	..	..	..	..	31	37
Other access	..	..	..	..	..	..	..	..	..	..	2	6
Microwave oven	..	..	..	..	55	62	70	74	79	78	83	85
Refrigerator*	73	88	93	95	..	..	..	..	..	..	..	..
Deep freezer*	..	..	49	66	83	86	89	91	93	92	93	94
Washing machine	66	71	78	81	87	88	90	90	92	91	93	92
Tumble drier	..	..	23	33	48	49	51	51	52	51	54	54
Dishwasher	..	..	4	6	14	16	20	20	24	23	26	28
Telephone (fixed or mobile)	42	54	75	81	88	90	93	94	96	96	98	98
fixed telephone†	..	..	..	..	..	..	..	..	..	..	93	93
mobile telephone†	..	..	..	..	..	..	..	..	..	..	58	70
Central heating	37	43	59	69	82	83	86	88	90	90	92	92
A car or van	43 (52)	45 (56)	44 (59)	45 (62)	44 (67)	45 (68)	45 (71)	46 (70)	44 (72)	45 (72)	45 (73)	44 (72)
- more than 1	9	11	14	17	23	23	26	24	28	27	28	28
Weighted base (000's) = 100%*										*24,450*	*24,575*	*24,592*
Unweighted sample*	*11663*	*11929*	*11718*	*9993*	*9955*	*9850*	*9757*	*9156*	*8636*		*8213*	*8984*

* Fridge freezers are attributed to both 'refrigerator' and 'deep freezer' from 1979 on.
† Data only available for 2000 and 2001. Percentages for fixed and mobile phones sum to greater than 100% because some households owned both.
** See the fourth footnote to Table 4.1.

Weighting to be revised in Spring 2003 following the 2001 census revisions of population estimates. See Appendix D.

Table 4.20 Consumer durables, central heating and cars by socio-economic classification of household reference person

Household reference persons *Great Britain: 2001*

Consumer durables	Socio-economic classification of household reference person*									
	Economically active								Economically inactive	Total
	Large employers and higher managerial	Higher professional	Lower managerial and professional	Intermediate	Small employers and own account	Lower supervisory and technical	Semi-routine	Routine		
Television										
colour	100	99	98	98	98	99	99	99	98	98
black and white	0	0	0	0	0	0	0	0	0	0
satellite TV/cable/digital	54	45	52	47	47	59	51	52	29	42
Video recorder	98	94	96	94	96	96	95	95	78	88
CD player	99	97	94	92	88	93	88	85	59	79
Home computer	82	86	76	59	66	57	48	43	24	49
Access to internet at home	76	79	66	48	51	42	33	32	17	40
Microwave oven	93	85	89	88	89	92	91	89	79	85
Deep freezer/ fridge freezer	98	97	97	93	96	98	96	95	92	94
Washing machine	98	98	97	94	96	97	94	93	86	92
Tumble drier	70	61	61	58	64	64	57	59	43	54
Dishwasher	67	50	42	25	43	27	18	16	15	28
Telephone (fixed or mobile)	100	100	100	99	100	99	98	98	96	98
fixed telephone†	99	99	96	93	98	92	91	87	91	93
mobile telephone†	93	88	89	82	86	86	78	81	45	70
Central heating	99	97	95	91	94	91	90	88	91	92
Car or van - more than 1	65	48	46	26	59	38	20	26	8	28
Weighted base (000's) = 100%	*1,026*	*1,661*	*3,856*	*1,392*	*1,590*	*1,792*	*1,807*	*1,646*	*9,166*	*24,227*
Unweighted sample	*381*	*604*	*1394*	*487*	*572*	*617*	*649*	*577*	*3491*	*8869*

* From April 2001 the National Statistics Social-economic Classification (NS-SEC) was introduced for all official statistics and surveys. It has replaced Social Class based on Occupation and Socio-economic Groups (SEG). Excludes full-time students and persons in inadequately described occupations.

Weighting to be revised in Spring 2003 following the 2001 census revisions of population estimates. See Appendix D.

Table 4.21 Consumer durables, central heating and cars by usual gross weekly household income

Households *Great Britain: 2001*

Consumer durables	Usual gross weekly household income (£)										
	0.01-100	100.01-150	150.01-200	200.01-250	250.01-300	300.01-350	350.01-400	400.01-450	450.01-500	500.01 or more	Total*
Percentage of households with:											
Television											
colour	97	98	99	98	99	97	98	99	100	99	98
black and white only	1	0	0	1	0	0	0	0	0	0	0
satellite/cable/digital	27	27	31	34	40	41	49	47	50	54	42
Video recorder	72	76	84	87	91	91	93	96	96	96	88
CD player	59	57	62	72	81	84	88	91	89	95	80
Home computer	27	22	29	31	41	42	50	55	58	75	50
Access to internet at home	20	14	20	23	27	29	37	40	46	66	40
Microwave oven	77	82	80	82	85	85	91	88	90	90	85
Deep freezer/fridge freezer	87	92	93	92	95	96	96	95	97	98	94
Washing machine	79	85	89	91	93	94	94	96	97	98	92
Tumble drier	42	40	44	47	52	53	52	57	58	65	54
Dishwasher	13	9	13	14	17	19	21	24	28	47	28
Telephone	94	96	98	97	99	98	100	99	99	100	98
fixed telephone†	84	87	91	90	91	89	94	94	96	98	93
mobile telephone†	49	46	48	57	68	69	75	79	81	89	70
Central heating	88	90	90	86	89	88	91	93	94	97	92
Car or van - more than 1	11	6	9	9	13	17	18	27	29	53	28
Weighted base (000's) = 100%	*2,884*	*2,043*	*1,831*	*1,564*	*1,405*	*1,267*	*1,212*	*974*	*1,089*	*7,895*	*24,592*
Unweighted sample	*1036*	*773*	*690*	*580*	*515*	*455*	*435*	*359*	*394*	*2859*	*8984*

* Total includes no answers to income.
† Percentages for fixed and mobile telephones sum to greater than 100 because some people owned both.

Weighting to be revised in Spring 2003 following the 2001 census revisions of population estimates. See Appendix D.

Table 4.22 Consumer durables, central heating and cars by household type

Households *Great Britain: 2001*

Consumer durables	Household type							
	1 adult aged 16-59	2 adults aged 16-59	Small family	Large family	Large adult household	2 adults, 1 or both aged 60 or over	1 adult aged 60 or over	Total
Percentage of households with:								
Television								
colour	95	99	100	99	100	100	97	98
black and white only	1	0	0	0	0	0	1	0
satellite TV/cable/digital	33	50	54	58	59	33	16	42
Video recorder	85	95	97	97	98	90	62	88
CD player	82	93	94	91	95	68	38	80
Home computer	45	62	68	73	73	30	8	50
Access to internet at home	36	54	55	55	58	22	5	40
Microwave oven	79	89	92	92	93	85	71	85
Deep freezer/fridge freezer	87	97	98	99	99	96	88	94
Washing machine	83	97	98	98	99	96	76	92
Tumble drier	38	58	66	74	68	52	33	54
Dishwasher	14	33	35	41	42	26	8	28
Telephone (fixed or mobile)	96	99	99	99	100	99	95	98
fixed telephone*	82	95	91	92	96	99	94	93
mobile telephone*	72	86	87	88	89	53	22	70
Central heating	88	94	95	95	94	92	89	92
Car or van - more than 1	5	45	37	40	57	19	1	28
Weighted base (000's) = 100%	*3,768*	*4,128*	*4,564*	*1,311*	*3,399*	*3,667*	*3,738*	*24,575*
Unweighted sample	*1164*	*1491*	*1738*	*514*	*1172*	*1480*	*1425*	*8984*

* Percentages for fixed and mobile telephones sum to greater than 100 because some households owned both.

Weighting to be revised in Spring 2003 following the 2001 census revisions of population estimates. See Appendix D.

Table 4.23 Consumer durables, central heating and cars: lone-parent families compared with other families

*Families with dependent children** *Great Britain: 2000 and 2001 combined*

Consumer durables	Lone-parent families	Other families
Percentage of households with:		
Television		
colour	99	100
black and white	0	0
satellite TV/cable/digital	46	60
Video recorder	94	98
CD player	90	95
Home computer	49	75
Access to internet at home	31	59
Microwave oven	89	92
Deep freezer/fridge freezer	97	99
Washing machine	96	99
Tumble drier	60	72
Dishwasher	18	45
Telephone (fixed or mobile)	98	99
fixed telephone†	83	96
mobile telephone†	76	85
Central heating	92	95
Car or van - one or more	51	93
*Unweighted sample**	*1348*	*3817*

* Dependent children are persons aged under 16, or aged 16-18 and in full-time education, and living in the household.
† Percentages for fixed and mobile telephones sum to greater than 100 because some households owned both.
** Weighted base not shown for combined data sets.

Chapter 5

Marriage and cohabitation

Over the last thirty years the GHS has collected details on current marital status. Periodically questions have been extended to include cohabitation reflecting the way society has changed. As a result the GHS is a key source of information on these topics.

- In 1979 questions on marital history for both men and women were introduced for the first time. In the same year, questions were introduced for women aged 18 to 49 relating to pre-marital cohabitation before the current or most recent marriage.
- In 1986 questions on pre-marital cohabitation were extended to include both men and women aged 16 to 59 and every marriage past and present.
- In 1998, a single question was added to ascertain the number of past cohabitations which did not end in marriage.
- In 2000 new questions[1] were included on the length of past cohabitations which did not end in marriage. These included the dates of the start and end of cohabitations and what people perceived to be the end of each cohabitation (the end of the relationship, the end of sharing accommodation or both).

Information relating to marital status is collected in two stages. Initially, at household level, the marital status of all adults aged 16 or over is collected from the respondent who answers the household questionnaire (usually the household reference person or their partner). Later each household member aged 16 to 59 is asked detailed questions about their marriage and cohabitation history. Where lack of privacy may affect reporting, interviewers offer respondents a self-completion questionnaire. In 2001, 3% of respondents chose this option (unweighted data).

Marital status

De facto marital status (that is, including cohabitation) was ascertained by combining the information on marital status with whether the respondent was currently cohabiting. Cohabiting couples were defined as people who were living together in a household as a couple without being married to each other. Respondents who were single, widowed, divorced or separated but who were cohabiting are here classified as cohabiting - rather than by their legal marital status - while those not cohabiting are classified by their marital status.

In 2001, the de facto marital status of adults aged 16 and over was as follows:

- 54% of men and 52% of women were married;
- 10% of men and 9% of women were cohabiting;
- 27% of men and 18% of women were single;
- 3% of men and 11% of women were widowed;
- 6% of men were either divorced or separated, compared with 9% of women.

Among the total adult population in 2001 over twice as many women as men were either married or cohabiting in the 16 to 24 age group; 7% of women were married compared with 3% of men, and 17% women were cohabiting compared with 8% of men. This difference decreased among those aged 25 to 34 with 70% of women married or cohabiting compared with 58% of men. Among people aged 35 to 44 there was no difference between the proportion of men and women who were married or cohabiting (76%). **Tables 5.1-5.2**

Current cohabitation

All marital status groups are represented among cohabiters, with the exception of married people living with their spouse, who, by definition, cannot be cohabiting.

Among people aged 16 to 59 in 2001:

- 12% of men and 13% of women were cohabiting[2];
- comparison by age showed that those most likely to be cohabiting were men aged 25 to 29 and women in their twenties (28% for men and 27% and 28% respectively for women aged 20 to 24 and 25 to 29 compared with no more than 18% of any other age/sex group).

Among non-married people (including those who were separated) aged 16 to 59 in 2001:

- 25% of men and 28% of women were cohabiting;
- nearly twice as many women as men aged 20 to 24 were cohabiting (30% of women and 16% of men). **Table 5.3**

Data from 2000 and 2001 were combined to provide a sufficiently large sample to analyse cohabitation by age and legal marital status.[3]

Figure 5A **Percentage of non-married men and women aged 16-59 cohabiting by age: Great Britain, 2001**

Figure 5B **Percentage of single, divorced and separated women* aged 18-49 cohabiting by legal marital status: Great Britain, 1979 to 2001**

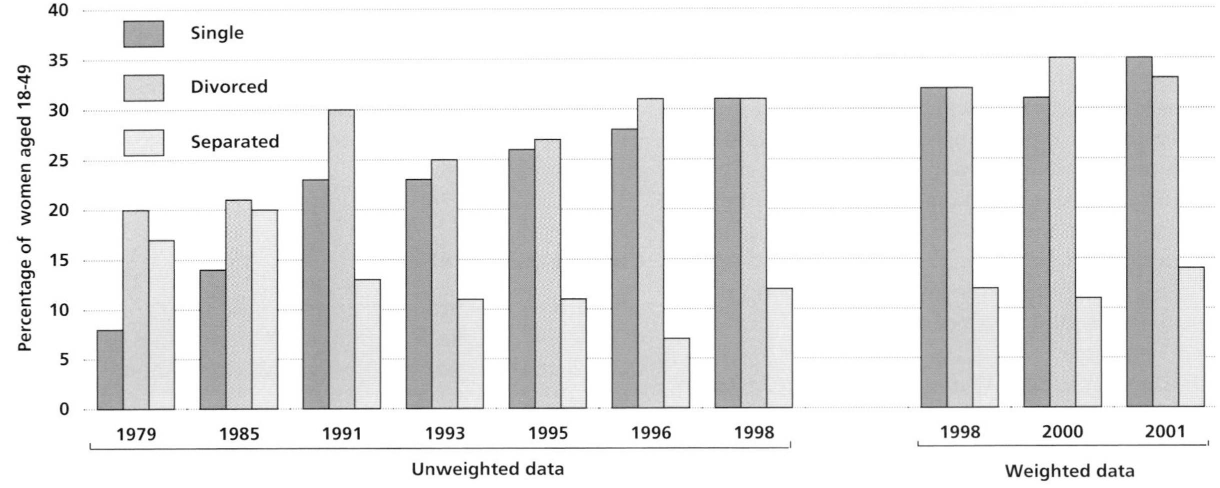

* Widows have not been included because their numbers are so small

- Among men aged 16 to 59, those who were divorced were more likely than those who were single or separated to be cohabiting, 34% compared with 22% of single or separated men.
- Of women aged 16 to 59 there was little difference between the proportions of divorced and single women who were cohabiting, 30% and 29% respectively.

However, analysis of those who were currently cohabiting showed:

- nearly three quarters of cohabiters were single (73% of cohabiting men and 71% of cohabiting women);
- older cohabiters were more likely to be divorced; among adults aged 50 to 59, 64% of cohabiting men and 76% of cohabiting women were divorced. **Tables 5.4 -5.5**

See also 5.6

Current cohabitation and trends over time among women

As noted earlier, questions relating to cohabitation on the GHS were initially asked only of women aged 18 to 49. Time series analysis for this group is therefore longer than for any other group and is presented in Tables 5.7 and 5.8.

Among women aged 18 to 49:

- Since 1979 the proportion married has shown a continuous decline from 74% in 1979 to 61% in 1991 and 50% in 2001;
- the proportion of single women has doubled from 18% in 1979 to 36% in 2001.

In terms of current cohabitation among women aged 18 to 49:

- there has been a marked increase in the proportion of non-married women who were

cohabiting, from 11% in 1979 to 32% in 2001;
- the proportion of single women cohabiting more than quadrupled, from 8% in 1979 to 35% in 2001. **Tables 5.7-5.8**

Women aged 16 to 59 and dependent children

A total of 49% of women aged 16 to 59 had no children living with them, while 42% had at least one dependent child and 9% only non-dependent children living with them. The proportion of women aged 16 to 59 with children varied according to their marital status.

Among women aged 16 to 59:

- 51% of married women and 37% of cohabiting women had at least one dependent child living with them compared with 20% of single women and 17% of widows;
- single women were the most likely to have no children living with them; 79% compared with 65% of widows, 61% of cohabiting women, and 35% of both married and separated women;
- 14% of married women and 13% of both divorced and separated women had non-dependent children living with them;
- nearly two thirds (65%) of women with dependent children were married, 12% were cohabiting and 10% were single. **Table 5.9**

Dependent children and current cohabitation among women

As has been seen in previous years non-married women aged 16 to 59 with dependent children were more likely than those without dependent children to be cohabiting. In 2001:

- 34% of non-married women with dependent children were cohabiting, compared with 25% of non-married women without dependent children;
- 45% of single women with dependent children were cohabiting, compared with 26% of single women without dependent children.

Among women aged 16 to 59 who were currently cohabiting:

- over two thirds (69%) with dependent children were single while 24% were divorced and 6% separated;
- just under three quarters (74%) of cohabiting women aged 16 to 59 without dependent children were single compared with 22% who were divorced and 3% separated.

Tables 5.10-5.11

Past cohabitations which did not end in marriage

In 2001, men and women aged 16 to 59 were asked details about past cohabitations which did not end in marriage. These questions were first asked in 2000, while the number of such cohabitations[4] had previously been asked in 1998. These periods of completed cohabitation did not include the current relationship of a respondent living as a couple at the time of interview. With the exception of those who chose the self-completion option, the majority of married and cohabiting respondents were interviewed in the presence of their partner; it is therefore possible that, for these groups, there was some under-reporting of previous cohabitations.

Among adults aged 16 to 59 in 2001:

- 13% reported at least one such cohabiting union that did not end in marriage;
- 10% had one of these relationships, 2% two and 1% three or more;
- there was no statistically significant difference between the proportions of men and women reporting at least one completed cohabitation not ending in marriage (14% of men and 13% of women);
- the highest proportions reporting at least one such relationship were found to be adults aged 25 to 39 (between 19% and 22%). This compares with between 5% and 9% of adults aged 45 to 59.

Table 5.12

Previous cohabitations by current marital status

As in 2000 the proportion of respondents reporting cohabiting unions that did not end in marriage varied by marital status for both men and women. Married respondents were less likely than others to report such relationships.

Among those aged 16 to 59:

- 8% of married men and 7% of married women said they had lived as a couple with someone whom they did not subsequently marry compared with 22% of currently cohabiting men and 22% of cohabiting women;
- the proportion of single women reporting at least one previous cohabitation (24%) was significantly greater than the proportion of single men (19%). **Table 5.13**

First cohabitations which did not end in marriage

Overall, 70% of first cohabitations, which did not end in marriage began by the age of 25.

- First cohabitations which did not end in marriage were most likely to begin when people were aged 20 to 24 (41%).
- Women were more likely than men to begin their first completed cohabitation at a younger age, 36% began their first cohabiting union by the age of 19 compared with 21% of men.

The age at which people started their first completed cohabitation also varied with the year in which the cohabitation began. For both men and women, those starting their first cohabitation between 1990 and 2002 tended to start at an older age than those who started their first completed cohabitation in the 1960-70s. For cohabitations started in the 1960-70s, 41% of women started a first cohabiting union by the age of 19 compared with 36% between 1990 and 2002; the equivalent figures for men were 27% and 16%. **Table 5.14**

Duration of past cohabitations not ending in marriage

For questions on duration of cohabitation, respondents were asked how long each completed cohabitation had lasted and give either the start date or the end date. The date which had not been given was then calculated and checked with the respondent, who could disagree and correct it. Length of cohabitation was based on the corrected dates where required.

First previous cohabitations which did not end in marriage tended to be longer than second such cohabitations.

- The mean length of time for first cohabitations which did not end in marriage was 39 months compared with 28 months for second cohabitations.
- Among people aged 16 to 59, 42% of first cohabitations lasted for less than 2 years compared with 57% of second cohabitations.

First cohabitations which were the only past cohabitation tended to be longer than those which were the first of two or more among people aged 16 to 59.

- The mean length of a first and only completed cohabitation was 40 months compared with a mean length of 34 months for a cohabitation which was the first of two or more.
- Differences were more more marked among women with a mean length of a first and only completed cohabitation of 44 months compared with 35 months for a cohabitation which was the first of two or more. **Table 5.15**

End of previous cohabitations

In order to identify what people meant by stopping living together respondents were asked whether it was the end of the relationship, the end of sharing accommodation or both. Those who said it meant the end of the relationship were then asked for the date of the end of sharing accommodation and vice versa. The answer to this question was then compared with the dates already given.

For first completed cohabitations 26% of men and women aged 16 to 59 said the end of 'living together' meant the end of the relationship, 17% said it meant the end of sharing accommodation and 53% said both (4% gave other answers which included a small percentage who volunteered the fact that they had stopped sharing accommodation but the relationship had continued, table not shown).

As in 2000 the dates did not always support their perception of what defined the end of 'living together'. For first completed cohabitations 58% of those who said the end of 'living together' meant the end of the relationship and 42% of those who said it meant the end of sharing accommodation gave the same dates for both of these events. Where the dates differed, those who said the end of 'living together' meant the end of sharing accommodation were more likely to give this as the first date than those who had said it meant the end of the relationship (37% compared with 19%). Thus, as was the case in 2000, it would appear that there was a closer match between the dates given and people's perceptions in the case where the end of 'living together' meant the end of sharing accommodation. **Table 5.16**

Notes and references

1 These were developed in conjunction with John Haskey at ONS. The results of the final development work can be found in: Lilly R. Developing questions on cohabitation histories. *Survey Methodology Bulletin*. No. 46. January 2000.
2 'Cohabiting' includes same sex cohabitees.
3 The section on marital history identified cases where the current or most recent marriage was in fact a cohabitation and also ascertained for cases where the spouse was not listed as a household member whether the marriage had broken down. This additional information was used to derive a modified version of marital status and it is this variable which is used in the rest of the chapter. Less than 1% of respondent's aged 16 to 59 were classified differently as a result of this exercise.
4 In 1998 the question specified cohabitations with 'someone of the opposite sex'. This part of the wording was dropped in 2000 but same sex couples were not specifically identified.

Table 5.1 **Sex by marital status**

All persons aged 16 and over *Great Britain: 2001*

Marital status*	Men		Women	
	%		%	
Married	54		52	
Cohabiting	10		9	
Single	27		18	
Widowed	3		11	
Divorced	5	6	7	9
Separated	2		3	
Weighted base (000's) = 100%	*22,342*		*23,290*	
Unweighted sample†	*7903*		*8782*	

* Marital status as recorded at the beginning of the interview.
† Total includes a very small number of same sex cohabitees.

Weighting to be revised in Spring 2003 following the 2001 census revisions of population estimates. See Appendix D.

Table 5.2 (a) Age and sex by marital status (b) Marital status by sex and age

Persons aged 16 and over *Great Britain: 2001*

Age	Marital status*						
	Married	Cohabiting	Single	Widowed	Divorced	Separated	Total
(a)	%	%	%	%	%	%	%
Men							
16-24	1	12	47	0	0	2	14
25-34	12	44	28	0	6	16	19
35-44	24	26	11	3	28	26	20
45-54	22	11	6	3	30	20	16
55-64	19	4	4	14	22	25	14
65-74	14	3	3	26	10	7	10
75 and over	8	0	1	55	3	5	7
Weighted base (000's) = 100%	*11,999*	*2,189*	*5,951*	*768*	*1,016*	*397*	*22,342*
Unweighted sample	*4562*	*762*	*1829*	*295*	*325*	*122*	*7903*
	%	%	%	%	%	%	%
Women							
16-24	2	23	53	0	0	3	13
25-34	16	41	22	0	10	22	18
35-44	24	20	11	1	24	34	19
45-54	23	10	4	5	25	23	16
55-64	18	4	3	11	22	10	13
65-74	11	1	3	28	13	3	11
75 and over	6	0	4	54	6	5	10
Weighted base (000's) = 100%	*12,012*	*2,181*	*4,295*	*2,668*	*1,526*	*600*	*23,290*
Unweighted sample	*4567*	*765*	*1624*	*1005*	*584*	*233*	*8782*
	%	%	%	%	%	%	%
Total							
16-24	1	18	50	0	0	2	14
25-34	14	42	26	0	8	20	18
35-44	24	23	11	2	26	31	20
45-54	23	11	5	5	27	22	16
55-64	18	4	4	11	22	16	13
65-74	13	2	3	28	12	5	10
75 and over	7	0	2	54	5	5	9
Weighted base (000's) = 100%	*24,011*	*4,370*	*10,246*	*3,436*	*2,542*	*996*	*45,632*
Unweighted sample†	*9129*	*1527*	*3453*	*1300*	*909*	*355*	*16685*

(b)		Married	Cohabiting	Single	Widowed	Divorced	Separated	*Weighted base (000's) = 100%*	*Unweighted sample†*
Men									
16-24	%	3	8	89	0	0	0	*3,169*	*987*
25-34	%	35	23	39	0	1	2	*4,251*	*1378*
35-44	%	64	12	15	0	6	2	*4,542*	*1556*
45-54	%	73	7	9	1	8	2	*3,645*	*1357*
55-64	%	75	3	8	3	7	3	*3,066*	*1151*
65-74	%	75	2	7	9	5	1	*2,203*	*905*
75 and over	%	63	0	5	29	2	1	*1,467*	*569*
Total	%	54	10	27	3	5	2	*22,342*	*7903*
Women									
16-24	%	7	17	76	0	0	1	*3,023*	*1077*
25-34	%	48	22	23	0	4	3	*4,093*	*1521*
35-44	%	66	10	10	1	8	5	*4,389*	*1663*
45-54	%	73	6	4	3	10	4	*3,810*	*1420*
55-64	%	71	3	4	10	11	2	*3,019*	*1219*
65-74	%	55	1	5	30	8	1	*2,524*	*977*
75 and over	%	28	0	7	59	4	1	*2,431*	*905*
Total	%	52	9	18	11	7	3	*23,290*	*8782*
Total									
16-24	%	5	12	83	0	0	0	*6,192*	*2064*
25-34	%	42	22	31	0	2	2	*8,345*	*2899*
35-44	%	65	11	13	1	7	3	*8,931*	*3219*
45-54	%	73	6	6	2	9	3	*7,455*	*2777*
55-64	%	73	3	6	6	9	3	*6,085*	*2370*
65-74	%	64	2	6	20	6	1	*4,727*	*1882*
75 and over	%	41	0	6	48	3	1	*3,898*	*1474*
Total	%	53	10	22	8	6	2	*45,632*	*16685*

* Marital status as recorded at the beginning of the interview.
† Total includes a very small number of same sex cohabitees.

Weighting to be revised in Spring 2003 following the 2001 census revisions of population estimates. See Appendix D.

Table 5.3 **Percentage currently cohabiting by sex and age**

Men and women aged 16-59 *Great Britain: 2001*

Age	All	Non-married*	Weighted base (000's) = 100%		Unweighted sample	
			All	*Non-married**	*All*	*Non-married**
	Percentage cohabiting					
Men						
16-19	2	2	*1,082*	*1,078*	*349*	*348*
20-24	15	16	*1,407*	*1,330*	*426*	*402*
25-29	28	36	*1,654*	*1,288*	*525*	*395*
30-34	19	37	*2,083*	*1,084*	*680*	*327*
35-39	14	35	*2,213*	*886*	*754*	*268*
40-44	9	27	*1,811*	*579*	*618*	*174*
45-49	8	29	*1,469*	*407*	*553*	*141*
50-54	5	19	*1,819*	*495*	*666*	*167*
55-59	4	16	*1,435*	*363*	*535*	*122*
Total	12	25	*14,972*	*7,511*	*5106*	*2344*
Women						
16-19	8	8	*1,130*	*1,110*	*416*	*409*
20-24	27	30	*1,414*	*1,235*	*491*	*431*
25-29	28	44	*1,651*	*1,080*	*618*	*412*
30-34	18	42	*2,210*	*964*	*817*	*364*
35-39	10	27	*2,182*	*814*	*830*	*316*
40-44	10	30	*2,016*	*644*	*762*	*250*
45-49	7	25	*1,665*	*497*	*613*	*179*
50-54	5	19	*1,996*	*517*	*749*	*189*
55-59	3	11	*1,632*	*498*	*639*	*185*
Total	13	28	*15,896*	*7,360*	*5935*	*2735*

* Men and women describing themselves as 'separated' were, strictly speaking, legally married. However, because the separated can cohabit, they have been included in the 'non-married' category.

Weighting to be revised in Spring 2003 following the 2001 census revisions of population estimates. See Appendix D.

Table 5.4 **Percentage currently cohabiting by legal marital status and age**

Men and women aged 16-59 *Great Britain: 2000 and 2001 combined*

Legal marital status*	16-24	(Non-married)	25-34	(Non-married)	35-49	(Non-married)	50-59	(Non-married)	Total	(Non-married)	Unweighted sample** 16-24	25-34	35-49	50-59	Total
	Percentage cohabiting														
Men															
Married	-		-		-		-		-		*49*	*907*	*2603*	*1757*	*5316*
Non-married															
Single	8		36		28		9		22		*1508*	*1238*	*638*	*199*	*3583*
Widowed	0	8	†	35	[16]	30	[13]	18	18	23	*0*	*3*	*22*	*36*	*61*
Divorced	0		37		38		26		34		*0*	*61*	*382*	*256*	*699*
Separated	†		[26]		21		19		22		*6*	*39*	*105*	*65*	*215*
Total	8		23		11		5		12		*1563*	*2248*	*3750*	*2313*	*9874*
Women															
Married	-		-		-		-		-		*122*	*1299*	*2842*	*1872*	*6135*
Non-married															
Single	18		44		32		6		29		*1577*	*1133*	*549*	*114*	*3373*
Widowed	†	18	†	41	14	29	7	14	8	27	*1*	*4*	*52*	*141*	*198*
Divorced	†		41		31		22		30		*3*	*180*	*599*	*340*	*1122*
Separated	†		11		15		7		12		*10*	*116*	*211*	*87*	*424*
Total	17		21		10		4		12		*1713*	*2732*	*4253*	*2554*	*11252*

* Men and women describing themselves as 'separated' were, strictly speaking, legally married. However, because the separated can cohabit they have been included in the 'non-married' category.

† Base too small to enable reliable analysis to be made.

** Weighted bases not shown for combined data sets.

Table 5.5 **Cohabiters: age by legal marital status**

Cohabiting persons aged 16-59 *Great Britain: 2000 and 2001 combined*

Legal marital status*	16-24	25-34	35-49	50-59	Total
Men					
	%	%	%	%	%
Married	-	-	-	-	-
Non-married					
Single	99	93	52	18	73
Widowed	0	1	1	5	1
Divorced	0	5	40	64	21
Separated	1	2	6	12	4
Unweighted sample	*128*	*530*	*404*	*120*	*1182*
Women					
Married	-	-	-	-	-
Non-married					
Single	99	86	43	7	71
Widowed	0	0	2	10	1
Divorced	1	12	46	76	24
Separated	0	2	8	6	4
Unweighted sample	*260*	*542*	*393*	*104*	*1299*

* Men and women describing themselves as 'separated' were, strictly speaking, legally married. However, because the separated can cohabit they have been included in the 'non-married' category.
** Weighted bases not shown for combined data sets.

Table 5.6 **Cohabiters: age by sex**

Cohabiting persons aged 16-59 *Great Britain: 2001*

Age	Men	Women
	%	%
16-19	1	4
20-24	12	18
25-29	25	23
30-34	22	20
35-39	17	11
40-44	9	10
45-49	6	6
50-54	5	5
55-59	3	3
Weighted base (000's) = 100%	*1,850*	*2,037*
Unweighted sample	*639*	*714*

Weighting to be revised in Spring 2003 following the 2001 census revisions of population estimates. See Appendix D.

Table 5.7 **Legal marital status of women aged 18-49: 1979 to 2001**

Women aged 18-49 *Great Britain*

Legal marital status*	Unweighted										Weighted		
	1979	1981	1983	1985	1989	1991	1993	1995	1996	1998	1998	2000	2001
	%	%	%	%	%	%	%	%	%	%	%	%	%
Married	74	72	70	68	63	61	59	58	57	53	53	51	50
Non-married													
Single	18	20	21	22	26	26	28	28	29	30	32	35	36
Widowed	1	1	1	1	1	1	1	1	1	1	1	0	1
Divorced	4	5	6	6	7	8	9	9	9	11	10	9	9
Separated	3	3	2	3	3	3	4	4	4	5	4	5	4
Weighted base (000's) = 100%†											*11,827*	*11,946*	*11,689*
Unweighted sample†	*6006*	*6524*	*5285*	*5364*	*5483*	*5359*	*5171*	*4953*	*4695*	*4181*		*3979*	*4325*

* Men and women describing themselves as 'separated' were, strictly speaking, legally married. However, because the separated can cohabit they have been included in the 'non-married' category.

† Trend tables show unweighted and weighted figures for 1998 to give an indication of the effect of the weighting. For the weighted data (1998, 2000 and 2001) the weighted base (000's) is the base for percentages. Unweighted data (up to 1998) are based on the unweighted sample.

Weighting to be revised in Spring 2003 following the 2001 census revisions of population estimates. See Appendix D.

Table 5.8 **Percentage of women aged 18-49 cohabiting by legal marital status: 1979 to 2001**

Women aged 18-49 *Great Britain*

Legal marital status*	Unweighted								Weighted		
	1979	1985	1989	1991	1993	1995	1996	1998	1998	2000	2001
	Percentage cohabiting										
Married	-	-	-	-	-	-	-	-			
Non-married	11	16	21	23	22	25	26	29	30	30	32
Single	8	14	19	23	23	26	28	31	32	31	35
Widowed	0	5	9	2	[8]	[8]	[5]	[8]	[11]	[15]	[11]
Divorced	20	21	30	30	25	27	31	31	32	35	33
Separated	17	20	17	13	11	11	7	12	12	11	14
Total	3	5	8	9	9	10	11	13	14	15	16
Weighted bases (000's) = 100%†											
Married									*6,212*	*6,051*	*5,899*
Non-married											
Single									*3,760*	*4,176*	*4,155*
Widowed									*99*	*55*	*99*
Divorced									*1,229*	*1,120*	*1,023*
Separated									*528*	*544*	*513*
Total									*11,828*	*11,946*	*11,689*
Unweighted sample†											
Married	*4461*	*3653*	*3457*	*3265*	*3053*	*2864*	*2683*	*2234*		*2032*	*2176*
Non-married											
Single	*1061*	*1175*	*1433*	*1416*	*1431*	*1405*	*1361*	*1268*		*1342*	*1523*
Widowed	*61*	*55*	*55*	*55*	*49*	*40*	*44*	*36*		*20*	*37*
Divorced	*256*	*338*	*387*	*448*	*453*	*437*	*421*	*443*		*393*	*389*
Separated	*167*	*143*	*151*	*175*	*185*	*206*	*186*	*200*		*192*	*200*
Total	*6006*	*5364*	*5483*	*5359*	*5171*	*4952*	*4695*	*4181*		*3979*	*4325*

* Men and women describing themselves as 'separated' were, strictly speaking, legally married. However, because the separated can cohabit they have been included in the 'non-married' category.

† See the second footnote to Table 5.7.

Weighting to be revised in Spring 2003 following the 2001 census revisions of population estimates. See Appendix D.

Table 5.9 (a) Whether had dependent children in the household by marital status (b) Marital status by whether had dependent children in the household

Women aged 16-59 *Great Britain: 2001*

Marital status		Children: Dependent children	Non dependent children only	No children	*Weighted base (000's) =100%*	*Unweighted sample*
(a)						
Married	%	51	14	35	*8,471*	*3176*
Non-married						
Cohabiting	%	37	2	61	*2,114*	*738*
Single	%	20	1	79	*3,392*	*1288*
Widowed	%	17	18	65	*301*	*110*
Divorced	%	47	13	40	*1,052*	*399*
Separated	%	52	13	35	*572*	*223*
Total	%	42	9	49	*15,901*	*5934*
					Total	
(b)		%	%	%	%	
Married		65	78	38	53	
Non-married						
Cohabiting		12	3	17	13	
Single		10	2	35	21	
Widowed		1	4	3	2	
Divorced		7	9	5	7	
Separated		4	5	3	4	
Weighted base (000's) =100%		*6,643*	*1,482*	*7,776*	*15,901*	
Unweighted sample		*2520*	*508*	*2906*	*5934*	

Weighting to be revised in Spring 2003 following the 2001 census revisions of population estimates. See Appendix D.

Table 5.10 Women aged 16-59: percentage cohabiting by legal marital status and whether has dependent children in the household

Women aged 16-59 *Great Britain: 2001*

Legal marital status	Has dependent children		No dependent children		Total		*Weighted bases (000's) = 100%: Has dependent children*	*No dependent children*	*Total**	*Unweighted sample: Has dependent children*	*No dependent children*	*Total**
	Percentage cohabiting											
Married	-		-		-		*4,336*	*4,137*	*8,511*	*1629*	*1548*	*3190*
Non-married		34		25		28						
Single	45		26		30		*1,201*	*3,645*	*4,872*	*458*	*1330*	*1798*
Widowed	[12]		6		7		*58*	*226*	*325*	*22*	*97*	*119*
Divorced	27		33		30		*675*	*828*	*1,524*	*263*	*303*	*573*
Separated	14		11		12		*343*	*307*	*653*	*139*	*111*	*251*
Total	12		14		13		*6,613*	*9,183*	*15,885*	*2511*	*3389*	*5931*

* Totals with dependent children and without dependent children do not sum to the total because the dependency of some children could not be established.

Weighting to be revised in Spring 2003 following the 2001 census revisions of population estimates. See Appendix D.

Table 5.11 Cohabiting women aged 16-59: whether has dependent children in the household by legal marital status

Cohabiting women aged 16-59 *Great Britain: 2001*

Legal marital status	Has dependent children	No dependent children	Total
	%	%	%
Non-married			
Single	69	74	72
Widowed	1	1	1
Divorced	24	22	22
Separated	6	3	4
Weighted base (000's) = 100%	*777*	*1,260*	*2,038*
Unweighted sample	*283*	*432*	*715*

Weighting to be revised in Spring 2003 following the 2001 Census revisions of population estimates. See Appendix D.

Table 5.12 Number of past cohabitations not ending in marriage by sex and age

Men and women aged 16-59 *Great Britain: 2001*

Age		Number of completed cohabitations*					*Weighted base (000's) = 100%*	*Unweighted sample*
		None	One	Two	Three or more	Total at least one		
Men								
16-19	%	98	2	0	0	2	*1,078*	*348*
20-24	%	89	8	2	1	11	*1,407*	*426*
25-29	%	80	15	3	2	20	*1,648*	*523*
30-34	%	76	18	4	2	24	*2,080*	*679*
35-39	%	81	13	3	3	19	*2,207*	*752*
40-44	%	86	8	3	2	14	*1,809*	*617*
45-49	%	90	7	2	1	10	*1,466*	*552*
50-54	%	92	5	1	1	8	*1,808*	*662*
55-59	%	94	4	1	1	6	*1,432*	*534*
Total	%	86	10	2	2	14	*14,934*	*5093*
Women								
16-19	%	96	4	0	0	4	*1,122*	*413*
20-24	%	86	13	1	0	14	*1,408*	*489*
25-29	%	77	18	4	0	23	*1,651*	*618*
30-34	%	80	14	5	1	20	*2,210*	*817*
35-39	%	81	15	3	1	19	*2,172*	*826*
40-44	%	86	11	2	1	14	*2,013*	*761*
45-49	%	91	7	2	1	9	*1,665*	*613*
50-54	%	95	4	1	0	5	*1,993*	*748*
55-59	%	97	3	1	0	3	*1,625*	*636*
Total	%	87	10	2	0	13	*15,859*	*5921*
All								
16-19	%	97	3	0	0	3	*2,200*	*761*
20-24	%	87	11	1	0	13	*2,815*	*915*
25-29	%	79	17	4	1	21	*3,299*	*1141*
30-34	%	78	16	4	2	22	*4,290*	*1496*
35-39	%	81	14	3	2	19	*4,379*	*1578*
40-44	%	86	10	3	1	14	*3,822*	*1378*
45-49	%	91	7	2	1	9	*3,131*	*1165*
50-54	%	94	5	1	1	6	*3,800*	*1410*
55-59	%	95	3	1	1	5	*3,057*	*1170*
Total	%	87	10	2	1	13	*30,793*	*11014*

* Excludes current cohabitations.

Weighting to be revised in Spring 2003 following the 2001 census revisions of population estimates. See Appendix D.

Table 5.13 Number of past cohabitations not ending in marriage by current marital status and sex

Men and women aged 16-59 *Great Britain: 2001*

Number of cohabitations*	Marital status						
	Married	Non-married					
		Cohabiting	Single	Widowed	Divorced	Separated	Total†
	%	%	%	%	%	%	%
Men							
None	92	78	81	[95]	79	84	86
One	6	15	13	[5]	13	8	10
Two	1	4	4	[0]	3	7	2
Three or more	0	2	2	[0]	5	1	2
Total at least one	8	22	19	[5]	21	16	14
Weighted base (000's) = 100%	*7,437*	*1,825*	*4,560*	*72*	*737*	*283*	*14,934*
Unweighted sample	*2756*	*630*	*1372*	*23*	*223*	*82*	*5093*
Women							
None	93	78	76	96	84	89	87
One	6	17	18	4	11	8	10
Two	1	4	5	0	5	3	2
Three or more	0	1	1	0	1	1	0
Total at least one	7	22	24	4	16	11	13
Weighted base (000's) = 100%	*8,559*	*2,012*	*3,379*	*298*	*1,075*	*528*	*15,859*
Unweighted sample	*3207*	*705*	*1282*	*109*	*407*	*207*	*5921*

* Excludes current cohabitations.
† Total includes a small number of same sex cohabitees.

Weighting to be revised in Spring 2003 following the 2001 census revisions of population estimates. See Appendix D.

Table 5.14 Age at first cohabitation which did not end in marriage by year cohabitation began and sex

Persons aged 16-59 who have cohabited *Great Britain: 2001*

Age at first cohabitation	Year first cohabitation began			
	1960-79	1980-89	1990-2002	All
	%	%	%	%
Men				
16-19	27	28	16	21
20-24	44	40	45	43
25-29	22	19	27	24
30-34	8	7	8	8
35-59	0	6	5	5
Weighted base (000's) =100%	*200*	*584*	*1,009*	*1,793*
Unweighted sample	*69*	*189*	*305*	*563*
Women				
16-19	41	36	36	36
20-24	40	39	38	39
25-29	12	15	13	14
30-34	7	8	7	7
35-59	0	2	6	4
Weighted base (000's) =100%	*212*	*667*	*985*	*1,864*
Unweighted sample	*76*	*250*	*365*	*691*
All				
16-19	34	32	26	29
20-24	42	40	41	41
25-29	17	17	20	19
30-34	7	7	8	7
35-59	0	4	5	4
Weighted base (000's) =100%	*412*	*1,250*	*1,995*	*3,657*
Unweighted sample	*145*	*439*	*670*	*1254*

Weighting to be revised in Spring 2003 following the 2001 census revisions of population estimates. See Appendix D.

Table 5.15 **Duration of past cohabitations which did not end in marriage by number of past cohabitations and sex**

Persons aged 16-59 who have cohabited *Great Britain: 2001*

Duration of cohabitation	First cohabitation			Second cohabitation
	One only	One of two or more	All	All
	%	%	%	%
Men				
Less than 1 year	25	25	25	37
1 year, less than 2	20	23	21	28
2 years, less than 3	17	19	18	14
3 years, less than 5	18	14	17	11
5 years or more	20	19	20	10
Mean length in months	37	33	36	24
Weighted base (000's) =100%	*1,319*	*473*	*1,794*	*496*
Unweighted sample	*419*	*144*	*563*	*152*
Women				
Less than 1 year	17	26	19	27
1 year, less than 2	21	15	20	20
2 years, less than 3	17	18	17	16
3 years, less than 5	19	17	19	20
5 years or more	26	22	25	17
Mean length in months	44	35	42	33
Weighted base (000's) =100%	*1,513*	*370*	*1,880*	*398*
Unweighted sample	*559*	*138*	*697*	*149*
All persons				
Less than 1 year	21	25	22	32
1 year, less than 2	21	20	20	25
2 years, less than 3	17	19	17	15
3 years, less than 5	19	16	18	15
5 years or more	23	21	22	13
Mean length in months	40	34	39	28
Weighted base (000's) =100%	*2,832*	*843*	*3,674*	*894*
Unweighted sample	*978*	*282*	*1260*	*301*

Weighting to be revised in Spring 2003 following the 2001 census revisions of population estimates. See Appendix D.

Table 5.16 **How people chose to date the end of 'living together', by the date given**

Persons aged 16-59 who specified end of relationship/sharing accommodation *Great Britain: 2001*

Comparison of dates given	Definition of end of 'living together'	
	End of relationship	End of sharing accommodation
	%	%
End of sharing accommodation before end of relationship	19	37
End of relationship before end of sharing accommodation	23	21
Same dates given	58	42
Weighted base (000's) =100%	*894*	*603*
Unweighted sample	*305*	*212*

Weighting to be revised in Spring 2003 following the 2001 census revisions of population estimates. See Appendix D.

Occupational and personal pension schemes

The GHS has included questions on occupational pensions in selected years since 1981 and on personal pensions since 1987. This chapter first presents information on occupational and personal pensions for employees (Tables 6.1 - 6.11), and then on the pension arrangements of the self-employed (Tables 6.12 - 6.14).

Currently all working people, both employees and the self-employed, are required to pay National Insurance contributions towards the basic state pension. Employees are also required to contribute either through National Insurance deductions to the second-tier state pension, SERPS (State Earnings Related Pension Scheme), or to make alternative provision through an occupational scheme or a personal pension arrangement. Self-employed people cannot contribute to SERPS so the only second pension choice for them is a personal pension.

A number of changes in pension provision have recently been introduced. In April 2001, coinciding with the start of fieldwork for the 2001 GHS, a new type of personal pension called the stakeholder pension was made available. The requirement on certain employers to offer access to a pension scheme, including a stakeholder pension, started a little later in October 2001. Stakeholder pensions offer greater flexibility than traditional personal pensions and are, for example, available to people who are not currently in employment. In April 2002, shortly after the completion of fieldwork for the 2001 GHS, the State Second Pension was introduced. The new pension reformed SERPS to provide a more generous additional pension for low and moderate earners, and for certain carers and people with a longstanding illness or disability.

Pension arrangements for employees

In 2001:

- two thirds of full-time employees (67% of men and 65% of women) were currently members of either an occupational or personal pension scheme, as were 39% of women working part time;
- overall 54% of men and 58% of women working full time belonged to their employer's pension scheme, representing the majority of employees with current pension arrangements;
- men were more likely than women to belong to a personal pension scheme (22% of men working full time compared with 13% of women).

It should be noted that the GHS questions asked only about the respondent's current employer, so some people may have held entitlements in the occupational pension scheme of a previous employer.

There was a strong association between pension arrangements and the age of the respondent, with low levels of membership among employees under the age of 25.

- Among full-time male employees, 63% of those aged 35 to 44 belonged to their current employer's scheme and 29% had a current personal pension compared with 25% and 4% respectively of men aged 18 to 24.
- Interestingly, however, among 18 to 24 year olds working full-time, women were more likely than men to have some pension provision; 38% compared with 27%. For both men and women, most of this provision came from occupational pensions. **Table 6.1**

In 2001:

- about one in ten employees who had a personal pension arrangement had a stakeholder pension - 8% of men and 11% of women who worked full time (table not shown).

Membership of current employer's pension scheme

Membership of an employer's pension scheme varied according to the sex of the respondent and whether they worked full or part time.

- Among both sexes, employees working full time were more likely than part-time workers to belong to their employer's pension scheme. For example, 58% of women working full time belonged to an occupational scheme compared with 33% working part time.
- Among part-time workers 33% of women compared with 12% of men belonged to their employer's pension scheme.

The variation in membership of an occupational scheme reflects differences in whether a scheme was available and whether the respondent thought that they were eligible to belong. Overall, more than two thirds of employees (71% of men and women) reported that their current employer offered an occupational pension scheme and about one in ten (8% of men and 9% of women) said that they were not eligible to belong to the scheme offered.

Employees who worked part time were less likely than those working full time to have access to an occupational pension scheme and were more likely to say that they were not eligible for the scheme.

- More than three quarters (78%) of women who worked full time reported that their current employer had a pension scheme compared with 63% of women working part time.
- 12% of women who worked part time said that they were not eligible for their employer's scheme compared with 6% of women working full time. (The proportions were 19% and 8% respectively when based on women whose employer actually ran a pension scheme.)

Table 6.2, Figure 6A

Employees who belong to an occupational pension scheme may make further contributions known as Additional Voluntary Contributions (AVCs). In 2001:

- 7% of men and women who worked full time were currently paying AVCs in addition to their contributions to an occupational pension scheme (table not shown).

Trends in membership of an occupational pension scheme

This discussion of trends in occupational pension scheme membership concentrates on the period since 1988 when important changes in pension provision for employees were introduced. Since 1988 employers have been allowed to contract out of SERPS if their pension scheme satisfies specific requirements. Also, individual employees who belong to an occupational scheme which is not contracted-out of SERPS and those who do not belong to an occupational scheme have had the option of contracting out of SERPS by starting their own personal pension plan. In such cases the employee receives a rebate on his or her National Insurance contribution from the Inland Revenue (formerly from the DSS).

A further change that introduced parity of access to occupational pension schemes for full-time and part-time employees was the ruling by the European Court of Justice in September 1994. This disallowed the exclusion of part-time employees from occupational pension schemes on the grounds of indirect discrimination against women.

Trends in membership of the current employer's pension scheme differ for men and women and for employees working full and part time.

- Among men working full time, current membership of an occupational pension scheme decreased from 64% in 1989 to 55% in 1998 and has since remained constant (54% in 2001).

Figure 6A **Membership of current employer's pension scheme by sex and whether working full time or part time: Great Britain, 2001**

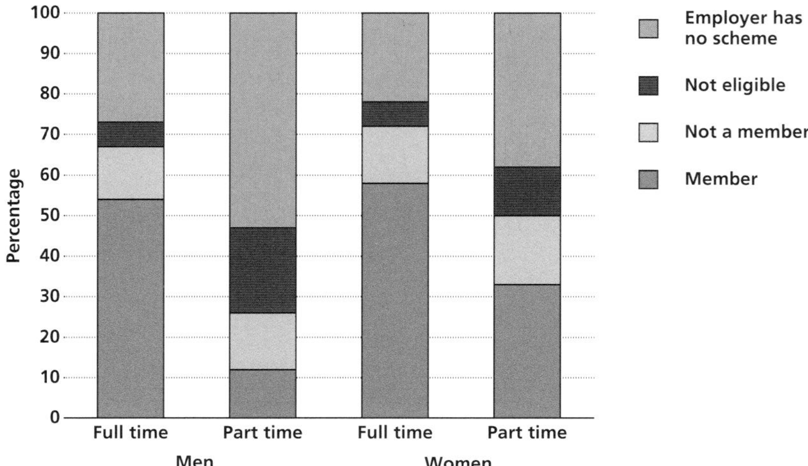

- The proportion of women working full time who are members of an occupational scheme has been more stable over this period (55% in 1989 and 58% in 2001).
- Among women in part time work, membership of the current employer's pension scheme increased from 15% in 1989 to 26% in 1998 and again to 33% in 2001.

Similar patterns are also seen in the proportions of respondents whose employer offered a pension scheme. For example:

- the proportion of men working full time who said that their current employer ran a pension scheme decreased from 79% in 1989 to 73% in 2001;
- the proportion of women working part time whose employer ran a pension scheme varied between 52% and 55% from 1989 to 1998, but increased to 63% in 2001. **Table 6.3**

Variation in pension scheme membership by employee characteristics

Pension scheme membership is strongly associated with a number of characteristics of employees and their type of employment, as shown in Tables 6.4 to 6.11. The following discussion mainly focuses on membership of occupational pension schemes as this is the most common type of pension arrangement for employees.

Socio-economic classification

In 2001, as in previous years, there were marked differences in the current pension arrangements of respondents in different occupational groups. From April 2001 the National Statistics Socio-economic Classification (NS-SEC) was introduced for all official statistics and surveys. It has replaced Social Class based on occupation and Socio-economic Groups (SEG). Because of small sample sizes when the results are shown separately for men and women working full or part time, the table shows only three broad categories of the NS-SEC.

Employees in professional or managerial occupations were more likely than those working either in intermediate occupations or in routine and manual occupations to belong to their current employer's pension scheme. This variation reflected differences both in the likelihood that the current employer ran a pension scheme and in the likelihood that employees belonged to a scheme. For example:

- among women working full time, 73% of those in professional or managerial occupations belonged to an occupational pension scheme, compared with 58% of those in intermediate occupations and 33% in routine and manual occupations;
- for the same groups, the proportion of respondents who said that their current employer ran a pension scheme were 86%, 80% and 64% respectively. **Tables 6.4 and 6.5**

Income

In general, the higher their gross weekly income, the more likely men and women working full time were to belong either to their employer's pension scheme or to a personal pension scheme. For example, in 2001 among those working full time:

- 73% of men and 80% of women with gross weekly earnings of more than £600 belonged to an occupational pension scheme compared with 20% of men and 26% of women earning between £100 and £200 per week;
- about three out of ten men (29%) and a quarter of women (23%) earning more than £600 belonged to a personal pension scheme compared with less than one in ten men and women earning between £100 and £200 per week. **Table 6.6**

Length of time with current employer

The likelihood of belonging to the current employer's pension scheme increased with the length of time respondents had worked for that employer. This variation reflected differences in whether the employer ran a pension scheme and whether the respondent was eligible. For example, among men working full time:

- about a quarter (27%) of male employees who had worked for their current employer for less than two years belonged to an occupational pension scheme compared with almost three quarters (73%) of those who had been with their employer for five years or more;
- for these two groups, the proportions who said that their employer ran a pension scheme were 60% and 82% respectively;
- one in seven (14%) men who had worked for their current employer for less than two years said that they were not eligible to belong to their employer's pension scheme compared with just 2% of those who had been with their employer for five years or more.

Tables 6.7 and 6.8, Figure 6B

Figure 6B **Membership of current employer's pension scheme by length of time with current employer: men working full time: Great Britain, 2001**

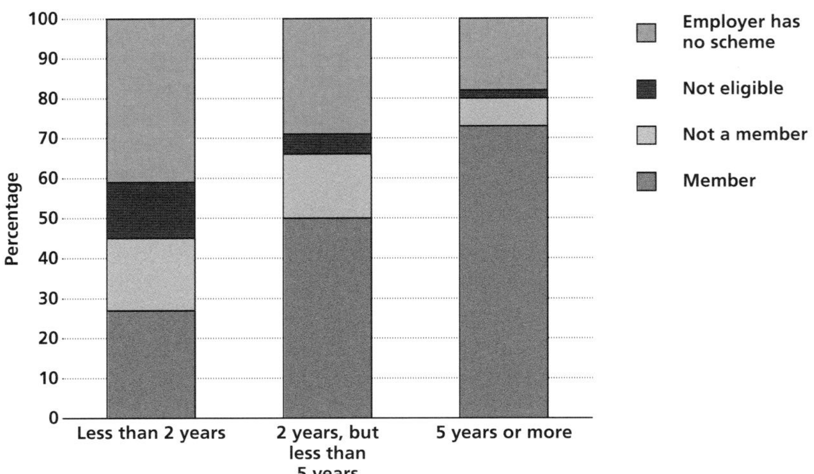

Size of establishment

Membership of an occupational pension scheme was strongly associated with the size of the establishment in which the respondent worked, and again closely reflected whether the employer offered an occupational scheme. For example:

- among women working full time, the proportion belonging to their employer's pension scheme ranged from 35% of those in establishments with 3-24 employees to 83% of those in establishments with 1000 or more employees;
- the proportion of respondents in these two groups who said that their employer ran an occupational scheme were 55% and 97% respectively. **Tables 6.9 and 6.10**

Industry

There was wide variation in membership of occupational pension schemes between industry groups. The sample sizes of some groups are, however, small and the results for these industries should be treated with caution. For the years 1998, 2000 and 2001 combined:

- for men working full time, occupational pension scheme membership ranged from 17% for those employed in agriculture, forestry and fishing to 78% among those working in public and personal services;
- the high level of pension scheme membership among employees in public and personal services was also seen for both full-time and part-time female employees (69% and 43%);
- the proportion of employees belonging to their employer's pension scheme was generally below average for workers in the distribution and construction industries (36% in each industry for men working full time). **Table 6.11**

Personal pension arrangements among the self-employed

Self-employed people, like employees, currently have to pay National Insurance contributions towards a basic state pension but they cannot contribute to SERPS. The second pension choice for them is a personal pension or, since April 2001, a stakeholder pension, although many self-employed people make provision for their retirement through other savings and investments.

Among self-employed people working full time, as with employees, men were more likely than women to have personal pension arrangements. In 2001:

- 54% of self-employed men and 37% of self-employed women working full time were currently in a personal pension scheme;
- among self-employed people working full time, one third (32%) of men had never had a personal pension compared with a half (50%) of women;
- about a quarter of the self-employed who worked part time were currently members of a personal pension scheme (24% of men and 29% of women);
- among self-employed people with a current personal pension, just 4% had a stakeholder pension in 2001 (table not shown). **Table 6.12**

Although the GHS provides trend data since 1991 on the personal pension arrangements among self-employed people, Table 6.13 shows data only for men working full time since the sample sizes for self-employed men working part time and for self-employed women are too small to give reliable estimates.

- The take up of personal pensions among self-employed men remained fairly stable between 1991 and 1998, at just under two thirds, but has since decreased from 64% in 1998 to 54% in 2001. **Table 6.13**

The likelihood of having a personal pension increased with the length of time spent in self-employment. Because of small sample numbers, the results are based on combined data for the most recent three years of the GHS.

- Men working full time who had been self-employed for five years or more were twice as likely to have a current personal pension as were those who had been self-employed for less than two years (66% compared with 30%).
- The pattern was similar for women. For example, for women working part time the comparable proportions were 35% and 10%. **Table 6.14**

Table 6.1 **Current pension scheme membership by age and sex**

Employees aged 16 and over excluding YT and ET *Great Britain: 2001*

Pension scheme members	Age 16-17	18-24	25-34	35-44	45-54	55 and over	Total
				Percentages			
Men full time							
Occupational pension*	[0]	25	52	63	63	57	54
Personal pension	[0]	4	23	29	24	16	22
Any pension	[0]	27	66	80	78	65	67
Women full time							
Occupational pension*	[7]	34	61	64	66	59	58
Personal pension	[0]	5	14	19	12	5	13
Any pension	[5]	38	69	72	73	62	65
Women part time							
Occupational pension*	1	5	38	44	40	29	33
Personal pension	0	0	13	10	9	8	8
Any pension	1	5	46	49	46	35	39
Weighted base (000's) =100%							
Men full time	*118*	*1,231*	*2,987*	*3,251*	*2,332*	*1,245*	*11,164*
Women full time	*66*	*953*	*1,808*	*1,609*	*1,511*	*512*	*6,459*
Women part time	*264*	*502*	*966*	*1,382*	*1,106*	*766*	*4,986*
Unweighted sample							
Men full time	*38*	*382*	*970*	*1117*	*880*	*473*	*3860*
Women full time	*25*	*335*	*652*	*607*	*562*	*200*	*2381*
Women part time	*101*	*175*	*362*	*522*	*411*	*305*	*1876*

* Including a few people who were not sure if they were in a scheme but thought it possible.

Weighting to be revised in Spring 2003 following the 2001 census revisions of population estimates. See Appendix D.

Table 6.2 **Membership of current employer's pension scheme by sex and whether working full time or part time**

Employees aged 16 and over excluding YT and ET *Great Britain: 2001*

Pension scheme coverage	Men: Working full time		Men: Working part time		Men: Total*		Women: Working full time		Women: Working part time		Women: Total*	
	%		%		%		%		%		%	
Present employer has a pension scheme												
Member†	54		12		51		58		33		47	
Not a member	12	73	14	47	12	71	14	78	17	63	15	71
Not eligible to belong	6		21		8		6		12		9	
Does not know if a member	0		0		0		0		0		0	
Present employer does not have a pension scheme	26		49		28		21		36		27	
Not known if present employer has a pension scheme	1		4		1		1		2		1	
Weighted base (000's) = 100%	*11,220*		*1,004*		*12,264*		*6,465*		*4,990*		*11,473*	
Unweighted sample	*3881*		*350*		*4245*		*2384*		*1878*		*4268*	

* Including a few people whose hours of work were not known.
† Including a few people who were not sure if they were in a scheme but thought it possible.

Weighting to be revised in Spring 2003 following the 2001 census revisions of population estimates. See Appendix D.

Table 6.3 **Membership of current employer's pension scheme by sex: 1983 to 2001**

*Employees aged 16 and over excluding YT and ET**

Great Britain

Pension scheme coverage	Unweighted									Weighted		
	1983	1987	1989	1991	1993	1994	1995	1996	1998	1998	2000	2001
	%	%	%	%	%	%	%	%	%	%	%	%
Men full time												
Present employer has a pension scheme	77	74	79	77	76	75	74	74	72	71	70	73
Member†	66	63	64	61	60	60	58	58	57	55	54	54
Not a member	10	12	14	16	16	15	16	16	15	15	16	19
Does not know if a member	1	0	0	1	0	0	0	0	0	0	0	0
Present employer does not have a pension scheme	22	22	19	21	22	24	25	25	28	29	29	26
Does not know if present employer has a pension scheme - not a member	2	3	2	2	2	1	1	1	1	1	1	1
*Weighted base (000's) = 100%***										*11,009*	*11,323*	*11,220*
*Unweighted sample***	*5087*	*5129*	*4906*	*4563*	*3976*	*4006*	*4062*	*3937*	*3697*		*3558*	*3881*
	%	%	%	%	%	%	%	%	%	%	%	%
Women full time												
Present employer has a pension scheme	72	68	76	77	77	73	76	73	73	73	75	78
Member†	55	52	55	55	54	53	55	53	56	55	58	58
Not a member	17	16	21	21	22	19	20	20	17	18	17	20
Does not know if a member	0	1	0	0	0	0	0	0	0	0	0	0
Present employer does not have a pension scheme	24	28	21	20	22	27	24	26	26	27	25	21
Does not know if present employer has a pension scheme - not a member	4	4	3	3	2	1	1	1	0	0	1	1
*Weighted base (000's) = 100%***										*6,429*	*6,353*	*6,465*
*Unweighted sample***	*2256*	*2562*	*2602*	*2484*	*2239*	*2345*	*2331*	*2143*	*2244*		*2089*	*2384*
	%	%	%	%	%	%	%	%	%	%	%	%
Women part time												
Present employer has a pension scheme	53	46	52	52	55	52	55	53	53	52	56	63
Member†	13	11	15	17	19	19	24	26	27	26	31	33
Not a member	39	34	37	34	35	33	32	28	26	26	25	29
Does not know if a member	0	0	0	1	0	0	0	0	0	0	0	0
Present employer does not have a pension scheme	40	44	40	39	38	45	42	44	45	46	42	36
Does not know if present employer has a pension scheme - not a member	7	10	7	8	7	3	3	2	2	3	2	2
*Weighted base (000's) = 100%***										*4,628*	*5,059*	*4,990*
*Unweighted sample***	*1638*	*2126*	*2102*	*1977*	*1938*	*1930*	*2038*	*1908*	*1674*		*1732*	*1878*

* Prior to 1985 full-time students are excluded. Figures since 1987 include full-time students who were working but exclude those on Government schemes.

† Including a few people who were not sure if they were in a scheme but thought it possible.

** Trend tables show unweighted and weighted figures for 1998 to give an indication of the effect of the weighting. For the weighted data (1998, 2000 and 2001) the weighted base (000's) is the base for percentages. Unweighted data (up to 1998) are based on the unweighted sample.

Weighting to be revised in Spring 2003 following the 2001 census revisions of population estimates. See Appendix D.

Table 6.4 **Current pension scheme membership by socio-economic classification**

Employees aged 16 and over excluding YT and ET *Great Britain: 2001*

Pension scheme members	Socio-economic classification			
	Managerial and professional	Intermediate	Routine and manual	Total†
		Percentages		
Men full time				
Occupational pension*	69	62	40	54
Personal pension	25	14	21	22
Any pension	81	69	56	67
Women full time				
Occupational pension*	73	58	33	58
Personal pension	15	11	10	13
Any pension	80	65	41	65
Women part time				
Occupational pension*	62	45	23	33
Personal pension	15	11	6	8
Any pension	69	53	28	39
Weighted base (000's) =100%				
Men full time	*4,913*	*929*	*5,216*	*11,164*
Women full time	*3,028*	*1,554*	*1,772*	*6,459*
Women part time	*925*	*1,020*	*2,616*	*4,986*
Unweighted sample				
Men full time	*1735*	*307*	*1788*	*3860*
Women full time	*1128*	*569*	*645*	*2381*
Women part time	*355*	*390*	*975*	*1876*

* Including a few people who were not sure if they were in a scheme but thought it possible.

† From April 2001 the National Statistics Socio-economic Classification (NS-SEC) was introduced for all official statistics and surveys. It has replaced Social Class based on Occupation and Socio-economic Groups (SEG). Full-time students, persons in inadequately described occupations, persons who have never worked and the long term unemployed are not shown as separate categories, but are included in the figure for all persons (see Appendix A).

Weighting to be revised in Spring 2003 following the 2001 census revisions of population estimates. See Appendix D.

Table 6.5 Membership of current employer's pension scheme by sex and socio-economic classification

Employees aged 16 and over excluding YT and ET *Great Britain: 2001*

Pension scheme coverage	Socio-economic classification							
	Managerial and professional		Intermediate		Routine and manual		Total*	
	%		%		%		%	
Men full time								
Present employer has a pension scheme								
Member†	69	81	62	82	40	64	54	73
Not a member **	12		20		24		19	
Present employer does not have a pension scheme	19		17		34		26	
Not known if employer has a pension scheme	0		1		1		1	
Weighted base (000's) =100%	*4,940*		*935*		*5,239*		*11,220*	
Unweighted sample	*1745*		*309*		*1797*		*3881*	
Women full time								
Present employer has a pension scheme								
Member†	73	86	58	80	33	64	58	78
Not a member **	12		22		31		20	
Present employer does not have a pension scheme	14		18		35		21	
Not known if employer has a pension scheme	0		1		1		1	
Weighted base (000's) =100%	*3,028*		*1,557*		*1,777*		*6,466*	
Unweighted sample	*1128*		*570*		*647*		*2384*	
Women part time								
Present employer has a pension scheme								
Member†	62	81	45	68	23	57	33	63
Not a member **	19		22		33		29	
Present employer does not have a pension scheme	19		32		40		36	
Not known if employer has a pension scheme	0		0		3		2	
Weighted base (000's) =100%	*925*		*1,022*		*2,619*		*4,990*	
Unweighted sample	*355*		*391*		*976*		*1878*	

* From April 2001 the National Statistics Socio-economic Classification (NS-SEC) was introduced for all official statistics and surveys. It has replaced Social Class based on Occupation and Socio-economic Groups (SEG). Full-time students, persons in inadequately described occupations, persons who have never worked and the long term unemployed are not shown as separate categories, but are included in the figure for all persons (see Appendix A).
† Including a few people who were not sure if they were in a scheme but thought it possible.
** Including people who were not eligible and a few people who did not know if they were a member.

Weighting to be revised in Spring 2003 following the 2001 census revisions of population estimates. See Appendix D.

Table 6.6 **Current pension scheme membership by sex and usual gross weekly earnings**

Employees aged 16 and over excluding YT and ET — *Great Britain: 2001*

Pension scheme members	Usual gross weekly earnings (£)							
	0.01-100.00	100.01-200.00	200.01-300.00	300.01-400.00	400.01-500.00	500.01-600.00	600.01 or more	Total†
	Percentages							
Men full time								
Occupational pension*	[38]	20	36	56	66	68	73	54
Personal pension	[17]	9	17	23	23	25	29	22
Any pension	[49]	29	48	71	79	85	86	67
Women full time								
Occupational pension*	[35]	26	53	68	78	83	80	58
Personal pension	[10]	8	12	12	18	13	23	13
Any pension	[42]	33	61	73	86	88	89	65
Women part time								
Occupational pension*	15	40	68	70	[52]	**	**	33
Personal pension	5	10	11	10	[27]	**	**	8
Any pension	19	46	72	74	[65]	**	**	39
Weighted base (000's) =100%								
Men full time	*133*	*668*	*2,141*	*2,177*	*1,505*	*948*	*1,948*	*11,164*
Women full time	*109*	*997*	*1,839*	*1,188*	*733*	*431*	*537*	*6,459*
Women part time	*2,075*	*1,689*	*545*	*156*	*51*	*29*	*31*	*4,986*
Unweighted sample								
Men full time	*46*	*221*	*724*	*741*	*522*	*332*	*688*	*3860*
Women full time	*41*	*363*	*679*	*440*	*271*	*159*	*195*	*2381*
Women part time	*779*	*630*	*208*	*61*	*20*	*11*	*11*	*1876*

* Including a few people who were not sure if they were in a scheme but thought it possible.
† Totals include no answers to income.
** Base too small for reliable analysis to be made.

Weighting to be revised in Spring 2003 following the 2001 census revisions of population estimates. See Appendix D.

Table 6.7 **Current pension scheme membership by sex and length of time with current employer**

Employees aged 16 and over excluding YT and ET — *Great Britain: 2001*

Pension scheme members	Length of time with current employer			
	Less than 2 years	2 years, but less than 5 years	5 years or more	Total†
		Percentages		
Men full time				
Occupational pension*	27	50	73	54
Personal pension	20	22	23	22
Any pension	41	64	85	67
Women full time				
Occupational pension*	37	55	75	58
Personal pension	11	13	13	13
Any pension	44	64	81	65
Women part time				
Occupational pension*	16	34	49	33
Personal pension	6	8	11	8
Any pension	21	37	56	39
Weighted base (000's) = 100%				
Men full time	*3,330*	*2,364*	*5,468*	*11,164*
Women full time	*2,107*	*1,433*	*2,913*	*6,459*
Women part time	*1,882*	*1,034*	*2,068*	*4,986*
Unweighted sample				
Men full time	*1104*	*798*	*1958*	*3860*
Women full time	*764*	*523*	*1092*	*2381*
Women part time	*699*	*389*	*787*	*1876*

* Including a few people who were not sure if they were in a scheme but thought it possible.
† Including a few where length of time in job was not known.

Weighting to be revised in Spring 2003 following the 2001 census revisions of population estimates. See Appendix D.

Table 6.8 Membership of current employer's pension scheme by sex and length of time with current employer

Employees aged 16 and over excluding YT and ET *Great Britain: 2001*

Pension scheme coverage	Length of time with current employer							
	Less than 2 years		2 years, but less than 5 years		5 years or more		Total*	
	%		%		%		%	
Men full time								
Present employer has a pension scheme								
Member†	27		50		73		54	
Not a member **	18	60	16	71	7	82	12	73
Not eligible to belong	14		5		2		6	
Present employer does not have a pension scheme	38		28		18		26	
Not known if employer has a pension scheme	3		0		0		1	
Weighted base (000's) =100%	*3,347*		*2,373*		*5,496*		*11,220*	
Unweighted sample	*1109*		*802*		*1969*		*3881*	
Women full time								
Present employer has a pension scheme								
Member†	37		55		75		58	
Not a member **	18	69	18	77	8	86	14	78
Not eligible to belong	14		4		2		6	
Present employer does not have a pension scheme	29		23		14		21	
Not known if employer has a pension scheme	2		0		0		1	
Weighted base (000's) =100%	*2,111*		*1,436*		*2,913*		*6,465*	
Unweighted sample	*766*		*524*		*1092*		*2384*	
Women part time								
Present employer has a pension scheme								
Member†	16		34		49		33	
Not a member **	16	49	20	63	17	74	17	63
Not eligible to belong	17		9		8		12	
Present employer does not have a pension scheme	47		34		25		36	
Not known if employer has a pension scheme	3		3		0		2	
Weighted base (000's) =100%	*1,882*		*1,035*		*2,070*		*4,990*	
Unweighted sample	*699*		*390*		*788*		*1878*	

* Including a few whose length of time in job was not known.
† Including a few people who were not sure if they were in a scheme but thought it possible.
** Including a few people who did not know if they were a member.

Weighting to be revised in Spring 2003 following the 2001 census revisions of population estimates. See Appendix D.

Table 6.9 Current pension scheme membership by sex and number of employees in the establishment

Employees aged 16 and over excluding YT and ET *Great Britain: 2001*

Pension scheme members	Number of employees at establishment					
	1-2	3-24	25-99	100-999	1000 or more	Total†
			Percentages			
Men full time						
Occupational pension*	37	32	51	67	81	54
Personal pension	25	26	27	18	11	22
Any pension	54	52	67	76	84	67
Women full time						
Occupational pension*	29	35	58	69	83	58
Personal pension	17	14	14	10	11	13
Any pension	41	47	66	73	85	65
Women part time						
Occupational pension*	6	18	40	50	73	33
Personal pension	15	8	7	9	9	8
Any pension	20	24	43	55	76	39
Weighted base (000's) = 100%						
Men full time	*312*	*2,831*	*3,001*	*3,792*	*1,195*	*11,164*
Women full time	*179*	*1,565*	*1,851*	*2,024*	*813*	*6,459*
Women part time	*305*	*1,991*	*1,287*	*1,062*	*321*	*4,986*
Unweighted sample						
Men full time	*111*	*968*	*1039*	*1321*	*409*	*3860*
Women full time	*65*	*581*	*677*	*748*	*300*	*2381*
Women part time	*112*	*744*	*487*	*405*	*121*	*1876*

* Including a few people who were not sure if they were in a scheme but thought it possible.
† Includes a few people for whom the number of employees at establishment was not known.

Weighting to be revised in Spring 2003 following the 2001 census revisions of population estimates. See Appendix D.

Table 6.10 **Membership of current employer's pension scheme by sex and number of employees at the establishment**

Employees aged 16 and over excluding YT and ET *Great Britain: 2001*

Pension scheme coverage	Number of employees at establishment					
	1-2	**3-24**	**25-99**	**100-999**	**1000 or more**	**Total***
	%	%	%	%	%	%
Men full time						
Present employer has a pension scheme	46	46	74	89	94	73
Member†	37	32	51	67	81	54
Not a member **	10	15	23	21	13	19
Present employer does not have a pension scheme	52	52	25	11	6	26
Not known if employer has a pension scheme	2	2	1	1	0	1
Weighted base (000's) =100%	*312*	*2,843*	*3,008*	*3,820*	*1,201*	*11,220*
Unweighted sample	*111*	*973*	*1042*	*1331*	*411*	*3881*
Women full time						
Present employer has a pension scheme	35	55	79	92	97	78
Member†	29	35	58	69	83	58
Not a member **	7	20	21	23	14	20
Present employer does not have a pension scheme	65	44	20	8	3	21
Not known if employer has a pension scheme	0	1	1	0	0	1
Weighted base (000's) =100%	*181*	*1,570*	*1,851*	*2,023*	*813*	*6,465*
Unweighted sample	*66*	*583*	*677*	*748*	*300*	*2384*
Women part time						
Present employer has a pension scheme	24	42	74	89	93	63
Member†	6	18	40	50	73	33
Not a member **	18	24	34	39	20	29
Present employer does not have a pension scheme	74	56	24	10	7	36
Not known if employer has a pension scheme	2	2	2	1	0	2
Weighted base (000's) =100%	*305*	*1,991*	*1,288*	*1,065*	*321*	*4,990*
Unweighted sample	*112*	*744*	*488*	*406*	*121*	*1878*

* Includes a few people for whom the number of employees at establishment was not known.
† Including a few people who were not sure if they were in a scheme but thought it possible.
* Including people who were not eligible and a few people who did not know if they were a member.

Weighting to be revised in Spring 2003 following the 2001 census revisions of population estimates. See Appendix D.

Table 6.11 **Current pension scheme membership by sex and industry group**

Employees aged 16 and over excluding YT and ET *Great Britain: 1998, 2000 and 2001 combined*

Pension scheme members	Industry group†										
	Agriculture, forestry, fishing	Coal mining, energy and water supply	Mining (excl coal), manufacture of metals, minerals and chemicals	Metal goods, engineering and vehicle	Other manufacturing	Construction	Distribution, hotels, catering repairs	Transport and communications	Banking, finance, insurance business services	Public and other personal services	Total
					Percentages						
Men full time											
Occupational pension*	17	73	48	58	52	36	36	61	53	78	55
Personal pension	40	21	23	25	25	28	27	18	28	13	23
Any pension	52	84	67	71	67	55	55	71	69	82	68
Women full time											
Occupational pension*	[19]	80	**	59	43	54	35	54	54	69	57
Personal pension	[20]	13	**	15	17	16	14	13	20	10	14
Any pension	[40]	81	**	64	53	64	44	60	66	74	65
Women part time											
Occupational pension*	[6]	**	**	26	26	16	15	33	30	43	30
Personal pension	[13]	**	**	13	11	20	6	10	17	8	9
Any pension	[16]	**	**	35	34	33	20	40	40	47	36
Unweighted sample††											
Men full time	*142*	*212*	*51*	*1755*	*1529*	*1032*	*1573*	*1023*	*1650*	*2083*	*11050*
Women full time	*25*	*55*	*8*	*344*	*656*	*104*	*992*	*336*	*1260*	*2899*	*6679*
Women part time	*32*	*12*	*1*	*114*	*268*	*69*	*1659*	*171*	*598*	*2337*	*5251*

* Including a few people who were not sure if they were in a scheme but thought it possible.
† Standard Industrial Classification, 1992.
** Base too small for reliable analysis to be made.
†† Weighted bases not shown for combined data sets.

Table 6.12 **Membership of personal pension scheme by sex and whether working full time or part time: self-employed persons**

Self-employed persons aged 16 and over *Great Britain: 2001*

Pension scheme coverage	Men			Women		
	Working full time	Working part time	Total*	Working full time	Working part time	Total*
	%	%	%	%	%	%
Informant belongs to a personal pension scheme	54	24	49	37	29	33
Informant no longer has a personal pension scheme	15	19	15	13	15	14
Informant has never had a personal pension scheme	32	57	36	50	57	53
Weighted base (000's) = 100%	*1,942*	*372*	*2,326*	*407*	*403*	*810*
Unweighted sample	*700*	*136*	*840*	*153*	*154*	*307*

* Including a few people whose hours of work were not known.

Weighting to be revised in Spring 2003 following the 2001 census revisions of population estimates. See Appendix D.

Table 6.13 Membership of a personal pension scheme for self-employed men working full time: 1991 to 2001

Self-employed persons aged 16 and over — *Great Britain*

Pension scheme coverage	Unweighted							Weighted		
	1991	1992	1993	1994	1995	1996	1998	1998	2000	2001
	Percentages									
Men working full time										
Informant belongs to a personal pension scheme	66	65	67	60	61	64	65	64	54	54
Informant no longer has a personal pension	7	9	9	10	11	11	10	10	12	15
Informant has never had a personal pension	27	26	24	30	28	25	26	27	34	32
*Weighted base (000's) =100%**								*1,958*	*1,904*	*1,942*
*Unweighted sample**	*929*	*869*	*852*	*842*	*879*	*696*	*683*		*625*	*700*

* Trend tables show unweighted and weighted figures for 1998 to give an indication of the effect of the weighting. For the weighted data (1998, 2000 and 2001) the weighted base (000's) is the base for percentages. Unweighted data (up to 1998) are based on the unweighted sample.

Weighting to be revised in Spring 2003 following the 2001 census revisions of population estimates. See Appendix D.

Table 6.14 Membership of personal pension scheme by sex and length of time in self-employment

Self-employed persons aged 16 and over — *Great Britain: 1998, 2000 and 2001 combined*

	Length of time in self-employment			
	Less than 2 years	2 years, but less than 5 years	5 years or more	Total
	Percentage of self-employed who belong to a personal pension scheme			
Men full time	30	44	66	57
Women full time	27	34	49	41
Women part time	10	16	35	24
*Unweighted sample**				
Men full time	*283*	*276*	*1437*	*1996*
Women full time	*86*	*96*	*251*	*433*
Women part time	*126*	*103*	*246*	*475*

* Weighted bases not shown for combined data sets.

Chapter 7

General health and use of health services

The GHS has asked a series of questions about health and the use of health services since the beginning of the survey in 1971. Although periodic changes have been made to the content of the health section, it is possible to monitor changes in self-reported health and the use of health services over a 30 year period.

The *Independent Inquiry into Inequalities in Health*[1] and *Our Healthier Nation*[2] both indicate that health inequalities exist. *The NHS Plan*[3] gives priority to addressing this problem, and following its publication, the Secretary of State set two national targets in February 2001 to reduce health inequalities in infant mortality and life expectancy. *Tackling Health Inequalities - Consultation on a plan for delivery*[4] builds on the NHS Plan, to develop further ways of reducing health inequalities. Analysis of GHS data makes it possible to monitor changes over time and health measures alongside other socio-economic factors.

Many of the tables in this chapter refer to data on adults and children. Questions on health and use of health services are asked of all adults aged 16 and over in the household . For the majority of questions, information is also collected from a responsible adult about all children in the household. (For more detail see Appendix F for the full questionnaire.)

Self-reported health

Questions on the self-perception of health have been asked since 1977. In 2001, the GHS found that 59% of adults said they had good health, 27% reported they had fairly good health and 14% said their health was not good. This remains broadly unchanged since 1998 and there has been no obvious trend in the data since 1977. In 2000 this question was introduced for children aged less than 16 and, as was the case for adults, there is no evidence of change between 2000 and 2001.

- 81% of children were reported by their parent or guardian as having good health, 15% were reported as having fairly good health and for 3% it was reported that their health was not good (table not shown). **Table 7.2**

Chronic sickness

Respondents are asked whether they have a longstanding illness, disability or infirmity.[5] This question has been included in the GHS in its present form since 1972. Those who report a longstanding illness are then asked if this limits their activities in any way. This question has been asked since 1973. The data include both adults and children.

In 2001, 32% reported a longstanding condition, while 19% said they had a condition which limited their activities in some way.

The prevalence of reported longstanding illness increased over the last three decades of the GHS from 21% in 1972 to 32% in 2001. The likelihood of reporting a longstanding illness increased steadily through the 1970s and early 1980s, and then ranged from 30% in 1985 to 35% in 1996, with no clear pattern over time. From 1998 to 2001, however, the proportion reporting longstanding illness has remained broadly unchanged.

The prevalence of limiting longstanding conditions has increased in line with longstanding conditions and has shown similar variations, although the overall increase has been smaller. In 1972, 15% reported a limiting condition compared with 19% in 2001. Between the 1970s and 2001 the proportion of children aged 0 to 4 and 5 to 15 who were reported to have a limiting longstanding illness has almost doubled from 2% to 4% for 0 to 4 year olds and 5% to 8% for 5 to 15 year olds.

In 2001, as in all previous years, the likelihood of reporting a chronic condition, whether limiting or otherwise, increased with age.

- The prevalence of longstanding illnesses, disabilities or infirmities increased from 14% of those aged under five to 63% of those aged 75 and over.
- The increase in prevalence was particularly marked among those aged 45 or over. Whereas one in five respondents aged under 45 reported a longstanding illness, nearly half of respondents aged 45 and over did so.
- The proportion reporting a limiting condition increased from 4% of children aged under 5 to 46% of adults in the 75 and over age group.
- One in ten respondents under the age of 45 reported a limiting longstanding illness, compared with nearly a third of older respondents.

It should be noted that these reports of chronic sickness are based on respondent's own assessments, therefore increases in the prevalence may reflect increased expectations which people have about their health as well as changes in the actual prevalence of sickness. A possible contributory factor is an increase in the absolute numbers of people with severe chronic conditions who are surviving now compared with the past, perhaps due to new treatments or the wider application of successful treatments. It should also be remembered that people vary in the extent to which they are troubled by the same symptoms, and that their need to limit activities will also depend on what they usually do.

Findings from other surveys have also suggested that older people are more likely to under-report chronic conditions. This is perhaps because they regard limitations in their daily activities as a normal part of growing old and not as evidence of illness or disability. A report from the 1998 GHS 'People aged 65 and over', discusses how the GHS data is likely to underestimate the incidence of longstanding conditions among older people.[6]

Overall, there were no statistically significant differences between men and women in the reported prevalence of longstanding or limiting longstanding illness, but there was a higher reported prevalence of longstanding illness among boys compared with girls. Among boys, 17% of those aged less than five and 20% aged 5 to 15 were reported to have a longstanding illness compared with 12% and 16% of girls respectively.

Table 7.1, Figure 7A

Acute sickness

Respondents were asked whether they had to cut down on their normal activities in the two weeks prior to interview as a result of illness or injury.

From 1972 to 1996, the proportion of those reporting restricted activity increased from 8% to 16% but since then it has declined to 14% in 2001. Reported acute sickness increased with age but not as sharply as for chronic conditions. About one in ten of those aged under 16 had an acute sickness which restricted their activities during the reference period, increasing to a quarter of those aged 75 and over.

In 2001, 13% of males and 15% of females reported restricted activity due to illness or injury during the two weeks prior to interview. The largest difference in reported acute sickness between men and women was in the 65 to 74 age group; 21% of women reported restricted activity compared with 16% of men. Women had on average 32 days restricted activity per year whereas men had 28.

Tables 7.1, 7.3

Self-reported sickness, socio-economic classification and economic activity status

Tackling Health Inequalities - consultation on a plan for delivery[4] states that, 'at the turn of the 21st century, opportunity for a healthy life is still linked to social circumstances'. The new socio-economic classification (NS-SEC) used for the first time in the 2001 GHS[7] confirms that social circumstances are still related to health.

Figure 7A **Percentages of males and females reporting (a) longstanding illness (b) limiting longstanding illness (c) restricted activity in the 14 days before interview: Great Britain, 1972 to 2001**
(data is not available for 1977, 1978, 1997 and 1999)

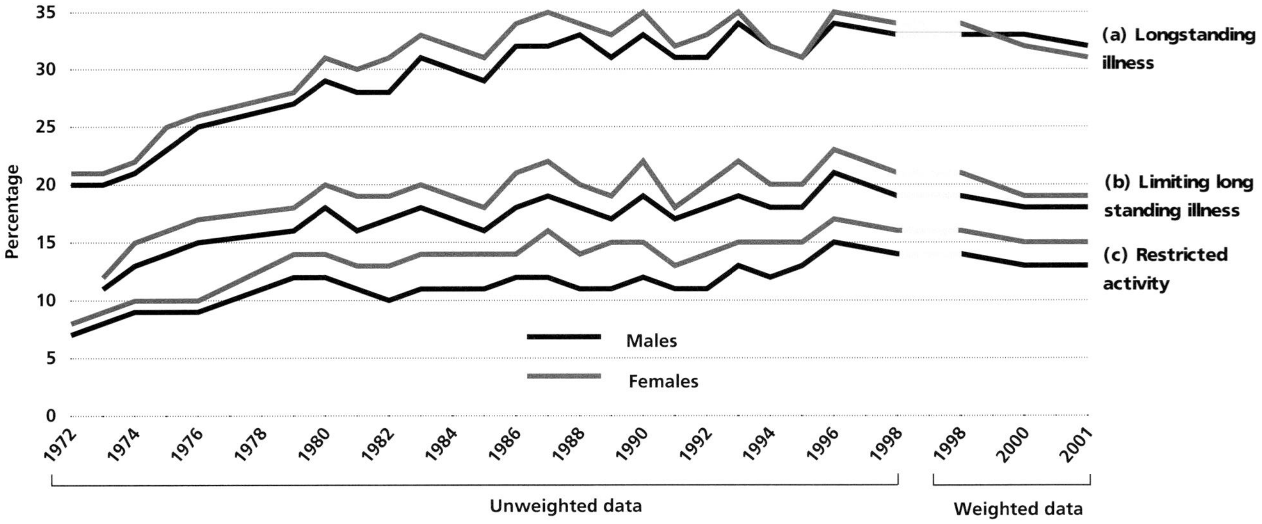

Tables 7.4 to 7.6 present data using NS-SEC and are also grouped into the following three main classes:

- Managerial and professional occupations
- Intermediate occupations
- Routine and manual occupations

There were differences between each of the three main NS-SEC groups in the proportion of respondents who reported longstanding illness.

- Respondents living in households whose reference person was in the routine and manual group had the highest prevalence of longstanding illness (37% of men and 36% of women), followed by the intermediate group (31% of men and 32% of women) and with the lowest prevalence in the managerial and professional group (27% of men and 26% of women).

A similar trend was evident among respondents who reported limiting longstanding illness and restricted activity in the 14 days before interview. However, among those who reported restricted activity, there were no significant differences between respondents whose household reference person was in the managerial and professional group and those in the intermediate group. The highest prevalence of reported restricted activity was among respondents whose household reference person was in the routine and manual group. For example:

- among men, 15% of those in routine and manual group households reported restricted activity compared with 11% of men in both intermediate group and managerial and professional group households.

Thus, of the three main NS-SEC groups, respondents who were living in households headed by someone who was in the routine and manual group were the most likely to report a longstanding illness, a limiting longstanding illness or restricted activity in the last two weeks and respondents whose household reference person was in the managerial and professional group were least likely to report a longstanding illness or limiting longstanding illness.

There were no statistically significant differences in reported sickness and restricted activity between respondents whose household reference person was in the routine and manual occupations group and those whose reference person had never worked or was long-term unemployed.

Tables 7.4-7.6

Our Healthier Nation[2] argues that 'being in work is good for your health' and states that joblessness had been clearly linked to poor physical and mental health. Among the GHS respondents, the unemployed were more likely than those in work to report longstanding illness but the difference was only significant for women[8]. However, both unemployed men and unemployed women reported significantly higher levels of limiting longstanding illness than those who were working.

- 19% of unemployed women reported a limiting longstanding condition, compared with 10% of those who were working at the time of the interview.
- Men who were unemployed were over one and a half times more likely than those who were working (15% compared with 9%) to report restricted activity in the two weeks before interview, but the differences were not significant for women (13% and 11% respectively).

The prevalence of longstanding illness, limiting illness and restricted activity was highest among economically inactive respondents. The difference between economically inactive and working respondents, who reported chronic and acute sickness, was significant across all age groups and was more pronounced among men than women.

- 10% of men and women who were working reported a limiting longstanding illness compared with 46% of men and 37% of women who were economically inactive.

Tables 7.7-7.9

Self-reported sickness and regional variations

People in Wales were more likely to report longstanding illness than those in Scotland or England, a difference which was statistically significant for males but not for females.

- Among males, 38% of those living in Wales reported a longstanding illness compared with 33% in Scotland and 31% in England.

In terms of Government Office Regions, people in London had the lowest incidence of longstanding illness (25% compared with 29-36% for other regions). People in the North East had the highest incidence of limiting longstanding illness (25% compared with 15-21% for other regions) and were at the upper end of the range of reported restricted activity (17% compared with 12-15% for other regions). There were no statistically significant differences between regions in the restriction of activities due to sickness in the 2 weeks before interview. Similar results were found for NHS Regional Office areas which are shown in Table 7.11.

Tables 7.10-7.11

Details of longstanding conditions

Respondents aged 16 and over who reported a longstanding illness or condition were asked 'What is the matter with you?' Details of the illness were recorded by the interviewer and coded during the interview using a computer-assisted coding frame.[9] The categories into which respondents' replies were coded were later collapsed into broad groups which approximate to the chapter headings of the International Classification of Diseases (ICD10). Studies of the validity of self-reported data have shown that there is a high level of agreement between incidence based on self-reporting and on medical examinations[10], and between self-reporting and doctor diagnosis of specific conditions.[11] The level of agreement is highest for those conditions which require ongoing treatment, have commonly recognised names and are salient to respondents because they cause discomfort or worry.[12]

Similar to previous years of the GHS, the most common conditions reported by respondents were musculoskeletal problems and conditions of the heart and circulatory system. Since 1998, there has been no change in the order of frequency of conditions. **Table 7.12**

For the majority of conditions a higher prevalence was found among older people than among young people. The difference was more marked for some complaints than others.

- A condition of the musculoskeletal system was reported at a rate of 66 per 1000 for those aged 16 to 44, compared with a rate of 313 per 1000 among people aged 75 and over.
- Whereas 19 per 1000 in the 16 to 44 age group reported a heart and circulatory system condition, the corresponding rate among those aged 75 and over was 327 per 1000.

Skin complaints were one of a few conditions that did not increase with age. For example, people aged 16 to 44 were more likely than those aged 45 to 64 to have a skin condition (9 per 1000 compared with 5 per 1000). Similarly, there was a higher prevalence of mental disorders among 45 to 64 year olds (35 per 1000) than among the two older age groups (12 and 18 per 1000). The GHS does not collect data on people living in institutions because the sample is based on private households. Therefore it is possible that rates of some disorders are an underestimation of the true population rates, particularly among those aged 75 and over.

Table 7.13

In line with the GHS results from previous years, women were more likely than men to report musculoskeletal problems, 153 compared to 138 per 1000 respectively. However, among those aged 16 to 44 this trend was reversed and the rate of reported musculoskeletal problems was higher among men than among women (74 per 1000 for men compared with 57 per 1000 for women). Overall there was no diffference between men and women in the reporting of heart and circulatory problems but for all age groups below the age of 75, rates of reported heart and circulatory problems were higher for men than for women. These differences increased with age and were largest among those aged 65 to 74.

- Among people aged 65 to 74, 313 per 1000 men reported heart and circulatory problems compared with 252 per 1000 women.

There was also a significantly higher prevalence of endocrine and metabolic conditions among women aged 65 and over compared with men of the same age. These differences were greatest in the oldest age group, where rates among women were 109 per 1000 compared with 65 per 1000 for men.

Tables 7.12 and 7.14

Table 7.15 shows the major disease groups separated into their component parts. This shows that the higher levels of women than men who reported musculoskeletal problems in the older age groups was mainly explained by the higher rate of arthritis and rheumatism among women (184 compared with 124 per 1000 among those aged 65 to 74 and 231 compared with 140 per 1000 among those aged 75 and over). Conversely, the higher levels of men compared with women who reported musculoskeletal problems in the youngest age group (16 to 44) can be explained by a higher rate of bone and joint problems among men.

Up to the age of 74, bronchitis and emphysema was significantly related to age, especially in men. There was almost no reporting among men aged 16 to 44, whereas 31 out of 1000 men aged 65-74 reported this condition. Hay fever was significantly higher among young men. The rates for men aged 16 to 44 were 5 per 1000 whereas there was no reporting from men aged 65 and over. **Table 7.15**

Tables 7.16 and 7.17 look at the rate of reporting selected longstanding conditions by socio-economic classification of the household reference person.

- Respondents whose household reference person was in the managerial and professional group had the lowest incidence of musculoskeletal and heart and circulatory problems.
- Respondents whose household reference person was in the semi-routine and routine group were almost twice as likely to report a musculoskeletal condition than those in the managerial and professional group (195 per 1000 compared with 111 per 1000). **Table 7.16-7.17**

Use of health services

The GHS provides data about the use of health services among children and adults in the general population. It complements other sources of data which refer to those who have made use of health services, as it also includes those who make little or no use of these services.

The topics covered include:

- whether they have seen a General Practitioner (GP) in the two weeks before interview;
- whether they have seen a practice nurse in the two weeks before interview;
- whether they have attended an outpatient or casualty department in the three months before interview;
- whether they have been a day patient in the last 12 months;
- whether they have been an inpatient in the last 12 months.

Overall, females were more likely than males to have made use of any of these services. Use was highest among children aged less than 5 and adults in the older age groups.

General Practitioner (GP) consultations

There has been very little change in the proportion of GP consultations for 2001 compared with those reported in 1998 and 2000. In 2001, 11% of males and 16% of females reported consulting a GP during the 14 days prior to interview. Similar to previous years, the difference between men and women was particularly marked in the 16 to 44 age group (8% compared with 15%). Many consultations by women of this age are likely to be associated with birth control or pregnancy which could account for some of the difference. The difference was also apparent among those aged 45 to 64, 13% of men compared with 18% of women of this age reported consulting a GP during the 14 days prior to interview.

- The likelihood of having consulted a GP was highest for adults aged 75 and over, at 22% of men and 20% of women.[13]
- The average number of consultations per year was the same as in 1998 and 2000; 4 for males and 5 for females. **Tables 7.18-7.19, Figure 7B**

Overall there was no change from 2000 in the proportions of consultations taking place at the surgery, at home or by telephone. Trend data from 1971 however, shows a reduction in the number of NHS GP consultations that take place at home and an increase in surgery and phone consultations.

- The proportion of consultations taking place in respondent's homes has fallen from 22% in 1971 to only 5% in 2001.
- In 1971, 73% of consultations took place in the surgery, but by 2001 this figure had increased to 85%.

Figure 7B **Percentage of males and females consulting an NHS GP in the 14 days before interview: Great Britain 1971 to 2001**
(data is not available for 1977, 1978, 1997 and 1999)

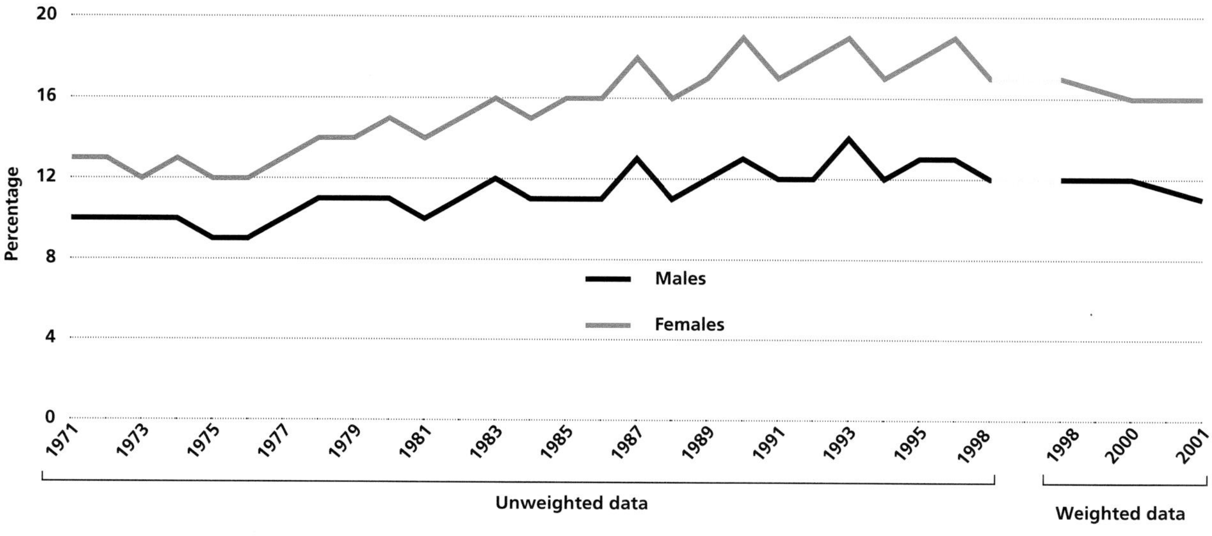

GP consultations over the phone have shown an increase over time. In 1971 only 4% of GP consultations took place over the phone, at a time when less than half of households owned a phone. During the 1980s and early 1990s, the proportion of GP consultations on the phone was between 7% and 8% and has remained at 10% since 1998. **Table 7.20**

Table 7.21 presents the percentage of consultations by site of consultation, and Table 7.22 shows the percentage of males and females of different ages consulting a doctor by site of consultation. The distributions within each table are fairly similar and the following figures refer to Table 7.22. Older people were more likely than younger people to report home consultations. Of people aged less than 65, between 1% and 4% reported having a consultation at home in the two weeks before interview compared with 6% of people aged 65 to 74 and 20% of those aged 75 and over. One reason for this may be that it is more difficult for older people to get to surgeries and health centres. **Tables 7.21-7.22**

A higher proportion of males living in households whose household reference person was in the routine and manual group consulted a doctor in the two weeks prior to interview than of those in intermediate group households and managerial and professional group households (13%, 10% and 10% respectively). These differences were not found among females.

Economically inactive men were over twice as likely to consult a doctor in the two weeks before interview than those who were working. The differences were evident in each age group.

- Men who were economically inactive had an average of 6 consultations per year, whereas those who were working had an average of 3.

Economically inactive women were also more likely to consult a doctor than those who were working, 20% compared to 14%.

Among people who had consulted a GP in the two weeks before interview, those living in households where the household reference person was in the routine and manual group were more likely to receive a prescription than those in managerial and professional households. Overall, men and women in the oldest age group (65 and over) and women aged 45 to 64 were more likely to receive a prescription than those in younger age groups. **Tables 7.23-7.25**

Similar to previous years, only a small percentage of GP consultations were with private doctors: 3% of all consultations. **Table 7.26**

Practice nurse consultations

Questions on practice nurses were introduced in 2000. Overall, one in twenty people (5%) reported consulting a practice nurse during the two weeks before interview, which remains unchanged since 2000. Older people were more likely to have visited a practice nurse than younger people; 12% of those aged 65 to 74 and of those aged 75 and over visited a practice nurse compared with 2-6% of younger people. The proportion of respondents aged 75 and over who had consulted a practice nurse increased from 9% in 2000 to 12% in 2001.

Overall, females were more likely than males to report consulting a practice nurse during the fortnight before interview. These differences were greatest among 16 to 44 year olds where 2% of men visited a practice nurse compared with 5% of women. This may be partly due to women visiting practice nurses for reasons associated with family planning and pregnancy.

- On average there were 2 consultations with a practice nurse per person, per year. This figure doubled for those for those aged 65 and over. **Table 7.27**

Children's use of other health services

It was reported that in the two weeks before interview:

- 2% of children had seen a practice nurse at the GP surgery;
- 4% of children had seen a health visitor at the GP surgery;
- 2% of children had gone to a child health clinic;
- less than 0.5% of children had gone to a child welfare clinic.

Children under five were more likely to have made use of the services. There were no significant differences between boys and girls. **Table 7.28**

Hospital visits

Outpatient visits

Fourteen percent of respondents reported visiting an outpatient or casualty department at least once in a three month period before interview. There has been a general increase since 1972, when 10% of all respondents reported such visits, although there is also evidence of a slight decline from 1998 onwards.

Figure 7C **Percentage of males and females reporting an inpatient stay in the 12 months before interview by age: Great Britain, 2001**

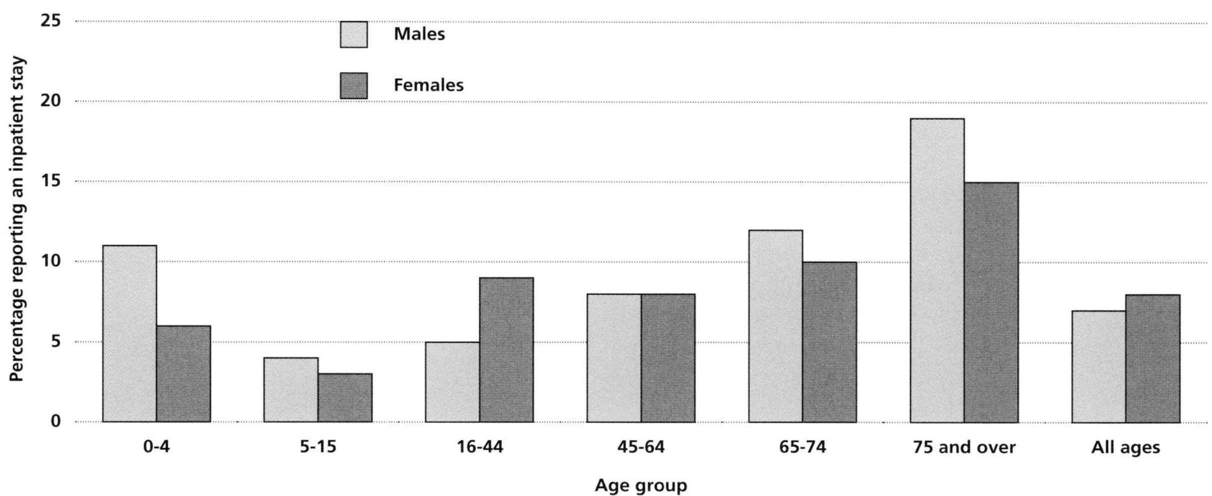

Older respondents were most likely to have reported attending an outpatient or casualty department. Among those aged 75 and over, men were more likely than women to have attended an outpatient or casualty department, 31% compared to 23%. **Table 7.29**

Day patients
In 2001, 7% of people reported attending hospital as a day patient in the 12 months before interview. The proportion of respondents attending hospitals as day patients has increased since this question was first asked in 1992 from 4% to 7%, although this figure has remained unchanged since 1998.

There were no statistically significant differences between males and females in the average number of separate days spent in hospital as day patients during the 12 months prior to interview. **Tables 7.30-7.31**

Inpatients
The proportion of respondents who reported an inpatient stay in the 12 months prior to interview remained unchanged since 2000, at 8% which reflects the overall trend of little change since 1982. Overall, females were slightly more likely to report an inpatient stay than males (8% compared with 7%) but within age groups this difference was only found among those aged 16 to 44 (9% compared with 5%). People aged 75 and over were more likely to report an inpatient stay than any other age group, 17% in this group did so.

Among those who had been an inpatient, the average number of nights spent in hospital during the 12 months before interview was 8. Among adults, the average number of nights increased with age from 4 nights for those aged 16 to 44, to 17 nights for those aged 75 or over. **Tables 7.32-7.34, Figure 7C**

Notes and references

1 *Independent Inquiry into Inequalities in Health.* The Stationery Office (London 1998).
2 *Our Healthier Nation.* Department of Health. The Stationery Office (London 1998).
3 *The NHS Plan.* Department of Health. The Stationery Office (London 2000).
4 *Tackling Health Inequalities - consultation on a plan for delivery.* Department of Health. The Stationery Office (London 2001).
5 Respondents are asked 'Do you have any longstanding illness, disability or infirmity? By longstanding, I mean anything that has troubled you over a period of time or that is likely to affect you over a period of time?' It is left to the respondent to define what is meant by longstanding illness, disability or infirmity.
6 Bridgwood A. *People aged 65 and over. Results of an independent study carried out on behalf of the Department of Health as part of the 1998 General Household Survey.* Office for National Statistics (London 2000).
7 From April 2001 the National Statistics Socio-economic classification (NS-SEC) was introduced for all official statistics and surveys. It has replaced Social Class based on occupation and Socio-economic Groups (SEG). See Appendix E for further information about NS-SEC.
8 This may be due to the small sample sizes in the unemployed group.
9 The interviewers checked whether respondents had more than one complaint. They recorded details of, and coded up to six complaints.
10 Blaxter M. Self-reported health in *The Health and Lifestyles Survey.* Health Promotion Research Trust (London 1987).

11 Bennett N et al. *Health Survey for England 1993: Appendix D*. HMSO (London 1995).

12 Discrepancies do not necessarily indicate that data from self-reported sources are inaccurate. Respondents may not have brought a condition to the attention of a doctor, medical records could be inaccurate, doctors may not have informed patients of their diagnosis, and lay descriptions may be different from those given by a doctor (see Blaxter and Bennett).

13 The GHS does not collect data on people living in institutions because the sample is based on private households. Therefore it is possible that rates of service use are an underestimation of the true population rates, particularly among those aged 75 and over.

Table 7.1 **Trends in self-reported sickness by sex and age, 1972 to 2001: percentage of persons who reported**
(a) longstanding illness
(b) limiting longstanding illness
(c) restricted activity in the 14 days before interview

All persons *Great Britain*

	Unweighted									Weighted			*Weighted base 2001 (000's) = 100%**	*Unweighted sample* 2001*
	1972	1975	1981	1985	1991	1993	1995	1996	1998	1998	2000	2001		
							(a) Longstanding illness							
Percentage who reported:														
Males														
0- 4	5	8	12	11	13	15	14	14	15	15	14	17	*1,737*	*675*
5-15†	9	11	17	18	17	21	20	19	21	21	23	20	*4,112*	*1579*
16-44†	14	17	22	21	23	26	23	27	24	24	23	22	*11,606*	*3806*
45-64	29	35	40	42	42	45	43	46	44	44	45	44	*6,612*	*2474*
65-74	48	50	51	55	61	62	55	61	59	59	61	58	*2,190*	*900*
75 and over	54	63	60	58	63	64	56	64	68	68	63	64	*1,451*	*564*
Total	20	23	28	29	31	34	31	34	33	33	33	32	*27,709*	*9998*
Females														
0- 4	3	6	7	9	10	12	11	13	15	15	13	12	*1,694*	*668*
5-15†	6	9	13	13	15	16	17	16	19	19	18	16	*4,047*	*1556*
16-44†	13	16	21	22	23	26	22	27	23	23	22	21	*11,295*	*4188*
45-64	31	33	41	43	41	45	39	47	43	43	42	42	*6,763*	*2613*
65-74	48	54	58	56	55	59	54	58	59	59	54	56	*2,519*	*975*
75 and over	65	61	70	65	65	69	66	68	65	65	64	63	*2,424*	*902*
Total	21	25	30	31	32	35	31	35	34	34	32	31	*28,742*	*10902*
All persons														
0- 4	4	7	10	10	12	13	13	13	15	15	14	14	*3,431*	*1343*
5-15†	8	10	15	16	16	19	19	18	20	20	20	18	*8,160*	*3135*
16-44†	13	16	21	22	23	26	23	27	24	24	22	22	*22,901*	*7994*
45-64	30	34	41	43	41	45	41	47	44	43	44	43	*13,375*	*5087*
65-74	48	52	55	56	58	60	55	59	59	59	57	57	*4,710*	*1875*
75 and over	62	62	67	63	65	67	63	66	66	66	64	63	*3,875*	*1466*
Total	21	24	29	30	31	34	31	35	33	33	32	32	*56,451*	*20900*
							(b) Limiting longstanding illness							
Percentage who reported:														
Males														
0- 4	..	3	3	4	4	5	5	4	4	4	4	5	*1,737*	*675*
5-15†	..	6	8	8	7	9	8	8	8	8	9	9	*4,110*	*1578*
16-44†	..	9	10	10	10	13	12	14	12	12	11	10	*11,606*	*3806*
45-64	..	24	26	27	25	28	28	31	28	28	27	28	*6,612*	*2474*
65-74	..	36	35	38	40	41	37	42	36	36	38	36	*2,188*	*899*
75 and over	..	46	44	43	46	45	41	50	48	48	44	47	*1,451*	*564*
Total	..	14	16	16	17	19	18	21	19	19	18	18	*27,704*	*9996*
Females														
0- 4	..	2	3	3	3	3	3	4	5	5	4	4	*1,694*	*668*
5-15†	..	4	6	6	5	8	8	8	8	8	8	8	*4,047*	*1556*
16-44†	..	9	11	11	11	15	13	16	13	13	11	12	*11,295*	*4188*
45-64	..	22	26	26	25	29	26	32	29	29	27	26	*6,763*	*2613*
65-74	..	39	41	38	34	39	37	40	39	39	35	37	*2,519*	*975*
75 and over	..	49	56	51	51	52	52	53	51	51	48	45	*2,422*	*901*
Total	..	16	19	18	18	22	20	23	21	21	19	19	*28,740*	*10901*
All persons														
0- 4	..	2	3	3	4	4	4	4	4	4	4	4	*3,431*	*1343*
5-15†	..	5	7	7	6	9	8	8	8	8	8	8	*8,157*	*3134*
16-44†	..	9	11	10	10	14	12	15	13	13	11	11	*22,901*	*7994*
45-64	..	23	26	26	25	29	27	32	28	28	27	27	*13,375*	*5087*
65-74	..	38	38	38	37	40	37	41	38	37	37	36	*4,707*	*1874*
75 and over	..	48	52	48	49	50	48	52	50	50	47	46	*3,873*	*1465*
Total	..	15	17	17	18	20	19	22	20	20	19	19	*56,444*	*20897*

* Trend tables show unweighted and weighted figures for 1998 to give an indication of the effect of the weighting. For the weighted data (1998, 2000 and 2001) the weighted base (000's) is the base for percentages. Unweighted data (up to 1998) are based on the unweighted sample. Unweighted bases for earlier years are of similar size to the unweighted sample and can be found in GHS reports for each year.

† These age-groups were 5-14 and 15-44 in 1972 to 1978.

Weighting to be revised in Spring 2003 following the 2001 census revisions of population estimates. See Appendix D.

Table 7.1 - *continued*

All persons *Great Britain*

	Unweighted									Weighted			*Weighted base 2001 (000's) = 100%**	*Unweighted sample* 2001*
	1972	1975	1981	1985	1991	1993	1995	1996	1998	1998	2000	2001		
	(c) Restricted activity in the 14 days before interview													
Percentage who reported:														
Males														
0- 4	5	10	13	13	11	13	11	12	10	10	11	9	*1,737*	*675*
5-15†	6	9	12	11	11	11	10	10	9	9	10	9	*4,120*	*1582*
16-44†	7	7	8	9	9	11	10	13	11	11	10	10	*11,609*	*3807*
45-64	9	10	12	11	12	15	15	18	18	18	17	17	*6,614*	*2475*
65-74	10	8	11	13	14	16	17	19	18	18	20	16	*2,186*	*898*
75 and over	10	12	15	17	18	17	20	23	24	24	23	23	*1,450*	*564*
Total	7	9	11	11	11	13	13	15	14	14	13	13	*27,715*	*10001*
Females														
0- 4	6	8	12	13	10	10	11	9	8	8	7	8	*1,694*	*668*
5-15†	5	7	11	12	9	11	10	9	11	11	11	10	*4,049*	*1557*
16-44†	8	10	11	13	12	13	13	15	13	13	12	12	*11,304*	*4191*
45-64	9	10	13	14	13	17	17	22	20	20	19	18	*6,766*	*2614*
65-74	10	12	17	18	16	19	20	21	23	23	21	21	*2,517*	*974*
75 and over	14	13	21	23	21	23	26	25	27	27	27	26	*2,424*	*902*
Total	8	10	13	14	13	15	15	17	16	16	15	15	*28,754*	*10906*
All persons														
0- 4	6	9	13	13	11	11	11	10	9	9	9	9	*3,431*	*1343*
5-15†	6	8	12	11	10	11	10	10	10	10	10	10	*8,169*	*3139*
16-44†	8	9	10	11	10	12	12	14	12	12	11	11	*22,914*	*7998*
45-64	9	10	12	12	13	16	16	20	19	19	18	17	*13,397*	*5089*
65-74	10	11	14	16	15	18	19	20	21	21	21	19	*4,702*	*1872*
75 and over	13	13	19	21	20	21	24	24	26	26	25	25	*3,874*	*1466*
Total	8	9	12	12	12	14	14	16	15	15	14	14	*56,469*	*20907*

* Trend tables show unweighted and weighted figures for 1998 to give an indication of the effect of the weighting. For the weighted data (1998, 2000 and 2001) the weighted base (000's) is the base for percentages. Unweighted data (up to 1998) are based on the unweighted sample. Unweighted bases for earlier years are of similar size to the unweighted sample and can be found in GHS reports for each year.
† These age-groups were 5-14 and 15-44 in 1972 to 1978.

Weighting to be revised in Spring 2003 following the 2001 census revisions of population estimates. See Appendix D.

Table 7.2 **Self perception of general health during the last 12 months: 1977 to 2001**

*Persons aged 16 and over** *Great Britain*

	Unweighted										Weighted		
	1977	1979	1981	1983	1985	1987	1990	1994	1996	1998	1998	2000	2001
	%	%	%	%	%	%	%	%	%	%	%	%	%
Percentage who reported their general health was:													
Good	58	60	62	60	63	60	60	60	55	59	60	59	59
Fairly good	30	27	26	28	25	28	28	27	33	27	27	27	27
Not good	12	13	12	12	12	12	12	13	12	14	14	13	14
*Weighted base (000's) =100%***											*40,884*	*42,467*	*41,990*
*Unweighted sample**	*23125*	*21962*	*23242*	*19056*	*18575*	*19477*	*17537*	*16778*	*15684*	*14410*		*14113*	*15385*

* This question was not asked of proxies.
** Trend tables show unweighted and weighted figures for 1998 to give an indication of the effect of the weighting. For the weighted data (1998, 2000 and 2001) the weighted base (000's) is the base for percentages. Unweighted data (up to 1998) are based on the unweighted sample.

Weighting to be revised in Spring 2003 following the 2001 census revisions of population estimates. See Appendix D.

Table 7.3 Acute sickness: average number of restricted activity days per person per year, by sex and age

All persons — *Great Britain: 2001*

	Number of days			*Weighted bases (000's) = 100%*			*Unweighted sample*		
	Males	Females	Total	*Males*	*Females*	*Total*	*Males*	*Females*	*Total*
Age									
0- 4	13	10	12	*1,737*	*1,694*	*3,431*	*675*	*668*	*1343*
5-15	12	15	14	*4,114*	*4,049*	*8,164*	*1580*	*1557*	*3137*
16-44	18	21	20	*11,606*	*11,304*	*22,911*	*3806*	*4191*	*7997*
45-64	42	40	41	*6,608*	*6,758*	*13,366*	*2473*	*2611*	*5084*
65-74	44	56	50	*2,186*	*2,517*	*4,702*	*898*	*974*	*1872*
75 and over	71	78	75	*1,450*	*2,424*	*3,874*	*564*	*902*	*1466*
Total	28	32	30	*27,701*	*28,746*	*56,447*	*9996*	*10903*	*20899*

Weighting to be revised in Spring 2003 following the 2001 census revisions of population estimates. See Appendix D.

Table 7.4 Chronic sickness: prevalence of reported longstanding illness by sex, age and socio-economic classification of household reference person

All persons — *Great Britain: 2001*

Socio-economic classification of household reference person*	Males										Females									
	Age										Age									
	0-15		16-44		45-64		65 and over		Total		0-15		16-44		45-64		65 and over		Total	
	Percentage who reported longstanding illness																			
Large employers and higher managerial	17		15		42		52		27		16		18		39		44		25	
Higher professional	18	17	18	19	31	38	45	54	23	27	10	13	15	18	33	38	50	53	22	26
Lower managerial and professional	17		20		40		57		28		13		20		39		56		28	
Intermediate	21	18	23	24	43	39	70	64	32	31	17	14	25	22	47	40	64	64	38	32
Small employers and own account	16		25		37		61		31		12		19		34		64		27	
Lower supervisory and technical	20		21		48		67		35		12		21		45		59		32	
Semi-routine	19	22	24	25	54	52	60	63	36	37	20	17	26	24	46	45	61	61	38	36
Routine	26		30		54		62		40		18		27		45		62		38	
Never worked and long-term unemployed	24		32		[44]		†		32		14		26		[64]		62		33	
All persons	19		22		44		60		32		15		21		42		60		31	

	Males 0-15	Males 16-44	Males 45-64	Males 65 and over	Males Total	Females 0-15	Females 16-44	Females 45-64	Females 65 and over	Females Total
Weighted bases (000's) = 100%										
Large employers and higher managerial	*345*	*778*	*442*	*225*	*1,790*	*437*	*771*	*415*	*152*	*1,776*
Higher professional	*568*	*1,265*	*622*	*268*	*2,722*	*485*	*1,037*	*547*	*215*	*2,284*
Lower managerial and professional	*1,205*	*2,625*	*1,491*	*675*	*5,996*	*1,182*	*2,655*	*1,630*	*879*	*6,346*
Intermediate	*434*	*849*	*397*	*191*	*1,871*	*388*	*956*	*616*	*577*	*2,538*
Small employers and own account	*606*	*1,109*	*787*	*380*	*2,882*	*655*	*993*	*677*	*344*	*2,668*
Lower supervisory and technical	*744*	*1,511*	*897*	*685*	*3,838*	*610*	*1,306*	*758*	*598*	*3,272*
Semi-routine	*799*	*1,299*	*871*	*520*	*3,488*	*761*	*1,376*	*1,030*	*983*	*4,150*
Routine	*759*	*1,409*	*942*	*646*	*3,756*	*793*	*1,334*	*899*	*977*	*4,003*
Never worked and long-term unemployed	*282*	*356*	*114*	*39*	*790*	*302*	*431*	*112*	*189*	*1,034*
All persons	*5,849*	*11,606*	*6,612*	*3,641*	*27,709*	*5,741*	*11,295*	*6,763*	*4,943*	*28,742*
Unweighted sample										
Large employers and higher managerial	*138*	*270*	*176*	*95*	*679*	*174*	*288*	*167*	*63*	*692*
Higher professional	*223*	*426*	*244*	*113*	*1006*	*193*	*391*	*223*	*86*	*893*
Lower managerial and professional	*467*	*868*	*580*	*283*	*2198*	*466*	*995*	*646*	*343*	*2450*
Intermediate	*166*	*271*	*146*	*82*	*665*	*150*	*352*	*233*	*225*	*960*
Small employers and own account	*225*	*369*	*294*	*151*	*1039*	*251*	*363*	*260*	*130*	*1004*
Lower supervisory and technical	*273*	*493*	*321*	*266*	*1353*	*223*	*467*	*285*	*222*	*1197*
Semi-routine	*315*	*424*	*318*	*202*	*1259*	*300*	*523*	*394*	*370*	*1587*
Routine	*294*	*462*	*338*	*251*	*1345*	*301*	*494*	*338*	*359*	*1492*
Never worked and long-term unemployed	*113*	*109*	*40*	*16*	*278*	*120*	*167*	*40*	*69*	*396*
All persons	*2254*	*3806*	*2474*	*1464*	*9998*	*2224*	*4188*	*2613*	*1877*	*10902*

* From April 2001 the National Statistics Socio-economic Classification (NS-SEC) was introduced for all official statistics and surveys. It has replaced Social Class based on Occupation and Socio-economic Groups (SEG). Full-time students and persons in inadequately described occupations are not shown as separate categories but are included in the figure for all persons (see Appendix A).

† Base too small for analysis.

Weighting to be revised in Spring 2003 following the 2001 census revisions of population estimates. See Appendix D.

Table 7.5 **Chronic sickness: prevalence of reported limiting longstanding illness by sex, age and socio-economic classification of household reference person**

All persons — *Great Britain: 2001*

Socio-economic classification of household reference person*	Males					Females				
	Age					Age				
	0-15	16-44	45-64	65 and over	Total	0-15	16-44	45-64	65 and over	Total
	Percentage who reported limiting longstanding illness									
Large employers and higher managerial	7	5	22	32	13	6	9	21	28	13
Higher professional	7 68	7 8	17 21	29 35	12 14	3 5	7 9	16 22	28 36	10 15
Lower managerial and professional	6	9	23	38	15	5	10	24	39	17
Intermediate	9 7	9 10	24 25	43 40	16 17	8 7	14 12	23 20	44 42	22 18
Small employers and own account	5	11	26	38	17	6	10	17	39	15
Lower supervisory and technical	7	10	32	47	21	6	12	29	40	20
Semi-routine	9 10	11 13	33 35	43 45	21 23	9 8	14 15	31 31	43 43	24 23
Routine	13	16	40	45	27	9	18	32	43	25
Never worked and long-term unemployed	9	27	[36]	†	22	8	20	[49]	44	24
All persons	8	10	28	41	18	7	12	26	41	19
Weighted bases (000's) = 100%										
Large employers and higher managerial	*345*	*778*	*442*	*225*	*1,790*	*437*	*771*	*415*	*152*	*1,776*
Higher professional	*568*	*1,265*	*622*	*268*	*2,722*	*485*	*1,037*	*547*	*215*	*2,284*
Lower managerial and professional	*1,205*	*2,625*	*1,491*	*675*	*5,996*	*1,182*	*2,655*	*1,630*	*879*	*6,346*
Intermediate	*434*	*849*	*397*	*191*	*1,871*	*388*	*956*	*616*	*577*	*2,538*
Small employers and own account	*606*	*1,109*	*787*	*380*	*2,882*	*655*	*993*	*677*	*344*	*2,668*
Lower supervisory and technical	*744*	*1,511*	*897*	*683*	*3,836*	*610*	*1,306*	*758*	*598*	*3,272*
Semi-routine	*799*	*1,299*	*871*	*520*	*3,488*	*761*	*1,376*	*1,030*	*981*	*4,148*
Routine	*759*	*1,409*	*942*	*646*	*3,756*	*793*	*1,334*	*899*	*977*	*4,003*
Never worked and long-term unemployed	*280*	*356*	*114*	*39*	*788*	*302*	*431*	*112*	*189*	*1,034*
All persons	*5,847*	*11,606*	*6,612*	*3,639*	*27,704*	*5,741*	*11,295*	*6,763*	*4,941*	*28,740*
Unweighted sample										
Large employers and higher managerial	*138*	*270*	*176*	*95*	*679*	*174*	*288*	*167*	*63*	*692*
Higher professional	*223*	*426*	*244*	*113*	*1006*	*193*	*391*	*223*	*86*	*893*
Lower managerial and professional	*467*	*868*	*580*	*283*	*2198*	*466*	*995*	*646*	*343*	*2450*
Intermediate	*166*	*271*	*146*	*82*	*665*	*150*	*352*	*233*	*225*	*960*
Small employers and own account	*225*	*369*	*294*	*151*	*1039*	*251*	*363*	*260*	*130*	*1004*
Lower supervisory and technical	*273*	*493*	*321*	*265*	*1352*	*223*	*467*	*285*	*222*	*1197*
Semi-routine	*315*	*424*	*318*	*202*	*1259*	*300*	*523*	*394*	*369*	*1586*
Routine	*294*	*462*	*338*	*251*	*1345*	*301*	*494*	*338*	*359*	*1492*
Never worked and long-term unemployed	*112*	*109*	*40*	*16*	*277*	*120*	*167*	*40*	*69*	*396*
All persons	*2253*	*3806*	*2474*	*1463*	*9996*	*2224*	*4188*	*2613*	*1876*	*10901*

* From April 2001 the National Statistics Socio-economic Classification (NS-SEC) was introduced for all official statistics and surveys. It has replaced Social Class based on Occupation and Socio-economic Groups (SEG). Full-time students and persons in inadequately described occupations are not shown as separate categories but are included in the figure for all persons (see Appendix A).

† Base too small for analysis.

Weighting to be revised in Spring 2003 following the 2001 census revisions of population estimates. See Appendix D.

Table 7.6 Acute sickness
(a) Prevalence of reported restricted activity in the 14 days before interview, by sex, age, and socio-economic classification of household reference person
(b) Average number of restricted activity days per person per year, by sex, age, and socio-economic classification of household reference person

All persons *Great Britain: 2001*

In the table, each column marked "(group)" gives the figure printed beside a boxed group of rows in the column to its left.

Socio-economic classification of household reference person*	Males										Females									
	Age										Age									
	0-15	(group)	16-44	(group)	45-64	(group)	65 and over	(group)	Total	(group)	0-15	(group)	16-44	(group)	45-64	(group)	65 and over	(group)	Total	(group)
(a) Percentage who reported restricted activity in the 14 days before interview																				
Large employers and higher managerial	14		9		15		14		12		14		10		15		19		13	
Higher professional	14	11	10	9	10	13	12	16	11	11	9	10	11	13	16	16	16	21	12	14
Lower managerial and professional	8		8		14		18		11		9		14		17		22		15	
Intermediate	11	9	7	10	9	12	16	17	9	11	10	9	9	10	14	13	28	26	15	13
Small employers and own account	7		12		14		18		12		9		10		12		23		12	
Lower supervisory and technical	7		11		19		26		15		8		9		19		23		14	
Semi-routine	7	8	9	11	19	22	20	22	13	15	10	9	10	11	20	21	23	24	16	16
Routine	9		14		26		19		17		9		12		23		26		17	
Never worked and long-term unemployed	12		20		[21]		†		17		7		13		[24]		25		15	
All persons	9		10		17		19		13		9		12		18		24		15	
(b) Average number of restricted activity days per person per year																				
Large employers and higher managerial	17		8		36		42		21		22		16		32		45		24	
Higher professional	17	12	18	13	15	32	35	46	19	21	10	13	17	21	30	35	39	54	21	27
Lower managerial and professional	9		12		37		52		22		11		24		37		59		30	
Intermediate	13	11	10	8	23	9	51	51	18	23	13	15	18	19	31	8	76	71	33	29
Small employers and own account	10		23		32		51		27		17		20		25		62		26	
Lower supervisory and technical	12		21		45		75		35		11		17		46		69		32	
Semi-routine	11	12	18	22	48	55	55	62	29	35	13	13	20	20	48	50	66	71	37	37
Routine	14		28		71		55		40		16		22		54		77		42	
Never worked and long-term unemployed	20		39		[71]		†		37		7		29		[80]		65		35	
All persons	12		18		42		55		28		13		21		40		66		32	

	Males 0-15	Males 16-44	Males 45-64	Males 65 and over	Males Total	Females 0-15	Females 16-44	Females 45-64	Females 65 and over	Females Total
Weighted bases (000's) = 100%										
Large employers and higher managerial	*345*	*778*	*442*	*225*	*1,790*	*437*	*771*	*415*	*152*	*1,776*
Higher professional	*568*	*1,265*	*622*	*264*	*2,719*	*485*	*1,037*	*547*	*215*	*2,284*
Lower managerial and professional	*1,205*	*2,622*	*1,488*	*675*	*5,990*	*1,182*	*2,655*	*1,630*	*879*	*6,346*
Intermediate	*434*	*849*	*399*	*193*	*1,875*	*388*	*959*	*616*	*575*	*2,539*
Small employers and own account	*604*	*1,109*	*784*	*380*	*2,877*	*655*	*993*	*674*	*344*	*2,666*
Lower supervisory and technical	*747*	*1,511*	*897*	*688*	*3,844*	*610*	*1,306*	*756*	*598*	*3,270*
Semi-routine	*801*	*1,302*	*873*	*520*	*3,497*	*763*	*1,382*	*1,030*	*983*	*4,158*
Routine	*762*	*1,409*	*940*	*641*	*3,751*	*793*	*1,334*	*899*	*979*	*4,005*
Never worked and long-term unemployed	*279*	*356*	*114*	*39*	*787*	*302*	*431*	*113*	*189*	*1,035*
All persons	*5,851*	*11,606*	*6,608*	*3,635*	*27,701*	*5,743*	*11,304*	*6,758*	*4,941*	*28,746*
Unweighted sample										
Large employers and higher managerial	*138*	*270*	*176*	*95*	*679*	*174*	*288*	*167*	*63*	*692*
Higher professional	*223*	*426*	*244*	*112*	*1005*	*193*	*391*	*223*	*86*	*893*
Lower managerial and professional	*467*	*867*	*579*	*283*	*2196*	*466*	*995*	*646*	*343*	*2450*
Intermediate	*166*	*271*	*147*	*83*	*667*	*150*	*353*	*233*	*224*	*960*
Small employers and own account	*224*	*369*	*293*	*151*	*1037*	*251*	*363*	*259*	*130*	*1003*
Lower supervisory and technical	*274*	*493*	*321*	*267*	*1355*	*223*	*467*	*284*	*222*	*1196*
Semi-routine	*316*	*425*	*319*	*202*	*1262*	*301*	*525*	*394*	*370*	*1590*
Routine	*295*	*462*	*337*	*249*	*1343*	*301*	*494*	*338*	*360*	*1493*
Never worked and long-term unemployed	*112*	*109*	*40*	*16*	*277*	*120*	*167*	*40*	*69*	*396*
All persons	*2255*	*3806*	*2473*	*1462*	*9996*	*2225*	*4191*	*2611*	*1876*	*10903*

* From April 2001 the National Statistics Socio-economic Classification (NS-SEC) was introduced for all official statistics and surveys. It has replaced Social Class based on Occupation and Socio-economic Groups (SEG). Full-time students and persons in inadequately described occupations are not shown as separate categories but are included in the figure for all persons (see Appendix A).

† Base too small for analysis.

Weighting to be revised in Spring 2003 following the 2001 census revisions of population estimates. See Appendix D.

Table 7.7 Chronic sickness: prevalence of reported longstanding illness by sex, age, and economic activity status

Persons aged 16 and over *Great Britain: 2001*

Economic activity status	Men				Women			
	Age				Age			
	16-44	45-64	65 and over	Total	16-44	45-64	65 and over	Total
	Percentage who reported longstanding illness							
Working	20	34	42	25	19	31	36	23
Unemployed	23	39	*	27	29	[42]	0	32
Economically inactive	37	76	61	60	28	59	60	51
All aged 16 and over	22	44	60	35	21	42	60	36
Weighted bases (000's) = 100%								
Working	*9,586*	*4,867*	*264*	*14,718*	*8,019*	*4,176*	*164*	*12,359*
Unemployed	*595*	*157*	*7*	*759*	*341*	*82*	*0*	*422*
Economically inactive	*1,424*	*1,584*	*3,370*	*6,379*	*2,932*	*2,505*	*4,779*	*10,217*
All aged 16 and over	*11,606*	*6,609*	*3,641*	*21,856*	*11,291*	*6,763*	*4,943*	*22,998*
Unweighted sample								
Working	*3180*	*1838*	*110*	*5128*	*2953*	*1588*	*61*	*4602*
Unemployed	*185*	*56*	*2*	*243*	*126*	*30*	*0*	*156*
Economically inactive	*441*	*579*	*1352*	*2372*	*1108*	*995*	*1816*	*3919*
All aged 16 and over	*3806*	*2473*	*1464*	*7743*	*4187*	*2613*	*1877*	*8677*

* Base too small for analysis.

Weighting to be revised in Spring 2003 following the 2001 census revisions of population estimates. See Appendix D.

Table 7.8 Chronic sickness: prevalence of reported limiting longstanding illness by sex, age, and economic activity status

Persons aged 16 and over *Great Britain: 2001*

Economic activity status	Men				Women			
	Age				Age			
	16-44	45-64	65 and over	Total	16-44	45-64	65 and over	Total
	Percentage who reported limiting longstanding illness							
Working	7	16	12	10	9	13	9	10
Unemployed	15	22	*	17	18	[19]	0	19
Economically inactive	30	67	43	46	21	47	42	37
All aged 16 and over	10	28	41	21	12	26	41	22
Weighted bases (000's) = 100%								
Working	*9,586*	*4,867*	*264*	*14,718*	*8,019*	*4,176*	*164*	*12,359*
Unemployed	*595*	*157*	*7*	*759*	*341*	*82*	*0*	*422*
Economically inactive	*1,424*	*1,584*	*3,368*	*6,377*	*2,932*	*2,505*	*4,777*	*10,214*
All aged 16 and over	*11,606*	*6,609*	*3,639*	*21,854*	*11,291*	*6,763*	*4,941*	*22,996*
Unweighted sample								
Working	*3180*	*1838*	*110*	*5128*	*2953*	*1588*	*61*	*4602*
Unemployed	*185*	*56*	*2*	*243*	*126*	*30*	*0*	*156*
Economically inactive	*441*	*579*	*1351*	*2371*	*1108*	*995*	*1815*	*3918*
All aged 16 and over	*3806*	*2473*	*1463*	*7742*	*4187*	*2613*	*1876*	*8676*

* Base too small for analysis.

Weighting to be revised in Spring 2003 following the 2001 census revisions of population estimates. See Appendix D.

Table 7.9 Acute sickness
(a) Prevalence of reported restricted activity in the 14 days before interview, by sex, age and economic activity status
(b) Average number of restricted activity days per person per year, by sex, age, and economic activity status

Persons aged 16 and over *Great Britain: 2001*

Economic activity status	Men				Women			
	Age				Age			
	16-44	45-64	65 and over	Total	16-44	45-64	65 and over	Total
	(a) Percentage who reported restricted activity in the 14 days before interview							
Working	8	10	3	9	10	12	10	11
Unemployed	15	16	*	15	12	[17]	0	13
Economically inactive	21	37	20	25	15	27	24	22
All aged 16 and over	10	17	19	14	12	18	24	16
	(b) Average number of restricted activity days per person per year							
Working	13	23	6	16	16	21	20	18
Unemployed	22	44	*	26	22	[50]	0	28
Economically inactive	51	101	59	67	33	71	68	59
All aged 16 and over	18	42	55	32	21	40	66	36
Weighted bases (000's) = 100%								
Working	*9,587*	*4,872*	*264*	*14,724*	*8,029*	*4,176*	*164*	*12,369*
Unemployed	*595*	*157*	*7*	*759*	*341*	*82*	*0*	*422*
Economically inactive	*1,424*	*1,575*	*3,364*	*6,364*	*2,932*	*2,500*	*4,777*	*10,209*
All aged 16 and over	*11,606*	*6,605*	*3,635*	*21,847*	*11,301*	*6,758*	*4,941*	*23,000*
Unweighted sample								
Working	*3180*	*1840*	*110*	*5130*	*2956*	*1588*	*61*	*4605*
Unemployed	*185*	*56*	*2*	*243*	*126*	*30*	*0*	*156*
Economically inactive	*441*	*576*	*1350*	*2367*	*1108*	*993*	*1815*	*3916*
All aged 16 and over	*3806*	*2472*	*1462*	*7740*	*4190*	*2611*	*1876*	*8677*

* Base too small for analysis.

Weighting to be revised in Spring 2003 following the 2001 census revisions of population estimates. See Appendix D.

Table 7.10 Self-reported sickness by sex and Government Office Region: percentage of persons who reported (a) longstanding illness (b) limiting longstanding illness (c) restricted activity in the 14 days before interview

All persons *Great Britain: 2001*

Government Office Region*	(a) Longstanding illness	(b) Limiting longstanding illness	(c) Restricted activity in the 14 days before interview	*Weighted base (000's) = 100%*	*Unweighted sample*
Males					
England					
North East	38	26	15	*1,205*	*440*
North West	33	21	14	*3,194*	*1235*
Yorkshire and the Humber	36	20	14	*2,212*	*887*
East Midlands	35	19	13	*2,179*	*733*
West Midlands	31	17	10	*2,440*	*944*
East of England	30	17	11	*2,636*	*1010*
London	25	15	12	*3,528*	*1117*
South East	29	14	10	*3,830*	*1374*
South West	31	16	13	*2,731*	*946*
All England	31	18	12	*23,955*	*8686*
Wales	38	23	16	*1,352*	*488*
Scotland	33	20	14	*2,397*	*822*
Great Britain	32	18	13	*27,704*	*9996*
Females					
England					
North East	34	24	18	*1,258*	*487*
North West	34	22	16	*3,341*	*1360*
Yorkshire and the Humber	35	22	14	*2,393*	*1000*
East Midlands	37	22	16	*2,175*	*772*
West Midlands	28	16	14	*2,380*	*960*
East of England	31	18	13	*2,632*	*1055*
London	25	15	13	*3,611*	*1245*
South East	30	18	14	*4,043*	*1506*
South West	32	19	14	*2,820*	*1023*
All England	31	19	14	*24,653*	*9408*
Wales	34	22	18	*1,521*	*563*
Scotland	31	19	16	*2,566*	*930*
Great Britain	31	19	15	*28,740*	*10901*
All persons					
England					
North East	36	25	17	*2,462*	*927*
North West	34	21	15	*6,535*	*2595*
Yorkshire and the Humber	35	21	14	*4,605*	*1887*
East Midlands	36	20	15	*4,354*	*1505*
West Midlands	30	17	12	*4,820*	*1904*
East of England	30	18	12	*5,268*	*2065*
London	25	15	12	*7,139*	*2362*
South East	29	16	12	*7,873*	*2880*
South West	32	18	14	*5,551*	*1969*
All England	31	18	13	*48,607*	*18094*
Wales	36	22	17	*2,873*	*1051*
Scotland	32	20	15	*4,963*	*1752*
Great Britain	32	19	14	*56,444*	*20897*

* The data have not been standardised to take account of age or socio-economic classification.

Weighting to be revised in Spring 2003 following the 2001 census revisions of population estimates. See Appendix D.

Table 7.11 Prevalence of:
(a) longstanding illness by sex and NHS Regional Office area
(b) limiting longstanding illness by sex and NHS Regional Office area
(c) reported restricted activity in the 14 days before interview, by sex and NHS Regional Office area

All persons *Great Britain: 2001*

NHS Regional Office area	Males	Females	All persons
		(a) Longstanding illness	
Northern and Yorkshire	36	33	35
Trent	37	38	38
West Midlands	31	28	30
North West	33	35	34
Eastern	30	31	31
London	25	25	25
South East	29	30	29
South West	31	33	32
England	31	31	31
Wales	38	34	36
Scotland	33	31	32
Great Britain	32	31	32
		(b) Limiting longstanding illness	
Northern and Yorkshire	22	22	22
Trent	21	23	22
West Midlands	17	16	17
North West	20	22	21
Eastern	17	18	18
London	15	15	15
South East	14	18	16
South West	16	19	18
England	18	19	18
Wales	23	22	22
Scotland	20	19	20
Great Britain	18	19	19
		(c) Restricted activity in the 14 days before interview	
Northern and Yorkshire	15	15	15
Trent	14	16	15
West Midlands	10	14	12
North West	14	16	15
Eastern	11	13	12
London	12	13	12
South East	11	14	13
South West	13	14	14
England	12	14	13
Wales	16	18	17
Scotland	14	16	15
Great Britain	13	15	14
Weighted bases (000's) =100%			
Northern and Yorkshire	*2,887*	*3,103*	*5,991*
Trent	*2,560*	*2,553*	*5,113*
West Midlands	*2,440*	*2,383*	*4,823*
North West	*3,114*	*3,252*	*6,367*
Eastern	*2,606*	*2,592*	*5,198*
London	*3,528*	*3,611*	*7,139*
South East	*4,116*	*4,369*	*8,484*
South West	*2,703*	*2,793*	*5,496*
England	*23,955*	*24,653*	*48,607*
Wales	*1,352*	*1,518*	*2,871*
Scotland	*2,397*	*2,566*	*4,963*
Great Britain	*27,704*	*28,740*	*56,444*

Weighting to be revised in Spring 2003 following the 2001 census revisions of population estimates. See Appendix D.

Table 7.11 - *continued*

All persons — *Great Britain: 2001*

NHS Regional Office area	Males	Females	All persons
Unweighted sample			
Northern and Yorkshire	*1108*	*1244*	*2352*
Trent	*902*	*955*	*1857*
West Midlands	*944*	*961*	*1905*
North West	*1207*	*1328*	*2535*
Eastern	*999*	*1040*	*2039*
London	*1117*	*1245*	*2362*
South East	*1473*	*1622*	*3095*
South West	*936*	*1014*	*1950*
England	*8686*	*9408*	*18094*
Wales	*488*	*562*	*1050*
Scotland	*822*	*930*	*1752*
Great Britain	*9996*	*10901*	*20897*

Weighting to be revised in Spring 2003 following the 2001 census revisions of population estimates. See Appendix D.

Table 7.12 **Chronic sickness: rate per 1000 reporting longstanding condition groups, by sex**

Persons aged 16 and over *Great Britain: 2001*

Condition group	Men	Women	Total
XIII Musculoskeletal system	138	153	146
VII Heart and circulatory system	110	102	106
VIII Respiratory system	63	61	62
III Endocrine and metabolic	37	51	44
IX Digestive system	28	33	31
VI Nervous system	27	32	30
V Mental disorders	30	30	30
VI Eye complaints	18	17	17
VI Ear complaints	19	15	17
X Genito-urinary system	11	12	11
II Neoplasms and benign growths	10	13	12
XII Skin complaints	8	7	8
IV Blood and related organs	3	6	5
Other complaints*	4	3	3
I Infectious diseases	3	2	2
Average number of conditions reported by those with a longstanding illness	1.5	1.5	1.5
Weighted bases (000's) = 100%	*22,342*	*23,290*	*45,632*
Unweighted sample	*7903*	*8782*	*16685*

* Including general complaints such as insomnia, fainting, generally run down, old age and general infirmity and non-specific conditions such as war wounds or road accident injuries where no further details were given.

Weighting to be revised in Spring 2003 following the 2001 census revisions of population estimates. See Appendix D.

Table 7.13 **Chronic sickness: rate per 1000 reporting longstanding condition groups, by age**

Persons aged 16 and over *Great Britain: 2001*

Condition group	16-44	45-64	65-74	75 and over
XIII Musculoskeletal system	66	198	252	313
VII Heart and circulatory system	19	133	281	327
VIII Respiratory system	55	60	89	79
III Endocrine and metabolic	14	60	110	92
IX Digestive system	17	42	41	59
VI Nervous system	23	39	33	37
V Mental disorders	33	35	12	18
VI Eye complaints	6	16	28	76
VI Ear complaints	8	18	30	49
X Genito-urinary system	7	13	18	24
II Neoplasms and benign growths	3	18	23	27
XII Skin complaints	9	5	7	8
IV Blood and related organs	3	4	11	10
Other complaints*	3	3	3	2
I Infectious diseases	2	2	1	2
Average number of conditions reported by those with a longstanding illness	1.3	1.5	1.7	1.8
Weighted bases (000's) = 100%	*23,467*	*13,540*	*4,727*	*3,898*
Unweighted sample	*8182*	*5147*	*1882*	*1474*

* Including general complaints such as insomnia, fainting, generally run down, old age and general infirmity and non-specific conditions such as war wounds or road accident injuries where no further details were given.

Weighting to be revised in Spring 2003 following the 2001 census revisions of population estimates. See Appendix D.

Table 7.14 **Chronic sickness: rate per 1000 reporting selected longstanding condition groups, by age and sex**

Persons aged 16 and over *Great Britain: 2001*

Condition group			16-44	45-64	65-74	75 and over	All ages
XIII	Musculoskeletal system	Men	74	203	212	255	138
		Women	57	194	287	349	153
VII	Heart and circulatory system	Men	22	150	313	333	110
		Women	15	115	252	322	102
VIII	Respiratory system	Men	57	56	94	97	63
		Women	54	63	85	68	61
III	Endocrine and metabolic	Men	12	56	93	65	37
		Women	16	64	124	109	51
IX	Digestive system	Men	15	41	39	55	28
		Women	20	43	43	62	33
VI	Nervous system	Men	19	36	30	49	27
		Women	26	42	36	30	32
Weighted bases (000's) = 100%		*Men*	*11,962*	*6,711*	*2,203*	*1,467*	*22,342*
		Women	*11,505*	*6,829*	*2,524*	*2,431*	*23,290*
Unweighted sample		*Men*	*3921*	*2508*	*905*	*569*	*7903*
		Women	*4261*	*2639*	*977*	*905*	*8782*

Weighting to be revised in Spring 2003 following the 2001 census revisions of population estimates. See Appendix D.

Table 7.15 Chronic sickness: rate per 1000 reporting selected longstanding conditions, by age and sex

Persons aged 16 and over *Great Britain: 2001*

Condition	Men					Women				
	16-44	45-64	65-74	75 and over	All ages	16-44	45-64	65-74	75 and over	All ages
Musculoskeletal (XIII)										
Arthritis and rheumatism	14	88	124	140	55	15	108	184	231	83
Back problems	30	62	46	38	42	29	50	36	33	36
Other bone and joint problems	30	52	43	77	41	13	36	67	85	33
Heart and circulatory (VII)										
Hypertension	9	59	99	63	36	6	65	108	102	44
Heart attack	1	32	75	113	25	0	16	39	53	15
Stroke	2	11	18	23	8	0	7	20	39	9
Other heart complaints	8	39	93	86	31	6	18	66	88	24
Other blood vessel/embolic disorders	1	7	27	44	8	2	6	12	35	8
Respiratory (VIII)										
Asthma	46	32	43	27	40	46	45	52	33	45
Bronchitis and emphysema	1	12	31	37	9	1	8	25	14	7
Hay fever	5	2	0	0	3	4	2	0	0	2
Other respiratory complaints	5	11	20	33	10	3	8	8	21	7
Weighted bases (000's) = 100%	*11,962*	*6,711*	*2,203*	*1,467*	*22,342*	*11,505*	*6,829*	*2,524*	*2,431*	*23,290*
Unweighted sample	*3921*	*2508*	*905*	*569*	*7903*	*4261*	*2639*	*977*	*905*	*8782*

Weighting to be revised in Spring 2003 following the 2001 census revisions of population estimates. See Appendix D.

Table 7.16 Chronic sickness: rate per 1000 reporting selected longstanding condition groups, by socio-economic classification of household reference person

Persons aged 16 and over *Great Britain: 2001*

Condition group		Managerial and professional	Intermediate	Small employers and own account	Lower supervisory and technical	Semi-routine and routine	All persons*
XIII	Musculoskeletal system	111	165	132	162	195	146
VII	Heart and circulatory system	77	130	97	128	141	106
VIII	Respiratory system	50	55	56	72	80	62
III	Endocrine and metabolic	40	43	45	52	51	44
IX	Digestive system	25	39	25	36	36	31
VI	Nervous system	26	31	27	30	34	30
Average number of condition groups reported by those with a longstanding illness		1.41	1.49	1.45	1.57	1.62	1.51
Weighted bases (000's) = 100%		*16,811*	*3,646*	*4,361*	*5,803*	*12,450*	*45,632*
Unweighted sample		*6297*	*1329*	*1593*	*2070*	*4532*	*16685*

* From April 2001 the National Statistics Social-economic Classification (NS-SEC) was introduced for all official statistics and surveys. It has replaced Social Class based on Occupation and Socio-economic Groups (SEG). Full-time students, persons in inadequately described occupations, persons who have never worked and the long-term unemployed are not shown as separate categories, but are included in the figure for all persons (see Appendix A for details).

Weighting to be revised in Spring 2003 following the 2001 census revisions of population estimates. See Appendix D.

Table 7.17 Chronic sickness: rate per 1000 reporting selected longstanding condition groups, by age and sex and socio-economic classification of household reference person

Persons aged 16 and over *Great Britain: 2001*

Condition group	Men				Women				All aged 16 and over			
	16-44	45-64	65 and over	Total	16-44	45-64	65 and over	Total	16-44	45-64	65 and over	Total
XIII Musculoskeletal system												
Managerial and professional	63	140	180	103	55	154	281	120	59	147	232	111
Intermediate	64	199	237	132	54	169	376	160	59	184	323	147
Routine and manual	94	270	260	183	63	244	319	186	79	257	294	184
VII Heart and circulatory system												
Managerial and professional	22	128	274	89	12	92	195	64	18	110	233	77
Intermediate	22	139	345	108	17	127	312	116	20	132	325	112
Routine and manual	22	182	352	140	19	134	318	134	20	158	332	137
VIII Respiratory system												
Managerial and professional	57	45	46	52	46	48	49	47	52	47	48	50
Intermediate	52	46	107	58	47	50	69	53	49	48	83	55
Routine and manual	59	75	125	78	65	80	92	77	62	78	106	77
III Endocrine and metabolic												
Managerial and professional	10	61	84	36	12	65	119	44	11	63	102	40
Intermediate	14	46	70	32	15	59	136	55	15	53	110	44
Routine and manual	15	58	86	43	22	69	108	59	18	63	99	51
IX Digestive system												
Managerial and professional	13	34	31	22	19	38	44	29	16	36	38	25
Intermediate	15	28	44	24	17	31	95	39	16	30	75	32
Routine and manual	17	56	55	37	21	52	42	36	19	54	47	36
VI Nervous system												
Managerial and professional	14	25	47	22	20	41	48	31	17	33	47	26
Intermediate	28	25	44	29	26	35	25	28	27	30	32	29
Routine and manual	23	53	31	34	24	44	29	32	23	49	30	33
Weighted bases (000's) = 100%												
Managerial and professional	*4,720*	*2,565*	*1,169*	*8,454*	*4,506*	*2,602*	*1,249*	*8,357*	*9,226*	*5,168*	*2,418*	*16,811*
Intermediate	*2,028*	*1,194*	*574*	*3,795*	*1,990*	*1,298*	*923*	*4,212*	*4,018*	*2,492*	*1,497*	*8,007*
Routine and manual	*4,304*	*2,731*	*1,859*	*8,894*	*4,089*	*2,708*	*2,562*	*9,359*	*8,393*	*5,439*	*4,421*	*18,253*
Unweighted sample												
Managerial and professional	*1581*	*1003*	*492*	*3076*	*1688*	*1040*	*493*	*3221*	*3269*	*2043*	*985*	*6297*
Intermediate	*663*	*444*	*234*	*1341*	*730*	*495*	*356*	*1581*	*1393*	*939*	*590*	*2922*
Routine and manual	*1407*	*984*	*722*	*3113*	*1511*	*1025*	*953*	*3489*	*2918*	*2009*	*1675*	*6602*

Weighting to be revised in Spring 2003 following the 2001 census revisions of population estimates. See Appendix D.

Table 7.18 **Trends in consultations with an NHS GP in the 14 days before interview: 1972 to 2001**

All persons *Great Britain*

	Unweighted									Weighted			*Weighted base 2001 (000's) = 100%**	*Unweighted sample* 2001*
	1972	1975	1981	1985	1991	1993	1995	1996	1998	1998	2000	*2001*		
	Percentage consulting GP													
Males														
0- 4	13	13	21	22	23	23	22	23	18	18	18	18	*1,737*	*675*
5-15†	7	7	8	9	10	11	9	9	8	8	8	7	*4,120*	*1582*
16-44†	8	7	7	7	9	11	10	10	9	9	8	8	*11,613*	*3808*
45-64	11	11	12	12	11	15	14	15	14	14	15	13	*6,617*	*2476*
65-74	12	12	13	15	17	21	17	19	17	17	20	18	*2,191*	*900*
75 and over	19	20	17	19	21	22	22	21	21	21	20	22	*1,454*	*565*
Total	10	9	10	11	12	14	13	13	12	12	12	11	*27,731*	*10006*
Females														
0- 4	15	13	17	21	21	22	21	20	18	18	14	18	*1,694*	*668*
5-15†	6	7	9	11	11	10	13	9	10	10	9	9	*4,046*	*1556*
16-44†	15	13	15	17	17	20	18	20	17	17	16	15	*11,304*	*4191*
45-64	12	12	13	15	17	19	17	19	18	18	17	18	*6,765*	*2614*
65-74	15	16	16	17	19	20	23	21	19	19	22	18	*2,517*	*974*
75 and over	20	17	20	20	19	23	23	23	20	20	22	20	*2,424*	*902*
Total	13	12	14	16	17	19	18	19	17	17	16	16	*28,751*	*10905*
All persons														
0- 4	14	13	19	21	22	22	21	22	18	18	16	18	*3,431*	*1343*
5-15†	7	7	9	10	10	11	11	9	9	9	8	8	*8,166*	*3138*
16-44†	12	10	11	12	13	16	14	15	13	13	12	11	*22,917*	*7999*
45-64	12	11	12	14	14	17	16	17	16	16	16	16	*13,382*	*5090*
65-74	14	14	15	16	18	21	20	20	18	18	21	18	*4,707*	*1874*
75 and over	20	18	19	20	19	22	23	22	21	20	21	21	*3,878*	*1467*
Total	12	11	12	14	14	17	16	16	14	14	14	13	*56,481*	*20911*

* † See the footnotes to Table 7.1.

Weighting to be revised in Spring 2003 following the 2001 census revisions of population estimates. See Appendix D.

Table 7.19 **Average number of NHS GP consultations per person per year: 1972 to 2001**

*All persons** | *Great Britain*

	Unweighted									Weighted		
	1972†	1975	1981	1985	1991	1993	1995	1996	1998	1998	2000	2001
Males												
0- 4	4	4	7	7	7	8	7	8	6	6	6	6
5-15**	2	2	2	3	3	3	3	3	2	2	2	2
16-44**	3	2	2	2	3	4	3	3	3	3	3	3
45-64	4	4	4	4	4	5	4	5	4	4	5	4
65-74	4	4	4	5	5	6	5	6	5	5	6	5
75 and over	7	7	6	6	7	7	8	7	7	7	6	7
Total	3	3	3	3	4	5	4	4	4	4	4	4
Females												
0- 4	5	4	5	7	7	7	7	6	6	6	4	6
5-15**	2	2	3	3	3	3	4	3	3	3	3	3
16-44**	5	4	5	5	5	6	6	7	5	5	5	5
45-64	4	4	4	5	5	6	5	6	6	6	5	6
65-74	5	5	5	5	6	6	7	7	6	6	7	5
75 and over	7	6	6	7	6	7	7	7	6	6	7	6
Total	4	4	4	5	5	6	6	6	5	5	5	5
All persons												
0- 4	4	4	6	7	7	8	7	7	6	6	5	6
5-15**	2	2	3	3	3	3	3	3	3	3	2	3
16-44**	4	3	4	4	4	5	4	5	4	4	4	4
45-64	4	4	4	4	4	5	5	5	5	5	5	5
65-74	4	4	4	5	6	6	6	6	6	6	6	5
75 and over	7	7	6	6	6	7	7	7	6	6	7	6
Total	4	4	4	4	5	5	5	5	4	4	4	4

* Trend tables show unweighted and weighted figures for 1998 to give an indication of the effect of the weighting. Bases for 2001 are shown in Table 7.1. Bases for earlier years can be found in GHS reports for each year.
† 1972 figures relate to England and Wales.
** These age-groups were 5-14 and 15-44 in 1972 to 1978.

Weighting to be revised in Spring 2003 following the 2001 census revisions of population estimates. See Appendix D.

Table 7.20 **(NHS) GP consultations: trends in site of consultation: 1971 to 2001**

Consultations in the 14 days before interview | *Great Britain*

Site of consultation	Unweighted									Weighted		
	1971	1975	1981	1985	1991	1993	1995	1996	1998	1998	2000	2001
	%	%	%	%	%	%	%	%	%	%	%	%
Surgery*	73	78	79	79	81	84	84	84	84	84	86	85
Home	22	19	14	14	11	9	9	8	6	6	5	5
Telephone	4	3	7	7	8	7	7	8	10	10	10	10
Weighted base (000's) = 100%†										*9,658*	*9,744*	*9,161*
Unweighted sample†	*5031*	*4455*	*4704*	*4123*	*4228*	*4873*	*4385*	*4341*	*3504*		*3294*	*3418*

* Includes consultations with a GP at a health centre and those who had answered 'elsewhere'.
† See the second footnote to Table 7.2.

Weighting to be revised in Spring 2003 following the 2001 census revisions of population estimates. See Appendix D.

Table 7.21 (NHS) GP consultations: consultations with doctors in the 14 days before interview, by sex and age of person consulting, and by site of consultation

Consultations in the 14 days before interview *Great Britain: 2000*

Site of consultation	Males						Females						All persons					
	Age						Age						Age					
	0-4	5-15	16-44	45-64	65-74	75 and over	0-4	5-15	16-44	45-64	65-74	75 and over	0-4	5-15	16-44	45-64	65-74	75 and over
	%	%	%	%	%	%	%	%	%	%	%	%	%	%	%	%	%	%
Surgery*	85	88	89	89	85	79	84	89	87	83	87	67	85	89	88	86	86	72
Home	4	1	1	2	6	15	2	1	3	3	6	23	3	1	2	3	6	20
Telephone	11	11	10	9	9	6	14	10	11	13	8	10	12	11	10	11	8	8
Weighted base (000's) = 100%	*400*	*366*	*1,177*	*1,019*	*432*	*385*	*377*	*422*	*2,029*	*1,466*	*519*	*569*	*778*	*788*	*3,205*	*2,485*	*952*	*954*
Unweighted sample	*159*	*138*	*374*	*375*	*179*	*152*	*148*	*158*	*750*	*567*	*203*	*215*	*307*	*296*	*1124*	*942*	*382*	*367*

* Includes consultations with a GP at a health centre and those who had answered 'elsewhere'.

Weighting to be revised in Spring 2003 following the 2001 census revisions of population estimates. See Appendix D.

Table 7.22 (NHS) GP consultations: percentage of persons consulting a doctor in the 14 days before interview, by sex and by site of consultation, and by age and by site of consultation

Persons who consulted in the 14 days before interview *Great Britain: 2001*

Site of consultation	Total	Males	Females	Age					
				0-4	5-15	16-44	45-64	65-74	75 and over
	%	%	%	%	%	%	%	%	%
Surgery	88	90	87	87	91	90	90	89	73
At home	5	4	5	4	1	2	3	6	20
Telephone	11	10	12	15	12	11	11	9	8
Weighted base (000's) = 100%	*7,598*	*3,134*	*4,464*	*620*	*663*	*2,585*	*2,090*	*838*	*803*
Unweighted sample	*2842*	*1147*	*1695*	*244*	*249*	*906*	*798*	*336*	*309*

* Percentages add to more than 100 because some people consulted at more than one site during the reference period.

Weighting to be revised in Spring 2003 following the 2001 census revisions of population estimates. See Appendix D.

Table 7.23 (NHS) GP consultations
(a) Percentage of persons who consulted a doctor in the 14 days before interview, by sex, age, and socio-economic classification of household reference person
(b) Average number of consultations per person per year, by sex, age, and socio-economic classification of household reference person

All persons *Great Britain: 2001*

(a) Percentage who consulted a GP in the 14 days before interview

Males

Socio-economic classification of household reference person*	0-4		5-15		16-44		45-64		65 and over		Total	
Large employers and higher managerial	[22]		5		7		9		22		10	
Higher professional	15	15	8	6	9	6	9	12	16	20	10	10
Lower managerial and professional	14		5		4		14		21		9	
Intermediate	[24]	15	10	8	6	8	9	12	19	17	10	10
Small employers and own account	9		6		9		13		16		11	
Lower supervisory and technical	22		6		10		14		21		13	
Semi-routine	17	22	11	8	7	10	13	14	20	20	12	13
Routine	26		8		13		16		20		15	
Never worked and long-term unemployed	[12]		12		16		[19]		†		14	
All persons	18		7		8		13		19		11	

Females

Socio-economic classification of household reference person*	0-4		5-15		16-44		45-64		65 and over		Total	
Large employers and higher managerial	23		7		17		11		17		14	
Higher professional	21	20	9	10	12	14	16	16	24	20	14	15
Lower managerial and professional	18		11		15		17		19		16	
Intermediate	[14]	13	8	6	13	14	17	18	20	19	15	15
Small employers and own account	13		6		15		20		18		15	
Lower supervisory and technical	23		8		15		20		19		16	
Semi-routine	17	20	11	9	14	15	19	20	17	18	16	16
Routine	19		8		16		19		19		16	
Never worked and long-term unemployed	[14]		11		15		[28]		24		17	
All persons	18		9		15		18		19		16	

(b) Average number of consultations per person per year

Males

Socio-economic classification of household reference person*	0-4		5-15		16-44		45-64		65 and over		Total	
Large employers and higher managerial	[6]		2		2		3		6		3	
Higher professional	5	5	2	2	3	2	2	3	5	6	3	3
Lower managerial and professional	5		1		1		4		7		3	
Intermediate	[7]	4	4	3	2	2	2	4	6	5	3	3
Small employers and own account	3		2		3		4		4		3	
Lower supervisory and technical	7		2		3		5		7		4	
Semi-routine	8	8	4	3	3	3	4	5	6	6	4	4
Routine	9		3		4		5		6		5	
Never worked and long-term unemployed	[4]		3		5		[6]		†		4	
All persons	6		2		3		4		6		4	

Females

Socio-economic classification of household reference person*	0-4		5-15		16-44		45-64		65 and over		Total	
Large employers and higher managerial	8		2		5		3		5		4	
Higher professional	8	7	2	3	4	5	5	5	7	6	4	5
Lower managerial and professional	6		3		5		5		6		5	
Intermediate	[5]	5	2	2	4	4	6	6	6	6	5	5
Small employers and own account	5		2		4		6		6		4	
Lower supervisory and technical	7		2		5		7		6		5	
Semi-routine	5	6	3	3	4	5	6	6	5	5	5	5
Routine	5		3		5		6		6		5	
Never worked and long-term unemployed	[4]		3		5		[10]		6		5	
All persons	6		3		5		6		6		5	

	Males 0-4	Males 5-15	Males 16-44	Males 45-64	Males 65 and over	Males Total	Females 0-4	Females 5-15	Females 16-44	Females 45-64	Females 65 and over	Females Total
Weighted bases (000's) = 100%												
Large employers and higher managerial	*101*	*244*	*778*	*442*	*225*	*1,790*	*134*	*303*	*771*	*415*	*152*	*1,776*
Higher professional	*193*	*375*	*1,265*	*622*	*268*	*2,722*	*162*	*323*	*1,037*	*547*	*215*	*2,284*
Lower managerial and professional	*339*	*865*	*2,625*	*1,491*	*675*	*5,996*	*351*	*828*	*2,655*	*1,630*	*879*	*6,343*
Intermediate	*108*	*326*	*849*	*399*	*193*	*1,875*	*116*	*272*	*959*	*613*	*577*	*2,538*
Small employers and own account	*169*	*437*	*1,112*	*787*	*380*	*2,885*	*151*	*504*	*993*	*677*	*344*	*2,668*
Lower supervisory and technical	*215*	*532*	*1,511*	*897*	*688*	*3,844*	*192*	*418*	*1,306*	*758*	*598*	*3,272*
Semi-routine	*202*	*599*	*1,302*	*873*	*520*	*3,497*	*217*	*545*	*1,382*	*1,033*	*983*	*4,161*
Routine	*259*	*502*	*1,412*	*942*	*646*	*3,762*	*217*	*576*	*1,334*	*899*	*977*	*4,003*
Never worked and long-term unemployed	*112*	*170*	*356*	*114*	*39*	*790*	*86*	*216*	*431*	*115*	*189*	*1,037*
All persons	*1,737*	*4,120*	*11,613*	*6,617*	*3,644*	*27,731*	*1,694*	*4,046*	*11,304*	*6,765*	*4,941*	*28,751*
Unweighted sample												
Large employers and higher managerial	*41*	*97*	*270*	*176*	*95*	*679*	*54*	*120*	*288*	*167*	*63*	*692*
Higher professional	*77*	*146*	*426*	*244*	*113*	*1006*	*67*	*126*	*391*	*223*	*86*	*893*
Lower managerial and professional	*134*	*333*	*868*	*580*	*283*	*2198*	*139*	*326*	*995*	*646*	*343*	*2449*
Intermediate	*42*	*124*	*271*	*147*	*83*	*667*	*46*	*104*	*353*	*232*	*225*	*960*
Small employers and own account	*65*	*160*	*370*	*294*	*151*	*1040*	*59*	*192*	*363*	*260*	*130*	*1004*
Lower supervisory and technical	*80*	*194*	*493*	*321*	*267*	*1355*	*73*	*150*	*467*	*285*	*222*	*1197*
Semi-routine	*80*	*236*	*425*	*319*	*202*	*1262*	*88*	*213*	*525*	*395*	*370*	*1591*
Routine	*97*	*198*	*463*	*338*	*251*	*1347*	*85*	*216*	*494*	*338*	*359*	*1492*
Never worked and long-term unemployed	*46*	*67*	*109*	*40*	*16*	*278*	*34*	*86*	*167*	*41*	*69*	*397*
All persons	*675*	*1582*	*3805*	*2476*	*1465*	*10006*	*668*	*1556*	*4191*	*2614*	*1876*	*10905*

* From April 2001 the National Statistics Socio-economic Classification (NS-SEC) was introduced for all official statistics and surveys. It has replaced Social Class based on Occupation and Socio-economic Groups (SEG). Full-time students and persons in inadequately described occupations are not shown as separate categories but are included in the figure for all persons (see Appendix A).

† Base too small for analysis.

Weighting to be revised in Spring 2003 following the 2001 census revisions of population estimates. See Appendix D.

Table 7.24 **(NHS) GP consultations**
(a) Percentage of persons who consulted a doctor in the 14 days before interview, by sex, age, and economic activity status
(b) Average number of consultations per person per year, by sex, age, and economic activity status

Persons aged 16 and over | *Great Britain: 2001*

Economic activity status	Men				Women			
	Age				Age			
	16-44	45-64	65 and over	Total	16-44	45-64	65 and over	Total
	(a) Percentage who consulted a GP in the 14 days before interview							
Working	7	10	12	8	13	15	13	14
Unemployed	12	16	*	13	16	[19]	0	17
Economically inactive	14	21	20	19	17	23	19	20
All aged 16 and over	8	13	20	12	14	18	19	16
	(b) Average number of consultations per person per year							
Working	2	3	3	3	4	4	4	4
Unemployed	4	5	*	4	7	5	0	6
Economically inactive	5	7	6	6	6	8	6	6
All aged 16 and over	3	4	6	4	5	6	6	5
Weighted base (000's) = 100%								
Working	*9,572*	*4,862*	*242*	*14,676*	*8,011*	*4,149*	*157*	*12,317*
Unemployed	*595*	*157*	*7*	*759*	*341*	*82*	*0*	*422*
Economically inactive	*1,424*	*1,584*	*3,373*	*6,382*	*2,932*	*2,508*	*4,777*	*10,217*
All aged 16 and over	*11,592*	*6,604*	*3,622*	*21,818*	*11,283*	*6,739*	*4,934*	*22,956*
Unweighted sample								
Working	*3175*	*1836*	*100*	*5111*	*2950*	*1578*	*58*	*4586*
Unemployed	*185*	*56*	*2*	*243*	*126*	*30*	*0*	*156*
Economically inactive	*441*	*579*	*1353*	*2373*	*1108*	*996*	*1815*	*3919*
All aged 16 and over	*3801*	*2471*	*1455*	*7727*	*4184*	*2604*	*1873*	*8661*

* Base too small for analysis.

Weighting to be revised in Spring 2003 following the 2001 census revisions of population estimates. See Appendix D.

Table 7.25 **(NHS) GP consultations: percentage of persons consulting a doctor in the 14 days before interview who obtained a prescription from the doctor, by sex, age and socio-economic classification of household reference person**

Persons who consulted in the 14 days before interview *Great Britain: 2001*

Socio-economic classification of household reference person*	Males					Females				
	Age					Age				
	0-15	16-44	45-64	65 and over	Total	0-15	16-44	45-64	65 and over	Total
	Percentage consulting who obtained a prescription									
Managerial and professional	54	55	58	62	57	62	57	66	74	63
Intermediate	71	56	54	75	62	69	60	67	69	65
Routine and manual	68	69	68	80	71	66	64	77	77	71
All persons consulting	65	62	63	73	65	65	61	72	74	67
Weighted base (000's) = 100%										
Managerial and professional	*182*	*292*	*303*	*233*	*1,011*	*267*	*634*	*417*	*247*	*1,565*
Intermediate	*100*	*146*	*142*	*97*	*485*	*85*	*277*	*235*	*174*	*772*
Routine and manual	*285*	*421*	*392*	*373*	*1,471*	*266*	*596*	*527*	*461*	*1,850*
All persons consulting	*615*	*942*	*867*	*708*	*3,132*	*668*	*1,641*	*1,223*	*933*	*4,464*
Unweighted sample										
Managerial and professional	*72*	*96*	*118*	*97*	*383*	*103*	*237*	*170*	*99*	*609*
Intermediate	*37*	*47*	*52*	*41*	*177*	*32*	*99*	*86*	*68*	*285*
Routine and manual	*110*	*135*	*142*	*146*	*533*	*103*	*220*	*203*	*173*	*699*
All persons consulting	*236*	*302*	*322*	*286*	*1146*	*257*	*603*	*476*	*359*	*1695*

* From April 2001 the National Statistics Social-economic Classification (NS-SEC) was introduced for all official statistics and surveys. It has replaced Social Class based on Occupation and Socio-economic Groups (SEG). Full-time students, persons in inadequately described occupations, persons who have never worked and the long-term unemployed are not shown as separate categories, but are included in the figure for all persons (see Appendix A for details).

Weighting to be revised in Spring 2003 following the 2001 census revisions of population estimates. See Appendix D.

Table 7.26 GP consultations: consultations with doctors in the 14 days before interview by whether consultation was NHS or private

Consultations in the 14 days before interview *Great Britain: 2001*

Type of consultation	Males	Females	All persons
	%	%	%
NHS	96	97	97
Private	4	3	3
Weighted base (000's) = 100%	*4,477*	*6,129*	*10,606*
Unweighted sample	*1624*	*2326*	*3950*

Weighting to be revised in Spring 2003 following the 2001 census revisions of population estimates. See Appendix D.

Table 7.27 Trends in reported consultations with a practice nurse by age and sex: 2000 to 2001 (a) percentage consulting a practice nurse in the 14 days before interview (b) average number of consultations with a practice nurse per person per year

All persons *Great Britain*

	2000	2001	2000	2001	*Weighted base (000's) = 100%*	*Unweighted sample*
	(a) percentage consulting a practice nurse		(b) average number of consultations with a practice nurse per person per year			
Males						
0- 4	4	3	1	1	*1,737*	*675*
5-15	2	2	0	1	*4,120*	*1582*
16-44	2	2	1	1	*11,609*	*3807*
45-64	5	6	1	2	*6,617*	*2476*
65-74	10	12	3	4	*2,191*	*900*
75 and over	8	13	3	4	*1,454*	*565*
Total	4	5	1	1	*27,727*	*10005*
Females						
0- 4	5	3	1	1	*1,694*	*668*
5-15	1	1	0	0	*4,049*	*1557*
16-44	5	5	1	1	*11,304*	*4191*
45-64	6	7	2	2	*6,765*	*2614*
65-74	10	11	3	4	*2,517*	*974*
75 and over	9	12	3	4	*2,424*	*902*
Total	5	6	2	2	*28,753*	*10906*
All persons						
0- 4	4	3	1	1	*3,431*	*1343*
5-15	1	2	0	1	*8,169*	*3139*
16-44	3	4	1	1	*22,914*	*7998*
45-64	6	6	2	2	*13,382*	*5090*
65-74	10	12	3	4	*4,707*	*1874*
75 and over	9	12	3	4	*3,878*	*1467*
Total	5	5	1	2	*56,481*	*20911*

Weighting to be revised in Spring 2003 following the 2001 census revisions of population estimates. See Appendix D.

Table 7.28 Percentage of children using health services in the 14 days before interview

All persons aged under 16 — *Great Britain: 2001*

	Male			Female			Total		
	0-4	5-15	Total	0-4	5-15	Total	0-4	5-15	Total
Percentage who reported:*									
Seeing a practice nurse at the GP surgery	3	2	2	3	1	2	3	2	2
Seeing a health visitor at the GP surgery	7	2	3	8	2	4	8	2	4
Going to a child health clinic	4	1	2	5	1	2	5	1	2
Going to a child welfare clinic	1	0	0	1	0	0	1	0	0
None of the above	87	95	93	85	96	93	86	96	93
Weighted base (000's) =100%	*1,737*	*4,120*	*5,857*	*1,694*	*4,049*	*5,743*	*3,431*	*8,169*	*11,600*
Unweighted sample	*675*	*1582*	*2257*	*668*	*1557*	*2225*	*1343*	*3139*	*4482*

* Percentages may sum to more than 100 as respondents could give more than one answer.

Weighting to be revised in Spring 2003 following the 2001 census revisions of population estimates. See Appendix D.

Table 7.29 Trends in percentages of persons who reported attending an outpatient or casualty department in a 3 month reference period: 1972 to 2001

*All persons** — *Great Britain*

	Unweighted									Weighted		
	1972†	1975	1981	1985	1991	1993	1995	1996	1998	1998	2000	2001
	Percentages											
Males												
0- 4	8	9	12	13	14	14	12	13	16	16	14	16
5-15**	9	8	11	12	11	12	11	12	12	12	11	10
16-44**	11	9	11	12	11	12	12	13	13	13	12	11
45-64	11	10	12	16	15	15	16	16	17	17	16	16
65-74	10	11	14	16	18	20	21	20	25	25	24	22
75 and over	10	12	14	15	22	24	26	25	29	29	26	31
Total	10	10	11	13	13	14	14	15	16	16	15	14
Females												
0- 4	6	8	9	11	11	10	12	9	13	13	10	11
5-15**	6	6	8	9	8	10	9	10	11	11	8	8
16-44**	9	9	11	12	12	12	12	13	13	13	13	12
45-64	11	10	13	15	16	17	17	18	18	18	16	18
65-74	12	12	16	17	18	18	21	22	21	21	21	21
75 and over	13	10	16	17	20	22	22	24	26	26	24	23
Total	10	9	12	13	14	14	14	15	16	16	15	14
All persons												
0- 4	7	9	10	12	13	12	12	11	14	15	12	13
5-15**	8	7	10	10	10	11	10	11	11	11	10	9
16-44**	10	9	11	12	12	12	12	13	13	13	13	12
45-64	11	10	13	15	16	16	16	17	18	18	16	17
65-74	11	11	15	17	18	19	21	21	23	23	22	21
75 and over	12	10	15	16	21	22	24	24	27	27	25	26
Total	10	9	12	13	13	14	14	15	16	16	15	14

* † ** See the footnotes to Table 7.19.

Weighting to be revised in Spring 2003 following the 2001 census revisions of population estimates. See Appendix D.

Table 7.30 **Trends in day-patient treatment in the 12 months before interview, 1992 to 2001**

All persons *Great Britain*

	Unweighted						Weighted			*Weighted base 2001 (000's) = 100%**	*Unweighted sample* 2001*
	1992	1993	1994	1995	1996	1998	1998	2000	2001		
	Percentage receiving day-patient treatment										
Males											
0- 4	4	4	4	4	5	6	6	6	7	*1,737*	*675*
5-15	2	3	3	3	3	4	4	5	4	*4,120*	*1582*
16-44	4	5	5	6	5	6	6	6	7	*11,609*	*3807*
45-64	4	4	5	7	6	7	7	8	8	*6,613*	*2475*
65-74	5	5	6	6	7	6	6	10	8	*2,193*	*901*
75 and over	4	3	5	5	6	12	11	7	10	*1,451*	*564*
Total	4	4	5	5	5	6	6	7	7	*27,723*	*10004*
Females											
0- 4	2	3	3	3	3	5	4	6	4	*1,694*	*668*
5-15	2	3	3	2	4	4	4	3	3	*4,049*	*1557*
16-44	5	6	7	6	7	8	8	8	8	*11,302*	*4190*
45-64	5	5	5	7	8	8	8	9	8	*6,768*	*2615*
65-74	4	5	5	5	6	6	6	12	8	*2,519*	*975*
75 and over	3	5	5	5	7	8	8	8	8	*2,422*	*901*
Total	4	5	5	5	6	7	7	8	7	*28,755*	*10906*
All persons											
0- 4	3	3	3	3	4	5	5	6	5	*3,431*	*1343*
5-15	2	3	3	3	3	4	4	4	4	*8,169*	*3139*
16-44	4	6	6	6	6	7	7	7	7	*22,911*	*7997*
45-64	5	5	5	7	7	8	8	8	8	*13,382*	*5090*
65-74	4	5	5	6	7	6	6	11	8	*4,712*	*1876*
75 and over	3	4	5	5	6	9	9	8	9	*3,873*	*1465*
Total	4	5	5	5	6	7	7	7	7	*56,478*	*20910*

* See the first footnote to Table 7.1.

Weighting to be revised in Spring 2003 following the 2001 census revisions of population estimates. See Appendix D.

Table 7.31 **Average number of separate days spent in hospital as a day-patient during the last 12 months**

All day-patients *Great Britain: 2001*

Age	Male	Female	Total	*Male*	*Female*	*Total*	*Male*	*Female*	*Total*
	Average number of days			*Weighted base (000's) = 100% (all day-patients)*			*Unweighted sample*		
0-4	2	1	2	*113*	*64*	*177*	*46*	*25*	*71*
5-15	2	3	2	*172*	*130*	*301*	*66*	*48*	*114*
16-44	2	2	2	*778*	*934*	*1,712*	*254*	*347*	*601*
45-64	2	2	2	*509*	*531*	*1,040*	*192*	*208*	*400*
65-74	2	3	2	*172*	*205*	*377*	*70*	*81*	*151*
75 and over	4	3	3	*151*	*203*	*354*	*61*	*75*	*136*
All persons	2	2	2	*1,895*	*2,067*	*3,962*	*689*	*784*	*1473*

Weighting to be revised in Spring 2003 following the 2001 census revisions of population estimates. See Appendix D.

Table 7.32 **Trends in inpatient stays in the 12 months before interview, 1982 to 2001**

All persons *Great Britain*

	Unweighted								Weighted			*Weighted base 2001 (000's) = 100%**	*Unweighted sample* 2001*
	1982	1985	1987	1991	1993	1995	1996	1998	1998	2000	2001		
	Percentage with inpatient stay												
Males													
0- 4	14	12	10	10	10	9	9	9	9	8	11	*1,737*	*675*
5-15	6	8	6	6	6	5	5	5	5	5	4	*4,120*	*1582*
16-44	5	6	6	6	6	5	5	5	5	4	5	*11,609*	*3807*
45-64	8	8	9	8	9	9	8	8	8	8	8	*6,617*	*2476*
65-74	12	13	12	13	14	15	13	15	15	13	12	*2,193*	*901*
75 and over	14	17	20	20	21	21	18	21	21	18	19	*1,454*	*565*
Total	7	8	8	8	8	8	7	8	8	7	7	*27,729*	*10006*
Females													
0- 4	12	8	8	8	7	8	7	10	10	6	6	*1,691*	*667*
5-15	4	5	5	4	5	4	4	4	4	3	3	*4,042*	*1554*
16-44	15	16	16	15	13	12	12	11	11	10	9	*11,302*	*4190*
45-64	8	8	9	9	9	8	10	8	9	7	8	*6,768*	*2615*
65-74	8	18	11	11	10	11	12	10	10	13	10	*2,519*	*975*
75 and over	12	13	14	16	16	20	16	15	15	18	15	*2,419*	*900*
Total	11	11	12	11	11	10	10	10	10	9	8	*28,743*	*10901*
All persons													
0- 4	13	10	9	9	9	9	8	9	9	7	9	*3,428*	*1342*
5-15	5	6	6	5	5	4	4	5	5	4	4	*8,162*	*3136*
16-44	10	11	11	10	9	8	9	8	8	7	7	*22,912*	*7997*
45-64	8	8	9	8	9	8	9	8	9	8	8	*13,385*	*5091*
65-74	10	10	12	12	12	13	12	12	12	13	11	*4,712*	*1876*
75 and over	13	15	16	18	18	20	17	17	17	18	17	*3,873*	*1465*
Total	9	10	10	10	9	9	9	9	9	8	8	*56,472*	*20907*

* See the first footnote to Table 7.1.

Weighting to be revised in Spring 2003 following the 2001 census revisions of population estimates. See Appendix D.

Table 7.33 Average number of nights spent in hospital as an inpatient during the last 12 months

All inpatients *Great Britain: 2001*

Age	Male	Female	Total	*Male*	*Female*	*Total*	*Male*	*Female*	*Total*
	Average number of nights			*Weighted base (000's) = 100% (all inpatients)*			*Unweighted sample*		
0-4	8	5	7	189	107	296	73	44	117
5-15	4	3	4	170	135	305	68	51	119
16-44	6	3	4	559	1,000	1,559	176	374	550
45-64	10	8	9	517	521	1,038	193	203	396
65-74	11	13	12	251	254	505	103	98	201
75 and over	13	20	17	265	352	617	103	132	235
All persons	9	8	8	1,951	2,368	4,319	716	902	1618

Weighting to be revised in Spring 2003 following the 2001 census revisions of population estimates. See Appendix D.

Table 7.34 Inpatient stays and outpatient attendances
(a) Average number of inpatient stays per 100 persons in a 12 month reference period, by sex and age
(b) Average number of outpatient attendances per 100 persons per year, by sex and age

All persons *Great Britain: 2001*

Age	(a) Average number of inpatient stays per 100 persons in a 12 month reference period			(b) Average number of outpatient attendances per 100 persons per year			*Weighted base (000's) = 100%*			*Unweighted sample*		
	Males	Females	Total	Males	Females	Total	*Males*	*Females*	*Total*	*Males*	*Females*	*Total*
0- 4	16	8	12	107	54	81	1,737	1,691	3,428	675	667	1342
5-15	6	5	5	68	53	61	4,120	4,042	8,162	1582	1554	3136
16-44	6	7	7	88	107	98	11,609	11,302	22,912	3807	4190	7997
45-64	11	11	11	144	152	148	6,617	6,768	13,385	2476	2615	5091
65-74	16	14	15	174	198	187	2,193	2,519	4,712	901	975	1876
75 and over	29	21	24	257	222	235	1,454	2,419	3,873	565	900	1465
Total	10	9	10	115	125	120	27,729	28,743	56,472	10006	10901	20907

Weighting to be revised in Spring 2003 following the 2001 census revisions of population estimates. See Appendix D.

Chapter 8

Smoking

Questions about smoking behaviour have been asked of GHS respondents aged 16 and over in alternate years since 1974. Following the review of the GHS, the smoking questions became part of the continuous survey and are being included every year from 2000 onwards.

This chapter updates information about trends in cigarette smoking presented in previous reports in this series, and comments on variations according to personal characteristics such as sex, age, socio-economic classification and economic activity status, and briefly on the prevalence of cigarette smoking in different parts of Great Britain. Other topics covered in the chapter include cigarette consumption, type of cigarette smoked, and dependency on cigarettes.

The reliability of smoking estimates

As noted in previous GHS reports, it is likely that the GHS underestimates cigarette consumption, and perhaps, though to a lesser extent, prevalence (that is, the proportion of people who smoke). The evidence suggests that when respondents are asked how many cigarettes a day they smoke, there is a tendency to round down to the nearest multiple of ten. Therefore, underestimates of consumption are likely to occur in all age groups.

In relation to prevalence, under-reporting is most likely to occur among young people. To protect their privacy, particularly when they are being interviewed in their parents' home, young people aged 16 and 17 complete the smoking and drinking sections of the questionnaire themselves, without the questions or their responses being heard by anyone else who may be present, but this is probably only partially successful in encouraging honest answers.[1]

When considering trends in smoking, it is usually assumed that any under-reporting remains constant over time. However, since the prevalence of smoking has fallen, this assumption may not be entirely justified: as smoking has become less acceptable as a social habit, some people may be less inclined to admit how much they smoke, or to admit to smoking at all.

The effect of weighting on the smoking data

Weighting for non-response was introduced on the GHS in 2000, and was described in detail in the GHS 2000 report.[2] The effect of weighting on the smoking data is slight: it increases the overall prevalence of cigarette smoking by one percentage point. In 1998 and 2000, the upward revision was due solely to a change of two percentage points among men: there was no difference in the weighted and unweighted prevalence rates among women. In 2001, however, weighting increases prevalence for both men and women by one percentage point. The change occurs because weighting reduces the contribution to the overall figure of those aged 60 and over, among whom prevalence is relatively low.

Targets for the reduction of smoking

In December 1998 *Smoking Kills - a White Paper on tobacco*[3] was released, which included targets for reducing the prevalence of cigarette smoking among adults in England from 28% in 1996 to 24% by 2010 (with an interim target of 26% by 2005). These targets were based on unweighted GHS data, and since they will now be monitored using weighted data, it is suggested that they should be revised upwards by one percentage point.

Reducing smoking is also one of three key commitments at the heart of the NHS Cancer Plan[4], since smoking is estimated to be the cause of about one third of all cancers. In particular, the Cancer Plan focuses on the need to reduce the comparatively high rates of smoking among those in manual socio-economic groups, which result in much higher death rates from cancer among unskilled workers than among professionals. The national target is to reduce the proportion of smokers in manual groups in England from 32% in 1998 to 26% by 2010. Comparisons of weighted and unweighted data suggest that, as with the *Smoking Kills* targets, these should also be increased by one percentage point. These figures may also need further revision in the light of the recent introduction of the new socio-economic classification NS-SEC.

Trends in the prevalence of cigarette smoking

- There was no change in the overall prevalence of cigarette smoking in Great Britain between 2000 and 2001: it remained at 27% of those aged 16 and over.

The prevalence of cigarette smoking fell substantially in the 1970s and the early 1980s - from 45% in 1974 to 35% in 1982. After 1982, the rate of decline slowed, with prevalence falling by only about one percentage point every two years until 1990, since when it has levelled out. It should be noted that even during periods when the prevalence of smoking in the general population is not changing, upward and downward movements in survey estimates are to be expected, because of sampling fluctuations. Thus although there was no overall change between 2000 and 2001, prevalence rose by one percentage point among women and fell by the same amount among men: neither of these changes is statistically significant.

- In 2001, 28% of men and 26% of women were cigarette smokers.

In the 1970s, men were much more likely than women to be smokers - in 1974, for example, 51% of men, compared with 41% of women, smoked cigarettes. Since then, the difference in smoking prevalence between men and women has reduced, although it has not disappeared completely.

This change results mainly from a combination of two factors.

- First, there is a cohort effect resulting from the fact that smoking became common among men several decades earlier than it did among women, so that in the 1970s there was a fall in the proportion of women aged 60 and over who had never smoked regularly.
- Second, men are more likely than women to have given up smoking cigarettes. It should be noted, however, that this difference conceals the fact that a proportion of men who give up smoking cigarettes remain smokers, since they continue to smoke cigars and pipes; this is much less common among women who stop smoking cigarettes.

The effect of weighting on the 1998 and 2000 data suggested that the difference in prevalence between men and women may have been slightly underestimated by the unweighted data shown in previous reports, but this is less clear from the 2001 data.

Smoking among different age groups is another key area of interest. Since the early 1990s, the prevalence of cigarette smoking has been higher among those aged 20 to 24 than among those in other age groups: up to the early twenties, more young people are starting to smoke than are giving up (almost one in five of those who smoke at some time in their lives take up the habit after the age of 20[5]).

Since the survey began, there has been considerable fluctuation in prevalence rates among those aged 16 to 19, but this is mainly because of the small sample size in this age group. Thus, although the prevalence of cigarette smoking fell from 30% in 2000 to 25% in 2001 among young men aged 16 to 19, and rose from 28% to 31% among young women of the same age, neither these changes nor the difference in 2001 between men and women in this age group are statistically significant.

Prevalence continues to be lowest, at 17% in 2001, among people aged 60 and over, who are less likely than younger people to have ever been smokers, and also more likely to have given up.

Figures 8A, 8B, Tables 8.1-8.3

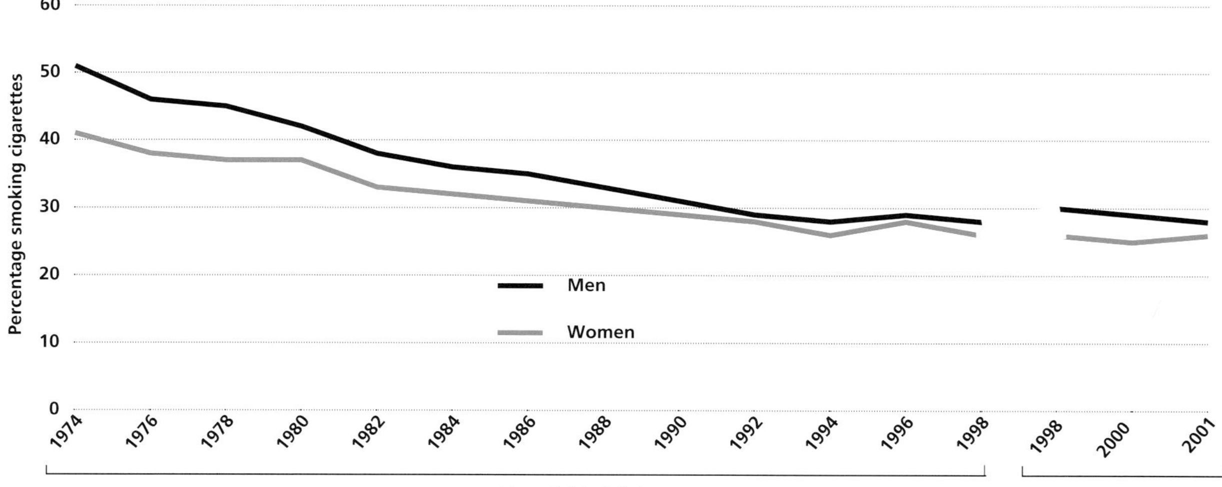

Figure 8B **Prevalence of cigarette smoking by sex and age: Great Britain, 1980 to 2001**

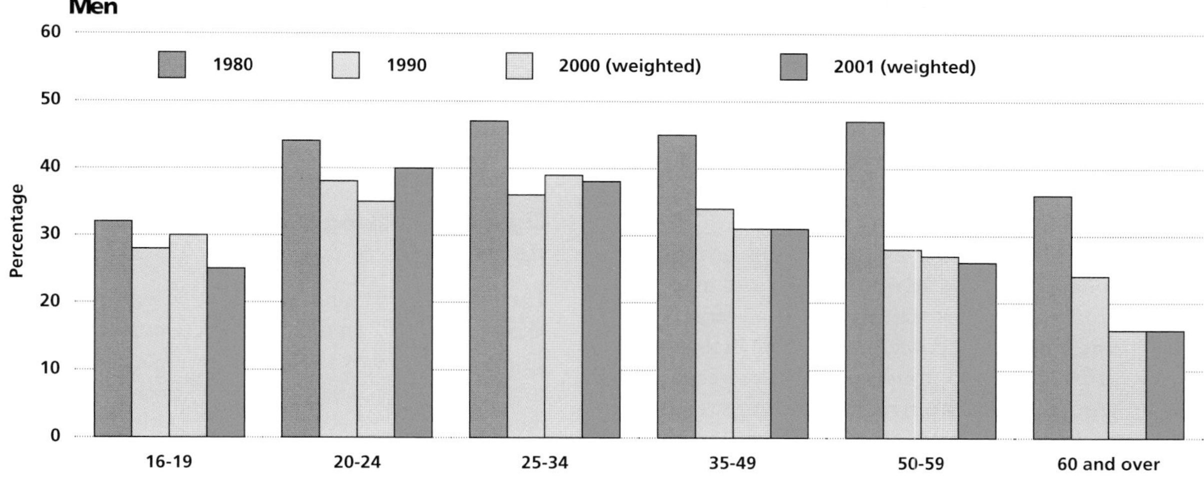

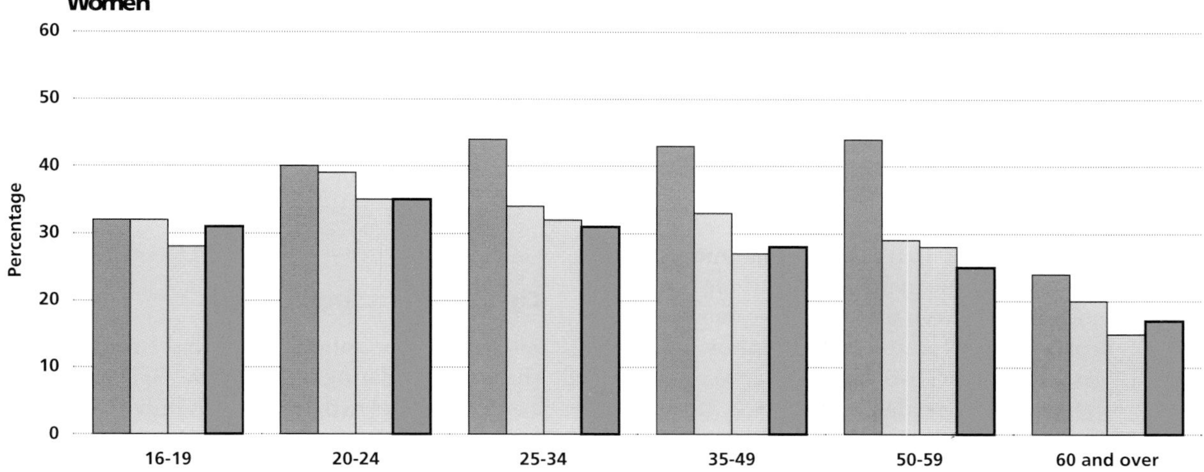

Cigarette smoking and marital status

The prevalence of cigarette smoking varies considerably according to marital status, and is much lower among married people than among those in any of the three other marital status categories (single, cohabiting, and widowed, divorced or separated). This is not explained by the association between age and marital status (for example, married people and those who are widowed, divorced or separated are older, on average, than single people). Table 8.5 shows that in every age group (although this is much less marked among those aged 60 and over) married people were less likely to be smokers than were other respondents. For example, among those aged 25 to 34, as many as 41% of those who were single or cohabiting were smokers, compared with only 25% of those who were married. **Tables 8.4-8.5**

Regional variation in cigarette smoking

The data presented so far have been for Great Britain, but the targets included in the White Paper *Smoking Kills* and in the NHS Cancer Plan relate to England only. Table 8.6 shows that in 2001, overall prevalence in England was 27%, the same as in Great Britain as a whole.

In 2001, as in previous years, prevalence was significantly higher in Scotland, at 31%, than in England or Wales (both 27%). In England, prevalence tended to be higher in the north of the country than in the midlands and the south.
Tables 8.6-8.8

Cigarette smoking and socio-economic classification

In 2001, a new socio-economic classification - the National Statistics Socio-economic classification (NS-SEC) - was introduced for all official statistics and surveys. NS-SEC classifies occupations according to different criteria compared with the Social Class and Socio-economic Group classifications which it replaces, and, in addition, the occupational classification underpinning the groupings also changed in 2001.

This follows another change introduced on the GHS in 2000, which was the replacement of the head of household with the household reference person as the basis for deriving a socio-economic variable reflecting the living standards of the household.[6] The definition of household reference person removes the precedence given to men in the head of household definition (see Appendix A).

The new NS-SEC does not allow categories to be collapsed into broad non-manual and manual groupings. So, since the Cancer Plan targets for England relate particularly to those in the manual socio-economic groups, the old socio-economic groupings have been recreated for this report in Table 8.9. Because of the new occupation coding, the classifications are not exactly the same, and comparisons with previous years should be treated with caution.

The GHS has consistently shown striking differences in the prevalence of cigarette smoking in relation to socio-economic group, with smoking being considerably more prevalent among those in manual groups than among those in non-manual groups. In the 1970s and 1980s, the prevalence of cigarette smoking fell more sharply among those in non-manual than in manual groups, so that differences between the groups became proportionately greater (table not shown). There was little further change in the relative proportions smoking cigarettes during the 1990s.

In England, the overall prevalence of cigarette smoking among those in manual socio-economic groups fell from 33% in 1998 to 31% in 2000, but showed no statistically significant change in 2001 at 32%, suggesting little progress in relation to the targets set out in the Cancer Plan. However, caution is advisable when making comparisons over this period because the data may have been affected by the change from head of household to household reference person as the basis for assessing socio-economic group and from the introduction of the revised occupation coding and socio-economic classification.

In England in 2001, 33% of men living in households in the manual group smoked cigarettes compared with 22% of those in non-manual households. The corresponding proportions for women were 30% and 20%.

Table 8.10 shows the prevalence of cigarette smoking in 2001 in relation to the eight- and three-category versions of NS-SEC. As was the case with the socio-economic groupings used previously, there were striking differences between the various classes. Prevalence was lowest among those in higher professional and higher managerial households (15% and 16% respectively) and highest, at 35%, among those whose household reference person was in a routine occupation.

Tables 8.9-8.10

Cigarette smoking and economic activity status

Those who were economically active were more likely to smoke than those who were not, but this is largely explained by the lower prevalence of smoking among those aged 60 and over, who form the majority of the economically inactive.

Indeed, among both men and women, prevalence was highest among the economically inactive aged 16 to 59, 35% of whom were cigarette smokers, compared with 29% of the economically active and only 17% of the economically inactive aged 60 and over. Prevalence was particularly high among economically inactive people aged 16 to 59 whose last job was a routine or manual one, 48% of whom were cigarette smokers. **Table 8.11**

Cigarette consumption

Although the prevalence of cigarette smoking changed little during the 1990s, the GHS has shown a continuing fall in the reported number of cigarettes smoked. The fall in consumption has occurred mainly among younger smokers: the number of cigarettes smoked by those aged 50 and over has changed very little since the mid-1970s.

Most of the decline in consumption in the 1990s is due to a reduction in the proportion of heavy smokers:

- the proportion of respondents smoking 20 or more cigarettes a day, on average, fell from 14% of men in 1990 to 10% in 1998, and from 9% to 7% of women over the same period, since when it has remained virtually unchanged among both men and women. The proportion of respondents who were light smokers also changed little throughout the 1990s.

In all age groups, respondents are more likely to be light than heavy smokers, the difference being most pronounced among the younger age groups.

- For example, in 2001, 22% of young men and 26% of young women aged 16 to 19 were light smokers, but only 3% and 4% respectively were heavy smokers. **Tables 8.12-8.13**

In 2001, as in previous years, male smokers smoked more cigarettes a day on average than female smokers: 15 compared with 13. Cigarette consumption also varied by age.

- Among both men and women smokers, those aged 35 to 59 smoked the most: men smokers in this age group smoked 17 or 18 cigarettes a day, on average, and women smoked 15 a day.

Earlier GHS reports have shown cigarette consumption levels to be higher among male and female smokers in manual socio-economic groups than among those in non-manual groups.[6] A similar pattern was evident in 2001 in relation to NS-SEC: smokers in households where the household reference person was in the routine and manual occupation group smoked an average of 15 cigarettes a day, compared with 13 a day for those in managerial or professional households.

Tables 8.14-8.15

Cigarette type

Filter cigarettes continue to be the most widely smoked type of cigarette, especially among women, but during the 1990s there was a marked increase in the proportion of smokers who said that they smoked mainly hand-rolled tobacco. In 1990, 18% of men smokers and 2% of women smokers said they smoked mainly hand-rolled cigarettes, but by 2001 this had risen to 31% and 12% respectively. There are likely to be two main reasons for this sharp increase in the use of hand-rolled cigarettes:

- the rise in the real price of packaged cigarettes - hand-rolled ones are cheaper;
- the reduction in tar yield of packaged cigarettes (see below) - depending on how they are rolled and smoked, hand-rolled ones can give a higher tar yield.

It is possible that the lessening of the restrictions on the amount of tobacco that can legally be brought into the country and an increase in smuggling have also contributed to the increase in the consumption of hand-rolled tobacco.

The use of hand-rolled tobacco was more common among men aged 35 to 59 than among men of other ages, but among women smokers, there was less variation with age, except that only 4% of women smokers aged 60 or over used hand-rolled tobacco.

Tables 8.16-8.17

Tar level[7]

Table 8.18 shows the dramatic reduction in the tar yield of cigarettes over the period during which the GHS has been collecting information about brand smoked. In 1986, 40% of those who smoked manufactured cigarettes smoked brands yielding more than 15mg of tar per cigarette. In the following ten years, the proportion smoking this type of cigarette fell to zero. Initially, this was partly due to smokers switching to lower tar brands, but the main factor has been that manufacturers have been required to reduce substantially the tar yields of existing brands: following legislation in 1992, they were required to reduce the tar yield to no more than 12mg per cigarette by the beginning of 1998. An EU Directive which comes into force at the end of 2002 will further reduce the maximum tar yield to 10 mg per cigarette by January 2004.

Although there has been a shift towards the cigarettes with the lowest tar yield, the biggest increase has been in what used to be the middle category - cigarettes with a tar yield of 10 but less than 15mg; in 2001, 71% of those who smoked manufactured cigarettes smoked brands in this category.

Among smokers under age 35, differences between men and women in the tar yield of their usual brand were small. Among those aged 35 and over, however, men were much less likely to smoke low tar brands.

There was also a difference in tar yield of cigarettes smoked according to the socio-economic class of the smoker's household.

- Cigarettes with the highest tar yield (12 mg or more) were more likely to be smoked by those in routine and manual households than by other smokers: 43% of men and 40% of women in manual groups smoked these cigarettes, compared with only 31% of men and 28% of women smokers in managerial and professional households. **Tables 8.18-8.20**

Cigar and pipe smoking

A decline in the prevalence of pipe and cigar smoking among men has been evident since the survey began, with most of the reduction occurring in the 1970s and 1980s. In 2001, only 5% of men smoked at least one cigar a month, compared with 34% in 1974. Only a small number of women smoked cigars in 1974, and since 1978, the percentages have been scarcely measurable on the GHS.

Overall, 2% of men in 2001 said they smoked a pipe. The proportion doing so was higher among men aged 60 and over (4%) than among any other age group; among men aged under 30, fewer than 0.5% smoked a pipe. Cigar smoking, on the other hand, was not so concentrated among older men; even among young men aged 16 to 19, 4% said they smoked at least one cigar a month.

Tables 8.21-8.22

Dependence on cigarette smoking

In order for the prevalence of cigarette smoking to reduce, young people have to be discouraged from starting to smoke and existing smokers have to be encouraged to stop. Since 1992, the GHS has asked three questions relevant to the likelihood of a smoker giving up: whether they would like to stop smoking, and two indicators of dependence - whether they think they would find it easy or difficult not to smoke for a whole day and how soon after waking they smoke their first cigarette.

There has been very little change since 1992 in any of the three dependence measures used, which is perhaps not unexpected, given that there has been little change in the prevalence of cigarette smoking over that period.

For an attempt to stop smoking to be successful, the smoker must want to stop, and in 2001, two thirds of all smokers (68% of men and 65% of women) said they would like to stop smoking altogether. The relationship between wanting to stop smoking and the number of cigarettes smoked is not straightforward. Although the difference in 2001 between those in the two highest consumption categories is very small - only one percentage point - in every survey since the questions were first included in 1992, the proportion wanting to give up has been highest among those smoking on average 10-19 cigarettes a week. It is interesting that it is not the heaviest smokers who are most likely to want to stop - it may be because they feel it would be too difficult or that they have been discouraged from wanting to stop by previous attempts that were unsuccessful. Furthermore, some previously heavy smokers who would like to give up may have cut down their consumption prior to an attempt to do so.

- In 2001, 55% of smokers felt that it would be either very or fairly difficult to go without smoking for a whole day.
- Not surprisingly, heavier smokers were more likely to say they would find it difficult: 80% of those smoking 20 or more cigarettes a day did so, compared with only 22% of those smoking fewer than 10 cigarettes a day.

Since women are less likely to be heavy smokers than men, it might be expected that women would be less likely to say they would find it hard to stop smoking for a day, but this was not the case.

- Overall, 58% of women, compared with 52% of men, said they would find it very difficult not to smoke for a day.
- Among those smoking 20 or more cigarettes a day the difference was particularly marked: 87% of women, compared with 74% of men, said they would find it very difficult.

In 2001, 15% of smokers had their first cigarette within five minutes of waking up.

- Heavy smokers were more likely than light smokers to smoke immediately on waking up: 32% of those smoking 20 or more cigarettes a day did so, compared with only 2% of those smoking fewer than 10 a day.

There was no statistically significant difference between the proportions of men and women who said they had their first cigarette within five minutes of waking.

Thus, women smokers are more likely to perceive themselves as dependent despite the fact that women smoke fewer cigarettes a day than men, there is no difference between men and women smokers in the proportions wanting to give up, nor in the more objective of the two indicators of dependence (how soon they smoke after waking up).

Tables 8.23-8.25

Notes and references

1 See Chapter 4, *General Household Survey 1992*, HMSO 1994. This includes a discussion of the differences found when smoking prevalence reported by young adults on the GHS was compared with prevalence reported on surveys of smoking among secondary school children.
2 See Appendix D, *Living in Britain: results from the 2000 General Household Survey.*
3 *Smoking kills - a White Paper on tobacco*, The Stationery Office, 1998.
4 *The NHS Cancer Plan*, Department of Health, 2000 (www.doh.gov.uk/cancer/cancerplan.htm)
5 See Table 8.26 in Chapter 8, *Living in Britain: results from the 2000 General Household Survey*
6 Prior to 1992, the method for assigning socio-economic group to GHS respondents involved classifying married or cohabiting women according to their partner's present (or last) job. No tables using this definition are included in this report.
7 An error was found recently in the automated procedure for coding the brand of cigarette smoked which was introduced when the GHS moved to computerised interviewing in April 1994. The net effect of this was that from 1994 to 2000, some brands were wrongly assigned to a low tar category. The coding procedure has been revised for the 2001 survey. Corrected data for 1998 and 2000 are given in Table 8.18.

Table 8.1 **Prevalence of cigarette smoking by sex and age: 1974 to 2001**

Persons aged 16 and over *Great Britain*

Age	Unweighted										Weighted			*Weighted base 2001 (000's) =100%**	*Unweighted sample* 2001*
	1974	1978	1982	1986	1988	1990	1992	1994	1996	1998	1998	2000	2001		
	Percentage smoking cigarettes														
Men															
16-19	42	35	31	30	28	28	29	28	26	30	30	30	25	*1,063*	*344*
20-24	52	45	41	41	37	38	39	40	43	42	41	35	40	*1,410*	*427*
25-34	56	48	40	37	37	36	34	34	38	37	38	39	38	*3,754*	*1211*
35-49	55	48	40	37	37	34	32	31	30	32	33	31	31	*5,536*	*1939*
50-59	53	48	42	35	33	28	28	27	28	27	28	27	26	*3,273*	*1208*
60 and over	44	38	33	29	26	24	21	18	18	16	16	16	16	*4,876*	*1926*
All aged 16 and over	51	45	38	35	33	31	29	28	29	28	30	29	28	*19,913*	*7055*
Women															
16-19	38	33	30	30	28	32	25	27	32	31	32	28	31	*1,119*	*412*
20-24	44	43	40	38	37	39	37	38	36	39	39	35	35	*1,418*	*493*
25-34	46	42	37	35	35	34	34	30	34	33	33	32	31	*3,887*	*1445*
35-49	49	43	38	34	35	33	30	28	30	28	29	27	28	*5,897*	*2218*
50-59	48	42	40	35	34	29	29	26	26	27	27	28	25	*3,647*	*1395*
60 and over	26	24	23	22	21	20	19	17	19	16	16	15	17	*6,020*	*2336*
All aged 16 and over	41	37	33	31	30	29	28	26	28	26	26	25	26	*21,987*	*8299*
Total															
16-19	40	34	30	30	28	30	27	27	29	31	31	29	28	*2,182*	*756*
20-24	48	44	40	39	37	38	38	39	39	40	40	35	37	*2,828*	*920*
25-34	51	45	38	36	36	35	34	32	36	35	35	35	34	*7,641*	*2656*
35-49	52	45	39	36	36	34	31	30	30	30	31	29	29	*11,433*	*4157*
50-59	51	45	41	35	33	29	29	27	27	27	28	27	26	*6,920*	*2603*
60 and over	34	30	27	25	23	21	20	17	18	16	16	16	17	*10,896*	*4262*
All aged 16 and over	45	40	35	33	32	30	28	27	28	27	28	27	27	*41,899*	*15354*

* Trend tables show unweighted and weighted figures for 1998 to give an indication of the effect of the weighting. For the weighted data (1998, 2000 and 2001) the weighted base (000's) is the base for percentages. Unweighted data (up to 1998) are based on the unweighted sample. Unweighted bases for earlier years are of similar size to the unweighted sample and can be found in GHS reports for each year.

Weighting to be revised in Spring 2003 following the 2001 census revisions of population estimates. See Appendix D.

Table 8.2 **Ex-regular cigarette smokers by sex and age: 1974 to 2001**

Persons aged 16 and over *Great Britain*

Age	Unweighted 1974	1978	1982	1986	1988	1990	1992	1994	1996	1998	Weighted 1998	2000	2001	*Weighted base 2001 (000's) =100%**	*Unweighted sample* 2001*
	Percentage of ex-regular cigarette smokers														
Men															
16-19	3	4	4	5	4	4	5	5	5	5	5	3	4	*1,063*	*344*
20-24	9	9	9	11	10	8	8	7	10	8	9	7	9	*1,410*	*427*
25-34	18	18	20	20	17	16	16	16	13	13	13	12	15	*3,754*	*1211*
35-49	21	26	32	33	31	32	29	27	27	22	21	20	20	*5,536*	*1939*
50-59	30	35	38	38	41	42	41	40	41	41	40	36	36	*3,273*	*1208*
60 and over	37	43	47	52	53	52	55	55	55	54	54	52	47	*4,876*	*1926*
All 16 and over	23	27	30	32	32	32	32	31	32	31	29	27	27	*19,913*	*7055*
Women															
16-19	4	5	6	7	5	6	5	6	5	7	8	6	6	*1,119*	*412*
20-24	9	8	9	9	8	8	9	10	11	8	8	11	12	*1,418*	*493*
25-34	12	14	15	16	16	14	15	14	13	14	14	13	16	*3,887*	*1445*
35-49	10	13	15	20	21	20	22	21	18	19	19	19	19	*5,897*	*2218*
50-59	13	18	19	18	19	20	22	22	25	25	25	24	24	*3,647*	*1395*
60 and over	11	16	20	23	25	27	29	29	28	29	29	29	29	*6,020*	*2336*
All 16 and over	11	14	16	18	19	19	21	21	20	21	20	20	21	*21,987*	*8299*

* See the footnote to Table 8.1.

Weighting to be revised in Spring 2003 following the 2001 census revisions of population estimates. See Appendix D.

Table 8.3 **Percentage who have never smoked cigarettes regularly by sex and age: 1974 to 2001**

Persons aged 16 and over *Great Britain*

Age	Unweighted 1974	1978	1982	1986	1988	1990	1992	1994	1996	1998	Weighted 1998	2000	2001	*Weighted base 2001 (000's) =100%**	*Unweighted sample* 2001*
	Percentage who have never smoked regularly														
Men															
16-19	56	61	65	65	69	68	67	67	69	64	65	67	71	*1,063*	*344*
20-24	38	46	50	47	53	54	52	53	47	49	50	58	51	*1,410*	*427*
25-34	26	33	39	43	46	48	50	50	49	50	49	49	47	*3,754*	*1211*
35-49	24	26	28	30	32	34	39	42	43	46	45	49	49	*5,536*	*1939*
50-59	16	17	20	26	26	31	31	33	31	32	32	37	38	*3,273*	*1208*
60 and over	18	18	20	19	22	24	24	27	28	30	30	32	36	*4,876*	*1926*
All 16 and over	25	29	32	34	35	37	38	40	40	41	42	44	45	*19,913*	*7055*
Women															
16-19	58	62	64	62	67	62	70	67	63	62	61	66	63	*1,119*	*412*
20-24	47	49	51	54	55	53	54	52	54	53	53	54	53	*1,418*	*493*
25-34	42	44	48	48	50	52	51	55	53	53	53	54	53	*3,887*	*1445*
35-49	41	44	47	46	44	48	49	51	52	52	52	54	53	*5,897*	*2218*
50-59	38	39	41	47	48	51	49	52	49	48	48	48	51	*3,647*	*1395*
60 and over	63	60	57	55	54	54	52	54	53	55	56	56	54	*6,020*	*2336*
All 16 and over	49	49	51	51	51	52	52	54	53	53	53	54	53	*21,987*	*8299*

* See the footnote to Table 8.1.

Weighting to be revised in Spring 2003 following the 2001 census revisions of population estimates. See Appendix D.

Table 8.4 Cigarette-smoking status by sex and marital status

Persons aged 16 and over *Great Britain: 2001*

Marital status		Current cigarette smokers			Current non-smokers of cigarettes		*Weighted base (000's) = 100%*	*Unweighted sample*
		Light (under 20 per day)	Heavy (20 or more per day)	Total	Ex-regular cigarette smokers	Never or only occasionally smoked cigarettes		
Men								
Single	%	26	8	34	13	53	*4,893*	*1494*
Married/cohabiting	%	15	10	25	31	44	*12,896*	*4839*
Married couple	%	13	9	22	34	44	*10,930*	*4156*
Cohabiting couple	%	27	16	43	18	39	*1,967*	*683*
Widowed/divorced/separated	%	21	13	35	31	34	*2,124*	*722*
All aged 16 and over	%	19	10	28	27	45	*19,913*	*7055*
Women								
Single	%	25	7	32	12	55	*3,736*	*1417*
Married/cohabiting	%	17	6	23	22	55	*13,574*	*5105*
Married couple	%	15	6	21	23	57	*11,472*	*4365*
Cohabiting couple	%	27	9	36	19	45	*2,102*	*740*
Widowed/divorced/separated	%	20	8	28	24	48	*4,676*	*1777*
All aged 16 and over	%	19	7	26	21	53	*21,987*	*8299*
Total								
Single	%	26	8	33	12	54	*8,629*	*2911*
Married/cohabiting	%	16	8	24	27	49	*26,471*	*9944*
Married couple	%	14	7	21	28	51	*22,402*	*8521*
Cohabiting couple	%	27	12	39	19	42	*4,069*	*1423*
Widowed/divorced/separated	%	20	10	30	26	44	*6,800*	*2499*
All aged 16 and over	%	19	8	27	24	49	*41,899*	*15354*

Weighting to be revised in Spring 2003 following the 2001 census revisions of population estimates. See Appendix D.

Table 8.5 Cigarette-smoking status by age and marital status

Pesons aged 16 and over — *Great Britain: 2001*

Marital status	Age					
	16-24	25-34	35-49	50-59	60 and over	Total
	Percentage smoking cigarettes					
Single	31	41	35	32	16	33
Married couple	28	25	24	22	15	21
Cohabiting couple	46	41	38	31	17	39
Widowed/divorced/separated	*	41	47	39	20	30
All aged 16 and over	33	34	29	26	17	27
Weighted base (000's) = 100%						
Single	*4,016*	*2,296*	*1,230*	*426*	*660*	*8,629*
Married couple	*267*	*3,194*	*7,575*	*5,048*	*6,318*	*22,402*
Cohabiting couple	*699*	*1,751*	*1,165*	*307*	*147*	*4,069*
Widowed/divorced/separated	*27*	*400*	*1,464*	*1,138*	*3,771*	*6,800*
All aged 16 and over	*5,009*	*7,641*	*11,433*	*6,920*	*10,896*	*41,899*
Unweighted sample						
Single	*1358*	*758*	*406*	*144*	*245*	*2911*
Married couple	*88*	*1147*	*2820*	*1942*	*2524*	*8521*
Cohabiting couple	*221*	*601*	*421*	*121*	*59*	*1423*
Widowed/divorced/separated	*9*	*150*	*510*	*396*	*1434*	*2499*
All aged 16 and over	*1676*	*2656*	*4157*	*2603*	*4262*	*15354*

* Base too small for analysis.

Weighting to be revised in Spring 2003 following the 2001 census revisions of population estimates. See Appendix D.

Table 8.6 Prevalence of cigarette smoking by sex and country of Great Britain: 1978 to 2001

Persons aged 16 and over — *Great Britain*

Country	Unweighted										Weighted			*Weighted base 2001 (000's) =100%**	*Unweighted sample* 2001*
	1978	1982	1984	1986	1988	1990	1992	1994	1996	1998	1998	2000	2001		
	Percentage smoking cigarettes														
Men															
England	44	37	35	34	32	31	29	28	28	28	29	29	28	*17,206*	*6128*
Wales	44	36	42	33	35	30	32	28	28	28	29	25	27	*949*	*342*
Scotland	48	45	43	37	36	33	34	31	33	33	35	30	32	*1,758*	*585*
Great Britain	45	38	36	35	33	31	29	28	29	28	30	29	28	*19,913*	*7055*
Women															
England	36	32	32	31	30	28	27	25	27	26	26	25	25	*18,851*	*7158*
Wales	37	34	32	30	28	31	33	27	27	26	27	24	26	*1,090*	*406*
Scotland	42	39	35	35	37	35	34	29	31	29	29	30	30	*2,046*	*735*
Great Britain	37	33	32	31	30	29	28	26	28	26	26	25	26	*21,987*	*8299*
Total															
England	40	35	33	32	31	29	28	26	28	27	28	27	27	*36,056*	*13286*
Wales	40	35	37	31	31	31	32	27	27	27	28	25	27	*2,039*	*748*
Scotland	45	42	39	36	37	34	34	30	32	30	31	30	31	*3,804*	*1320*
Great Britain	40	35	34	33	32	30	28	27	28	27	28	27	27	*41,899*	*15354*

* Trend tables show unweighted and weighted figures for 1998 to give an indication of the effect of the weighting. For the weighted data (1998, 2000 and 2001) the weighted base (000's) is the base for percentages. Unweighted data (up to 1998) are based on the unweighted sample. Unweighted bases for earlier years are of similar size to the unweighted sample and can be found in GHS reports for each year.

Weighting to be revised in Spring 2003 following the 2001 census revisions of population estimates. See Appendix D.

Table 8.7 **Prevalence of cigarette smoking by sex and Government Office Region: 1998 to 2001**

Persons aged 16 and over *Great Britain*

Government Office Region	Weighted 1998	2000	2001	*Weighted base 2001 (000's) = 100%**	*Unweighted sample* 2001*
	Percentage smoking cigarettes				
Men					
England					
North East	28	27	33	*926*	*330*
North West	29	29	28	*2,258*	*865*
Yorkshire and the Humber	30	29	30	*1,601*	*621*
East Midlands	27	27	28	*1,612*	*542*
West Midlands	32	27	27	*1,719*	*652*
East of England	26	27	27	*1,824*	*689*
London	34	31	29	*2,538*	*773*
South East	28	28	26	*2,874*	*1016*
South West	26	30	27	*1,854*	*640*
All England	29	29	28	*17,206*	*6128*
Wales	29	25	27	*949*	*342*
Scotland	35	30	32	*1,758*	*585*
Great Britain	30	29	28	*19,913*	*7055*
Women					
England					
North East	30	28	26	*985*	*376*
North West	32	30	29	*2,522*	*1031*
Yorkshire and the Humber	28	26	28	*1,816*	*748*
East Midlands	26	24	27	*1,725*	*617*
West Midlands	26	24	22	*1,795*	*719*
East of England	24	23	25	*1,946*	*789*
London	27	24	26	*2,659*	*893*
South East	21	23	23	*3,252*	*1199*
South West	25	24	22	*2,150*	*786*
All England	26	25	25	*18,851*	*7158*
Wales	27	24	26	*1,090*	*406*
Scotland	29	30	30	*2,046*	*735*
Great Britain	26	25	26	*21,987*	*8299*
All persons					
England					
North East	29	27	29	*1,911*	*706*
North West	31	30	29	*4,781*	*1896*
Yorkshire and the Humber	29	28	29	*3,417*	*1369*
East Midlands	27	25	28	*3,336*	*1159*
West Midlands	29	26	24	*3,514*	*1371*
East of England	25	25	26	*3,771*	*1478*
London	31	27	27	*5,197*	*1666*
South East	24	25	24	*6,125*	*2215*
South West	25	27	24	*4,004*	*1426*
All England	28	27	27	*36,056*	*13286*
Wales	28	25	27	*2,039*	*748*
Scotland	31	30	31	*3,804*	*1320*
Great Britain	28	27	27	*41,899*	*15354*

* The tables show unweighted and weighted figures for 1998 to give an indication of the effect of the weighting. For the weighted data (1998, 2000 and 2001) the weighted base (000's) is the base for percentages. Unweighted data (up to 1998) are based on the unweighted sample. Unweighted bases for earlier years are of similar size to the unweighted sample and can be found in GHS reports for each year.

Weighting to be revised in Spring 2003 following the 2001 census revisions of population estimates. See Appendix D.

Table 8.8 Cigarette-smoking status by age and sex: England

Persons aged 16 and over *England: 2001*

Cigarette-smoking status and number of cigarettes smoked per day	Age							
	16-24	25-34	35-44	45-54	55-64	65-74	75 and over	Total
	%	%	%	%	%	%	%	%
Men								
Current smokers:								
Less than 10	10	14	8	5	4	5	4	8
10, less than 20	17	15	12	10	8	6	3	11
20 or more	5	9	12	14	11	5	2	9
Total current cigarette smokers*	33	38	31	29	22	16	10	28
Ex-regular smokers	7	15	18	31	39	48	57	27
Never or only occasionally smoked cigarettes	61	47	51	40	38	37	33	45
Weighted base (000's) = 100%	*2,126*	*3,240*	*3,545*	*2,847*	*2,417*	*1,825*	*1,206*	*17,206*
Unweighted sample	*662*	*1048*	*1212*	*1063*	*910*	*761*	*472*	*6128*
Women								
Current smokers:								
Less than 10	13	12	8	6	6	6	5	8
10, less than 20	15	12	11	9	11	8	5	10
20 or more	5	6	9	10	7	5	2	7
Total current cigarette smokers*	33	30	28	25	24	19	11	25
Ex-regular smokers	9	17	18	22	25	30	32	21
Never or only occasionally smoked cigarettes	57	52	54	53	52	51	57	54
Weighted base (000's) = 100%	*2,168*	*3,432*	*3,650*	*3,135*	*2,447*	*2,045*	*1,975*	*18,851*
Unweighted sample	*776*	*1277*	*1391*	*1172*	*998*	*803*	*741*	*7158*
Total								
Current smokers:								
Less than 10	12	13	8	6	5	5	5	8
10, less than 20	16	14	11	9	9	7	4	11
20 or more	5	8	10	12	9	5	2	8
Total current cigarette smokers*	33	34	30	27	23	17	11	27
Ex-regular smokers	8	16	18	26	32	38	41	24
Never or only occasionally smoked cigarettes	59	50	53	47	45	44	48	50
Weighted base (000's) = 100%	*4,293*	*6,673*	*7,194*	*5,981*	*4,864*	*3,869*	*3,181*	*36,056*
Unweighted sample	*1438*	*2325*	*2603*	*2235*	*1908*	*1564*	*1213*	*13286*

* Includes those for whom number of cigarettes was not known.

Weighting to be revised in Spring 2003 following the 2001 census revisions of population estimates. See Appendix D.

Table 8.9 Prevalence of cigarette smoking by sex and whether household reference person is in a non-manual or manual socio-economic group: England, 1992 to 2001*

Persons aged 16 and over *England*

Socio-economic group of household reference person†	Unweighted 1992	Unweighted 1994	Unweighted 1996	Unweighted 1998	Weighted 1998	Weighted 2000	Weighted 2001	*Weighted base 2001 (000's) = 100%***	*Unweighted sample** 2001*
	Percentage smoking cigarettes								
Men									
Non-manual	22	21	21	21	22	24	22	*8,401*	*3039*
Manual	35	34	35	34	35	34	33	*8,307*	*2939*
Total††	29	28	28	28	29	29	28	*17,173*	*6117*
Women									
Non-manual	23	21	22	21	22	22	20	*9,894*	*3814*
Manual	30	30	33	31	31	29	30	*8,142*	*3050*
Total††	27	25	27	26	26	25	25	*18,756*	*7126*
All persons									
Non-manual	23	21	22	21	22	23	21	*18,295*	*6853*
Manual	33	32	34	32	33	31	32	*16,450*	*5989*
Total††	28	26	28	27	28	27	27	*35,929*	*13243*

* Figures for 1992 to 1996 are taken from the Department of Health bulletin *Statistics on Smoking: England, 1978 onwards.* Figures for 2001 are based on the new NS-SEC classification recoded to produce SEG and should therefore be treated with caution. See Appendix E.

† Head of household in years before 2000.

** Trend tables show unweighted and weighted figures for 1998 to give an indication of the effect of the weighting. For the weighted data (1998, 2000 and 2001) the weighted base (000's) is the base for percentages. Unweighted data (up to 1998) are based on the unweighted sample. Unweighted bases for earlier years are of similar size to the unweighted sample and can be found in GHS reports for each year.

†† Persons whose head of household/household reference person was a full time student, in the Armed forces, had an inadequately described occupation or had never worked are not shown as separate categories but are included in the total.

Weighting to be revised in Spring 2003 following the 2001 census revisions of population estimates. See Appendix D.

Table 8.10 Prevalence of cigarette smoking by sex and socio-economic classification based on the current or last job of the household reference person

Persons aged 16 and over *Great Britain: 2001*

Socio-economic classification of household reference person	Men		Women		Total	
			Percentage smoking cigarettes			
Managerial and professional						
Large employers and higher managerial	16		15		16	
Higher professional	17	21	13	18	15	19
Lower managerial and professional	24		20		22	
Intermediate						
Intermediate	28	29	26	26	27	27
Small employers and own account	30		26		28	
Routine and manual						
Lower supervisory and technical	33		29		31	
Semi routine	33	35	32	31	33	33
Routine	38		33		35	
Total*	28		26		27	
Weighted base (000's) = 100%						
Large employers and higher managerial	*1,324*		*1,277*		*2,601*	
Higher professional	*2,003*		*1,728*		*3,731*	
Lower managerial and professional	*4,406*		*4,953*		*9,358*	
Intermediate	*1,344*		*2,080*		*3,424*	
Small employers and own account	*2,009*		*1,889*		*3,898*	
Lower supervisory and technical	*2,825*		*2,506*		*5,331*	
Semi routine	*2,410*		*3,249*		*5,660*	
Routine	*2,725*		*3,101*		*5,826*	
*Total**	*19,839*		*21,838*		*41,677*	
Unweighted sample						
Large employers and higher managerial	*496*		*495*		*991*	
Higher professional	*727*		*672*		*1399*	
Lower managerial and professional	*1591*		*1903*		*3494*	
Intermediate	*466*		*784*		*1250*	
Small employers and own account	*718*		*708*		*1426*	
Lower supervisory and technical	*988*		*917*		*1905*	
Semi routine	*849*		*1235*		*2084*	
Routine	*955*		*1151*		*2106*	
*Total**	*7031*		*8247*		*15278*	

* From April 2001 the National Statistics Socio-economic classification (NS-SEC) was introduced for all official statistics and surveys. It has replaced Social Class based on Occupation and Socio-economic Groups (SEG). Persons whose household reference person was a full-time student, had an inadequately described occupation, had never worked or was long term unemployed are not shown as separate categories but are included in the figure for all persons (see Appendix A).

Weighting to be revised in Spring 2003 following the 2001 census revisions of population estimates. See Appendix D.

Table 8.11 Prevalence of cigarette smoking by sex and socio-economic classification based on own current or last job, whether economically active or inactive, and, for economically inactive persons, age

Persons aged 16 and over *Great Britain: 2001*

Socio-economic classification*	Men					Women					All persons				
	Active	Inactive 16-59	Inactive 60 and over	Total inactive	Total	Active	Inactive 16-59	Inactive 60 and over	Total inactive	Total	Active	Inactive 16-59	Inactive 60 and over	Total inactive	Total
	Percentage smoking cigarettes														
Managerial and professional	21	30	9	13	19	19	20	11	14	18	20	23	10	14	19
Intermediate	31	45	16	23	29	26	25	14	18	23	28	29	15	19	25
Routine and manual	40	55	20	29	36	33	45	20	30	32	37	48	20	30	34
Total	31	37	16	23	28	27	34	17	24	26	29	35	17	24	27
Weighted bases (000's) = 100%															
Managerial and professional	*5,360*	*293*	*1,284*	*1,577*	*6,937*	*4,070*	*571*	*957*	*1,528*	*5,597*	*9,429*	*864*	*2,241*	*3,105*	*12,534*
Intermediate	*2,575*	*162*	*550*	*712*	*3,287*	*3,105*	*702*	*1,198*	*1,901*	*5,005*	*5,679*	*864*	*1,749*	*2,612*	*8,292*
Routine and manual	*5,273*	*708*	*2,126*	*2,834*	*8,107*	*4,278*	*1,848*	*2,996*	*4,844*	*9,126*	*9,551*	*2,557*	*5,122*	*7,679*	*17,233*
*Total**	*13,967*	*1,953*	*3,993*	*5,946*	*19,913*	*12,225*	*4,248*	*5,510*	*9,758*	*21,987*	*26,192*	*6,200*	*9,504*	*15,704*	*41,900*
Unweighted sample															
Managerial and professional	*1895*	*105*	*530*	*635*	*2530*	*1530*	*225*	*380*	*605*	*2135*	*3425*	*330*	*910*	*1240*	*4665*
Intermediate	*885*	*56*	*219*	*275*	*1160*	*1160*	*270*	*476*	*746*	*1906*	*2045*	*326*	*695*	*1021*	*3066*
Routine and manual	*1811*	*237*	*821*	*1058*	*2869*	*1577*	*696*	*1144*	*1840*	*3418*	*3388*	*933*	*1965*	*2898*	*6287*
*Total**	*4832*	*640*	*1583*	*2223*	*7055*	*4554*	*1611*	*2133*	*3744*	*8299*	*9386*	*2251*	*3716*	*5967*	*15354*

* From April 2001 the National Statistics Socio-economic classification (NS-SEC) was introduced for all official statistics and surveys. It has replaced Social Class based on Occupation and Socio-economic Groups (SEG). Full-time students, persons in inadequately described occupations, those who had never worked and the long term unemployed are not shown as separate categories but are included in the figure for all persons (see Appendix A).

Weighting to be revised in Spring 2003 following the 2001 census revisions of population estimates. See Appendix D.

Table 8.12 **Cigarette-smoking status by sex: 1974 to 2001**

Persons aged 16 and over *Great Britain*

	Unweighted										Weighted		
	1974	1978	1982	1986	1988	1990	1992	1994	1996	1998	1998	2000	2001
	Percentages												
Men													
Current cigarette smokers													
Light (under 20 per day)	25	22	20	20	18	17	17	17	17	18	19	18	19
Heavy (20 or more per day)	26	23	18	15	15	14	12	12	11	10	11	10	10
Total current cigarette smokers	51	45	38	35	33	31	29	28	29	28	30	29	28
Ex-regular cigarette smokers	23	27	30	32	32	32	32	31	32	31	29	27	27
Never or only occasionally smoked cigarettes	25	29	32	34	35	37	38	40	40	41	42	44	45
*Weighted base (000's) = 100%**											*19,229*	*20,350*	*19,913*
*Unweighted sample**	*9852*	*10480*	*9199*	*8874*	*8673*	*8106*	*8417*	*7642*	*7172*	*6579*		*6593*	*7055*
Women													
Current cigarette smokers													
Light (under 20 per day)	28	23	22	21	20	20	19	18	19	19	19	19	19
Heavy (20 or more per day)	13	13	11	10	10	9	9	8	8	7	7	6	7
Total current cigarette smokers	41	37	33	31	30	29	28	26	28	26	26	25	26
Ex-regular cigarette smokers	11	14	16	18	19	19	21	21	20	21	20	20	21
Never or only occasionally smoked cigarettes	49	49	51	51	51	52	52	54	53	53	53	54	53
Weighted base (000's) = 100%											*21,654*	*22,044*	*21,987*
*Unweighted sample**	*11480*	*12156*	*10641*	*10304*	*10122*	*9445*	*9764*	*9108*	*8501*	*7830*		*7496*	*8299*

* Trend tables show unweighted and weighted figures for 1998 to give an indication of the effect of the weighting. For the weighted data (1998, 2000 and 2001) the weighted base (000's) is the base for percentages. Unweighted data (up to 1998) are based on the unweighted sample.

Weighting to be revised in Spring 2003 following the 2001 census revisions of population estimates. See Appendix D.

Table 8.13 **Cigarette-smoking status by sex and age**

Persons aged 16 and over *Great Britain: 2001*

Age		Current cigarette smokers			Current non-smokers of cigarettes		*Weighted base (000's) = 100%*	*Unweighted sample*
		Light (under 20 per day)	Heavy (20 or more per day)	All current smokers	Ex-regular cigarette smokers	Never or only occasionally smoked cigarettes		
Men								
16-19	%	22	3	25	4	71	*1,063*	*344*
20-24	%	33	7	40	9	51	*1,410*	*427*
25-34	%	29	9	38	15	47	*3,754*	*1211*
35-49	%	18	13	31	20	49	*5,536*	*1939*
50-59	%	14	12	26	36	38	*3,273*	*1208*
60 and over	%	10	7	16	47	36	*4,876*	*1926*
All aged 16 and over	%	19	10	28	27	45	*19,913*	*7055*
Women								
16-19	%	26	4	31	6	63	*1,119*	*412*
20-24	%	30	5	35	12	53	*1,418*	*493*
25-34	%	24	7	31	16	53	*3,887*	*1445*
35-49	%	17	10	28	19	53	*5,897*	*2218*
50-59	%	16	9	25	24	51	*3,647*	*1395*
60 and over	%	13	4	17	29	54	*6,020*	*2336*
All aged 16 and over	%	19	7	26	21	53	*21,987*	*8299*
Total								
16-19	%	24	4	28	5	67	*2,182*	*756*
20-24	%	31	6	37	11	52	*2,828*	*920*
25-34	%	27	8	34	15	50	*7,641*	*2656*
35-49	%	18	12	29	19	51	*11,433*	*4157*
50-59	%	15	10	26	30	45	*6,920*	*2603*
60 and over	%	12	5	17	37	46	*10,896*	*4262*
All aged 16 and over	%	19	8	27	24	49	*41,899*	*15354*

Weighting to be revised in Spring 2003 following the 2001 census revisions of population estimates. See Appendix D.

Table 8.14 **Average daily cigarette consumption per smoker by sex and age: 1974 to 2001**

Current cigarette smokers aged 16 and over *Great Britain*

Age	Unweighted										Weighted			*Weighted base 2001 (000's) =100%**	*Unweighted sample* 2001*
	1974	1978	1982	1986	1988	1990	1992	1994	1996	1998	1998	2000	2001		
	Mean number of cigarettes per day														
Men															
16-19	16	14	12	12	12	13	12	10	12	10	10	12	11	*262*	*85*
20-24	19	17	16	15	16	16	13	13	14	14	13	12	12	*559*	*171*
25-34	19	19	17	16	17	16	14	15	15	13	13	13	13	*1,428*	*454*
35-49	20	20	20	19	19	19	19	18	18	17	18	17	17	*1,721*	*583*
50-59	18	20	18	17	19	17	18	20	17	18	18	17	18	*860*	*305*
60 and over	14	15	16	15	15	15	15	14	15	16	16	15	15	*796*	*307*
All aged 16 and over	18	18	17	16	17	17	16	16	16	16	15	15	15	*5,628*	*1905*
Women															
16-19	12	13	11	11	11	11	10	10	10	10	10	10	12	*342*	*120*
20-24	14	14	14	12	14	13	13	13	11	12	11	10	11	*496*	*169*
25-34	15	16	16	14	15	15	14	14	13	12	12	12	12	*1,203*	*453*
35-49	15	16	15	16	16	15	16	15	16	15	15	14	15	*1,634*	*612*
50-59	13	14	14	14	15	15	15	15	16	15	15	15	15	*917*	*344*
60 and over	10	11	11	12	12	12	12	13	13	12	12	12	12	*1,039*	*401*
All aged 16 and over	13	14	14	14	14	14	14	14	14	13	13	13	13	*5,631*	*2099*

* See the footnote to Table 8.1.

Weighting to be revised in Spring 2003 following the 2001 census revisions of population estimates. See Appendix D.

Table 8.15 **Average daily cigarette consumption per smoker by sex, and socio-economic classification based on the current or last job of the household reference person**

Current cigarette smokers aged 16 and over *Great Britain: 2001*

Socio-economic classification of household reference person*	Men		Women		Total	
	Average number of cigarettes a day					
Managerial and professional						
Large employers and higher managerial	13		12		12	
Higher professional	13	13	11	12	12	13
Lower managerial and professional	14		12		13	
Intermediate						
Intermediate	14	15	12	12	13	14
Small employers and own account	16		13		14	
Routine and manual						
Lower supervisory and technical	16		13		15	
Semi routine	15	16	14	14	14	15
Routine	17		14		16	
Total*	15		13		14	
Weighted base (000's) = 100%						
Large employers and higher managerial	*211*		*191*		*403*	
Higher professional	*334*		*217*		*552*	
Lower managerial and professional	*1,033*		*1,012*		*2,045*	
Intermediate	*375*		*538*		*913*	
Small employers and own account	*601*		*486*		*1,087*	
Lower supervisory and technical	*929*		*720*		*1,648*	
Semi routine	*807*		*1,042*		*1,850*	
Routine	*1,024*		*1,017*		*2,041*	
*Total**	*5,619*		*5,599*		*11,218*	
Unweighted sample						
Large employers and higher managerial	*73*		*73*		*146*	
Higher professional	*115*		*81*		*196*	
Lower managerial and professional	*357*		*383*		*740*	
Intermediate	*126*		*202*		*328*	
Small employers and own account	*207*		*179*		*386*	
Lower supervisory and technical	*309*		*260*		*569*	
Semi routine	*274*		*394*		*668*	
Routine	*348*		*379*		*727*	
*Total**	*1902*		*2088*		*3990*	

* From April 2001 the National Statistics Socio-economic classification (NS-SEC) was introduced for all official statistics and surveys. It has replaced Social Class based on Occupation and Socio-economic Groups (SEG). Persons whose household reference person was a full-time student, had an inadequately described occupation, had never worked or was long term unemployed are not shown as separate categories but are included in the figure for all persons (see Appendix A).

Weighting to be revised in Spring 2003 following the 2001 census revisions of population estimates. See Appendix D.

Table 8.16 **Type of cigarette smoked by sex: 1974 to 2001**

Current cigarette smokers aged 16 and over — *Great Britain*

Type of cigarette smoked	Unweighted										Weighted		
	1974	1978	1982	1986	1988	1990	1992	1994	1996	1998	1998	2000	2001
	%	%	%	%	%	%	%	%	%	%	%	%	%
Men													
Mainly filter	69	75	72	78	79	80	80	78	75	74	74	69	68
Mainly plain	18	11	7	4	3	2	2	2	1	1	1	1	1
Mainly hand-rolled	13	14	21	18	18	18	18	21	23	25	25	31	31
*Weighted base (000's) = 100%**											*5,687*	*5,802*	*5,643*
*Unweighted sample**	*4993*	*4646*	*3469*	*3072*	*2849*	*2510*	*2473*	*2150*	*2052*	*1857*		*1796*	*1911*
Women													
Mainly filter	91	95	94	96	96	97	97	96	93	92	92	89	87
Mainly plain	8	4	3	1	1	1	1	1	1	1	1	1	1
Mainly hand-rolled	1	1	3	2	2	2	2	4	6	7	8	10	12
*Weighted base (000's) = 100%**											*5,735*	*5,619*	*5,635*
*Unweighted sample**	*4600*	*4421*	*3522*	*3192*	*3076*	*2748*	*2698*	*2336*	*2341*	*2044*		*1900*	*2101*

* See the footnote to Table 8.12.

Weighting to be revised in Spring 2003 following the 2001 census revisions of population estimates. See Appendix D.

Table 8.17 **Type of cigarette smoked by age and sex**

Current cigarette smokers aged 16 and over — *Great Britain: 2001*

Type of cigarette smoked	Age					
	16-24	25-34	35-49	50-59	60 and over	All aged 16 and over
	%	%	%	%	%	%
Men						
Mainly filter	79	70	64	62	67	68
Mainly plain	2	0	1	0	2	1
Mainly hand-rolled	20	29	36	38	31	31
Weighted base (000's) = 100%	*824*	*1,428*	*1,727*	*863*	*801*	*5,643*
Unweighted sample	*257*	*454*	*585*	*306*	*309*	*1911*
Women						
Mainly filter	85	86	85	88	94	87
Mainly plain	3	1	0	0	1	1
Mainly hand-rolled	12	13	15	12	4	12
Weighted base (000's) = 100%	*838*	*1,203*	*1,636*	*917*	*1,041*	*5,635*
Unweighted sample	*289*	*453*	*613*	*344*	*402*	*2101*
Total						
Mainly filter	82	77	74	75	82	78
Mainly plain	2	1	0	0	2	1
Mainly hand-rolled	16	22	26	25	16	22
Weighted base (000's) = 100%	*1,663*	*2,631*	*3,363*	*1,780*	*1,842*	*11,279*
Unweighted sample	*546*	*907*	*1198*	*650*	*711*	*4012*

Weighting to be revised in Spring 2003 following the 2001 census revisions of population estimates. See Appendix D.

Table 8.18 **Tar yield per cigarette: 1986 to 2001**

Current smokers of manufactured cigarettes *Great Britain*

Tar yield	Unweighted					Weighted		
	1986	1988	1990	1992	1998*	1998*	2000*	2001
	%	%	%	%	%	%	%	%
<10mg	19	21	24	25	28	28	27	26
10<15mg	32	58	54	68	70	69	71	71
15+mg	40	17	19	4	0	0	0	0
No regular brand/new brand/ don't know	10	4	4	3	2	2	2	2
Weighted base (000's) =100%†						*9,568*	*9,104*	*8,850*
Unweighted sample†	*5620*	*5363*	*4739*	*4662*	*3288*		*2955*	*3174*

* Data for 1998 and 2000 revised due to error in automated coding procedure. See Chapter 8.
† See footnote to Table 8.12.

Weighting to be revised in Spring 2003 following the 2001 census revisions of population estimates. See Appendix D.

Table 8.19 **Tar yields by sex and age**

Current smokers of manufactured cigarettes aged 16 and over* *Great Britain: 2001*

		Tar yield						*Weighted base (000's) = 100%*	*Unweighted sample*
		Less than 4mg	4<8mg	8<10mg	10<12mg	12<15mg	No regular brand/ don't know tar yield		
Men									
16-19	%	0	16	0	43	36	5	*218*	*71*
20-24	%	1	23	1	40	33	1	*445*	*136*
25-34	%	2	26	3	29	39	2	*1,008*	*322*
35-49	%	2	11	4	44	36	3	*1,111*	*378*
50-59	%	2	5	6	43	43	1	*534*	*191*
60 and over	%	4	7	7	46	34	2	*549*	*214*
Total	%	2	15	4	40	37	2	*3,865*	*1312*
Women									
16-19	%	1	15	4	38	41	1	*304*	*108*
20-24	%	2	24	8	32	33	1	*438*	*149*
25-34	%	3	25	7	30	33	2	*1,047*	*396*
35-49	%	3	14	10	36	36	1	*1,390*	*523*
50-59	%	4	15	13	26	38	3	*809*	*302*
60 and over	%	4	15	13	30	34	4	*997*	*384*
Total	%	3	18	10	32	36	2	*4,984*	*1862*
Total									
16-19	%	1	16	2	40	39	3	*521*	*179*
20-24	%	1	24	5	36	33	1	*883*	*285*
25-34	%	3	25	5	29	36	2	*2,055*	*718*
35-49	%	2	12	7	39	36	2	*2,501*	*901*
50-59	%	3	11	10	33	40	2	*1,344*	*493*
60 and over	%	4	12	11	36	34	3	*1,546*	*598*
Total	%	3	17	7	35	36	2	*8,850*	*3174*

* Thirty-one per cent of male smokers and 12 per cent of female smokers said they mainly smoked hand-rolled cigarettes and have been excluded from this analysis.

Weighting to be revised in Spring 2003 following the 2001 census revisions of population estimates. See Appendix D.

Table 8.20 Tar yields by socio-economic classification based on the current or last job of the household reference person

Current smokers of manufactured cigarettes aged 16 and over* *Great Britain: 2001*

Socio-economic classification of household reference person†		Tar yields						*Weighted base (000's) = 100%*	*Unweighted sample*
		Less than 4mg	4<8mg	8<10mg	10<12mg	12<15mg	No regular brand don't know tar yield		
Men									
Managerial and professional	%	3	26	3	34	31	3	*1,274*	*438*
Intermediate	%	2	20	6	40	32	1	*625*	*214*
Routine and manual	%	1	5	4	44	43	3	*1,730*	*589*
Total	%	2	15	4	40	37	2	*3,856*	*1309*
Women									
Managerial and professional	%	4	30	7	28	28	2	*1,339*	*508*
Intermediate	%	3	18	14	29	33	3	*900*	*337*
Routine and manual	%	2	10	11	34	40	2	*2,415*	*897*
Total	%	3	18	10	32	36	2	*4,958*	*1853*
All persons									
Managerial and professional	%	4	28	5	31	30	2	*2,613*	*946*
Intermediate	%	3	19	11	33	33	2	*1,525*	*551*
Routine and manual	%	2	8	8	38	41	2	*4,145*	*1486*
Total	%	3	16	7	35	36	2	*8,814*	*3162*

* See the footnote to Table 8.19.
† See the footnote to Table 8.15.

Weighting to be revised in Spring 2003 following the 2001 census revisions of population estimates. See Appendix D.

Table 8.21 **Prevalence of smoking by sex and type of product smoked: 1974 to 2001**

Persons aged 16 and over *Great Britain*

	Unweighted										Weighted		
	1974	1978	1982	1986	1988	1990	1992	1994	1996	1998	1998	2000	2001
	Percentage smoking												
Men													
Cigarettes*	51	45	38	35	33	31	29	28	29	28	30	29	28
Pipe	12	10	..	6	4	4	4	3	2	2	2	2	2
Cigars†	34	16	12	10	9	8	7	6	6	6	6	5	5
All smokers**	64	55	45††	44	40	38	36	33	33	33	34	32	32
Weighted base (000's) = 100%§											*19,225*	*20,350*	*19,972*
Unweighted sample§	*9862*	*10439*	*9171*	*8884*	*8673*	*8119*	*8427*	*7662*	*7186*	*6579*		*6593*	*7074*
Women													
Cigarettes*	41	37	33	31	30	29	28	26	28	26	26	25	26
Cigars†	3	1	0	1	0	0	0	0	0	0	0	0	0
All smokers**	41	37	34	31	31	29	28	26	28	26	27	26	26
Weighted base (000's) = 100%§											*21,653*	*22,044*	*22,032*
Unweighted sample§	*11419*	*12079*	*10559*	*10312*	*10122*	*9455*	*9772*	*9137*	*8512*	*7830*		*7496*	*8317*

* Figures for cigarettes include all smokers of manufactured and hand-rolled cigarettes.
† For 1974 the figures include occasional cigar smokers, that is, those who smoked less than one cigar a month.
** The percentages for cigarettes, pipes and cigars add to more than the percentage for all smokers because some people smoked more than one type of product.
†† In 1982 men were not asked about pipe smoking, and therefore the figures for all smokers exclude those who smoked only a pipe.
§ See the footnote to Table 8.12.

Weighting to be revised in Spring 2003 following the 2001 census revisions of population estimates. See Appendix D.

Table 8.22 **Prevalence of smoking by type of product smoked by sex and age**

Persons aged 16 and over *Great Britain: 2001*

Age	Men						Women				
	Cigarettes*	Pipe†	Cigars†	All smokers**	*Weighted base (000's) = 100%*	*Unweighted sample*	Cigarettes*	Cigars†	All smokers**	*Weighted base (000's) = 100%*	*Unweighted sample*
	Percentage smoking						Percentage smoking				
16-19	24	0	4	24	*1,102*	*356*	30	1	30	*1,149*	*424*
20-24	40	0	3	41	*1,410*	*427*	35	1	35	*1,418*	*493*
25-29	40	0	5	41	*1,658*	*526*	35	0	35	*1,659*	*621*
30-34	37	1	6	39	*2,105*	*687*	28	0	28	*2,228*	*824*
35-49	31	1	5	35	*5,539*	*1940*	28	0	28	*5,902*	*2220*
50-59	26	2	7	32	*3,273*	*1208*	25	0	25	*3,644*	*1394*
60 and over	16	4	4	22	*4,886*	*1930*	17	0	17	*6,032*	*2341*
All aged 16 and over	28	2	5	32	*19,972*	*7074*	26	0	26	*22,032*	*8317*

* Figures for cigarettes include all smokers of both manufactured and hand-rolled cigarettes.
† Young people aged 16-17 were not asked about cigar or pipe-smoking.
** The percentages for cigarettes, pipes and cigars add to more than the percentage for all smokers because some people smoked more than one type of product.

Weighting to be revised in Spring 2003 following the 2001 census revisions of population estimates. See Appendix D.

Table 8.23 Proportion of smokers who would like to give up smoking altogether, by sex and number of cigarettes smoked per day: 1992 to 2001

Current cigarette smokers aged 16 and over *Great Britain*

Number of cigarettes smoked a day	Unweighted				Weighted			*Weighted base 2001 (000's) = 100%**	*Unweighted sample** 2001*
	1992	1994	1996	1998	1998	2000	2001		
	Percentage who would like to stop altogether								
Men									
20 or more	68	70	66	69	69	74	70	*1,923*	*665*
10-19	70	72	69	73	73	76	71	*2,196*	*737*
0-9	58	61	62	62	62	64	62	*1,509*	*503*
All smokers	66	69	66	69	69	72	68	*5,643*	*1,911*
Women									
20 or more	70	69	69	68	68	73	66	*1,525*	*575*
10-19	72	71	70	75	75	76	67	*2,349*	*875*
0-9	58	62	59	65	65	63	60	*1,757*	*649*
All smokers	68	68	67	70	70	71	65	*5,638*	*2,102*
Total									
20 or more	69	70	68	69	69	74	68	*3,448*	*1,240*
10-19	71	71	70	74	74	76	69	*4,544*	*1,612*
0-9	58	61	60	64	64	63	61	*3,266*	*1,152*
All smokers	67	68	67	69	69	72	66	*11,281*	*4,013*

* Trend tables show unweighted and weighted figures for 1998 to give an indication of the effect of the weighting. For the weighted data (1998, 2000 and 2001) the weighted base (000's) is the base for percentages. Unweighted data (up to 1998) are based on the unweighted sample. Unweighted bases for earlier years are of similar size to the unweighted sample and can be found in GHS reports for each year.

Weighting to be revised in Spring 2003 following the 2001 census revisions of population estimates. See Appendix D.

Table 8.24 Proportion of smokers who would find it difficult to go without smoking for a day, by sex and number of cigarettes smoked per day: 1992 to 2001

Current cigarette smokers aged 16 and over *Great Britain*

Number of cigarettes smoked a day	Unweighted				Weighted			*Weighted base 2001 (000's) = 100%**	*Unweighted sample** 2001*
	1992	1994	1996	1998	1998	2000	2001		
	Percentages								
Men									
20 or more	76	78	78	78	78	78	74	*1,917*	*663*
10-19	54	57	54	54	54	56	55	*2,179*	*731*
0-9	20	17	20	25	23	14	21	*1,507*	*502*
All smokers	55	56	56	56	56	53	52	*5,619*	*1,902*
Women									
20 or more	86	86	87	87	86	88	87	*1,523*	*574*
10-19	68	68	66	66	65	67	65	*2,335*	*870*
0-9	23	20	24	24	25	22	24	*1,754*	*648*
All smokers	61	60	61	59	59	58	58	*5,617*	*2,094*
Total									
20 or more	80	82	83	82	82	82	80	*3,440*	*1,237*
10-19	61	63	60	61	60	62	61	*4,514*	*1,601*
0-9	21	19	23	24	24	18	22	*3,261*	*1,150*
All smokers	58	59	58	58	57	56	55	*11,236*	*3,996*

* Trend tables show unweighted and weighted figures for 1998 to give an indication of the effect of the weighting. For the weighted data (1998, 2000 and 2001) the weighted base (000's) is the base for percentages. Unweighted data (up to 1998) are based on the unweighted sample. Unweighted bases for earlier years are of similar size to the unweighted sample and can be found in GHS reports for each year.

Weighting to be revised in Spring 2003 following the 2001 census revisions of population estimates. See Appendix D.

Table 8.25 Proportion of smokers who have their first cigarette within five minutes of waking, by sex and number of cigarettes smoked per day: 1992 to 2001

Current cigarette smokers aged 16 and over — *Great Britain*

Number of cigarettes smoked a day	Unweighted				Weighted			*Weighted base 2001 (000's) = 100%**	*Unweighted sample** 2001*
	1992	1994	1996	1998	1998	2000	2001		
	Percentage smoking within 5 minutes of waking								
Men									
20 or more	29	31	29	31	32	30	30	*1,923*	*665*
10-19	10	13	9	11	11	13	11	*2,196*	*737*
0-9	2	2	3	2	2	2	3	*1,498*	*499*
All smokers	16	18	16	16	17	16	15	*5,630*	*1,906*
Women									
20 or more	29	34	32	31	31	32	35	*1,522*	*574*
10-19	10	9	11	12	12	12	12	*2,349*	*875*
0-9	1	0	1	1	1	2	2	*1,746*	*645*
All smokers	14	14	15	14	14	14	15	*5,624*	*2,097*
Total									
20 or more	29	33	30	31	31	31	32	*3,445*	*1,239*
10-19	10	11	10	12	12	13	11	*4,544*	*1,612*
0-9	2	1	2	2	2	2	2	*3,244*	*1,144*
All smokers	15	16	15	15	15	15	15	*11,254*	*4,003*

* Trend tables show unweighted and weighted figures for 1998 to give an indication of the effect of the weighting. For the weighted data (1998, 2000 and 2001) the weighted base (000's) is the base for percentages. Unweighted data (up to 1998) are based on the unweighted sample. Unweighted bases for earlier years are of similar size to the unweighted sample and can be found in GHS reports for each year.

Weighting to be revised in Spring 2003 following the 2001 census revisions of population estimates. See Appendix D.

Chapter 9

Drinking

Questions about drinking alcohol were included in the General Household Survey every two years from 1978 to 1998. From 2000, questions about drinking in the last 7 days form part of the continuous survey and are asked every year. Prior to 1988, alcohol questions were asked only of those aged 18 and over, but since 1988, respondents aged 16 and 17 have answered the questions using a self-completion questionnaire.

Measuring alcohol consumption

Obtaining reliable information about drinking behaviour is difficult and, in consequence, social surveys consistently record lower levels of consumption than would be expected from data on alcohol sales. This is partly because people may consciously or unconsciously under-estimate how much alcohol they consume. Drinking at home is particularly likely to be under-estimated because the quantities consumed are not measured and are likely to be larger than those dispensed in licensed premises.

There are different methods for obtaining survey information on drinking behaviour. One approach is to ask people to recall all episodes of drinking during a set period.[1] However, this is time consuming to administer and is therefore not suitable for the GHS, where drinking is only one of a number of subjects covered.

In 2001, as in 1998 and 2000, the GHS used two measures of alcohol consumption:

- Maximum daily amount drunk last week
- Weekly alcohol consumption level

Maximum daily amount drunk last week

These questions were included for the first time on the GHS in 1998, following the publication in 1995 of an inter-departmental review of the effects of drinking.[2] This concluded that it was more appropriate to set benchmarks for daily than for weekly consumption of alcohol, partly because of concern about the health and social risks associated with single episodes of intoxication.

- The report considered that regular consumption of between three and four units[3] a day for men and two to three units a day for women does not carry a significant health risk, but that consistently drinking more than four units a day for men, or more than three for women, is not advised.

The government's advice on sensible drinking is now based on these daily benchmarks, and GHS data are used to monitor the extent to which people are following the advice given. Respondents are asked on how many days they drank alcohol during the previous week. They are then asked how much of each of six different types of drink (normal strength beer, strong beer (6% or greater ABV[4]), wine, spirits, fortified wines and alcopops) they drank on their heaviest drinking day during the previous week. These amounts are added to give an estimate of the maximum the respondent had drunk on any one day.

Weekly alcohol consumption level

The current measure of average weekly alcohol consumption has been used on the GHS since 1986, and was developed in response to earlier medical guidelines on drinking which related to maximum recommended weekly amounts of alcohol. Its use has been continued to provide a consistent measure of alcohol consumption by means of which trends can continue to be monitored. Respondents are asked how often over the last year they have drunk each of the six types of drink listed in the previous section (normal strength beer, strong beer, wine, spirits, fortified wines and alcopops), and how much they have usually drunk on any one day. This information is combined to give an estimate of the respondent's weekly alcohol consumption (averaged over a year) in units of alcohol.[5]

Frequency of drinking during the last week

Patterns of drinking behaviour in 2001 were broadly the same as those described in earlier GHS reports.

Men were more likely than women to have had an alcoholic drink in the previous week than were women:

- 75% of men and 59% of women had a drink on at least one day during the previous week.

The proportions drinking last week also varied between age groups.

- Among men, those aged 16 to 24 and those aged 65 and over were least likely to report drinking alcohol during the reference period.
- Among women, however, the 25 to 44 age group were most likely and those aged 65 and over least likely to have drunk alcohol during the previous week.

Men also drank on more days of the week than women:

- more than one in five men (22%) compared with one in eight women (13%) had drunk on at least five of the preceding seven days
- 12% of men, but only 8% of women, had drunk alcohol every day during the previous week.

Among both men and women, older people drank more frequently than younger people. For example, 21% of men and 12% of women aged 65 and over had drunk every day during the previous week compared with only 5% of men and 3% of women aged 16 to 24. **Table 9.1 Figure 9A**

Maximum daily amount drunk last week

Two measures of daily consumption are shown in the tables. The first is the proportion exceeding the recommended daily benchmarks: that is, men drinking more than four units in one day and women drinking more than three units.[2] The second measure is intended to indicate heavy drinking that would be likely to lead to intoxication. People vary in their susceptibility to the effect of alcohol, but as a rough guide, this level is taken as more than eight units on one day for men and more than six units for women.

Trends in daily drinking

The GHS included questions about the maximum daily amount drunk last week for only the third time in 2001, so these data provide no evidence on long term trends. However, Table 9.2 shows that there were no significant changes between 1998 and 2001 in the proportions of men and women and of different age groups who had an alcoholic drink in the previous week, nor in the number of days on which they had done so.

There does appear to be an increase in heavy drinking among women between 1998 and 2001: the proportion of women who had drunk more than 6 units on at least one day in the previous week rose from 8% in 1998 to 10% in 2000 and remained at that level in 2001.

The increase over this period occurred only among women under age 45: among those aged 16 to 24 the proportion who had drunk more than 6 units on at least one day in the previous week rose from 24% to 27%, and the equivalent proportion among women aged 25 to 44 rose from11% to 14%. **Table 9.2 Figures 9B and 9C**

Daily drinking and sex, age and marital status

Men were much more likely than women to have exceeded the daily benchmarks on at least one day during the previous week

- 39% of men compared with 22% of women had done so and they were twice as likely as women to have drunk heavily (21% compared with 10%).

It was noted earlier that young people drink less frequently than older people. However, among both men and women, those aged 16 to 24 were significantly more likely than respondents in other age groups to have exceeded the recommended number of daily units on at least one day.

- One half of young men (49%) aged 16 to 24 had exceeded four units on at least one day during

Figure 9A **Percentage of men and women who had drunk alcohol on 5 days or more in the week prior to interview by age: Great Britain, 2001**

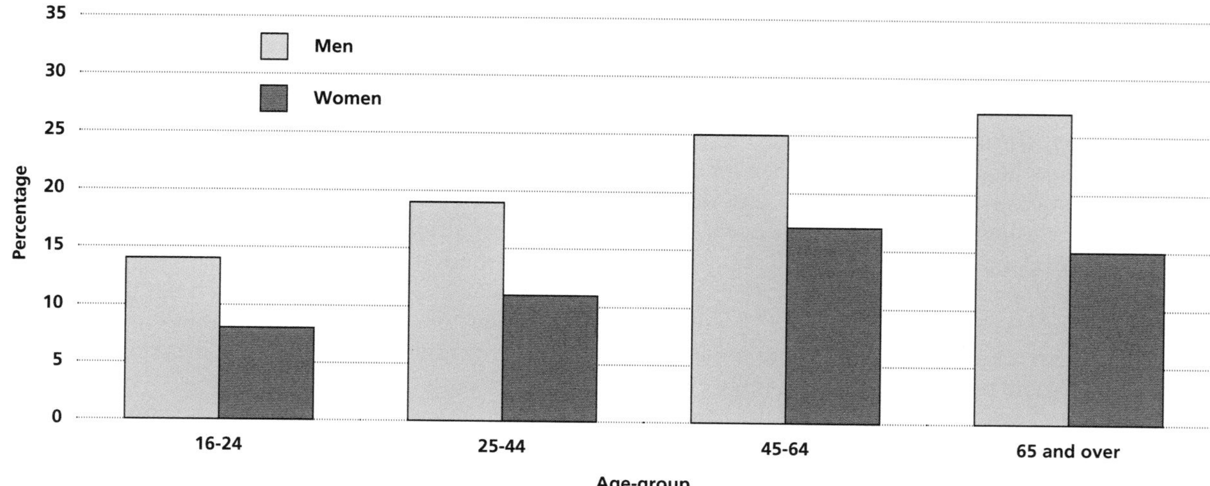

Figure 9B **Percentage exceeding daily benchmarks by age: men: Great Britain, 2001**

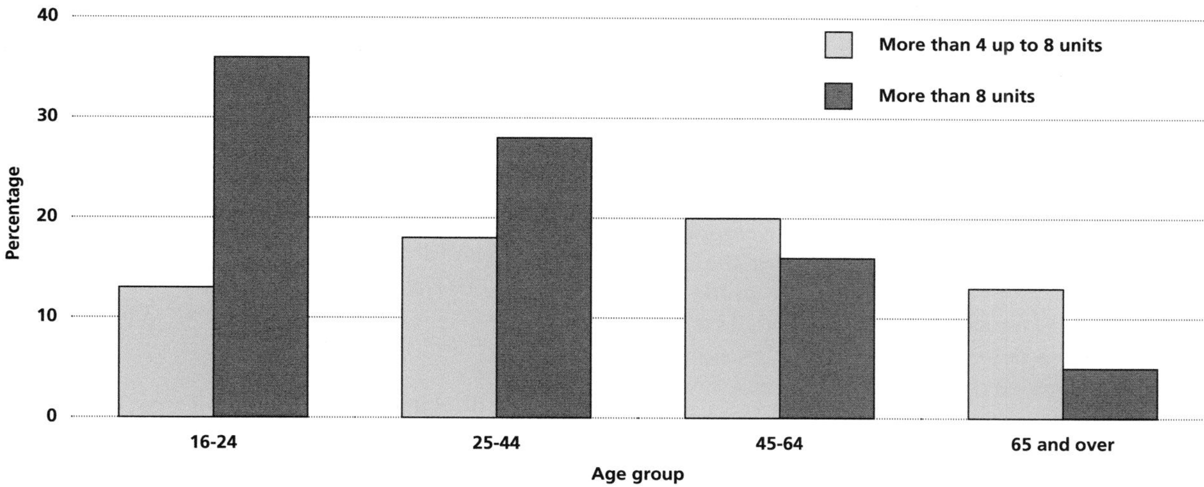

Figure 9C **Percentage exceeding daily benchmarks by age: women: Great Britain, 2001**

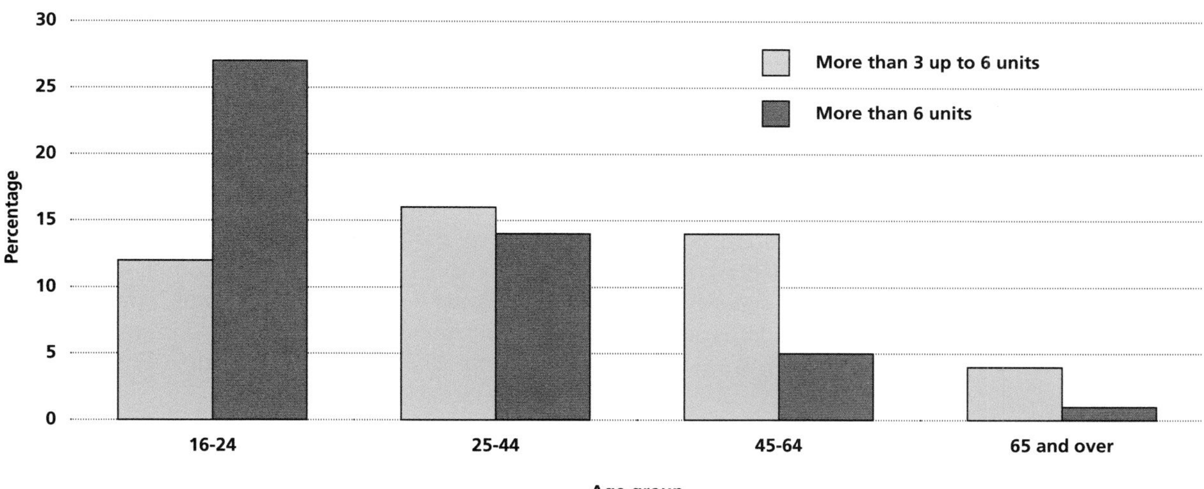

the previous week compared with 18% of men aged 65 and over.

- Among women, 39% of those in the youngest age group had exceeded three units on at least one day compared with only 5% of those aged 65 and over.

Similar patterns were evident for heavy drinking:

- 36% of men aged 16 to 24, but only 5% of those aged 65 and over, had drunk more than eight units on at least one day during the previous week;
- among women aged 16 to 24, 27% had drunk heavily on at least one day during the preceding week compared with only 1% of women in the oldest age group. **Table 9.3**

Analysis of alcohol consumption by marital status is complicated by the strong association between marital status and age, and this is only partly controlled for in Table 9.4, where two age groups are shown. For example, among those aged 16 to 44, single men are more likely than married men to drink heavily, but this may be due to the fact that within this age group single men are, on average, younger than married men, and the difference may be due to their age rather than their marital status.

However, it is clear that alcohol consumption is higher than average among divorced and separated men aged 45 and over: 20% of this group had drunk more than 8 units on at least one day in the last week, compared with only 12% of married/cohabiting men in that age group. Divorced and separated women aged 45 and over, however, were no more likely than women in general in that age group to have drunk heavily in the previous week.

Table 9.4

Daily drinking and socio-economic characteristics

The link between alcohol consumption and socio-economic characteristics is an important focus of analysis for the GHS. A recent review of information on inequalities in health, undertaken by the Department of Health, noted that both mortality and morbidity show a clear association with socio-economic position, rates being much higher among unskilled men than among those in professional households.[6] However, the GHS has shown over many years that there is little difference in usual weekly alcohol consumption between those in non-manual and manual households, and where differences do exist it has been those in the non-manual categories who tended to have the higher consumption.

The National Statistics Socio-economic Classification (NS-SEC) was introduced in April 2001 for all official statistics and surveys. NS-SEC classifies occupations according to different criteria compared with the Social Class and Socio-economic Group classifications which it replaces, and, in addition, the occupational classification underpinning the groupings also changed in 2001. The new NS-SEC is not designed to be collapsed into broad non-manual and manual groupings.

This follows another change introduced on the GHS in 2000, which was the replacement of the head of household with the household reference person as the basis for deriving a socio-economic variable reflecting the living standards of the household.

Tables 9.5 to 9.8 show four indicators of last week's drinking in relation to the eight- and three-category versions of NS-SEC based on the current or last job of the household reference person. These are the proportions of adults who:

- drank alcohol in the previous week;
- drank on five or more days last week;
- drank more than 4/3 units on at least one day last week;
- drank more than 8/6 units on at least one day last week.

Both men and women in managerial and professional households were more likely than other men and women to have drunk alcohol in the last week, and more likely to have done so on five or more days. Differences were particularly marked for women: among those in large employer/higher managerial households, 77% had a drink in the last week and 21% had done so on five or more days, compared with only 48% and 6% respectively of women in households where the household reference person was in a routine occupation. **Tables 9.5-9.6**

Variations in amounts drunk, however, were much less marked. Among men, indeed, there were no clear patterns of difference according to household socio-economic class: in nearly all groups about two fifths had drunk more than 4 units, and just over one fifth more than 8 units, on at least one day in the previous week. Among women, however, those in the three managerial and professional classes of household were more likely than other women to drink more than 3 units (26% compared with 20%) and also more likely to drink more than 6 units (11% compared with 8-9%). **Tables 9.7-9.8**

Daily drinking and household income

In general, the higher the level of gross weekly household income, the more likely both men and women were to have drunk alcohol in the previous week, and the more likely they were to have exceeded the recommended number of units for daily consumption.

- 84% of men in households with a gross weekly income of over £1,000 had a drink in the previous week and 47% had drunk more than four units on at least one day, but only 63% of men in households with an income of £200 or less had a drink and only 28% had drunk more than four units on any one day.

Similar differences according to household income were evident among women, although the proportions drinking and the proportions exceeding recommended levels were lower than for men.

Men and women in households with a gross weekly income of over £1,000 were almost twice as likely as those with a gross weekly household income of £200 or less to have drunk more than eight and six units respectively on at least one day in the previous week. **Table 9.9**

Daily drinking, economic activity status and earnings from employment

Among men aged 16 to 64, those in employment were more likely than men who were economically inactive to have drunk heavily during the previous week (27% of working men, 23% of unemployed men, and 15% of the economically inactive had done so). Lower levels of drinking among economically inactive men are partly due to the large proportion of this group who are aged 60 to 64.

One in seven working women (14%) aged 16 to 64 and the same proportion of those who were unemployed had drunk more than six units on at least one day during the previous week. This compares with 9% of women who were economically inactive. **Table 9.10**

Among those working full time, there was some variation in drinking behaviour in relation to earnings from employment, but the pattern of association was different to that described above in relation to household income.

There was a strong association between earnings and the frequency of drinking in the previous week - men and women who were high earners were more likely to have drunk alcohol at all, and more likely to have drunk on five or more days. Furthermore, differences between men and women were much smaller among high earners than among those at the other end of the earnings scale: among those with gross earnings of more than £800 a week, 90% of both men and women had drunk alcohol in the previous week, whereas among those earning £200 or less, 74% of men and only 62% of women had done so.

Variation in maximum amounts drunk on any one day in the previous week was, on the whole, less marked, and the pattern of association less clear. Among men, high earners were no more likely than other men in full-time work to have drunk more than four units on any one day in the previous week, and indeed they were less likely to have drunk more than eight units: 23% of men earning more than £800 a week had drunk more than eight units on at least one day in the last week, compared with 28% of all men in full-time employment.

Among women in full-time work, high earners were more likely than other women to have drunk more than three units on at least one day in the previous week, but much less likely to have drunk more than six units: 10% of women earning more than £800 a week had drunk more than six units on at least one day in the last week, compared with 19% of women earning £200 or less. **Table 9.11**

Regional variation in daily drinking

In 2001, men and women living in Scotland continued to be more likely than those living in England and Wales to have drunk heavily on at least one day in the previous week: 28% of men in Scotland had drunk more than eight units of alcohol on at least one day during the previous week compared with 21% in England and 20% in Wales. There was a similar pattern of differences among women: 13% of women in Scotland had drunk more than six units on at least one day in the previous week, compared with 9% of women in England and 11% of those in Wales.

Earlier GHS reports showed that among the regions of England, average weekly alcohol consumption tended to be higher in the north than in the south, but that this was mainly the case for men - differences for women were much less marked.

Maximum recommended daily amounts, however, appear to be much more likely to be exceeded by both men and women in the north (North East, North West, Yorkshire and the Humber, and East Midlands) than in the rest of England.

In the North East and North West, the English regions with the highest proportions drinking more than the daily benchmark amounts (47% of men and 28% of women), the proportions doing so were similar to those in Scotland (45% and 26% respectively). The equivalent figures for the South East were 33% of men and 20% of women. **Table 9.12**

Average weekly alcohol consumption

As noted in the introduction, the main GHS measure of drinking behaviour until 1998 was average weekly alcohol consumption, and this has been retained, primarily to give a continuing indication of trends in drinking behaviour.[7]

Average weekly alcohol consumption should not necessarily be expected to show the same patterns of variation in relation to respondents' characteristics as does the measure of daily consumption.

Trends in weekly alcohol consumption

Consideration of trends is complicated by the introduction of weighting in 2000. This increased the proportion of men drinking more than 21 units a week in 1998 by about one percentage point. The comparison of weighted and unweighted figures for 2000 and 2001, although not shown in the tables, is similar.

Over the period covered by the GHS, there has been a slight increase in overall weekly alcohol consumption among men, and a much more marked one among women, but in 2001, there was indication of a slight decline. The proportion of men drinking more than 21 units a week on average fell from 29% to 27% and there was a similar fall in the proportion of women drinking more than 14 units a week, from 17% in 2000 to 15% in 2001. There was no significant change in the proportion of men drinking on average more than 50 units a week, nor in the proportion of women drinking more than 35 units. **Table 9.13**

These changes are partially reflected in estimates of the average weekly alcohol consumption, which have been available since 1992, although the differences between the figures for 2000 and 2001 were not statistically significant .

- In 2001, men drank an average of 16.8 units a week (equivalent to almost 8.5 pints of beer), compared with 17.4 units in 2000. Women drank an average of 7.4 units a week, less than half as much as men, but this compared with 7.1 units in 2000.

The average consumption among young women aged 16 to 24 continues to rise: it increased from 12.6 units in 2000 to 14.0 units in 2001 - it has almost doubled in the ten years since 1992.

Among both men and women, alcohol consumption was highest among those aged 16 to 24, and then declined with increasing age. Overall, in 2001, men's consumption was more than twice that of women but the difference was less marked among younger than among older people. This again reflects the trend that has occurred in recent years for women's consumption to increase relative to that of men, particularly among younger age groups. **Table 9.14**

Weekly alcohol consumption and household socio-economic classification

The relationship between weekly alcohol consumption and socio-economic classification was similar to that shown earlier in relation to daily amounts, and also to that shown by previous surveys in relation to socio-economic group. There is no clear socio-economic gradient in relation to alcohol consumption among men: the highest weekly average was 19.1 units among men in the intermediate group, and the lowest, 15.5 units, among men in households where the reference person was in a semi-routine occupation.

The pattern among women was slightly clearer - average weekly consumption was highest, at 8.3 units, in the managerial and professional group, and lowest, at 6.4 units, among those in routine and manual worker households. **Table 9.15**

Weekly alcohol consumption, income and economic activity status

Average weekly alcohol consumption was higher among men and women in high income households than among other men and women: among those living in households with a gross income of more than £1,000 a week, men drank on average 19.1 units a week, and women, 9.4 units, compared with 15.2 units and 5.8 units respectively among those in households with an income of £200 or less.

Among those in full-time employment, however, there was no significant variation in average weekly alcohol consumption according to earnings. **Tables 9.16-9.18**

Weekly alcohol consumption and Government Office Region

The pattern of regional differences in England in relation to average weekly alcohol consumption was very similar to that seen for maximum amounts consumed on any day in the previous week. Overall, weekly consumption was highest in the same four regions (North East, North West, Yorkshire and the Humber, and East Midlands). This was also the case for women, but for men, the South West showed the fourth highest average weekly consumption, rather than the East Midlands.

However, the higher maximum daily amounts in Scotland are not reflected in average weekly consumption, which was lower in Scotland than England for both men and women: overall weekly consumption was 11.2 units in Scotland, compared with 12.0 in England. **Table 9.19**

Notes and references

1 Goddard E. *Obtaining information about drinking through surveys of the general population*. National Statistics Methodology Series NSM24 (ONS 2001).
2 *Sensible drinking: the report of an inter-departmental group*, Department of Health 1995.
3 One unit of alcohol is obtained from half a pint of normal strength beer, lager or cider, a single measure of spirits, one glass of wine, or one small glass of port, sherry or other fortified wine.
4 Alcohol by volume.
5 The method used to calculate an individual's average weekly alcohol consumption is to multiply the number of units of each type drunk on a usual drinking day by the frequency with which it was drunk, using the factors shown below, and totalling across all drinks.

Drinking frequency	Multiplying factor
Almost every day	7.0
5 or 6 days a week	5.5
3 or 4 days a week	3.5
Once or twice a week	1.5
Once or twice a month	0.375 (1.5/4)
Once every couple of months	0.115 (6/52)
Once or twice a year	0.029 (1.5/52)

6 Drever F, Bunting J, Harding D. *Male mortality from major causes of death* (in Drever F, Whitehead M, Eds. *Health inequalities: decennial supplement*: DS Series no.15. London: The Stationery Office, 1997) quoted in *Independent Inquiry into Inequalities in Health Report*. London: The Stationery Office 1998.
7 The earliest year shown in these trend tables is 1988, the first year in which data were collected from 16 and 17 year olds.

Table 9.1 Whether drank last week and number of drinking days by sex and age

Persons aged 16 and over *Great Britain: 2001*

Drinking days last week	Age 16-24	5–7	25-44	5–7	45-64	5–7	65 and over	5–7	Total	5–7
	%		%		%		%		%	
Men										
0	30		22		24		32		25	
1	21		18		18		17		18	
2	17		18		15		12		16	
3	11		13		10		8		11	
4	8		9		7		5		8	
5	5		6		6		3		5	
6	4	14	4	19	5	25	3	27	4	22
7	5		9		15		21		12	
% who drank last week	70		78		76		68		75	
Weighted base (000's) = 100%	*2,487*		*7,798*		*6,142*		*3,488*		*19,916*	
Unweighted sample	*775*		*2589*		*2289*		*1403*		*7056*	
	%		%		%		%		%	
Women										
0	41		34		39		55		41	
1	23		21		19		16		19	
2	13		17		12		7		13	
3	9		10		9		4		8	
4	5		6		5		2		5	
5	3		4		4		2		3	
6	2	8	2	11	2	17	1	15	2	13
7	3		5		11		12		8	
% who drank last week	59		66		61		45		59	
Weighted base (000's) = 100%	*2,550*		*8,105*		*6,562*		*4,765*		*21,981*	
Unweighted sample	*911*		*3044*		*2534*		*1808*		*8297*	
	%		%		%		%		%	
All persons										
0	35		28		32		45		33	
1	22		20		18		16		19	
2	15		17		14		9		14	
3	10		12		9		6		10	
4	7		8		6		3		6	
5	4		5		5		3		4	
6	3	11	3	15	3	21	2	20	3	17
7	4		7		13		15		10	
% who drank last week	65		72		68		55		67	
Weighted base (000's) = 100%	*5,037*		*15,903*		*12,704*		*8,253*		*41,897*	
Unweighted sample	*1686*		*5633*		*4823*		*3211*		*15353*	

Weighting to be revised in Spring 2003 following the 2001 census revisions of population estimates. See Appendix D.

Table 9.2 Drinking last week by sex and age: 1998 to 2001

Persons aged 16 and over *Great Britain*

Alcohol consumption last week	Weighted data														
	Age														
	16-24			25-44			45-64			65 and over			Total		
	1998	2000	2001	1998	2000	2001	1998	2000	2001	1998	2000	2001	1998	2000	2001
	Percentages														
Drank last week															
Men	70	70	70	79	78	78	77	77	76	65	67	68	75	75	75
Women	62	64	59	65	67	66	61	61	61	45	43	45	59	60	59
Drank on 5 or more days															
Men	13	11	14	21	19	19	29	26	25	25	28	27	23	22	22
Women	8	7	8	12	11	11	15	15	17	14	14	15	13	13	13
Drank more than 4/3 units* on at least one day															
Men	52	50	49	48	45	46	37	38	36	16	16	18	39	39	39
Women	42	42	39	28	31	30	17	19	19	4	4	5	21	23	22
Drank more than 8/6 units* on at least one day															
Men	39	37	36	29	27	28	17	17	16	4	5	5	22	21	21
Women	24	27	27	11	13	14	5	5	5	1	1	1	8	10	10
Weighted base (000's) =100%															
Men	*2,366*	*2,687*	*2,485*	*7,528*	*7,936*	*7,799*	*5,868*	*6,212*	*6,139*	*3,412*	*3,534*	*3,488*	*19,174*	*20,369*	*19,911*
Women	*2,580*	*2,633*	*2,549*	*7,995*	*8,091*	*8,104*	*6,306*	*6,588*	*6,566*	*4,744*	*4,742*	*4,765*	*21,625*	*22,054*	*21,985*
Unweighted sample															
Men	*699*	*791*	*774*	*2400*	*2311*	*2589*	*2132*	*2186*	*2288*	*1330*	*1310*	*1403*	*6561*	*6598*	*7054*
Women	*809*	*814*	*911*	*2910*	*2732*	*3044*	*2364*	*2357*	*2536*	*1738*	*1588*	*1808*	*7821*	*7491*	*8299*

* The first of each pair of figures shown relates to men, and the second, to women.

Weighting to be revised in Spring 2003 following the 2001 census revisions of population estimates. See Appendix D.

Table 9.3 **Maximum daily amount drunk last week by sex and age**

Persons aged 16 and over *Great Britain: 2001*

Maximum daily amount	Age 16-24		25-44		45-64		65 and over		Total	
	%		%		%		%		%	
Men										
Drank nothing last week	30		22		24		32		26	
Up to 4 units	21		31		39		50		36	
More than 4, up to 8 units	13	49	18	46	20	36	13	18	17	39
More than 8 units	36		28		16		5		21	
Weighted base (000's) =100%	*2,485*		*7,799*		*6,139*		*3,488*		*19,911*	
Unweighted sample	*774*		*2589*		*2288*		*1403*		*7054*	
	%		%		%		%		%	
Women										
Drank nothing last week	41		34		39		55		41	
Up to 3 units	20		36		42		40		37	
More than 3, up to 6 units	12	39	16	30	14	19	4	5	13	22
More than 6 units	27		14		5		1		10	
Weighted base (000's) =100%	*2,549*		*8,104*		*6,566*		*4,765*		*21,985*	
Unweighted sample	*911*		*3044*		*2536*		*1808*		*8299*	
	%		%		%		%		%	
All persons*										
Drank nothing last week	36		28		32		45		34	
Up to 4/3 units	21		34		41		44		36	
More than 4/3, up to 8/6 units	13	44	17	38	17	27	8	10	15	30
More than 8/6 units	31		21		11		3		15	
Weighted base (000's) =100%	*5,034*		*15,903*		*12,705*		*8,253*		*41,895*	
Unweighted sample	*1685*		*5633*		*4824*		*3211*		*15353*	

* The first of each pair of figures shown relates to men, and the second, to women.

Weighting to be revised in Spring 2003 following the 2001 census revisions of population estimates. See Appendix D.

Table 9.4 **Drinking last week, by sex, age and marital status**

Persons aged 16 and over *Great Britain: 2001*

Marital status	Men			Women			Total		
	16-44	45 and over	Total	16-44	45 and over	Total	16-44	45 and over	Total
				Percentage who drank last week					
Single	73	62	71	61	43	58	68	54	66
Married/cohabiting	79	75	76	67	60	63	72	68	70
Divorced/separated	73	73	73	58	50	54	64	60	61
Widowed	*	66	66	*	43	43	[69]	48	48
Total	76	73	75	64	54	59	70	63	67
				Percentage who drank on five or more days last week					
Single	14	28	16	9	14	9	12	22	13
Married/cohabiting	21	26	24	12	18	15	16	22	19
Divorced/separated	13	26	21	9	12	11	11	18	15
Widowed	*	22	21	*	14	14	[7]	16	16
Total	18	26	22	11	16	13	14	21	17
				Percentage who drank more than 4/3 units on at least one day last week					
Single	50	30	47	39	10	35	45	21	41
Married/cohabiting	45	29	36	30	16	23	37	23	29
Divorced/separated	49	39	43	29	12	19	36	23	28
Widowed	*	20	21	*	6	7	[40]	9	10
Total	47	30	39	32	13	22	40	21	30
				Percentage who drank more than 8/6 units on at least one day last week					
Single	35	14	32	24	4	21	30	10	27
Married/cohabiting	27	12	18	13	4	9	20	8	13
Divorced/separated	29	20	23	15	4	8	20	11	14
Widowed	*	6	6	*	1	1	[16]	2	2
Total	30	12	21	17	3	10	23	7	15
Weighted base (000's) =100%									
Single	*4,152*	*745*	*4,897*	*3,191*	*550*	*3,741*	*7,343*	*1,295*	*8,638*
Married/cohabiting	*5,607*	*7,290*	*12,897*	*6,559*	*7,015*	*13,574*	*12,165*	*14,305*	*26,471*
Divorced/separated	*506*	*865*	*1,371*	*856*	*1,234*	*2,090*	*1,362*	*2,099*	*3,461*
Widowed	*20*	*727*	*746*	*47*	*2,532*	*2,579*	*67*	*3,259*	*3,326*
Total	*10,284*	*9,627*	*19,911*	*10,653*	*11,332*	*21,985*	*20,937*	*20,958*	*41,895*
Unweighted sample									
Single	*1241*	*254*	*1495*	*1214*	*206*	*1420*	*2455*	*460*	*2915*
Married/cohabiting	*1976*	*2863*	*4839*	*2377*	*2728*	*5105*	*4353*	*5591*	*9944*
Divorced/separated	*140*	*293*	*433*	*346*	*457*	*803*	*486*	*750*	*1236*
Widowed	*6*	*281*	*287*	*18*	*953*	*971*	*24*	*1234*	*1258*
Total	*3363*	*3691*	*7054*	*3955*	*4344*	*8299*	*7318*	*8035*	*15353*

* Base too small for analysis.

Weighting to be revised in Spring 2003 following the 2001 census revisions of population estimates. See Appendix D.

Table 9.5 Whether drank last week by sex, and socio-economic classification based on the current or last job of the household reference person

Persons aged 16 and over *Great Britain: 2001*

Socio-economic classification household reference person*	Men		Women		Total	
	Percentage who drank last week					
Managerial and professional						
Large employers and higher managerial	87		77		82	
Higher professional	83	82	73	71	78	76
Lower managerial and professional	80		68		74	
Intermediate						
Intermediate	75	74	58	59	64	66
Small employers/own account	74		60		67	
Routine and manual						
Lower supervisory and technical	74		58		66	
Semi-routine	63	68	48	51	54	59
Routine	67		48		57	
Total*	75		59		67	
Weighted bases (000's) =100%						
Large employers and higher managerial	*1,328*		*1,275*		*2,604*	
Higher professional	*2,000*		*1,730*		*3,730*	
Lower managerial and professional	*4,404*		*4,947*		*9,351*	
Intermediate	*1,344*		*2,079*		*3,423*	
Small employers/own account	*2,015*		*1,889*		*3,904*	
Lower supervisory and technical	*2,814*		*2,505*		*5,319*	
Semi-routine	*2,409*		*3,246*		*5,655*	
Routine	*2,730*		*3,103*		*5,833*	
*Total**	*19,842*		*21,835*		*41,677*	
Unweighted sample						
Large employers and higher managerial	*498*		*494*		*992*	
Higher professional	*726*		*673*		*1399*	
Lower managerial and professional	*1590*		*1901*		*3491*	
Intermediate	*466*		*784*		*1250*	
Small employers/own account	*720*		*708*		*1428*	
Lower supervisory and technical	*985*		*917*		*1902*	
Semi-routine	*849*		*1234*		*2083*	
Routine	*956*		*1151*		*2107*	
*Total**	*7032*		*8246*		*15278*	

* From April 2001 the National Statistics Socio-economic Classification (NS-SEC) was introduced for all official statistics and surveys. It has replaced Social Class based on Occupation and Socio-economic Groups (SEG). Full-time students, persons in inadequately described occupations, persons who have never worked and the long term unemployed are not shown as separate categories, but are included in the figure for all persons (see Appendix A).

Weighting to be revised in Spring 2003 following the 2001 census revisions of population estimates. See Appendix D.

Table 9.6 **Percentage who drank on 5 or more days last week, by sex, and socio-economic classification based on the current or last job of the household reference person**

Persons aged 16 and over *Great Britain: 2001*

Socio-economic classification of household reference person*	Men		Women		Total	
	Percentage who drank on 5 or more days last week					
Managerial and professional						
Large employers and higher managerial	35		21		28	
Higher professional	29	29	22	19	25	24
Lower managerial and professional	26		17		21	
Intermediate						
Intermediate	19	22	14	14	16	18
Small employers/own account	23		15		19	
Routine and manual						
Lower supervisory and technical	19		12		16	
Semi-routine	14	16	8	9	11	12
Routine	13		6		10	
Total*	22		13		17	
Weighted bases (000's) =100%						
Large employers and higher managerial	*1,328*		*1,275*		*2,604*	
Higher professional	*2,000*		*1,730*		*3,730*	
Lower managerial and professional	*4,404*		*4,947*		*9,351*	
Intermediate	*1,344*		*2,079*		*3,423*	
Small employers/own account	*2,015*		*1,889*		*3,904*	
Lower supervisory and technical	*2,814*		*2,505*		*5,319*	
Semi-routine	*2,409*		*3,246*		*5,655*	
Routine	*2,730*		*3,103*		*5,833*	
*Total**	*19,842*		*21,835*		*41,677*	
Unweighted sample						
Large employers and higher managerial	*498*		*494*		*992*	
Higher professional	*726*		*673*		*1399*	
Lower managerial and professional	*1590*		*1901*		*3491*	
Intermediate	*466*		*784*		*1250*	
Small employers/own account	*720*		*708*		*1428*	
Lower supervisory and technical	*985*		*917*		*1902*	
Semi-routine	*849*		*1234*		*2083*	
Routine	*956*		*1151*		*2107*	
*Total**	*7032*		*8246*		*15278*	

* From April 2001 the National Statistics Socio-economic Classification (NS-SEC) was introduced for all official statistics and surveys. It has replaced Social Class based on Occupation and Socio-economic Groups (SEG). Full-time students, persons in inadequately described occupations, persons who have never worked and the long term unemployed are not shown as separate categories, but are included in the figure for all persons (see Appendix A).

Weighting to be revised in Spring 2003 following the 2001 census revisions of population estimates. See Appendix D.

Table 9.7 **Percentage who drank more than 4 units (men) and 3 units (women) on at least one day last week, by sex, and socio-economic classification based on the current or last job of the household reference person**

Persons aged 16 and over *Great Britain: 2001*

Socio-economic classification of household reference person*	Men		Women		Total	
	Percentage who drank more than 4/3 units on at least one day last week					
Managerial and professional						
Large employers and higher managerial	41	39	27	26	34	33
Higher professional	38		25		32	
Lower managerial and professional	40		26		32	
Intermediate						
Intermediate	39	38	21	20	28	29
Small employers/own account	38		19		29	
Routine and manual						
Lower supervisory and technical	41	38	22	20	32	28
Semi-routine	35		19		26	
Routine	37		20		28	
Total*	39		22		30	
Weighted bases (000's) =100%						
Large employers and higher managerial	*1,328*		*1,277*		*2,606*	
Higher professional	*1,997*		*1,730*		*3,727*	
Lower managerial and professional	*4,407*		*4,953*		*9,359*	
Intermediate	*1,340*		*2,079*		*3,420*	
Small employers/own account	*2,012*		*1,889*		*3,901*	
Lower supervisory and technical	*2,823*		*2,502*		*5,325*	
Semi-routine	*2,409*		*3,243*		*5,653*	
Routine	*2,726*		*3,105*		*5,831*	
*Total**	*19,837*		*21,839*		*41,675*	
Unweighted sample						
Large employers and higher managerial	*498*		*495*		*993*	
Higher professional	*725*		*673*		*1398*	
Lower managerial and professional	*1591*		*1903*		*3494*	
Intermediate	*465*		*784*		*1249*	
Small employers/own account	*719*		*708*		*1427*	
Lower supervisory and technical	*987*		*916*		*1903*	
Semi-routine	*849*		*1233*		*2082*	
Routine	*955*		*1152*		*2107*	
*Total**	*7030*		*8248*		*15278*	

* From April 2001 the National Statistics Socio-economic Classification (NS-SEC) was introduced for all official statistics and surveys. It has replaced Social Class based on Occupation and Socio-economic Groups (SEG). Full-time students, persons in inadequately described occupations, persons who have never worked and the long term unemployed are not shown as separate categories, but are included in the figure for all persons (see Appendix A).

Weighting to be revised in Spring 2003 following the 2001 census revisions of population estimates. See Appendix D.

Table 9.8 Percentage who drank more than 8 units (men) and 6 units (women) on at least one day last week, by sex, and socio-economic classification based on the current or last job of the household reference person

Persons aged 16 and over *Great Britain: 2001*

Socio-economic classification of the household reference person*	Men		Women		Total	
	Percentage who drank more than 8/6 units on at least one day last week					
Managerial and professional						
Large employers and higher managerial	22		11		16	
Higher professional	21	22	9	11	15	16
Lower managerial and professional	22		11		16	
Intermediate						
Intermediate	21	22	9	8	14	15
Small employers/own account	23		8		16	
Routine and manual						
Lower supervisory and technical	21		10		16	
Semi-routine	19	21	10	9	14	14
Routine	21		8		14	
Total*	21		10		15	
Weighted bases (000's) =100%						
Large employers and higher managerial	*1,328*		*1,277*		*2,606*	
Higher professional	*1,997*		*1,730*		*3,727*	
Lower managerial and professional	*4,407*		*4,953*		*9,359*	
Intermediate	*1,340*		*2,079*		*3,420*	
Small employers/own account	*2,012*		*1,889*		*3,901*	
Lower supervisory and technical	*2,823*		*2,502*		*5,325*	
Semi-routine	*2,409*		*3,243*		*5,653*	
Routine	*2,726*		*3,105*		*5,831*	
*Total**	*19,837*		*21,839*		*41,675*	
Unweighted sample						
Large employers and higher managerial	*498*		*495*		*993*	
Higher professional	*725*		*673*		*1398*	
Lower managerial and professional	*1591*		*1903*		*3494*	
Intermediate	*465*		*784*		*1249*	
Small employers/own account	*719*		*708*		*1427*	
Lower supervisory and technical	*987*		*916*		*1903*	
Semi-routine	*849*		*1233*		*2082*	
Routine	*955*		*1152*		*2107*	
*Total**	*7030*		*8248*		*15278*	

* From April 2001 the National Statistics Socio-economic Classification (NS-SEC) was introduced for all official statistics and surveys. It has replaced Social Class based on Occupation and Socio-economic Groups (SEG). Full-time students, persons in inadequately described occupations, persons who have never worked and the long term unemployed are not shown as separate categories, but are included in the figure for all persons (see Appendix A).

Weighting to be revised in Spring 2003 following the 2001 census revisions of population estimates. See Appendix D.

Table 9.9 **Drinking last week by sex and usual gross weekly household income**

Persons aged 16 and over *Great Britain: 2001*

Drinking last week	Usual gross weekly household income (£)						
	Up to 200.00	200.01 -400.00	400.01 -600.00	600.01 -800.00	800.01 -1000.00	1000.01 or more	Total*
				Percentages			
Drank last week							
Men	63	71	76	79	82	84	75
Women	47	54	63	67	69	76	59
All persons	53	62	70	74	76	80	67
Drank on 5 or more days							
Men	17	20	20	21	24	34	22
Women	11	12	14	12	15	21	13
All persons	13	16	17	16	20	28	17
Drank more than 4/3 units† on at least one day							
Men	28	34	43	44	45	47	39
Women	16	20	27	27	28	30	22
All persons	21	27	35	36	37	39	30
Drank more than 8/6 units† on at least one day							
Men	14	17	27	25	27	26	21
Women	7	8	12	12	14	13	10
All persons	10	12	19	18	21	19	15
Weighted base (000's) = 100%							
Men	*3,696*	*4,148*	*3,574*	*2,683*	*1,793*	*2,467*	*19,916*
Women	*5,632*	*4,573*	*3,564*	*2,529*	*1,572*	*2,244*	*21,981*
All persons	*9,328*	*8,721*	*7,138*	*5,213*	*3,365*	*4,711*	*41,897*
Unweighted sample							
Men	*1296*	*1460*	*1265*	*953*	*636*	*877*	*7056*
Women	*2143*	*1742*	*1341*	*944*	*586*	*840*	*8297*
All persons	*3439*	*3202*	*2606*	*1897*	*1222*	*1717*	*15278*

* Includes people for whom income data was not known.
† The first of each pair of figures shown relates to men, and the second, to women.

Weighting to be revised in Spring 2003 following the 2001 census revisions of population estimates. See Appendix D.

Table 9.10 Drinking last week by sex and economic activity status

Persons aged 16-64 — *Great Britain: 2001*

Drinking last week	Economic activity status			
	Working	Unemployed	Economically inactive	Total
	Percentages			
Drank last week				
Men	80	62	62	76
Women	68	59	52	63
All persons	74	61	56	69
Drank on 5 or more days				
Men	22	11	18	21
Women	14	9	12	13
All persons	18	11	14	17
Drank more than 4/3 units on at least one day*				
Men	46	35	32	43
Women	30	31	21	27
All persons	38	34	25	35
Drank more than 8/6 units on at least one day*				
Men	27	23	15	25
Women	14	14	9	12
All persons	21	20	11	19
Weighted base (000's) =100%				
Men	*13,054*	*668*	*2,702*	*16,423*
Women	*11,657*	*408*	*5,151*	*17,216*
All persons	*24,710*	*1,075*	*7,853*	*33,639*
Unweighted sample				
Men	*4516*	*214*	*921*	*5651*
Women	*4344*	*150*	*1996*	*6490*
All persons	*8860*	*364*	*2917*	*12141*

* The first of each pair of figures shown relates to men, and the second, to women.

Weighting to be revised in Spring 2003 following the 2001 census revisions of population estimates. See Appendix D.

Table 9.11 Drinking last week by sex and usual gross weekly earnings

Persons aged 16-64 in full-time employment *Great Britain: 2001*

Drinking last week	Usual gross weekly earnings (£)						
	Up to 200.00	200.01 -300.00	300.01 -400.00	400.01 -600.00	600.01 -800.00	800.01 or more	Total*
				Percentages			
Drank last week							
Men	74	77	78	83	87	90	81
Women	62	69	74	75	82	90	71
All persons	69	73	76	80	86	90	77
Drank on 5 or more days							
Men	20	17	17	21	36	35	22
Women	11	12	13	16	30	30	14
All persons	16	15	16	20	34	34	19
Drank more than 4/3 units† on at least one day							
Men	44	46	47	50	47	47	47
Women	33	31	35	34	41	39	33
All persons	39	39	43	45	46	46	42
Drank more than 8/6 units† on at least one day							
Men	28	28	30	29	25	23	28
Women	19	16	16	14	14	10	16
All persons	23	23	25	24	23	21	23
Weighted base (000's) = 100%							
Men	*1,337*	*2,357*	*2,386*	*2,708*	*1,116*	*1,143*	*11,485*
Women	*1,291*	*1,894*	*1,214*	*1,197*	*321*	*251*	*6,352*
All persons	*2,629*	*4,252*	*3,601*	*3,905*	*1,437*	*1,394*	*17,837*
Unweighted sample							
Men	*454*	*802*	*816*	*945*	*391*	*406*	*3966*
Women	*472*	*700*	*451*	*442*	*117*	*91*	*2342*
All persons	*926*	*1502*	*1267*	*1387*	*508*	*497*	*6308*

* Includes people for whom income data was not known.
† The first of each pair of figures shown relates to men, and the second, to women.

Weighting to be revised in Spring 2003 following the 2001 census revisions of population estimates. See Appendix D.

Table 9.12 **Drinking last week, by sex and Government Office Region**

Persons aged 16 and over *Great Britain: 2001*

Government Office Region	Drinking last week					
	Drank last week	Drank on 5 or more days last week	Drank more than 4/3 units on at least one day*	Drank more than 8/6 units on at least one day*	*Weighted base (000's) = 100%*	*Unweighted sample*
			Percentages			
Men						
North East	70	17	47	28	*929*	*331*
North West	78	21	47	27	*2,260*	*865*
Yorkshire and the Humber	78	21	43	26	*1,601*	*621*
East Midlands	75	22	42	21	*1,612*	*542*
West Midlands	72	23	33	17	*1,723*	*654*
East of England	72	22	33	19	*1,826*	*690*
London	70	22	35	19	*2,540*	*773*
South East	75	25	33	17	*2,874*	*1016*
South West	79	24	37	19	*1,842*	*636*
England	74	22	38	21	*17,207*	*6128*
Wales	72	19	36	20	*949*	*342*
Scotland	77	16	45	28	*1,755*	*584*
Great Britain	75	22	39	21	*19,911*	*7054*
Women						
North East	55	11	28	15	*985*	*376*
North West	63	12	28	13	*2,514*	*1027*
Yorkshire and the Humber	60	14	24	12	*1,818*	*749*
East Midlands	65	16	26	12	*1,724*	*617*
West Midlands	54	12	17	7	*1,799*	*721*
East of England	59	15	20	8	*1,945*	*789*
London	54	11	17	8	*2,662*	*894*
South East	61	16	20	7	*3,252*	*1199*
South West	64	16	23	8	*2,152*	*787*
England	60	14	22	9	*18,851*	*7159*
Wales	54	13	21	11	*1,088*	*405*
Scotland	57	10	26	13	*2,046*	*735*
Great Britain	59	13	22	10	*21,985*	*8299*
Total						
North East	62	14	37	21	*1,914*	*707*
North West	70	16	37	19	*4,774*	*1892*
Yorkshire and the Humber	68	17	33	19	*3,419*	*1370*
East Midlands	70	19	34	17	*3,336*	*1159*
West Midlands	63	18	25	12	*3,522*	*1375*
East of England	65	18	27	13	*3,772*	*1479*
London	62	16	26	13	*5,202*	*1667*
South East	68	20	26	12	*6,126*	*2215*
South West	71	19	29	13	*3,993*	*1423*
England	67	18	30	15	*36,058*	*13287*
Wales	63	16	28	15	*2,037*	*747*
Scotland	66	13	35	20	*3,801*	*1319*
Great Britain	67	17	30	15	*41,895*	*15353*

* The first of each pair of figures shown relates to men, and the second, to women.

Weighting to be revised in Spring 2003 following the 2001 census revisions of population estimates. See Appendix D.

Table 9.13 Weekly alcohol consumption: percentage exceeding specified amounts by sex and age: 1988 to 2001

Persons aged 16 and over *Great Britain*

Age	Men								Women							
	Unweighted					Weighted			Unweighted					Weighted		
	1988	1992	1994	1996	1998	1998	2000	2001	1988	1992	1994	1996	1998	1998	2000	2001
	Percentage who drank more than 21 units								Percentage who drank more than 14 units							
16-24	31	32	29	35	36	38	41	39	15	17	19	22	25	25	33	31
25-44	34	31	30	30	27	28	30	30	14	14	15	16	16	16	19	17
45-64	24	25	27	26	30	30	28	26	9	11	12	13	16	15	14	14
65 and over	13	15	17	18	16	16	17	15	4	5	7	7	6	6	7	6
Total	26	26	27	27	27	28	29	27	10	11	13	14	15	15	17	15
	Percentage who drank more than 50 units								Percentage who drank more than 35 units							
16-24	10	9	9	10	13	14	14	14	3	4	4	5	6	7	9	10
25-44	9	8	7	6	6	6	7	7	2	2	2	2	2	2	3	3
45-64	6	6	6	5	6	7	6	5	1	1	2	2	2	2	2	2
65 and over	2	2	3	3	3	3	3	2	0	0	1	1	1	1	1	1
Total	7	6	6	6	6	7	7	6	2	2	2	2	2	2	3	3
*Weighted base (000's) =100%**																
16-24						*2,370*	*2,681*	*2,484*						*2,577*	*2,620*	*2,550*
25-44						*7,529*	*7,933*	*7,798*						*7,994*	*8,072*	*8,105*
45-64						*5,876*	*6,208*	*6,130*						*6,312*	*6,582*	*6,564*
65 and over						*3,413*	*3,536*	*3,485*						*4,753*	*4,736*	*4,765*
Total						*19,188*	*20,358*	*19,897*						*21,636*	*22,011*	*21,983*
*Unweighted sample**																
16-24	*1356*	*1144*	*951*	*880*	*701*		*789*	*774*	*1530*	*1271*	*1069*	*968*	*807*		*812*	*911*
25-44	*3185*	*3056*	*2855*	*2612*	*2400*		*2310*	*2589*	*3530*	*3492*	*3437*	*3179*	*2909*		*2729*	*3044*
45-64	*2557*	*2598*	*2376*	*2214*	*2135*		*2185*	*2285*	*2749*	*2828*	*2560*	*2508*	*2366*		*2356*	*2535*
65 and over	*1575*	*1597*	*1454*	*1445*	*1331*		*1311*	*1402*	*2313*	*2156*	*2038*	*1836*	*1741*		*1589*	*1808*
Total	*8673*	*8395*	*7636*	*7151*	*6567*		*6595*	*7050*	*10122*	*9747*	*9104*	*8491*	*7823*		*7486*	*8298*

* Trend tables show unweighted and weighted figures for 1998 to give an indication of the effect of the weighting. For the weighted data (1998, 2000 and 2001) the weighted base (000's) is the base for percentages. Unweighted data (up to 1998) are based on the unweighted sample.

Weighting to be revised in Spring 2003 following the 2001 census revisions of population estimates. See Appendix D.

Table 9.14 **Average weekly alcohol consumption by sex and age: 1992 to 2001**

Persons aged 16 and over *Great Britain*

Age	Unweighted				Weighted			*Weighted base 2001 (000's) = 100%**	*Unweighted sample* 2001*
	1992	1994	1996	1998	1998	2000	2001		
	Mean number of units per week								
Men									
16-24	19.1	17.4	20.3	23.6	25.5	25.9	24.1	*2.484*	*774*
25-44	18.2	17.5	17.6	16.5	17.1	17.7	17.9	*7,798*	*2589*
45-64	15.6	15.5	15.6	17.3	17.4	16.8	15.9	*6,130*	*2285*
65 and over	9.7	10.0	11.0	10.7	10.6	11.0	10.7	*3,485*	*1402*
Total	15.9	15.4	16.0	16.4	17.1	17.4	16.8	*19,897*	*7050*
Women									
16-24	7.3	7.7	9.5	10.6	11.0	12.6	14.0	*2,550*	*94*
25-44	6.3	6.2	7.2	7.1	7.1	8.1	8.2	*8,104*	*3044*
45-64	5.3	5.3	5.9	6.4	6.4	6.2	6.8	*6,564*	*2535*
65 and over	2.7	3.2	3.5	3.3	3.2	3.5	3.6	*4,765*	*1808*
Total	5.4	5.4	6.3	6.4	6.5	7.1	7.4	*21,983*	*8298*
All persons									
16-24	12.9	12.3	14.7	16.6	18.0	19.3	18.9	*5,033*	*1685*
25-44	11.8	11.4	11.9	11.4	12.0	12.9	13.0	*15,903*	*5633*
45-64	10.2	10.2	10.5	11.6	11.7	11.4	11.2	*12,694*	*4820*
65 and over	5.6	6.0	6.8	6.5	6.3	6.7	6.6	*8,250*	*3210*
Total	10.2	10.0	10.7	11.0	11.5	12.0	11.9	*41,880*	*15348*

* Trend tables show unweighted and weighted figures for 1998 to give an indication of the effect of the weighting. For the weighted data (1998, 2000 and 2001) the weighted base (000's) is the base for percentages. Unweighted data (up to 1998) are based on the unweighted sample. Unweighted bases for earlier years are of similar size to the unweighted sample and can be found in GHS reports for each year.

Weighting to be revised in Spring 2003 following the 2001 census revisions of population estimates. See Appendix D.

Table 9.15 **Average weekly alcohol consumption, by sex and socio-economic classification based on the current or last job of the household reference person**

Persons aged 16 and over *Great Britain: 2001*

Socio-economic classification of household reference person*	Men		Women		Total	
	Mean number of units per week					
Managerial and professional						
Large employers and higher managerial	17.4	16.7	8.7	8.3	13.1	12.4
Higher professional	16.2		8.2		12.5	
Lower managerial and professional	16.7		8.1		12.2	
Intermediate						
Intermediate	19.1	17.6	6.8	7.0	11.7	11.9
Small employers/own account	16.6		7.2		12.0	
Routine and manual						
Lower supervisory and technical	16.5	16.0	7.0	6.4	12.0	10.9
Semi-routine	15.5		5.8		9.9	
Routine	16.0		6.5		10.9	
Total*	16.8		7.4		11.9	
Weighted bases (000's) =100%						
Large employers and higher managerial	*1,328*		*1,277*		*2,606*	
Higher professional	*1,997*		*1,730*		*3,727*	
Lower managerial and professional	*4,407*		*4,950*		*9,357*	
Intermediate	*1,344*		*2,079*		*3,423*	
Small employers/own account	*2,010*		*1,889*		*3,899*	
Lower supervisory and technical	*2,808*		*2,505*		*5,313*	
Semi-routine	*2,409*		*3,244*		*5,653*	
Routine	*2,727*		*3,103*		*5,830*	
*Total**	*19,823*		*21,837*		*41,660*	
Unweighted sample						
Large employers and higher managerial	*498*		*495*		*993*	
Higher professional	*725*		*673*		*1398*	
Lower managerial and professional	*1591*		*1902*		*3493*	
Intermediate	*466*		*784*		*1250*	
Small employers/own account	*718*		*708*		*1426*	
Lower supervisory and technical	*983*		*917*		*1900*	
Semi-routine	*849*		*1233*		*2082*	
Routine	*955*		*1151*		*2106*	
*Total**	*7026*		*8247*		*15273*	

* From April 2001 the National Statistics Socio-economic Classification (NS-SEC) was introduced for all official statistics and surveys. It has replaced Social Class based on Occupation and Socio-economic Groups (SEG). Full-time students, persons in inadequately described occupations, persons who have never worked and the long term unemployed are not shown as separate categories, but are included in the figure for all persons (see Appendix A).

Weighting to be revised in Spring 2003 following the 2001 census revisions of population estimates. See Appendix D.

Table 9.16 Average weekly alcohol consumption, by sex and usual gross weekly household income

Persons aged 16 and over — *Great Britain: 2001*

Usual gross weekly household income (£)	Men	Women	Total	Weighted base (000's) =100%			Unweighted sample		
				Men	Women	Total	Men	Women	Total
	Mean number of units per week								
Up to 200.00	15.2	5.8	9.6	3,686	5,628	9,314	1293	2141	3434
200.01-400.00	14.7	6.7	10.5	4,145	4,573	8,718	1459	1742	3201
400.01-600.00	18.0	8.2	13.1	3,574	3,566	7,140	1265	1342	2607
600.01-800.00	17.5	8.0	12.9	2,681	2,529	5,210	952	944	1896
800.01-1000.00	19.6	9.3	14.8	1,793	1,572	3,365	636	586	1222
1000.01 or more	19.1	9.4	14.5	2,467	2,246	4,713	877	841	1718
Total	16.8	7.4	11.9	19,897	21,983	41,880	7050	8298	15348

Weighting to be revised in Spring 2003 following the 2001 census revisions of population estimates. See Appendix D.

Table 9.17 Average weekly alcohol consumption, by sex and economic activity status

Persons aged 16 and over — *Great Britain: 2001*

Economic activity status	Men	Women	Total	Weighted base (000's) =100%			Unweighted sample		
				Men	Women	Total	Men	Women	Total
	Mean number of units per week								
Working	18.5	9.1	14.0	13,056	11,656	24,713	4516	4344	8860
Unemployed	18.4	9.1	14.9	670	408	1,078	215	150	365
Economically inactive	16.5	7.2	10.4	2,686	5,150	7,836	917	1995	2912
Total	18.1	8.5	13.2	16,412	17,214	33,626	5648	6489	12137

Weighting to be revised in Spring 2003 following the 2001 census revisions of population estimates. See Appendix D.

Table 9.18 Average weekly alcohol consumption, by sex and usual gross weekly earnings

Persons aged 16-64 in full time employment — *Great Britain: 2001*

Usual gross weekly earnings (£)	Men	Women	Total	Weighted base (000's) =100%			Unweighted sample		
				Men	Women	Total	Men	Women	Total
	Mean number of units per week								
Up to 200.00	19.1	10.0	14.6	1,335	1,291	2,626	453	472	925
200.01-300.00	19.4	9.9	15.1	2,357	1,894	4,252	802	700	1502
300.01-400.00	17.7	9.3	14.9	2,386	1,214	3,601	816	451	1267
400.01-600.00	18.7	9.7	16.0	2,711	1,197	3,908	946	442	1388
600.01-800.00	18.7	9.7	16.7	1,114	321	1,434	390	117	507
800.01 or more	18.5	10.0	17.0	1,143	251	1,394	406	91	497
Total	18.5	9.7	15.4	11,483	6,352	17,835	3965	2342	6307

Weighting to be revised in Spring 2003 following the 2001 census revisions of population estimates. See Appendix D.

Table 9.19 **Average weekly alcohol consumption, by sex and Government Office Region**

Persons aged 16 and over — *Great Britain: 2001*

Government Office Region	Men	Women	Total	*Weighted base (000's) =100%*			*Unweighted sample*		
				Men	*Women*	*Total*	*Men*	*Women*	*Total*
	Mean number of units per week								
North East	21.5	8.4	14.8	*929*	*985*	*1,914*	*331*	*376*	*707*
North West	18.8	8.4	13.3	*2,256*	*2,517*	*4,773*	*864*	*1028*	*1892*
Yorkshire and the Humber	19.0	8.9	13.6	*1,598*	*1,818*	*3,416*	*620*	*749*	*1369*
East Midlands	16.9	8.8	12.7	*1,609*	*1,724*	*3,333*	*541*	*617*	*1158*
West Midlands	16.4	6.8	11.5	*1,723*	*1,797*	*3,519*	*654*	*720*	*1374*
East of England	15.0	6.8	10.8	*1,826*	*1,943*	*3,769*	*690*	*788*	*1478*
London	14.7	5.7	10.1	*2,531*	*2,662*	*5,193*	*771*	*894*	*1665*
South East	15.8	7.3	11.3	*2,874*	*3,252*	*6,126*	*1016*	*1199*	*2215*
South West	17.8	7.5	12.2	*1,845*	*2,149*	*3,994*	*637*	*786*	*1423*
England	16.9	7.5	12.0	*17,192*	*18,847*	*36,039*	*6124*	*7157*	*13281*
Wales	16.5	7.3	11.5	*946*	*1,091*	*2,037*	*341*	*406*	*747*
Scotland	16.1	6.9	11.2	*1,759*	*2,046*	*3,804*	*585*	*735*	*1320*
Great Britain	16.8	7.4	11.9	*19,897*	*21,983*	*41,880*	*7050*	*8298*	*15348*

Weighting to be revised in Spring 2003 following the 2001 census revisions of population estimates. See Appendix D.

Chapter 10

Mobility difficulties and mobility aids

Questions about difficulties with mobility and the possession of mobility aids have previously been asked on the GHS in 1993 and 1996. The information from these questions is used to provide estimates of the proportion of people who need aids to get about, the proportion who have mobility aids and also the proportion of aids that people have but do not use. All respondents aged 16 and over were asked if they had any mobility difficulties and also if they had any mobility aids.

Prevalence of mobility difficulties

In 2001, 8% of adults reported having difficulties with getting around their home and/or going out of doors and walking down the road without assistance. This was the same proportion as in 1993 and 1996. Eight percent of all adults said they had a permanent difficulty with mobility and 1% said they had a temporary difficulty with mobility due to either an accident or illness.[1]

As one would expect, the likelihood of having difficulties with mobility increased with age. It should be noted that the GHS does not collect data on people living in institutions because the sample is based on private households. Therefore it is possible that the proportions of those with mobility difficulties are an underestimation of the true population figures, particularly among those aged 75 and over.

Figure 10A **Number of mobility aids per person*: Great Britain, 2001**

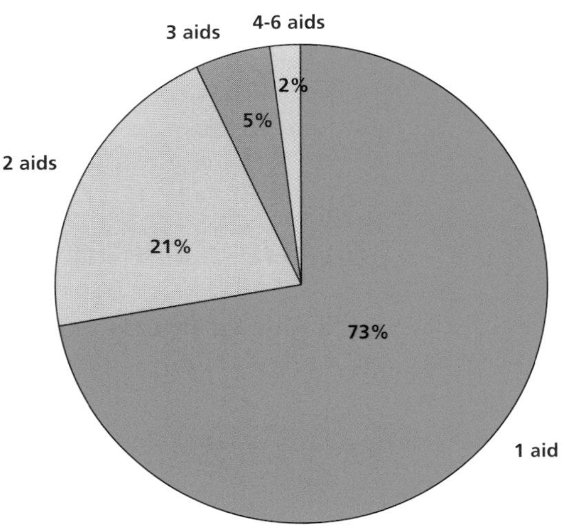

- Among men, 4% aged 16 to 64 reported having mobility difficulties compared with over half of men (52%) aged 85 and over.
- Four percent of women aged 16 to 64 reported having a mobility difficulty whereas 68% of women aged 85 and over did so.

Overall, women were more likely than men to report having a difficulty with mobility (9% compared with 7%). The greatest difference was among the very elderly; 52% of men aged 85 and over reported having mobility difficulties compared with 68% of women in the same age group. This is consistent with the finding in Chapter 7 (health) that women particularly in the older age groups were more likely than men to report a musculoskeletal problem. **Table 10.1**

Possession of mobility aids

Table 10.2 shows the proportion of people with at least one mobility aid by sex and age. In 2001, 9% of all adults reported that they had at least one aid. As would be expected, the likelihood of having a mobility aid increased with age. Although there were no statistically significant differences between men and women within each age group, overall women were slightly more likely than men to have at least one mobility aid (9% compared with 8%).

- Among adults who reported they had a mobility difficulty, 72% said they possessed at least one aid.
- 26% of those who reported permanent mobility difficulties said that they did not have a mobility aid of any kind.
- 3% of all adults who did not report a problem with mobility possessed at least one aid; around the same level as in 1993 and 1996.
- Among those who did not report mobility difficulties, adults in the oldest age group (75 and over) were the most likely to have a mobility aid; 16% did so compared with 8% of those aged 65 to 74 and 1% of those aged 16 to 64.

Figure 10A, Tables 10.2-10.4

People with mobility difficulties

Over half (52%) of adults with mobility difficulties said that they experienced difficulties indoors and outdoors, 43% of adults experienced difficulties outdoors only and 4% experienced difficulties indoors only. There was little association between where mobility difficulties were experienced and age. **Table 10.5**

As in 1996, people who experienced problems getting about both indoors and outdoors were the most likely (82%) to have a mobility aid. By contrast, 64% of the people who only had problems getting about outdoors and 46% of the people who only had difficulties getting about their home had an aid. **Table 10.6**

Respondents who had mobility difficulties were asked about the type of assistance they required, which included whether they needed a walking aid or wheelchair, and what aids they currently had. Table 10.7 shows the percentage of people who had a walking aid and/or wheelchair that they required for indoor and/or outdoor use. The category 'walking aids' includes: walking sticks, crutches, walking frames, tripods, zimmer frames and trolleys.

- Nearly all of those who thought they needed a walking aid to help them get about outdoors or indoors said they had one (99% in both cases).
- 95% of people who reported needing a wheelchair indoors and 91% of people who reported needing a wheelchair outdoors said they had one.

These results suggest there is a level of unmet need, particularly among people who felt they required wheelchairs, but it should be remembered that these results are based on the perception of need rather than professional assessment. The usefulness of mobility aids will also depend upon the nature and severity of a person's mobility difficulty and any other underlying conditions such as dementia. **Table 10.7**

Source and types of mobility aid

The Health Service or Social Services provided 45% of all mobility aids. Aids bought by the respondent or their spouse accounted for 35% of all aids, 15% came from friends or relatives and 1% came from voluntary organisations. Aids provided by the Health Service and Social Services or obtained by the respondent or their spouse were more likely to be in use than those provided by friends and relatives. **Table 10.8**

By far the most common of all the aids respondents possessed were walking sticks (69%), with the next largest proportion being manual wheelchairs (9%). Crutches and walking frames, tripods or zimmer frames each represented 8% of mobility aids. Two percent of all aids were trolleys, as were electric wheelchairs and buggies or scooters. One reason for the high proportion of walking sticks respondents possessed may be because they can be purchased relatively easily and at low expense compared with other types of mobility aid.

Overall, 85% of all mobility aids which people possessed were in use, although there was noticeable variation according to the type of aid. In line with the results from 1993 and 1996, mechanical aids (wheelchairs and buggies or scooters) were more likely to be in use than the less expensive walking aids. In 2001, 94% of mechanical aids were in use compared with 84% of walking aids. It is interesting to note that crutches, which are perhaps the most likely aid to be issued for temporary problems, were least likely to be in use. Only 71% of all crutches were in use at the time of the survey.

Among all mobility aids that were in use, 70% of mechanical aids were in constant or regular use compared with 66% of all other types of walking aid but this difference was not statistically significant. **Tables 10.9-10.10**

As would be expected, whether an aid was used indoors or outdoors varied by the type of aid. For example:

- Walking sticks were over six times more likely to be used outdoors only than indoors only, 49% compared with 8%.
- 5% of manual wheelchairs were used indoors only compared with 62% of walking frames, tripods or zimmer frames. **Table 10.11**

Respondents who used a manual or electric wheelchair were also asked whether they could manage it alone or if they needed someone else's help to push or control it. Over a quarter (26%) of people who used wheelchairs said they could manage their wheelchair alone compared with 61% who said they always needed some assistance and 14% who said they sometimes needed assistance. **Table 10.12**

Notes and references

1 These percentages do not add up to the total percentage because of rounding.

Table 10.1 Percentage of persons reporting mobility difficulties, by sex and by age

Persons aged 16 and over *Great Britain: 2001*

	Men						Women						Total
	16-64	65-74	75-79	80-84	85 and over	All men	16-64	65-74	75-79	80-84	85 and over	All women	
	Percentage reporting mobility difficulties												
Permanent difficulties	4	13	21	25	50	6	4	15	30	37	65	9	8
Temporary difficulties	1	0	2	2	2	1	0	1	2	2	3	1	1
All with difficulties*	4	14	23	26	52	7	4	16	32	38	68	9	8
Weighted base (000's) = 100%†	*16,464*	*2,106*	*699*	*452*	*235*	*19,956*	*17,239*	*2,449*	*1,102*	*743*	*474*	*22,007*	*41,963*
Unweighted sample†	*5663*	*866*	*275*	*175*	*89*	*7068*	*6498*	*947*	*415*	*274*	*173*	*8307*	*15375*

* Includes persons who did not specify whether difficulties were permanent or temporary.
† Base numbers represent the number of people who specified whether difficulties were permanent or temporary.

Weighting to be revised in Spring 2003 following the 2001 census revisions of population estimates. See Appendix D.

Table 10.2 Percentage of people with mobility aid(s), by sex and by age

Persons aged 16 and over *Great Britain: 2001*

	Men						Women						Total
	16-64	65-74	75-79	80-84	85 and over	All men	16-64	65-74	75-79	80-84	85 and over	All women	
	%	%	%	%	%	%	%	%	%	%	%	%	%
Has mobility aid	5	18	31	38	59	8	4	18	31	40	62	9	9
No mobility aid	95	82	69	62	41	92	96	82	69	60	38	91	91
Weighted base (000's) = 100%	*16,472*	*2,106*	*699*	*453*	*234*	*19,964*	*17,252*	*2,451*	*1,102*	*743*	*473*	*22,021*	*41,987*
Unweighted sample	*5666*	*866*	*275*	*175*	*89*	*7071*	*6503*	*948*	*415*	*274*	*173*	*8313*	*15384*

Weighting to be revised in Spring 2003 following the 2001 census revisions of population estimates. See Appendix D.

Table 10.3 Percentage of people with mobility aid(s) by type of mobility difficulties

Persons aged 16 and over *Great Britain: 2001*

Whether has mobility aid	Whether has mobility difficulties			
	No difficulties	Temporary difficulties	Permanent difficulties	All with difficulties
	%	%	%	%
Has mobility aid	3	57	74	72
No mobility aid	97	43	26	28
Weighted base (000's) = 100%	*38,469*	*289*	*3,205*	*3,518*
Unweighted sample	*14066*	*108*	*1201*	*1318*

Weighting to be revised in Spring 2003 following the 2001 census revisions of population estimates. See Appendix D.

Table 10.4 Percentage of people with mobility aid(s) by age and whether has mobility difficulties

Persons aged 16 and over *Great Britain: 2001*

Whether has mobility difficulties	Age			
	16-64	65-74	75 and over	Total
	Percentage with mobility aid(s)			
Has difficulties	64	75	80	72
No difficulties	1	8	16	3
Weighted bases (000's) = 100%				
Has difficulties	*1,474*	*681*	*1,363*	*3,518*
No difficulties	*32,252*	*3,876*	*2,341*	*38,469*
Unweighted sample				
Has difficulties	*543*	*264*	*511*	*1318*
No difficulties	*11626*	*1550*	*890*	*14066*

Weighting to be revised in Spring 2003 following the 2001 census revisions of population estimates. See Appendix D.

Table 10.5 Where mobility difficulties were experienced by age

Persons aged 16 and over with mobility difficulties *Great Britain: 2001*

Where mobility difficulties are experienced	Age			
	16-64	65-74	75 and over	Total
Indoors only	6	5	2	4
Outdoors only	41	46	44	43
Indoors and outdoors	52	50	54	52
Weighted bases (000's) = 100%	*1,473*	*681*	*1,363*	*3,517*
Unweighted sample	*543*	*264*	*511*	*1318*

Weighting to be revised in Spring 2003 following the 2001 census revisions of population estimates. See Appendix D.

Table 10.6 Percentage of people with mobility aid(s) by where mobility difficulties were experienced

Persons aged 16 and over with mobility difficulties *Great Britain: 2001*

Whether or not has at least one mobility aid	Where mobility difficulties are experienced		
	Indoors only	Outdoors only	Indoors and outdoors
	%	%	%
Has mobility aid	46	64	82
No mobility aid	54	36	18
Weighted base (000's) = 100%	*158*	*1,516*	*1,844*
Unweighted sample	*62*	*569*	*687*

Weighting to be revised in Spring 2003 following the 2001 census revisions of population estimates. See Appendix D.

Table 10.7 Percentage of people with the type of equipment they required ('met need')

Population: all aged 16 and over who need a walking aid or wheelchair *Great Britain: 2001*

Type of assistance required	Percentage with equipment that they required	*Weighted base (000's) = 100%*	*Un-weighted sample*
Need walking aid indoors	99	*1,289*	*479*
Need wheelchair indoors	95	*240*	*87*
Need walking aid outdoors	99	*1,799*	*674*
Need wheelchair outdoors	91	*401*	*147*

Weighting to be revised in Spring 2003 following the 2001 census revisions of population estimates. See Appendix D.

Table 10.8 Source of mobility aids and percentage in use by source

All mobility aids *Great Britain: 2001*

Origin	Percentage of all aids	Percentage in use	*Weighted base (000's) = 100%*	*Un-weighted sample*
	%			
Health/Social Services	45	89	*2,252*	*833*
Self/spouse	35	87	*1,723*	*661*
Relative/friend	15	76	*745*	*280*
Voluntary organisation	1	[100]	*64*	*24*
Other	4	70	*198*	*72*
Total in use		86	*4,982*	*1870*
Weighted base (000's) = 100%	*4,982*			
Unweighted sample	*1870*			

Weighting to be revised in Spring 2003 following the 2001 census revisions of population estimates. See Appendix D.

Table 10.9 Type of mobility aid as a percentage of all mobility aids and percentage in use according to type of aid

All mobility aids *Great Britain: 2001*

Type of aid	Percentage of all aids	Percentage in use		*Weighted base (000's) = 100%*	*Un-weighted sample*
Walking stick	69	85		*3,306*	*1251*
Crutches	8	71	84	*373*	*136*
Walking frame/tripod/zimmer	8	87		*385*	*144*
Trolley	2	[93]		*90*	*32*
Manual wheelchair	9	94		*441*	*163*
Electric wheelchair	2	[92]	94	*98*	*37*
Buggy/scooter	2	[97]		*115*	*42*
Total in use		85		*4,807*	*1805*
Weighted base (000's) = 100%	*4,807*				
Unweighted sample	*1805*				

Weighting to be revised in Spring 2003 following the 2001 census revisions of population estimates. See Appendix D.

Table 10.10 **Regularity of use outdoors of mobility aids by type**

All aids in use *Great Britain: 2001*

Type of aid		When aid used: All the time/ regularly		Occasionally		*Weighted base (000's) = 100%*	*Unweighted sample*
Walking stick	%	67		33		*2,586*	*979*
Crutches	%	53	66	47	34	*226*	*81*
Walking frame/zimmer/tripod	%	66		[34]		*125*	*47*
Trolley	%	*		*		*46*	*16*
Manual wheelchair	%	69	70	31	30	*393*	*145*
Electric wheelchair	%	[67]		[33]		*69*	*26*
Buggy/scooter	%	[78]		[22]		*108*	*40*

* Base too small for analysis.

Weighting to be revised in Spring 2003 following the 2001 census revisions of population estimates. See Appendix D.

Table 10.11 **Where mobility aids were used by type**

All aids in use *Great Britain: 2001*

Type of aid		Where aid used: Indoors only		Outdoors only		Indoors and outdoors		*Weighted base (000's) = 100%*	*Unweighted sample*
Walking stick	%	8		49		43		*2,807*	*1060*
Crutches	%	13		31		56		*263*	*96*
Walking frame/ zimmer/tripod	%	62	14	14	44	24	42	*334*	*125*
Trolley	%	[44]		[36]		[20]		*84*	*30*
Manual wheelchair	%	5		66		29		*415*	*153*
Electric wheelchair	%	[22]	7	[51]	69	[27]	25	*90*	*34*
Buggy/scooter	%	[0]		[93]		[7]		*111*	*41*

Weighting to be revised in Spring 2003 following the 2001 census revisions of population estimates. See Appendix D.

Table 10.12 **Percentage of people who use wheelchairs by whether they require assistance**

Population: all aged 16 and over who use a wheelchair *Great Britain: 2001*

Whether requires assistance	Percentage of those using wheelchairs
Manages alone	26
Always need assistance	61
Sometimes need assistance	14
Weighted base (000's) = 100%*	*505*
Unweighted base	*187*

* Includes those who use a manual or electric wheelchair.

Weighting to be revised in Spring 2003 following the 2001 census revisions of population estimates. See Appendix D.

Appendix A

Definitions and terms

Definitions and terms used in the report are listed in alphabetical order.

Acute sickness

See Sickness

Adults

Adults are defined as persons aged 16 or over in all tables except those showing dependent children where single persons aged16-18 who are in full-time education are counted as dependent children.

Bedroom standard

This concept is used to estimate occupation density by allocating a standard number of bedrooms to each household in accordance with its age/sex/ marital status composition and the relationship of the members to one another. A separate bedroom is allocated to each married couple, any other person aged 21 or over, each pair of adolescents aged 10-20 of the same sex, and each pair of children under 10. Any unpaired person aged 10-20 is paired if possible with a child under 10 of the same sex, or, if that is not possible, is given a separate bedroom, as is any unpaired child under 10. This standard is then compared with the actual number of bedrooms (including bedsitters) available for the sole use of the household, and deficiencies or excesses are tabulated. Bedrooms converted to other uses are not counted as available unless they have been denoted as bedrooms by the informants; bedrooms not actually in use are counted unless uninhabitable.

Central heating

Central heating is defined as any system whereby two or more rooms (including kitchens, halls, landings, bathrooms and WCs) are heated from a central source, such as a boiler, a back boiler to an open fire, or the electricity supply. This definition includes a system where the boiler or back boiler heats one room and also supplies the power to heat at least one other room.

Under-floor heating systems, electric air systems, and night storage heaters are included.

Where a household has only one room in the accommodation, it is treated as having central heating if that room is heated from a central source along with other rooms in the house or building.

Chronic sickness

See Sickness

Cohabitation

See Marital Status

Co-ownership or equity sharing schemes

Co-ownership or equity sharing schemes are those where a share in the property is bought by the occupier under an agreement with the housing association. The monthly charges paid for the accommodation include an amount towards the repayment of the collective mortgage on the scheme. The co-owner never becomes the sole owner of the property, but on leaving the scheme usually receives a cash sum.

See also **Tenure**

Dependent children

Dependent children are persons aged under 16, or single persons aged 16 but under 19 and in full-time education, in the family unit and living in the household.

Doctor consultations

Data on doctor consultations presented in this report relate to consultations with National Health Service general medical practitioners during the two weeks before interview. Visits to the surgery, home visits, and telephone conversations are included, but contacts only with a receptionist are excluded. Consultations with practice nurses were excluded prior to 2000, but since then are identified separately. The GHS also collects information about consultations paid for privately.

The average number of consultations per person per year is calculated by multiplying the total number of consultations within the reference period, for any particular group, by 26 (the number of two-week periods in a year) and dividing the product by the total number of persons in the sample in that group.

Economic activity

Economically active persons are those over the minimum school-leaving age who were working or unemployed in the week before the week of interview. These persons constitute the labour force.

Working persons

This category includes persons aged 16 and over who, in the week before the week of interview, worked for wages, salary or other form of cash payment such as commission or tips, for any number of hours. It covers persons absent from work in the reference week because of holiday, sickness, strike, or temporary lay-off, provided they had a job to return to with the same employer. It also includes persons attending an educational establishment during the specified week if they were paid by their employer while attending it, people on Government training schemes and unpaid family workers.

Persons are excluded if they worked in a voluntary capacity for expenses only, or only for payment in kind, unless they worked for a business, firm or professional practice owned by a relative.

Full-time students are classified as 'working', 'unemployed' or 'inactive' according to their own reports of what they were doing during the reference week.

Unemployed persons

The GHS uses the International Labour Organisation (ILO) definition of unemployment. This classifies anyone as unemployed if he or she was out of work and had looked for work in the four weeks before interview, or would have but for temporary sickness or injury, and was available to start work in the two weeks after interview. Otherwise, anyone out of work is classified as economically inactive.

The treatment of all categories on the GHS is in line with that used on the Labour Force Survey (LFS).

Ethnic group

In line with National Statistics guidelines and to maintain a harmonised approach to data collection and outputs, the 2001 GHS introduced the new National Statistics ethnic classification. The new classification has a separate category for people from mixed ethnic backgrounds. In the previous system, people with these backgrounds had to select a specific ethnic group or categorise themselves as 'other'.

Household members are classified as:

- British, other White background
- White and Black Caribbean; White and Black African; White and Asian; Other Mixed background
- Indian; Pakistani; Bangladeshi; Other Asian background
- Black Caribbean; Black African; Other Black background
- Chinese; Other ethnic group

by the person answering the Household Schedule.

See Appendix E for more details.

Family

A family is defined as:

(a) a married or opposite sex cohabiting couple on their own, or

(b) a married or opposite sex cohabiting couple/ lone parent and their never-married children, provided these children have no children of their own.

Persons who cannot be allocated to a family as defined above are said to be persons not in the family.

In general, families cannot span more than two generations, ie grandparents and grandchildren cannot belong to the same family. The exception to this is where it is established that the grandparents are responsible for looking after the grandchildren (eg while the parents are abroad).

Adopted and step-children belong to the same family as their adoptive/step-parents. Foster-children, however, are not part of their foster-parents' family (since they are not related to their foster-parents) and are counted as separate family units.

See also Lone-parent family.

Full-time working

Full-time working is defined as more than 30 hours a week with the exception of occupations in education where more than 26 hours a week was included as full time.

Government Office Region (GOR)

Government Office Regions came into force in 1998. They replaced the Standard Statistical Regions as the primary classification for the presentation of English regional statistics. Standard Statistical Region was retained for some long term trend tables up to 2000. See also NHS Regional Office.

GP Consultations

See Doctor consultations

Hospital visits

Inpatient stays

Inpatient data relate to stays overnight or longer (in

a twelve month reference period) in NHS or private hospitals. All types of cases are counted, including psychiatric and maternity, except babies born in hospital who are included only if they remained in hospital after their mother was discharged.

Outpatient attendances
Outpatient data relate to attendances (in a reference period of three calendar months) at NHS or private hospitals, other than as an inpatient. Consultative outpatient attendances, casualty attendances, and attendances at ancillary departments are all included and a separate count is made of attendances at a casualty department.

Day patient
Day patients are defined as patients admitted to a hospital bed during the course of a day or to a day ward where a bed, couch or trolley is available for the patient's use. They are admitted with the intention of receiving care or treatment which can be completed in a few hours so that they do not require to remain in hospital overnight. If a patient admitted as a day patient then stays overnight they are counted as an inpatient.

Household

A household is defined as:

> a single person or a group of people who have the address as their only or main residence and who either share one meal a day or share the living accommodation. (See L McCrossan, *A Handbook for Interviewers.* HMSO, London 1991.)

A group of people are not counted as a household solely on the basis of a shared kitchen or bathroom.

A person is in general regarded as living at the address if he or she (or the informant) considers the address to be his or her main residence. There are, however, certain rules which take priority over this criterion.

(a) Children aged 16 or over who live away from home for purposes of either work or study and come home only for holidays are *not* included at the parental address under any circumstances.
(b) Children of any age away from home in a temporary job and children under 16 at boarding school are *always* included in the parental household.
(c) Anyone who has been away from the address *continuously* for six months or longer is excluded.
(d) Anyone who has been living continuously at the address for six months or longer is included even if he or she has his or her main residence elsewhere.
(e) Addresses used only as second homes are never counted as a main residence.

Householder

The householder: the member of the household in whose name the accommodation is owned or rented, or is otherwise responsible for the accommodation.

Non-household members are never defined as householders even though they may own or rent the accommodation in question.

Household Reference Person (HRP)

For some topics it is necessary to select one person in the household to indicate the characteristics of the household more generally. In common with other government surveys, in 2000, the GHS replaced the Head of Household with the Household Reference Person for this purpose.

The household reference person is defined as follows:

- In households with a *sole* householder that person is the household reference person
- In households with *joint* householders the person with the *highest income* is taken as the household reference person.
- If both householders have exactly the same income, the *older* is taken as the household reference person.

Note that this definition does not require a question about people's actual incomes; only a question about who has the highest income.

Main changes from the HOH definition
Female householders with the highest income are now taken as the HRP. In the case of joint householders, income then age, rather than sex then age is used to define the HRP. This means that in both cases more women are defined as HRP than were classified as the HOH.

Appendix A in 'Living in Britain 2000' suggested that in the GHS, the HRP would not be the same as the HOH in about 14% of households. Households consisting of a single adult or a sole male householder do not change and in many other households the new definition in practice results in the same person being selected. Part of the change is due to sole female householders who are living with a non-householder partner: they were not classified as the HOH, but they are the HRP, and they account for 4% of households. The remainder is due to the use of income (or age) to choose between joint householders resulting in a different person being selected.

Household type

There are many ways of grouping or classifying households into household types; most are based on the age, sex and number of household members.

The main classification of household type uses the following categories:

1 adult aged 16-59

2 adults aged 16-59

small family

1 or 2 persons aged 16 or over and 1 or 2 persons aged under 16

large family

1 or more persons aged 16 or over and 3 or more persons aged under 16, or 3 or more persons aged 16 or over and 2 persons aged under 16

large adult household

3 or more persons aged 16 or over, with or without 1 person aged under 16

2 adults, 1 or both aged 60 or over

1 adult aged 60 or over

The term 'family' in this context does not necessarily imply any relationship.

Chapter 3 also uses a modified version of household type which takes account of the age of the youngest household member. 'Small family', 'large family' and 'large adult household' are replaced by the following:

youngest person aged 0-4

1 or more persons aged 16 or over and 1 or more persons aged under 5

youngest person aged 5-15

1 or more persons aged 16 or over and 1 or more persons aged 5-15

3 or more adults

3 or more persons aged 16 or over and no-one aged under 16

The first two categories above are combined in some tables.

In Chapter 3, households are also classified according to the families they contain (see Family for definition), into the following categories:

non-family households containing
- 1 person only
- 2 or more non-family* adults

one family households† containing
- married couple with dependent children
- married couple with independent children only
- married couple with no children
- cohabiting couple with dependent children
- cohabiting couple with independent children only
- cohabiting couple with no children
- lone parent with dependent children
- lone parent with independent children only

households containing two or more families.

Some of the above categories are combined for certain tables and figures.

** Individuals may, of course, be related without constituting a family. A household consisting of a brother and sister, for example, is a non-family household of two or more non-family adults.*
† Other individuals who were not family members may also have been present.

Income

Usual gross weekly income

Total income for an individual refers to income at the time of the interview, and is obtained by summing the components of earnings, benefits, pensions, dividends, interest and other regular payments. Gross weekly income of employees and those on benefits is calculated if interest and dividends are the only components missing.

If the last pay packet/cheque was unusual, for example in including holiday pay in advance or a tax refund, the respondent is asked for usual pay. No account is taken of whether a job is temporary or permanent. Payments made less than weekly are divided by the number of weeks covered to obtain a weekly figure.

Usual gross weekly household income is the sum of usual gross weekly income for all adults in the household. Those interviewed by proxy are also included.

Labour force

See Economic activity.

Lone-parent family

A lone-parent family consists of one parent, irrespective of sex, living with his or her never-married dependent children, provided these children have no children of their own.

Married or cohabiting women with dependent children, whose partners are not defined as resident in the household, are not classified as one-parent families because it is known that the majority of them are only temporarily separated from their husbands for a reason that does not imply the breakdown of the marriage (for example, because the husband usually works away from home). (See the GHS 1980 Report p.9 for further details.)

Longstanding conditions and complaints

See Sickness

Marriage and cohabitation

From 1971 to 1978 the Family Information section was addressed only to married women aged under 45 who were asked questions on their present marriage and birth expectations. In 1979 the section was expanded to include questions on cohabitation prior to marriage, previous marriages and all live births, and was addressed to all women aged 16-49 except non-married women aged 16 and 17. In 1986 the section was extended to cover all women and men aged 16-59. In 1998 all adults aged 16-59 were asked about any periods of cohabitation not leading to marriage. This section was extended in 2000.

Marital status

Since 1996 separate questions have been asked at the beginning of the questionnaire to identify the legal marital status and living arrangements of respondents in the household. The latter includes a category for cohabiting.

Cohabiting

Before 1996, unrelated adults of the opposite sex were classified as cohabiting if they considered themselves to be living together as a couple. From 1996, this has included a small number of same sex couples.

Married/non-married

In this dichotomy 'married' generally includes cohabiting and 'non- married' covers those who are single, widowed, separated or divorced and not cohabiting.

Living arrangements (de facto marital status)

Before 1996, additional information from the Family Information section of the individuals' questionnaire has been used to determine living arrangements (previously known as 'defacto marital status') and the classification has only applied to those aged 16-59 who answer the marital history questions. For this population it only differed from the main marital status for those who revealed in the Family Information section that they were cohabiting rather than having the marital status given at the beginning of the interview. 'Cohabiting' took priority over other categories. Since 1996, information on legal marital status and living arrangements, has been taken from the beginning of the interview where both are now asked.

Legal marital status

This classification applies to persons aged 16-59 who answer the marital history questions. Cohabiting people are categorised according to formal marital status. The classification differs from strict legal marital status in accepting the respondents' opinion of whether their marriage has terminated in separation rather than applying the criterion of legal separation.

Median

See Quantiles.

NHS Regional Office

NHS Regional Offices came into force in 1996.

England and Wales: Health Authority Areas, 1999-2001

Pensions

The GHS asks questions about any pension scheme, either occupational or personal, that the respondent belonged to on the date of interview. It is quite possible that some respondents have belonged to an occupational or a personal pension scheme in the past. The GHS measures current membership and not the percentage of respondents who will get an occupational or personal pension when they retire.

Since July 1988, all employees have been given the choice of starting their own personal pension in place of SERPS (State Earnings Related Pension Scheme). Previously employees not in an occupational scheme could arrange to pay for a personal pension plan, but they could not leave SERPS.

Some respondents may be contributing to both an occupational and personal pension scheme.

Qualification levels

Degree or equivalent

Higher degrees
First degrees
University diplomas and certificates, qualifications from colleges of technology etc and from professional institutions, of degree standard

Higher education below degree level

Non-graduate teaching qualifications HNC/HND; City and Guilds Full Technological Certificate; BEC/TEC/BTEC Higher/ SCOTECH Higher University diplomas and certificates, qualifications from colleges of technology etc and from professional institutions, below degree but above GCE 'A' level standard, Nursing qualifications

GCE 'A' level or equivalent

1 or more subjects at GCE 'A' level/AS level/ Scottish Certificate of Education (SCE) Higher; Scottish Universities Preliminary Examination (SUPE) Higher; and/or Higher School Certificate; Scottish Leaving Certificate (SLC) Higher; Certificate of Sixth Year Studies City and Guilds Advanced/ Final level; ONC/OND; BEC/TEC/BTEC/National/General certificate or diploma

GCSE Grades A-C or equivalent

1 or more subjects at GCE 'O' level (Grades A-C)/GCSE (Grades A-C)/CSE Grade 1/SCE Ordinary (Bands A-C); SUPE Lower or Ordinary; and/or School Certificates; SLC Lower City and Guilds Craft/Ordinary level/ SCOTVEC

GCSE Grades D-E or equivalent

GCSE (grades D-E)/CSE Grades 2-5/GCE 'O' level (Grades D and E)/SCE Ordinary (Bands D and E); Clerical and commercial qualifications; Apprenticeship

Foreign and other qualifications

Foreign qualifications (outside UK)
Other qualifications

None

- excludes those who never went to school (omitted from the classification altogether).

The qualification levels do not in all cases correspond to those used in statistics published by the Department for Education and Employment.

Quantiles

The quantiles of a distribution, eg of household income, divide it into equal parts.

Median: the median of a distribution divides it into two equal parts. Thus half the households in a distribution of household income have an income higher than the median, and the other half have an income lower than the median.

Quartiles: the quartiles of a distribution divide it into quarters. Thus the upper quartile of a distribution of household income is the level of income that is expected by 25% of the households in the distribution; and 25% of the households have an income less than the lower quartile. It follows that 50% of the households have an income between the upper and lower quartiles.

Quintiles: the quintiles of a distribution divide it into fifths. Thus the upper quintile of a distribution of household income is the level of income that is expected by 20% of the households in the distribution; and 20% of the households have an income less than the lower quintile. It follows that 60% of the households have an income between the upper and lower quintiles.

Relatives in the household

The term 'relative' includes any household member related to the head of household by blood, marriage, or adoption. Foster-children are therefore not regarded as relatives.

Rooms

These are defined as habitable rooms, including (unless otherwise specified) kitchens, whether eaten in or not, but excluding rooms used solely for business purposes, those not usable throughout the year (eg conservatories), and those not normally used for living purposes such as toilets, cloakrooms, store rooms, pantries, cellars and garages.

Sickness

Acute sickness

Acute sickness is defined as restriction of the level of normal activity, because of illness or injury, at any time during the two weeks before interview. Since the two-week reference period covers weekends, normal activities include leisure activities as well as school attendance, going to work, or doing housework. Anyone with a chronic condition that caused additional restriction during the reference period is counted among those with acute sickness.

The average number of restricted activity days per person per year is calculated in the same way as the average number of doctor consultations.

Chronic sickness

Information on chronic sickness was obtained from the following two-part question:

'Do you have any longstanding illness, disability or infirmity? By longstanding I mean anything that has troubled you over a period of time or that is likely to affect you over a period of time.

IF YES
Does this illness or disability limit your activities in any way?'

'Longstanding illness' is defined as a positive answer to the first part of the question, and 'limiting longstanding illness' as a positive answer to both parts of the question.

The data collected are based on people's subjective assessment of their health, and therefore changes over time may reflect changes in people's expectations of their health as well as changes in incidence or duration of chronic sickness. In addition, different sub-groups of the population may have varying expectations, activities and capacities of adaptation.

Longstanding conditions and complaints

The GHS collects information about the nature of longstanding illness. Respondents who report a longstanding illness are asked 'What is the matter with you?' and details of the illness or disability are recorded by the interviewers and coded into a number of broad categories. Interviewers are instructed to focus on the symptoms of the illness, rather than the cause, and code what the respondent said was currently the matter without probing for cause. This approach has been used in 1988, 1989, 1994 to 1996, 1998, 2000 to 2001.

The categories used when coding the conditions correspond broadly to the chapter headings of the International Classification of Diseases (ICD). However, the ICD is used mostly for coding conditions and diseases according to cause whereas the GHS coding is based only on the symptoms reported. This gives rise to discrepancies in some areas between the two classifications.

National Statistics Socio-economic classification (NS-SEC)

From April 2001 the National Statistics Socio-economic Classification (NS-SEC) was introduced for all official statistics and surveys. It has replaced Social Class based on occupation and Socio-economic Groups (SEG). Full details can be found in '*The National Statistics Socio-economic Classification User Manual 2002*' ONS 2002.

Descriptive definition	*NS-SEC categories*
Large employers and higher managerial occupations	L1, L2
Higher professional occupations	L3
Lower managerial and professional occupations	L4, L5, L6
Intermediate occupations	L7
Small employers and own account workers	L8, L9
Lower supervisory and technical occupations	L10, L11
Semi-routine occupations	L12
Routine occupations	L13
Never worked and long-term unemployed	L14

The three residual categories: L15 (full time students); L16 (occupation not stated or inadequately described) and L17 (not classifiable for other reasons) are excluded when the classification is collapsed into its analytical classes.

The categories can be further grouped into:

Managerial and professional occupations	L1-L6
Intermediate occupations	L7-L9
Routine and manual occupations	L10-L13

This results in the exclusion of those who have never worked and the long term unemployed, in addition to the groups mentioned above.

The main differences users need to be aware of are:

- the introduction of SOC2000 which includes various new technology occupations not previously defined in SOC90;
- definitional variations in employment status in

particular with reference to the term 'supervisor';

- the inclusion of armed forces personnel in the appropriate occupation group;
- the separate classification of full-time students, whether or not they have been or are presently in paid employment;
- the separate classification of long term unemployed who previously were classified by their most recent occupation.

This change has resulted in a discontinuity in time series data. The operational categories of NS-SEC can be aggregated to produce an approximated version of the previous Socio-economic Group. These approximations have been shown to achieve an overall continuity level of 87%. Some tables in Chapter 8 (Smoking) have used this approximation. For further details about NS-SEC see Appendix E.

Step-family

See Family.

Tenure

From 1981, households who were buying a share in the property from a housing association or co-operative through a shared ownership (equity sharing) or co-ownership scheme are included in the category of owner-occupiers. In earlier years such households were included with those renting from a housing association or co-operative.

Renting from a council includes renting from a local authority or New town corporation or commissions or Scottish Homes (formerly the Scottish Special Housing Association).

Renting from a housing association also includes co-operatives and charitable trusts. It also covers fair rent schemes. Since 1996, housing associations are more correctly described as Registered Social Landlords (RSLs). RSLs are not-for-profit organisations which include: charitable housing associations, industrial and provident societies and companies registered under the Companies Act 1985.

Social sector renters include households renting from a local authority or New Town corporation or commission or Scottish Homes and those renting from housing associations, cooperatives and charitable trusts.

Private renters include those who rent from a private individual or organisation and those whose accommodation is tied to their job even if the landlord is a local authority, housing association or Housing Action Trust, or if the accommodation is rent free. Squatters are also included in this category.

Unemployed

See Economic activity

Working

See Economic activity

Appendix B

Sample design and response

The GHS samples around 13,000 addresses each year and aims to interview all adults aged 16 or over at every household at the sampled address[1]. It uses a probability, stratified two-stage sample design. The Primary Sampling Units (PSUs) are postcode sectors, which are similar in size to wards and the secondary sampling units are addresses within those sectors.

Sample design

The revised 2000 survey design introduced new stratifiers[2]. Stratification involves the division of the population into sub-groups, or strata, from which independent samples are taken. This ensures that a representative sample will be drawn with respect to the stratifiers (i.e. the proportion of units sampled from any particular stratum will equal the proportion in the population with that characteristic). Stratification of a sample can lead to substantial improvements in the precision of survey estimates. Optimal precision is achieved where the factors used as strata are those which correlate most highly with the survey variables. From 2000, the stratification factors were based on an area classifier and selected indicators from the 1991 census. Details of how these were selected were reported in the January 2000 edition of the ONS Survey Methodology bulletin[3].

Initially, postcode sectors were allocated to 30 major strata. These were based on the 10 Government Office Regions in England, 5 subdivisions in Scotland and 2 in Wales. The English regions were divided between the former Metropolitan and non-Metropolitan counties. In addition London was subdivided into quadrants (Northwest, Northeast, Southwest and Southeast) with each quadrant being divided into inner and outer areas[4]. Using a finer division of London in the regional stratifier had a large effect on the increase in precision.

Within each major stratum, postcode sectors were then stratified according to the selected indicators taken from the 1991 Census. Sectors were initially ranked according to the proportion of households with no car, then divided into three bands containing approximately the same number of households. Within each band, sectors were re-ranked according to the proportion of households with head of household in socio-economic groups 1 to 5 and 13, and these bands were then sub-divided into three further bands of approximately equal size. Finally, within each of these bands, sectors were re-ranked according to the proportion of people who were pensioners. In order to minimise the difference between one band and the next, the ranking by the pensioners and socio-economic group criteria were in the reverse order in consecutive bands, as shown in Figure B.A.

Major strata were then divided into minor strata with equal numbers of addresses, the number of minor strata per major strata being proportionate to the size of the major stratum. Since 1984 the frame has been divided into 576 minor strata and one PSU has been selected from each per year. Of the 576 PSUs selected, 48 are randomly allocated to each month of the year.

Figure BA

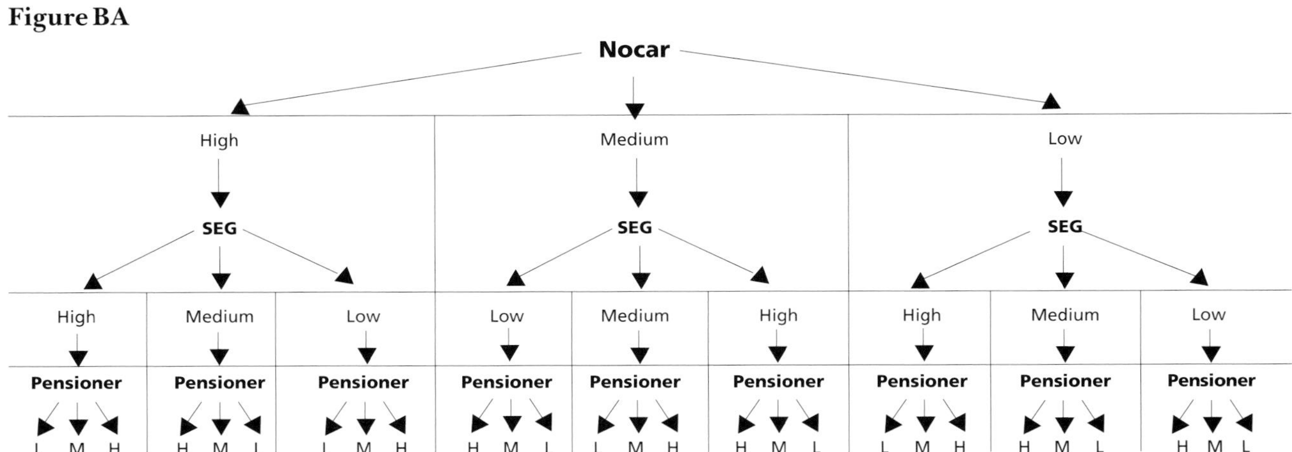

Each PSU forms a quota of work for an interviewer. Within each PSU 23 addresses are randomly selected. In June 2001, most interviewers from the Social Survey Division of ONS were required to take part in the Census Coverage Survey and were therefore not available to conduct GHS interviews. Examination of a number of key variables in the GHS showed little evidence of short term seasonal variation, so it was agreed that the 48 quotas for June should be randomly distributed across the rest of the survey year. Each month had four extra quotas except April and July which had six extra quotas. This plan was devised taking into consideration the shortened field time available in May because of the start of the Census Coverage Survey. Since GHS data is analysed on a yearly basis the rearrangement should mean there is no discernible effect on the overall results.

Conversion of multi-occupancy addresses to households

Most addresses contain just one private household, a few - such as institutions and purely business addresses[5] - contain no private households, while others contain more than one private household. For addresses containing more than one household, set procedures are laid down in order to give each household one and only one chance of selection.

As the PAF does not give names of occupants of addresses, it is not possible to use the number of different surnames at an address as an indicator of the number of households living there. A rough guide to the number of households at an address is provided on the PAF by the multi-occupancy (MO) count. The MO count is a fairly accurate indicator in Scotland but is less accurate in England and Wales, so it is used only when sampling at addresses in Scotland.

All addresses in England and Wales, and those in Scotland with an MO count of two or less, are given only one chance of selection for the sample. At such addresses, interviewers interview all the households they find up to a maximum of three. If there are more than three households at the address, the interviewer selects the households for interview by listing all households at the address systematically then making a random choice by referring to a household selection table.

Addresses in Scotland with an MO count of three or more, where the probability that there is more than one household is fairly high, are given as many chances of selection as the value of the MO count. When the interviewer arrives at such an address, he or she checks the actual number of households and interviews a proportion of them according to instructions. The proportion is set originally by the MO count and adjusted according to the number of households actually found, with a maximum of three households being interviewed at any address. The interviewer selects the households for interview by listing all households at the address systematically and making a random choice, as above, by means of a table.

No addresses are deleted from the sample to compensate for the extra interviews that may result from these multi-household addresses but a maximum of four extra interviews per quota of addresses is allowed. Once four extra interviews have been carried out in an interviewer's quota, only the first household selected at each multi-occupancy address is included. As a result of the limits on additional interviews, households in concealed multi-occupied addresses may be slightly under-represented in the GHS sample.

Data collection

Information for the GHS is collected week by week throughout the year by personal interview. In 2001, interviews took place from April 2001 to March 2002.[6] The survey is carried out using Computer Assisted Personal Interviewing (CAPI) on laptop computers and Blaise software[7] by face-to-face interviewers. Since 2000, telephone interviewers have also been employed on the GHS and they use Computer Assisted Telephone Interviewing (CATI) on computers in an interviewing booth. Interviews are sought with all adult members (aged 16 or over) of the sample of private households and some information about children in the household is also collected.

A letter is sent in advance of an interviewer calling at an address[8]. The letter briefly describes the purpose and nature of the survey and prepares the recipient for a visit by an interviewer. In 2001, postage stamps were included in the advance letter (see 'Improving response').

Data quality

The face-to-face and telephone interviewers who work on the GHS are recruited only after careful selection procedures after which they take part in an initial training course. Before working on the GHS they attend a briefing and new recruits are always supervised either by being accompanied in the field by a Field Manager or monitored by a Telephone Interviewing Unit (TIU) supervisor. All interviewers who continue to work on the GHS are observed regularly in their work.

Proxy interviews and the Proxy Conversion exercise

On occasion it may prove impossible, despite repeated calls, to contact a particular member of a household in person and, in strictly controlled circumstances, interviewers are permitted to conduct a proxy interview with a close household member. In these cases opinion-type questions and questions on smoking and drinking behaviour, qualifications, health, family information and income are omitted.

During the review of the GHS[9] the conversion of proxy interviews to full interviews was examined in order to improve the quality of data. This was achieved by re-contacting the household member, who was unavailable during the initial face-to-face interview, to answer the questions that were not asked of the proxy respondent on his/her behalf. The most efficient way of re-contacting these respondents was by employing Telephone Interviewing Unit (TIU) interviewers who could contact a widely dispersed population more efficiently than would be possible by conducting face-to-face interviews.

Response

The GHS is conducted with people who volunteer their time to answer questions about themselves. The voluntary nature of the survey means that people who do not wish to take part in the survey can refuse to do so. Reasons for not participating in the survey vary from a dislike of surveys to poor health that prevents them from taking part. The sample is designed to ensure that the results of the survey represent the population of Great Britain. The representativeness of the survey is likely to be reduced with every refusal or noncontact with a sampled household (survey nonresponse). One measure of the quality of survey results is therefore the response rate.

Table B.1 shows the outcome of visits to the addresses selected for the 2001 sample and the resultant number of households interviewed. Out of the 13,248 addresses that were selected, 12,103 were eligible and this yielded a sample of 12,223 eligible households. In 8,746 households, interviews (including proxy interviews) were achieved with every member of the household. In a further 243 households interviews were achieved with some but not all members of the household. This produced a total of 8,989 full or partial interviews. **Table B1**

Partial household response can arise for a variety of reasons: some individual members of households refuse to take part, some cannot be contacted and others are interviewed by proxy and, as noted above, are not then asked all the questions. Depending on whether or not these various categories of partial response are included, three response rates are calculated.

1 The *minimum* response rate, which accepts only completely co-operating households as responders (category 1 in Table B.2) and treats all partial household interviews as nonresponse. In 2001 the minimum response rate was 65%.

2 The *maximum* response rate, which accepts all partial household interviews as response (categories 2, 3a and 3b in Table B.2). In 2001 this rate was 74%.

3 The *middle* response rate, which accepts some of the partial household interviews as response - that is, it includes households where information has been collected by proxy and is therefore missing certain sections (category 2 in Table B.2), but does not include those where information is missing altogether for one or more household members (categories 3a and 3b in Table B.2). In other words, this middle rate can be thought of as the proportion of the eligible sample of households from whom all or nearly all the information was obtained. In 2001 the middle response rate was 72%.

Harmonised outcome codes[10] and definitions of response rates will be introduced for the first time on the 2002/3 GHS and other large household surveys. Household surveys using the codes will include all types of partial household interview in their overall response rates. Although the middle

Table B1 **The sample of addresses and households**

Great Britain: 2001

Selected addresses		13248
Ineligible addresses:		
Demolished or derelict		
Used wholly for business purposes		
Empty		
Institutions		1145
Other ineligible		
No sample selected at address		
Address not traced		
Eligible addresses		12103
Number of households at eligible addresses		12223
Number of households where all individual interviews achieved (including proxies)	8746	8989
Number of households where some but not all individual interviews achieved	243	

Table B2 Quarterly and annual response

Households | *Great Britain: 2001*

Outcome category	First quarter		Second quarter		Third quarter		Fourth quarter		Year	
	No.	%	No.	%	No.	%	No.	%	No.	%
1 Complete household co-operation	1531	68.1	2296	68.6	2166	65	1925	58.4	7918	64.8
2 Non-interview of one or more household members, proxy taken	126	5.6	219	6.5	202	6.1	281	8.5	828	6.8
3a Non-contact with one or more household members, no proxy taken	31	1.4	24	0.7	51	1.5	46	1.4	152	1.2
3b Refusal by at least one household member, no proxy taken	17	0.8	28	0.8	21	0.6	31	0.9	97	0.8
4 Whole household refused	401	17.8	574	17.1	648	19.5	732	22.2	2355	19.3
5 HQ refusal	51	2.3	89	2.7	93	2.8	104	3.2	337	2.8
6 Non-contact with household	92	4.1	119	3.6	150	4.5	175	5.3	536	4.4
Unweighted sample base = 100% (total effective sample, ie total categories 1-6 plus small data losses)	*2249**		*3349*		*3331*		*3294*		*12223*	
Middle response rate: (codes 1 and 2 as percentage of the effective sample)		73.7		75.1		71.1		67.0		71.6
Maximum response rate: (codes 1, 2, 3a and 3b as percentage of the effective sample)		75.8		76.6		73.3		69.3		73.6

* Due to the census coverage survey there were no GHS interviews in June 2001.

Table B3 Middle response rates by Government Office Region

Households | *Great Britain: 2001*

Government Office Region	First quarter		Second quarter		Third quarter		Fourth quarter		Year	
	%	Rank	%	Rank	%	Rank	%	Rank	%	Rank
North East	70.0	8	74.7	8	71.2	7	68.6	5	71.4	9
North West	74.5	4	76.9	6	71.3	6	72.3	1	73.7	3
Yorkshire and the Humber	84.1	2	78.9	4	73.2	3	68.7	4	75.8	1
East Midlands	73.7	5	80.3	2	71.8	5	67.6	6	73.2	4
West Midlands	69.3	10	68.0	10	72.3	4	66.4	8	69.0	10
East of England	72.6	7	72.5	9	74.6	1	66.1	9	71.5	8
London	65.5	11	64.5	11	66.2	11	57.7	11	63.2	11
South East (excluding Greater London)	72.9	6	77.4	5	70.9	8	69.3	2	72.6	5
South West	77.8	3	81.6	1	74.2	2	67.0	7	75.1	2
Wales	88.2	1	74.8	7	68.6	9	65.0	10	72.2	6
Scotland	69.6	9	79.1	3	68.5	10	69.0	3	71.8	7
Great Britain	73.7		75.1		71.1		67.0		71.6	

response rate has been used as a performance indicator in the past for the GHS, this year the maximum response rate has also been included in Table B.2 in order to provide a useful comparison for the forthcoming method of measuring overall response. The middle response rate figures for each region in 2001 are shown in Table B.3.

In total, 26% of households selected for interview in 2001 were lost to the sample altogether, because they did not wish to take part (22%) or because they could not be contacted (4%).

The proxy conversion exercise does not affect the middle response rate but it is worth noting that follow-up proxy interviews increased the proportion of full individual interviews from 70.7% to 72.7% (table not shown). This improves data quality by reducing item nonresponse.

Tables B.2-B.3

Trends in response

Since 1971, the middle response rate has shown some fluctuation, as shown in Table B.4. The decline in response rate since the early 90s is due to an increase in the proportion of households refusing to participate (12% in 1991 rising to 22% in 2001) rather than failure to contact people. This decline reflects a general trend in decreasing response experienced by all survey organisations.[11]

Tables B.2 - B.4

Improving response

One ongoing method of improving response has been to reissue addresses to interviewers where there is a possibility of obtaining a better outcome, for example if there was initially a non-contact or a circumstantial refusal. During the 2001/2 GHS survey, various new initiatives were also employed to reduce nonresponse. The advance letter was changed to mention that the survey had been running for 30 years and a 30-year leaflet was produced for interviewers to give to respondents. These changes were made to show respondents how important the survey is and how many people have taken part in it. Other surveys, like the Family Resources Survey, have found that including postage stamps with the advance letter also increases survey response. One theory is that

Table B4 **Trends in the middle response rate: 1971 to 2001**

Households *Great Britain*

Year	Response Rate
	%
1971	83
1972	81
1973	81
1974	83
1975	84
1976	84
1977	83
1978	82
1979	83
1980	82
1981	84
1982	84
1983	82
1984	81
1985	82
1986	84
1987	85
1988	85
1989	84
1990	81
1991	84
1992	83
1993	82
1994	80
1995	80
1996	76
1998	72
2000	67
2001	72

Table B5 **Unweighted bases: number of household reference persons in GHS 2001 by age, sex, region and country**

Household reference persons *Great Britain: 2001*

	Age							All
	16-24	25-34	35-44	45-54	55-64	65-74	75+	
Sex								
Male	153	893	1232	1129	977	817	508	5709
Female	171	558	605	464	438	451	593	3280
Government Office Region								
North East	19	68	79	60	76	57	48	407
North West	38	192	206	203	194	174	114	1121
Yorkshire and the Humber	35	132	164	126	137	100	121	815
East Midlands	23	99	134	130	97	108	82	673
West Midlands	30	113	156	134	139	120	88	780
East of England	34	128	190	160	125	124	94	855
London	29	225	241	174	143	99	94	1005
South East	43	179	255	241	177	184	177	1256
South West	15	128	165	140	115	127	131	821
Country								
England	266	1264	1590	1368	1203	1093	949	7733
Wales	17	60	84	83	71	69	61	445
Scotland	41	127	163	142	141	106	91	811
Total	324	1451	1837	1593	1415	1268	1101	8989

Shaded figures also show the number of households in each region and country.

respondents are more likely to remember the advance letter if stamps are included and this in turn can help interviewers to sell the survey on the doorstep. In 2001, a Response Working Group was set up in Social Survey Division and part of the GHS's contribution to the project was to carry out a split sample stamp experiment. The experiment involved a book of four postage stamps being included in the advance letters for half the GHS sample from December 2001 to March 2002[12]. During that period response was found to be 3% higher among households who had received stamps. Since August 2002, postage stamps have been included in all advance letters.

Another factor which is thought to have had a positive effect on the response of the 2001 GHS was the 2001 decennial Census. In the run up to the Census there was a significant amount of media coverage about ONS and it was suggested that this higher profile improved response across all ONS social surveys.

Sample sizes

Tables B.5 and B.6 show the numbers of households and individuals interviewed on the 2001 GHS by age, sex, region and country.

Tables B.5-B.6

Table B6 **Unweighted bases: number of people in GHS 2001 by age, sex, region and country**

All persons *Great Britain: 2001*

	Age									All
	0-4	5-15	16-24	25-34	35-44	45-54	55-64	65-74	75+	
Sex										
Male	678	1585	987	1378	1556	1357	1151	905	569	10166
Female	670	1562	1077	1521	1663	1420	1219	977	905	11014
Government Office Region										
North East	64	110	111	133	131	123	119	80	66	937
North West	162	395	267	365	365	360	308	256	155	2633
Yorkshire and the Humber	137	296	177	258	278	226	236	152	154	1914
East Midlands	72	208	159	188	235	217	173	156	111	1519
West Midlands	139	276	195	246	287	252	236	180	120	1931
East of England	142	342	186	276	338	282	209	185	132	2092
London	179	388	229	460	398	281	210	144	120	2409
South East	151	413	271	363	467	404	330	271	247	2917
South West	130	332	164	252	298	243	204	198	168	1989
Country										
England	1176	2760	1759	2541	2797	2388	2025	1622	1273	18341
Wales	78	153	117	120	152	140	124	100	79	1063
Scotland	94	234	188	238	270	249	221	160	122	1776
Total	1348	3147	2064	2899	3219	2777	2370	1882	1474	21180

Notes and references

[1] A limit is put on the number of households that are contacted per address. This is explained in detail at the 'Conversion of multi-occupancy addresses to households' section of Appendix B.

[2] From 1984 to 1998, the stratifiers used were a regional variable (based on the standard statistical region until 1996 and on the Government Office Region in 1998) and variables that measured the prevalence of privately rented accommodation, local authority accommodation and people in professional and managerial socio-economic groups.

[3] Insalaco F Choosing stratifiers for the General Household Survey *ONS Social Survey Division, Survey Methodology Bulletin*, No. 46, January 2000.

[4] The GOR regional stratifier

1. North East Met
2. North East Non Met
3. North West Met
4. North West Non Met
5. Merseyside
6. Yorks and Humberside Met
7. Yorks and Humberside Non Met
8. East Midlands
9. West Midlands Met
10. West Midlands Non Met
11. Eastern Outer Met
12. Eastern Other
13. Inner London North-East
14. Inner London North-West
15. Inner London South-East
16. Inner London South-West
17. Outer London North-East
18. Outer London North-West
19. Outer London South-East
20. Outer London South-West
21. South East Outer Met
22. South East Other
23. South West
24. Wales 1 - Glamorgan, Gwent
25. Wales 2 - Clwydd, Gwenneyd, Dyfed, Powys
26. Highlands, Grampian, Tayside
27. Fife, Central, Lothian
28. Glasgow Met
29. Strathclyde (excl. Glasgow)
30. Borders, Dumfries, Galloway

[5] Most institutions and business addresses are not listed on the small-user PAF. If an address was found in the field to be non-private (e.g. boarding house containing four or more boarders at the time the interviewer calls), the interviewer was instructed not to take an interview. However, a household member in hospital at the time of interview was included in the sample provided that he or she had not been away from home for more than six months and was expected to return. In this case a proxy interview was taken.

[6] From 1988, the GHS interviewing year was changed from a calendar year to a financial year basis.

[7] In 1994, the GHS was carried out for the first time using Computer Assisted Personal Interviewing (CAPI).

[8] An advance letter has been sent to residents since 1987, on the GHS. Clarke L et al. General Household Survey Advance Letter Experiment. *OPCS Social Survey Division, Survey Methodology Bulletin* No. 21, September 1987.

[9] Walker A et al *Living in Britain Results from the 2000 General Household Survey: Appendix E.* TSO London 2002. Also available on the web: www.statistics.gov.uk/lib

[10] Lynn P, Beerten R, Laiho J and Martin J. *Recommended Standard Final Outcome Categories and Standard Definition of Response Rate for Social Surveys.* ISER Working Papers. Number 2001-23. http://www.iser.essex.ac.uk/pubs/workpaps/pdf/2001-23.pdf

[11] The decline is being addressed through a number of different initiatives and through the use of weighting for nonresponse (see Appendix D).

[12] The results of this experiment will be published at a later date.

Appendix C

Sampling errors

Tables in this appendix present estimates for sampling errors for some of the main variables used in this report, taking into account the complex sample design of the survey.

Sources of error in surveys

Survey results are subject to various sources of error. The total error in a survey estimate is the difference between the estimate derived from the data collected and the true value for the population. The total error can be divided into two main types: systematic and random error.

Systematic error

Systematic error, or bias, covers those sources of error which will not average to zero over repeats of the survey. Bias may occur, for example, if a certain section of the population is excluded from the sampling frame, because non-respondents to the survey have different characteristics to respondents, or if interviewers systematically influence responses in one way or another. Substantial efforts have been made to avoid systematic errors.

Random error

An important component of random error is sampling error, which is the error that arises because the estimate is based on a survey rather than a full census of the population. The results obtained for any single sample may, by chance, vary from the true values for the population but the variation would be expected to average to zero over a number of repeats of the survey. The amount of variation depends on both the size of the sample and the sample design.

Random error may also result from other sources such as variation in respondent's interpretation of the questions, or interviewer variation. Efforts are made to minimise these effects through pilot work and interviewer training.

Sampling errors for complex sample designs

The GHS uses a multi-stage sample design which involves both clustering and stratification.
In considering the reliability of estimates, standard errors calculated on the basis of a simple random sample design will not reflect the true variation because of the complex sample design. Clustering can lead to a substantial increase in standard error if the household or individuals within primary sampling units (PSUs) are relatively homogenous but the PSUs differ from one another.
Stratification tends to reduce standard error and is of most advantage where the stratification factor is related to the characteristics of interest on the survey.

Standard error

In a complex sample design, the size of the standard error depends on how the characteristic of interest is spread within and between the PSUs and strata, and this is taken into account in the way data are grouped in order to calculate the standard error. The method explicitly allows for the fact that the percentages and means are ratios of two survey estimates: the number with the characteristic of interest is the numerator (y) and the sample size is the denominator (x), both of which are subject to random error. The formula used to estimate the variance of a ratio estimator (r, where r=y/x) is shown below.

$$var(r) = \frac{1}{x^2}\left[var(y) + r^2 var(x) - 2r\,cov(y,x)\right]$$

Var (r) is the estimate of the variance of the ratio, *r*, expressed in terms of *var(y)* and *var(x)* which are the estimated variances of *y* and *x*, and *cov(y,x)* which is their estimated covariance. The resulting estimate is only valid if the denominator is not too variable.[1] The method compares the differences between totals for adjacent PSUs (postal sectors) in the characteristic of interest. The ordering of PSUs reflects the ranking of postal sectors on the stratifiers used in the sample design.

Design factors (deft)

The design factor, or deft, is the ratio of the complex standard error to the standard error that would have resulted had the survey design been a simple random sample of the same size. This is often used to give a broad indication of the effect of the clustering. The size of the design factor varies between survey variables reflecting the degree to which a characteristic is clustered within PSUs, or is distributed between strata. For a single variable the size of the factor also varies according to the size of the subgroup on which the estimate is based, and on the distribution of the subgroup between PSUs and strata. Design factors below 1.0 show that the complex sample design improved on the estimate that would have expected from a simple random sample, probably due to the benefits of stratification. Design factors greater than 1.0 show less reliable estimates than might be gained from a simple random sample, due to the effects of clustering. The standard error of a proportion (p) based on a simple random sample multiplied by the deft gives the standard error of a complex design.

$$se(p) = deft \times se(p)_{srs}$$

Where:

$$se(p)srs=\sqrt{(p(100-p)/n)}$$

The formula to calculate the standard error of the difference between two percentages for a complex sample design is:

$$se(p1-p_2)=\sqrt{[deft^2_1(p_1(100-p_1)/n_1)+ deft^2_2(p_2(100-p_2)/n_2)]}$$

where p1 and p2 are observed percentages for the two subsamples and n1 and n2 are the subsample sizes.

Confidence intervals

The estimate produced from a sample survey will rarely be identical to the population value, but statistical theory allows us to measure the accuracy of any survey result. The standard error can be estimated from the values obtained for the sample and allows the calculation of confidence intervals which give an indication of the range in which the true population value is likely to fall.

It is common when quoting confidence intervals to refer to the 95% confidence interval around a survey estimate. This is calculated at 1.96 times the standard error on either side of the estimated percentage or mean since, under a normal distribution, 95% of values lie within 1.96 standard errors of the mean value. If it were possible to repeat the survey under the same conditions many times, 95% of these confidence intervals would contain the population values but, when assessing the results of a single survey, it is usual to assume that there is only a 5% chance that the true population value falls outside the 95% confidence interval calculated for the survey estimate.

The 95% confidence interval for the difference between two percentages is then given by:

$$(p_1-p_2) +/- 1.96 \times se(p_1-p_2)$$

If this confidence interval includes zero then the observed difference is considered to be a result of chance variation in the sample. If the interval does not include zero then it is unlikely (less than 5% probability) that the observed difference could have occurred by chance.

Standard errors for the 2001 GHS

The standard errors were calculated on weighted data using STATA.[2] Weighting for different sampling probabilities results in larger sampling errors than for an equal-probability sample without weights. However, using population totals to control for differential non-response tends to lead to a reduction in the errors. The method used to calculate the sampling errors correctly allows for the inflation in the sampling errors caused by the first type of weighting but, in treating the second type of weighting in the same way as the first, incorrectly inflates the estimates further. Therefore the standard errors and defts presented are likely to be slight over-estimates. Weighted data were used so that the values of the percentages and means were the same as those in the substantive chapters of the report.

Tables C.1 to C.12 show the standard error, the 95% confidence intervals and defts for selected survey estimates. The tables do not cover all the topics discussed in the report but show a selection of estimates. Over half (51%) of the estimates based on households had defts of less than 1.1 and for almost three quarters of household based estimates the deft was less than 1.2 (73% percent of the estimates given). In three cases (8%) the deft was 1.5 or greater; the higher defts were for tenure and accommodation type (see Table C.1). Defts below 1 were found for 11% of the estimates, some of those for the number of persons in the household and household type, indicating that stratification has increased the precision of the sample over a simple random sample for these estimates of household variables.

For the design factors of person based estimates, 8% were below 1, indicating that stratification has improved the precision of the estimates upon those from a simple random sample. Over two fifths of defts were below 1.1, and 72% were below 1.2. Four percent were 1.5 or greater.

These results show that the effects of clustering tend to lead to a loss of precision on some estimates compared with that from a simple random sample. This is particularly true of estimates of ethnic origin (Table C5). However, there are examples where the stratification has increased the precision from a simple random sample (the design factor is less than 1), for example, for some of the NS-SEC estimates. (see Table C8).

Estimating standard errors for other survey measures

The standard errors of survey measures which are not presented in the tables and for sample subgroups may be estimated by applying an appropriate value of deft to the sampling error. The choice of an appropriate value of deft will vary according to whether the basic survey measure is included in the tables. Since most deft values are relatively small (1.2 or less) the absolute effect of adjusting sampling errors to take account of the survey's complex design will be small. In most cases it will result in an increase of less than 20% over the standard error assuming a simple random sample. Whether it is considered necessary to use deft or to use the basic estimates of standard errors assuming a simple random sample is a matter of judgement and depends chiefly on the use to which the survey results are to be put.

Notes and references

1 This variability can be measured by the coefficient of variation of x, denoted by $cv(x)$, which is the standard error of x expressed as a proportion of x

$$cv(x) = \frac{se(x)}{x}$$

It has been suggested that the ratio estimator should not be used if $cv(x)$ is greater than 0.2. The coefficient of variation of x did not exceed 0.2 for any of the estimates presented in this Appendix.

2 STATA is a statistical analysis software package. For further details of the method of calculation see: Elliot D. A comparison of software for producing sampling errors on social surveys. *SSD Survey Methodology Bulletin* 1999; **44**: 27-36.

Table C.1 Standard errors and 95% confidence intervals for households's tenure, household type and accommodation type

Base	Characteristic	% (*p*)	Unweighted sample size	Standard error of *p*	95% confidence intervals	Deft
All households						
	Household type					
	1 adult aged 16-59	15.4	8989	0.42	14.6 - 16.2	1.10
	2 adults aged 16-59	16.8	8989	0.41	16.0 - 17.6	1.04
	Youngest person aged 0-4	11.1	8989	0.34	10.4 - 11.8	1.03
	Youngest person aged 5-15	15.7	8989	0.37	14.9 - 16.4	0.97
	3 or more adults	11.0	8989	0.35	10.3 - 10.7	1.06
	2 adults, 1 or both aged 60 or over	14.9	8989	0.38	14.2 - 15.7	1.01
	1 adult aged 60 or over	15.2	8989	0.40	14.4 - 16.0	1.06
	Tenure					
	Owner occupied, owned outright	27.2	8989	0.56	26.1 - 28.3	1.19
	Owner occupied, with mortgage	41.4	8989	0.57	40.3 - 42.5	1.10
	Rented from council	15.0	8989	0.57	13.9 - 16.2	1.51
	Rented from housing association	6.3	8989	0.35	5.6 - 7.0	1.37
	Rented privately, unfurnished	7.0	8989	0.32	6.4 - 7.6	1.19
	Rented privately, furnished	3.2	8989	0.26	2.7 - 3.7	1.41
	Accommodation type					
	Detatched house	21.1	8989	0.55	20.0 - 22.2	1.28
	Semi-detatched house	31.2	8989	0.70	29.9 - 32.6	1.43
	Terraced house	27.5	8989	0.72	26.1 - 28.9	1.53
	Purpose-built flat or masionette	16.1	8989	0.55	15.0 - 17.1	1.42
	Converted flat or maisonette/rooms	4.1	8989	0.32	3.4 - 4.7	1.54
	With business premises/other	0.1	8989	0.03	0.0 - 0.1	1.08

Table C.2 Standard errors and 95% confidence intervals for number of persons and cars at each household

Base	Characteristic	% (*p*)	Unweighted sample size	Standard error of *p*	95% confidence intervals	Deft
All households						
	Number of persons					
	1	30.6	8989	0.51	29.6 - 31.6	1.05
	2	34.2	8989	0.51	33.2 - 35.2	1.02
	3	15.8	8989	0.37	15.0 - 16.5	0.96
	4	13.5	8989	0.35	12.8 - 14.2	0.97
	5	4.2	8989	0.21	3.8 - 4.6	1.00
	6 or more	1.8	8989	0.15	1.6 - 2.1	1.06
	Number of cars/light vans					
	1	42.9	8989	0.56	41.8 - 44.0	1.07
	2 or more	30.0	8989	0.54	29.0 - 31.1	1.12
	none	27.1	8989	0.51	26.1 - 28.1	1.09

Table C.3 Standard errors and 95% confidence intervals for households' ownership of a video, compact disc player, home computer, microwave oven, freezer, washing machine, tumble drier and dish washer

Base	Characteristic	% (*p*)	Unweighted sample size	Standard error of *p*	95% confidence intervals	Deft
All households						
	Video recorder	88.4	8987	0.34	87.7 - 89.1	1.01
	Compact disc (CD) player	79.5	8988	0.46	78.6 - 80.4	1.08
	Home computer	49.6	8988	0.61	48.4 - 50.8	1.16
	Microwave oven	85.3	8988	0.39	84.6 - 86.1	1.04
	Deep freezer/fridge freezer	94.5	8988	0.27	93.9 - 95.0	1.12
	Washing machine	92.2	8988	0.33	91.5 - 92.8	1.16
	Tumble drier	54.0	8988	0.62	52.8 - 55.2	1.18
	Dishwasher	27.4	8988	0.59	26.3 - 28.6	1.25

Table C.4 Standard errors and 95% confidence intervals for age and sex

Base	Characteristic	% (*p*)	Unweighted sample size	Standard error of *p*	95% confidence intervals	Deft
All persons	**Sex**					
	Male	49.3	21180	0.25	48.8 - 49.8	0.73
	Female	50.7	21180	0.25	50.2 - 51.2	0.73
All persons	**Age**					
	0-4	6.0	21180	0.19	5.6 - 6.4	1.16
	5-15	14.3	21180	0.29	13.7 - 14.9	1.21
	16-44	41.0	21180	0.42	40.2 - 41.8	1.24
	45-64	23.7	21180	0.37	22.9 - 24.4	1.27
	65-74	8.3	21180	0.23	7.8 - 8.7	1.22
	75 and over	6.8	21180	0.22	6.4 - 7.2	1.27
All males	0-4	6.2	10166	0.25	5.7 - 6.7	1.05
	5-15	14.6	10166	0.40	13.9 - 15.4	1.14
	16-44	42.4	10166	0.53	41.4 - 43.4	1.08
	45-64	23.8	10166	0.43	23.0 - 24.6	1.02
	65-74	7.8	10166	0.28	7.3 - 8.4	1.05
	75 and over	5.2	10166	0.22	4.8 - 5.6	1.00
All females	0-4	5.9	11014	0.23	5.4 - 6.3	1.03
	5-15	14.0	11014	0.35	13.3 - 14.7	1.06
	16-44	39.6	11014	0.48	38.7 - 40.6	1.03
	45-64	23.5	11014	0.44	22.6 - 24.4	1.09
	65-74	8.7	11014	0.28	8.1 - 9.2	1.04
	75 and over	8.4	11014	0.31	7.8 - 9.0	1.17

Table C.5 **Standard errors and 95% confidence intervals for marital status**

Base	Characteristic	% (p)	Unweighted sample size	Standard error of p	95% confidence intervals	Deft
All persons aged 16 and over	Marital Status					
	Married	52.6	16685	0.55	51.5 - 53.7	1.42
	Cohabiting	9.6	16685	0.33	8.9 - 10.2	1.45
	Single	22.5	16685	0.43	21.6 - 23.3	1.33
	Widowed	7.5	16685	0.22	7.1 - 8.0	1.08
	Divorced	5.6	16685	0.18	5.2 - 5.9	1.01
	Separated	2.2	16685	0.11	2.0 - 2.4	0.99
Men aged 16 and over	Married	53.7	7903	0.64	52.5 - 55.0	1.14
	Cohabiting	9.8	7903	0.34	9.1 - 10.5	1.02
	Single	26.6	7903	0.63	25.4 - 27.9	1.27
	Widowed	34.4	7903	0.19	3.1 - 3.8	0.36
	Divorced	4.6	7903	0.25	4.1 - 5.0	1.07
	Separated	1.8	7903	0.15	1.5 - 2.1	1.01
Women aged 16 and over	Married	51.6	8782	0.58	50.4 - 52.7	1.09
	Cohabiting	9.4	8782	0.32	8.7 - 10.0	1.03
	Single	18.4	8782	0.42	17.6 - 19.3	1.01
	Widowed	11.5	8782	0.37	10.7 - 12.2	1.09
	Divorced	6.6	8782	0.25	6.1 - 7.0	0.95
	Separated	2.6	8782	0.18	2.2 - 2.9	1.07
All persons aged 16 to 24	Married	4.6	2064	0.58	3.5 - 5.7	1.26
	Cohabiting	12.4	2064	1.00	10.4 - 14.3	1.38
	Single	82.6	2064	1.09	80.4 - 84.7	1.31
	Widowed	0.1	2064	0.05	0.0 - 0.1	1.02
	Divorced	0.1	2064	0.05	0.0 - 0.1	1.02
	Separated	0.4	2064	0.14	0.1 - 0.7	1.03
All persons aged 25 to 34	Married	41.3	2899	1.16	39.0 - 43.5	1.27
	Cohabiting	22.3	2899	0.92	20.4 - 24.1	1.19
	Single	31.4	2899	1.15	29.1 - 33.6	1.33
	Widowed	0.1	2899	0.05	0.0 - 0.2	0.95
	Divorced	2.5	2899	0.28	2.0 - 3.0	0.97
	Separated	2.3	2899	0.29	1.8 - 2.9	1.04
All persons aged 35 to 44	Married	64.6	3219	1.02	62.6 - 66.6	1.21
	Cohabiting	11.3	3219	0.68	10.0 - 12.6	1.22
	Single	12.6	3219	0.67	11.3 - 13.9	1.14
	Widowed	0.6	3219	0.14	0.4 - 0.9	1.00
	Divorced	7.3	3219	0.46	6.4 - 8.2	1.00
	Separated	3.5	3219	0.35	2.8 - 4.1	1.09
All persons aged 45 to 54	Married	72.9	2777	0.99	71.0 74.9	1.17
	Cohabiting	6.2	2777	0.62	5.0 - 7.5	1.35
	Single	6.4	2777	0.47	6.5 - 7.4	1.01
	Widowed	2.1	2777	0.29	1.5 - 2.7	1.07
	Divorced	9.3	2777	0.60	8.1 - 10.5	1.09
	Separated	2.9	2777	0.35	2.2 - 3.6	1.10
All persons aged 55 to 64	Married	72.6	2370	1.05	70.6 - 74.7	1.15
	Cohabiting	2.9	2370	0.45	2.1 - 3.8	1.30
	Single	6.1	2370	0.55	6.0 - 7.1	1.12
	Widowed	6.5	2370	0.51	5.5 - 7.5	1.01
	Divorced	9.3	2370	0.60	8.1 - 10.4	1.01
	Separated	2.6	2370	0.37	1.9 - 3.4	1.13
All persons aged 65 to 74	Married	64.4	1882	1.39	61.6 - 67.1	1.26
	Cohabiting	1.8	1882	0.36	1.1 - 2.5	1.18
	Single	6.2	1882	0.59	5.0 - 7.4	1.06
	Widowed	20.2	1882	1.04	18.2 - 22.3	1.12
	Divorced	6.4	1882	0.65	5.1 - 7.3	1.15
	Separated	1.0	1882	0.25	0.5 - 1.5	1.10
All persons aged 75 and over	Married	41.4	1474	1.46	38.6 - 44.2	1.14
	Cohabiting	0.3	1474	0.13	0.0 - 0.5	0.98
	Single	6.3	1474	0.67	5.0 - 7.6	1.06
	Widowed	47.8	1474	1.37	45.1 - 50.5	1.05
	Divorced	3.0	1474	0.45	2.1 - 3.9	1.01
	Separated	1.2	1474	0.30	0.6 - 1.8	1.05

Table C.6 **Standard errors and 95% confidence intervals for ethnic origin***

Base	Characteristic	% (*p*)	Unweighted sample size	Standard error of *p*	95% confidence intervals	Deft
All persons aged 16 and over	White	92.5	16634	0.45	91.6 - 93.4	2.20
	Mixed race	0.7	16634	0.08	0.5 - 0.9	1.24
	Asian-Indian	1.5	16634	0.23	1.1 - 2.0	2.42
	Asian-Pakistani, Bangladeshi other	2.2	16634	0.31	1.6 - 2.8	2.74
	Black Caribbean	1.0	16634	0.12	0.7 - 1.2	1.58
	Black African	0.9	16634	0.12	0.6 - 1.1	1.66
	Other	1.3	16634	0.11	1.1 - 1.5	1.26

* Other includes other Black groups. Information on those giving no answer has not been presented.

Table C.7 **Standard errors and 95% confidence intervals for education level**

Base	Characteristic	% (*p*)	Unweighted sample size	Standard error of *p*	95% confidence intervals	Deft
All persons aged 16 to 69	Higher education	31.3	13035	0.58	30.2 - 32.5	1.43
	Other qualifications	45.9	13035	0.53	44.8 - 46.9	1.21
	None	22.8	13035	0.53	21.8 - 23.9	1.44
All men aged 16 to 69	Higher education	34.6	6085	0.74	33.2 - 36.1	1.21
	Other qualifications	44.9	6085	0.74	43.5 - 46.4	1.16
	None	20.4	6085	0.64	19.2 - 21.7	1.24
All women aged 16 to 69	Higher education	28.2	6950	0.65	26.9 - 29.5	1.20
	Other qualifications	46.7	6950	0.65	45.4 - 48.0	1.09
	None	25.1	6950	0.63	23.9 - 26.3	1.21

Table C.8 Standard errors and 95% confidence intervals for socio-economic group and employment status of adults

Base	Characteristic	% (*p*)	Unweighted sample size	Standard error of *p*	95% confidence intervals	Deft
All persons aged 16 and over	Higher managerial and professional	10.3	15684	0.35	9.6 - 11.0	1.44
	Lower managerial and professional	20.6	15684	0.39	19.9 - 21.4	1.21
	Intermediate	13.1	15684	0.29	12.5 - 13.6	1.08
	Small employers and own account	7.7	15684	0.26	7.2 - 8.2	1.22
	Lower supervisory and technical	10.6	15684	0.28	10.1 - 11.2	1.14
	Semi-routine	17.7	15684	0.35	17.0 - 18.4	1.15
	Routine	15.0	15684	0.35	14.3 - 15.7	1.23
	Never worked and long-term unemployed	5.0	15684	0.24	4.5 - 5.5	1.38
All men aged 16 and over	Higher managerial and professional	15.8	7420	0.51	14.8 - 16.8	1.20
	Lower managerial and professional	19.9	7420	0.51	18.9 - 20.9	1.10
	Intermediate	6.4	7420	0.31	5.7 - 7.0	1.10
	Small employers and own account	11.0	7420	0.42	10.2 - 11.8	1.16
	Lower supervisory and technical	15.4	7420	0.45	14.5 - 16.3	1.07
	Semi-routine	12.4	7420	0.38	11.7 - 13.1	0.99
	Routine	15.4	7420	0.49	14.4 - 16.4	1.17
	Never worked and long-term unemployed	3.8	7420	0.27	3.2 - 4.3	1.22
All women aged 16 and over	Higher managerial and professional	5.1	8264	0.31	4.5 - 5.7	1.28
	Lower managerial and professional	21.3	8264	0.49	20.3 - 22.2	1.09
	Intermediate	19.5	8264	0.46	18.5 - 20.4	1.06
	Small employers and own account	4.6	8264	0.23	4.1 - 5.0	1.00
	Lower supervisory and technical	6.1	8264	0.28	5.5 - 6.6	1.07
	Semi-routine	22.8	8264	0.52	21.8 - 23.8	1.13
	Routine	14.6	8264	0.43	13.8 - 15.5	1.11
	Never worked and long-term unemployed	6.2	8264	0.33	5.5 - 6.8	1.25
All persons aged 16 to 44	Higher managerial and professional	11.6	7276	0.62	10.5 - 12.6	1.39
	Lower managerial and professional	22.1	7276	0.57	21.0 - 23.2	1.17
	Intermediate	13.8	7276	0.45	12.9 - 14.7	1.11
	Small employers and own account	6.9	7276	0.35	6.2 - 7.6	1.18
	Lower supervisory and technical	10.1	7276	0.38	9.3 - 10.9	1.08
	Semi-routine	16.1	7276	0.45	15.2 - 17.0	1.04
	Routine	12.9	7276	0.47	12.0 - 13.8	1.20
	Never worked and long-term unemployed	7.0	7276	0.36	6.2 - 7.7	1.21
All persons aged 45 to 64	Higher managerial and professional	10.3	5068	0.49	9.4 - 11.3	1.15
	Lower managerial and professional	21.5	5068	0.67	20.2 - 22.8	1.16
	Intermediate	12.3	5068	0.45	11.5 - 13.2	0.97
	Small employers and own account	9.4	5068	0.50	8.4 - 10.4	1.22
	Lower supervisory and technical	10.5	5068	0.46	9.6 - 11.4	1.07
	Semi-routine	18.3	5068	0.58	17.2 - 19.5	1.07
	Routine	14.7	5068	0.56	13.6 - 15.8	1.13
	Never worked and long-term unemployed	2.9	5068	0.25	2.4 - 3.4	1.07
All persons aged 65 to 74	Higher managerial and professional	8.0	1875	0.62	6.8 - 9.2	0.99
	Lower managerial and professional	16.2	1875	0.88	14.5 - 17.9	1.03
	Intermediate	11.6	1875	0.75	10.1 - 13.0	1.02
	Small employers and own account	7.4	1875	0.65	6.2 - 8.7	1.07
	Lower supervisory and technical	11.1	1875	0.78	9.6 - 12.6	1.08
	Semi-routine	21.0	1875	1.06	18.9 - 23.0	1.13
	Routine	21.2	1875	1.11	19.0 - 23.4	1.18
	Never worked and long-term unemployed	3.6	1875	0.48	2.6 - 4.5	1.12
All persons aged 75 and over	Higher managerial and professional	6.3	1466	0.62	5.1 - 7.5	0.98
	Lower managerial and professional	15.0	1466	0.90	13.2 - 16.7	0.97
	Intermediate	13.3	1466	0.85	11.6 - 15.0	0.96
	Small employers and own account	6.5	1466	0.63	5.3 - 7.8	0.98
	Lower supervisory and technical	13.3	1466	0.93	11.4 - 15.1	1.05
	Semi-routine	20.3	1466	1.12	18.1 - 22.5	1.07
	Routine	19.8	1466	1.10	17.6 - 21.9	1.06
	Never worked and long-term unemployed	5.6	1466	0.70	4.3 - 7.0	1.16
All persons aged 16 and over	In employment	60.4	16443	0.54	59.3 - 61.4	1.42
	Unemployed	2.6	16443	0.14	2.4 - 2.9	1.12
	Economically inactive	37.0	16443	0.53	36.0 - 38.0	1.41
All men aged 16 and over	In employment	67.3	7757	0.63	66.1 - 68.6	1.18
	Unemployed	3.5	7757	0.23	3.0 - 3.9	1.11
	Economically inactive	29.2	7757	0.60	28.0 - 30.4	1.16
All women aged 16 and over	In employment	53.8	8686	0.61	52.6 - 54.9	1.14
	Unemployed	1.8	8686	0.15	1.5 - 2.1	1.04
	Economically inactive	44.4	8686	0.61	43.2 - 45.6	1.14

Table C.9 Standard errors and 95% confidence intervals for health measures

Base	Characteristic	% (*p*)	Unweighted sample size	Standard error of *p*	95% confidence intervals	Deft
All persons	Longstanding illness	31.5	20900	0.44	30.7 - 32.4	1.37
	Limiting longstanding illness	18.6	20897	0.34	17.9 - 19.2	1.26
	Restricted activity in the last 14 days	13.7	20907	0.29	13.1 - 14.3	1.22
All males	Longstanding illness	31.6	9998	0.55	30.6 - 32.7	1.18
	Limiting longstanding illness	18.1	9996	0.43	17.2 - 18.9	1.12
	Restricted activity in the last 14 days	12.7	10001	0.36	12.0 - 13.4	1.08
All females	Longstanding illness	31.4	10902	0.53	30.4 - 32.5	1.19
	Limiting longstanding illness	19.1	10901	0.40	18.3 - 19.9	1.06
	Restricted activity in the last 14 days	14.7	10906	0.38	13.9 - 15.4	1.12
All persons aged 0 to 4	Longstanding illness	14.2	1343	0.98	12.3 - 16.2	1.03
	Limiting longstanding illness	4.3	1343	0.57	3.2 - 5.4	1.03
	Restricted activity in the last 14 days	8.7	1343	0.89	6.9 - 10.4	1.16
All persons aged 5 to 15	Longstanding illness	18.2	3135	0.71	16.8 - 19.6	1.03
	Limiting longstanding illness	8.5	3134	0.53	7.4 - 9.5	1.07
	Restricted activity in the last 14 days	9.6	3139	0.63	8.3 - 10.8	1.20
All persons aged 16 to 44	Longstanding illness	21.7	7994	0.54	20.7 - 22.8	1.17
	Limiting longstanding illness	11.3	7994	0.38	10.6 - 12.0	1.07
	Restricted activity in the last 14 days	10.9	7998	0.38	10.1 - 11.6	1.09
All persons aged 45 to 64	Longstanding illness	42.8	5087	0.81	41.2 - 44.3	1.17
	Limiting longstanding illness	26.8	5087	0.69	25.4 - 28.1	1.11
	Restricted activity in the last 14 days	17.1	5089	0.59	15.9 - 18.2	1.12
All persons aged 65 to 74	Longstanding illness	56.9	1875	1.23	54.5 - 59.4	1.08
	Limiting longstanding illness	36.4	1874	1.20	34.1 - 38.8	1.08
	Restricted activity in the last 14 days	19.1	1872	0.93	17.3 - 21.0	1.02
All persons aged 75+	Longstanding illness	63.2	1466	1.43	60.4 - 66.0	1.14
	Limiting longstanding illness	45.9	1465	1.45	43.0 - 48.7	1.11
	Restricted activity in the last 14 days	25.1	1466	1.22	22.7 - 27.5	1.08

Table C.10 Standard errors and 95% confidence intervals for cigarette smoking

Base	Characteristic	% (*p*)	Unweighted sample size	Standard error of *p*	95% confidence intervals	Deft
All persons aged 16 and over	Current smoker	26.9	15354	0.47	26.0 - 27.8	1.31
	Ex-regular smoker	23.6	15354	0.42	22.8 - 24.4	1.23
	Never regularly smoked	49.5	15354	0.49	48.5 - 50.4	1.21
All men aged 16 and over	Current smoker	28.3	7055	0.60	27.2 - 29.5	1.12
	Ex-regular smoker	26.6	7055	0.56	25.5 - 27.7	1.06
	Never regularly smoked	45.0	7055	0.64	43.8 - 46.3	1.08
All women aged 16 and over	Current smoker	25.6	8299	0.54	24.6 - 26.7	1.13
	Ex-regular smoker	20.9	8299	0.53	19.8 - 21.9	1.19
	Never regularly smoked	53.5	8299	0.61	52.3 - 54.7	1.11

Table C.11 Standard errors and 95% confidence intervals for alcohol consumption (maximum daily amount)

Base	Characteristic	% (*p*)	Unweighted sample size	Standard error of *p*	95% confidence intervals	Deft
All men aged 16 and over	Drank nothing last week	25.6	7054	0.67	24.3 - 26.9	1.29
	Drank up to 4 units	35.8	7054	0.64	34.5 - 37.1	1.12
	Drank more than 4 and up to 8 units	17.2	7054	0.48	16.2 - 18.1	1.07
	Drank more than 8 units	21.5	7054	0.56	20.4 - 22.4	1.15
All women aged 16 and over	Drank nothing last week	40.8	8299	0.69	39.4 - 42.1	1.28
	Drank up to 4 units	36.8	8299	0.59	35.6 - 37.9	1.11
	Drank more than 4 and up to 8 units	12.6	8299	0.41	11.8 - 13.4	1.12
	Drank more than 8 units	9.8	8299	0.40	9.0 - 10.6	1.22
All aged 16 to 24	Drank nothing last week	35.6	1685	1.42	32.8 - 38.4	1.22
	Drank up to 4 units	20.6	1685	0.99	18.6 - 22.5	1.01
	Drank more than 4 and up to 8 units	12.7	1685	0.95	10.8 - 14.6	1.17
	Drank more than 8 units	31.1	1685	1.31	28.6 - 33.7	1.16
All aged 25 to 44	Drank nothing last week	28.2	5633	0.78	26.6 - 29.7	1.30
	Drank up to 4 units	33.7	5633	0.73	32.2 - 35.1	1.16
	Drank more than 4 and up to 8 units	17.3	5633	0.53	16.3 - 18.4	1.05
	Drank more than 8 units	20.8	5633	0.65	19.6 - 22.1	1.20
All aged 45 to 64	Drank nothing last week	31.7	4824	0.83	30.1 - 33.4	1.24
	Drank up to 4 units	40.8	4824	0.82	39.2 - 42.4	1.16
	Drank more than 4 and up to 8 units	16.9	4824	0.58	15.8 - 18.0	1.07
	Drank more than 8 units	10.6	4824	0.52	9.6 - 11.6	1.17
All aged 65 and over	Drank nothing last week	40.5	1813	1.40	37.8 - 43.3	1.21
	Drank up to 4 units	45.1	1813	1.38	42.4 - 47.8	1.18
	Drank more than 4 and up to 8 units	10.5	1813	0.76	9.0 - 12.0	1.06
	Drank more than 8 units	3.9	1813	0.48	2.9 - 4.8	1.06
All aged 16 and over	Drank nothing last week	33.6	15353	0.60	32.4 - 34.7	1.57
	Drank up to 4 units	36.3	15353	0.50	35.3 - 37.3	1.29
	Drank more than 4 and up to 8 units	14.8	15353	0.33	14.1 - 15.4	1.15
	Drank more than 8 units	15.4	15353	0.39	14.6 - 16.1	1.34

Table C.12 **Standard errors and 95% confidence intervals for number of cohabitations**

Base	Characteristic	% (*p*)	Unweighted sample size	Standard error of *p*	95% confidence intervals	Deft
All women aged 16 to 59	None	87.0	5930	0.45	86.1 - 87.9	1.03
	One	10.3	5930	0.41	9.5 - 11.1	1.04
	Two or more	2.7	5930	0.21	2.3 - 3.1	0.99
All men aged 16 to 59	None	86.3	5100	0.50	85.3 - 87.3	1.04
	One	9.8	5100	0.45	8.9 - 10.7	1.08
	Two or more	3.9	5100	0.29	3.4 - 4.8	1.07
All people aged 16 to 24	None	91.6	1678	0.76	90.1 - 93.1	1.12
	One	7.3	1678	0.71	5.9 - 8.7	1.12
	Two or more	1.1	1678	0.26	0.6 - 1.6	1.01
All people aged 25 to 34	None	78.3	2637	0.90	76.6 - 80.1	1.12
	One	16.4	2637	0.81	14.8 - 18.0	1.12
	Two or more	5.3	2637	0.46	4.4 - 6.2	1.06
All people aged 35 to 44	None	83.4	2960	0.74	81.9 - 84.8	1.08
	One	12.2	2960	0.63	11.0 - 13.5	1.05
	Two or more	4.4	2960	0.42	3.6 - 5.2	1.11
All people aged 45 to 54	None	92.2	2581	0.53	91.2 - 93.3	1.01
	One	5.6	2581	0.45	4.7 - 6.5	0.99
	Two or more	2.2	2581	0.31	1.6 - 2.8	1.08
All people aged 55 to 59	None	95.3	1174	0.70	93.9 - 96.7	1.14
	One	3.1	1174	0.57	2.0 - 4.2	1.13
	Two or more	1.6	1174	0.42	0.7 - 2.4	1.16
All people aged 16 to 59	None	86.7	11030	0.36	85.9 - 87.4	1.11
	One	10.0	11030	0.32	9.4 - 10.7	1.12
	Two or more	3.3	11030	0.18	2.9 - 3.7	1.06

Appendix D

Weighting and grossing

All surveys accept that there will be some degree of nonresponse, although great efforts are made to keep nonresponse to a minimum[1]. During the review of the GHS in 1999, two methods of compensating for nonresponse were examined with the aim of improving the quality of data. The method adopted to compensate for **total nonresponse** (where all survey information for a sampled household is missing) will be described here. The method adopted to reduce **item nonresponse** (where information for particular questions is missing as the result of conducting proxy interviews) is discussed in Appendix B.

The 2001 GHS is weighted using a two-step approach. In the first step, the data is weighted to compensate for nonresponse (sample-based weighting). The second step weights the sample distribution so that it matches the population distribution in terms of region, age-group and sex (population-based weighting).[2]

Weighting for nonresponse

Weighting for total nonresponse involves giving each respondent a weight so that they represent the non-respondents who are similar to them in terms of survey characteristics. To be able to use this method, information about non-respondents is needed. By their very nature, non-responding households yield little information. Although some surveys collect information about the characteristics of these households, information about non-respondents is not routinely collected on the GHS. An alternative approach to gaining information about the GHS's non-responding households was needed to carry out such a weighting procedure.

Sample-based weighting using the Census

The decennial Census was found to be the most appropriate source of information about non-responding addresses on the GHS. Unlike the GHS which is conducted by respondents on a voluntary basis, the Census is mandatory therefore nonresponse is kept to an absolute minimum.

After the 1991 Census, methodological work was conducted to match Census addresses with the sampled addresses of some of the large continuous surveys, of which the GHS was one. In this way it was possible to match the address details of the GHS respondents as well as the non-respondents with corresponding information gathered from the Census for the same address. It was then possible to identify any types of household that were being under-represented in the survey. Similar work is being conducted using the 2001 census, however information will not be available until 2003.

The information collected during the 1991 Census/ GHS matching work was used to weight the 2001/02 GHS data by identifying types of households that differed in terms of response rates. A combination of household variables such as household type, social class, region and car ownership were analysed using the software package Answer Tree (using the chi-squared statistic CHAID)[3] to identify which characteristics were most significant in distinguishing between responding and non-responding households. These characteristics are sorted by the program to produce the weighting classes shown in Figure D.A. The variables used to identify the weighting classes were restricted to those that appear annually on the GHS.

Figure D.A

Population-based weighting (grossing)

Population-based weighting schemes address deficiencies in the data due to sample-non coverage.

The GHS sample is based on private households, which means that the population totals used in the weighting need to relate to people in private households. These totals are taken from the Labour Force Survey (LFS). The LFS derives household population estimates by excluding residents of institutions initially from population projections based on mid-year estimates[4]. Since the LFS estimates are based on population projections as well as estimates, they are generally available earlier than the mid-year estimates, so in 2000, when weighting was introduced, the GHS was able to use the 2000 LFS household population estimates.

The situation regarding the weighting of the 2001 results presented in this report was less straightforward. We knew that by the time the results were published, the 2001 census figures would be available which would lead to some revision of all forms of population estimates and could also lead to confusion over which set of LFS 2001 population estimates the GHS had used. We had started the preparation of the weights using LFS

Figure D.A **Weighting classes formed in the CHAID analysis**

Level 1 split	Level 2 split	Level 3 split	Level 4 split	Weight class
Region North East Merseyside Yorks & Humbs W Midlands South East Scotland	**No. of Cars** 0 or 1	**No. of dependent children** 0 or 1	**Household type 1** 1 adult 16-59 Youngest 5-15 3+ adults no child	1
			Household type 1 2 adults 16-59 Youngest 0-4 2 adults, 1 or 2 60+ 1 adult only 60+	2
		No. of dependent children 2 or more		3
	No. of Cars 2 or more			4
Region North West E Midlands Eastern South West	**Pensioner HH** Pensioner in HH	**SEG (grouped)** Skilled Manual Partly-skilled manual Unskilled manual & others Not employed in last 10 years		5
		SEG (grouped) Professional Manager/employer Intermediate/jnr		6
	Pensioner HH No pensioner in HH	**No. of adults** 1		7
		No. of adults 2 or more	**Social Class** I, II, IV Not employed in last 10 years	8
			Social Class IIInm, IIIm, V Other	9
Region London	**Type of building** Detached Semi-detached Terraced Converted flat/other			10
	Type of building Purpose built flat			11
Region Wales				12

2000 population estimates, so this was continued as the basis for the population element of the weighting of the 2001 data. Since the weighted bases themselves are not recommended as a source for population estimates[5], it was not the intention to revise the GHS figures in the light of the census results.

The results from the 2001 Census, published on 30 September 2002, showed that previous estimates of the total UK population were around one million too high, with disparities being most apparent among men aged 25 to 39. These disparities were larger than expected and thus have two implications for figures presented in this report.

- Some of the percentages may need revision as they are based on old population figures
- The weighted bases will all change to some degree because of the reduction in estimated population size.

Thus, for this 2001 report the general caution regarding the use of weighted bases is re-iterated. Weighted bases should primarily be considered as bases for the percentages shown rather than estimates of population size.

ONS published interim revised estimates of the population in October 2002 but this was too far along the GHS reporting process to be incorporated.

Revised GHS estimates will be released in Spring 2003 based on new LFS population estimates following the release of the final census-based revisions of population data in February 2003. For more details about the revised census-based estimates see **www.statistics.gov.uk/census2001.**

The population information and GHS data were grouped into 12 age and sex categories within 6 region categories to form weighting classes as shown in Figure D.B[6]. The population data and the GHS data were then matched using the age and sex categories within region giving corresponding population totals for each of these sub-groups within the GHS sample.

The population-based and sample-based weighting methods were used in conjunction to produce the final weight. The final weight was created using a calibration procedure called CALMAR (a SAS-based Macro)[6] which used the pre-weighted (sample-based weighted) data.

Figure D.B

Presentation and interpretation of weighted data

Weighted data cannot be meaningfully compared to unweighted data from previous years without knowledge of how the weighting changes the estimates. In trend tables in the 2001 report weighted and unweighted data is presented for 1998 data and the weighted data only is shown for 2000 and 2001. Care should be taken when interpreting trend data or individual tables compared with other years as part of a time series.

As described above, population estimates from which the weighted bases in the tables are derived have been shown to require some revision. Weighted bases are given solely for the interpretation of table percentages, and are not a completely accurate representation of population numbers.

Tables D.1 and D.2 identify the effects of weighting by comparing unweighted and weighted data for 2001 and showing the differences between the weighted and unweighted estimates for 1998, 2000 and 2001 on a selection of household and individual level variables.

Tables D.1 and D.2

Figure D.B **Weighting classes used for CALMAR analysis**

Age/sex	Region
0-4	London
5-15	Scotland
16-24 Male	Wales
16-24 Female	Other metropolitan
25-44 Male	Other non-metropolitan
25-44 Female	South East
45-64 Male	
45-64 Female	
65-74 Male	
65-74 Female	
75+ Male	
75+ Female	

Effects of weighting on data

A comparison of the characteristics recorded on the 1991 Census forms of respondents and non-respondents in the 1991 GHS sample showed that households comprising one adult aged 16 to 59 or a couple with non-dependent children were under-represented[7]. Households containing dependent children were over-represented in the responding sample. As would be expected, weighting has changed the value of the estimate for some variables, but the overall changes have been relatively small. For the 2001 estimates, the most marked effect of weighting was seen in the following variables. None of the effects are large.

Increase in value of estimate.

- 1 person households from 29% to 31%.
- male current cigarette smokers from 27% to 28%.
- 1 adult households from 34% to 35%.

Decrease in value of estimate.

- 2 adult households from 51% to 49%.
- owns home outright from 29% to 27%.
- households containing a married couple with no children 25% to 23%.

The differences between the weighted and unweighted data for 1998 and 2000 are also shown in Tables D.1 and D.2. It can be seen that the differences produced by weighting in 2001 were similar to those in 1998 and 2000 for the same variables.

Tables D.1 and D.2

Notes and references

[1] Appendix B describes the variation in response for the GHS since it began in 1971.

[2] Barton, J. Developing a Weighting and Grossing System for the General Household Survey : *Social Survey Methodology Bulletin* (Issue 49 July 2001).

[3] CHAID is an acronym that stands for Chi-squared Automatic Interaction Detection. As is suggested by its name, CHAID uses chi-squared statistics to identify optimal splits or groupings of independent variables in terms of predicting the outcome of a dependent variable, in this case response.

[4] These estimates are revised when mid year estimates for the appropriate year are available.

[5] Missing answers are excluded from the tables and in some cases this is reflected in the weighted bases, i.e. these numbers vary between tables. For this reason, the bases themselves are not recommended as a source for population estimates. Recommended data sources for population estimates for most socio-demographic groups are: ONS mid-year estimates, the Labour Force Survey, or Housing Statistics from the Office of the Deputy Prime Minister.

[6] CALMAR uses a calibration procedure, also known as raking ratio or rim weighting, which divides the sample into weighting classes which in this case will have known population totals. The weighting classes used were those that were recommended for the GHS by Elliot, D. (1999) Report of the Task Force on Weighting and Estimation, *GSS Methodology Series.*

[7] *Foster K et al. General Household Survey 1993.* HMSO 1995. Appendix C.

Table D1 **Weighted versus unweighted data for years 1998 to 2001**

Household level variables

% of households		2001		Effect of weighting		
		Unweighted (a)	Weighted (b)	Weighted 1998-Unweighted 1998	Weighted 2000-Unweighted 2000	Weighted 2001-Unweighted 2001 (b-a)
Household size						
1 person		28.9	30.6	1.9	2.4	1.7
2 persons		35.6	34.2	-1.3	-1.6	-1.4
3 persons		15.6	15.8	0.2	0.2	0.2
4 persons		13.8	13.5	-0.4	-0.5	-0.3
5 persons		4.3	4.2	-0.1	-0.3	-0.1
6 or more persons		1.9	1.7	-0.2	-0.1	-0.2
	Base	*8989*				
Number of adults						
1 adult		34.3	35.5	1.4	1.9	1.2
2 adults		51.1	49.1	-2.7	-2.6	-2.0
3 adults		10.5	10.9	0.5	0.3	0.4
4 or more adults		4.1	4.5	0.7	0.5	0.4
	Base	*8989*				
Number of children						
No children		72.2	73.3	1.5	1.5	1.1
1 child		11.8	11.8	0.3	0.0	0.0
2 children		11.4	10.7	-1.0	-0.8	-0.7
3 or more children		4.6	4.2	-0.8	-0.6	-0.4
	Base					
Household type						
1 person only		28.8	30.7	1.9	2.4	1.9
2 or more unrelated adults		2.7	2.9	0.4	0.3	0.2
Married couple, dependent children		18.9	18.3	-0.8	-0.8	-0.6
Married couple, independent children		5.7	6.0	0.3	0.4	0.3
Married couple, no children		25	23.3	-2.0	-2.3	-1.7
Lone parent, dependent children		7.2	6.7	-0.4	-0.5	-0.5
Lone parent, independent children		2.3	2.5	0.1	0.2	0.2
2 or more families (inc.same sex cohab)		1	1.1	-0.1	0.0	0.1
Cohabiting couple, with children		3.3	3.3	0.0	0.0	0.0
Cohabiting couple, no children		4.9	5.2	0.4	0.4	0.3
	Base	*8961*				
Tenure - harmonised						
Owns outright		28.9	27.2	-1.7	-1.9	-1.7
Buying on mortgage		40.9	41.4	0.3	0.1	0.5
Rents from LA		14.8	15.0	0.1	0.5	0.2
Rents from HA		6.2	6.3	0.1	0.1	0.1
Rents privately - unfurnished/nk		6.6	7.0	0.4	0.5	0.4
Rents privately - furnished		2.6	3.2	0.6	0.6	0.6
	Base		*8989*			
Ownership of consumer durables						
Video		88.6	88.4	-0.4	-0.6	-0.2
Freezer		94.8	94.4	-0.6	-0.6	-0.4
Washing machine		92.8	92.2	-0.8	-0.7	-0.6
Drier		54.9	54.0	-1.1	-1.4	-0.9
Dishwasher		28.4	27.5	-1.0	-1.4	-0.9
Microwave oven		85.7	85.3	-0.6	-0.6	-0.4
Telephone		98.2	98.1	-0.3	-0.2	-0.1
Cd player		79.1	79.5	0.8	0.0	0.4
Home computer		49.2	49.5	0.4	-0.1	0.3
	Base	*8989*				
Central heating		92.4	92.2	-0.3	-0.3	-0.2
	Base	*8989*				
Car ownership						
No car		27.0	27.6	0.6	1.1	0.6
1 car		43.8	44.2	0.6	0.4	0.4
2 cars		23.8	22.8	-1.1	-1.3	-1.0
3 or more cars		5.4	5.4	-0.1	-0.2	0.0
	Base	*8989*				

Table D2 Weighted versus unweighted data for years 1998 to 2001

Individual level variables

% of individuals	2001 Unweighted (a)	2001 Weighted (b)	Effect of weighting: Weighted 1998-Unweighted 1998	Effect of weighting: Weighted 2000-Unweighted 2000	Effect of weighting: Weighted 2001-Unweighted 2001 (b-a)
Limiting longstanding Illness					
Male	18.4	18.1	-0.2	-0.3	-0.3
Female	19.2	19.1	-0.1	0.0	-0.1
Total	18.8	18.6	-0.1	-0.1	-0.2
Non-limiting longstanding Illness					
Male	13.8	13.6	-0.4	-0.2	-0.2
Female	12.4	12.3	0.0	-0.1	-0.1
Total	13.1	12.9	-0.2	-0.1	-0.2
No longstanding Illness					
Male	67.8	68.4	0.6	0.5	0.6
Female	68.4	68.6	0.1	-0.1	0.2
Total	68.1	68.5	0.4	0.2	0.4
General health					
Good					
Male	65.5	65.5	0.6	0.1	0.0
Female	62.6	62.5	0.2	-0.3	-0.1
Total	64.0	64.0	0.5	-0.1	0.0
Fairly good					
Male	23.4	23.4	-0.2	0.0	0.0
Female	25.4	25.4	0.0	0.2	0.0
Total	24.4	24.5	-0.2	0.0	0.1
Not good					
Male	11.1	11.0	-0.4	0.0	-0.1
Female	12.0	12.1	-0.2	0.1	0.1
Total	11.6	11.6	-0.3	0.0	0.0
Restricted activity in the last 14 days					
Male	12.6	12.7	0.0	-0.1	0.1
Female	14.6	14.6	0.0	0.1	0.0
Total	13.6	13.7	-0.1	-0.1	0.1
Cigarette smoking by sex					
Men					
Current cigarette smokers	27.1	28.3	1.4	1.2	1.2
Ex-regular cigarette smokers	28.0	26.6	-2.0	-2.0	-1.4
Never or (only occasionally) smoked	44.9	45.0	0.6	0.8	0.1
Women					
Current cigarette smokers	25.3	25.6	0.4	0.2	0.3
Ex-regular cigarette smokers	20.9	20.9	-0.3	-0.3	0.0
Never or (only occasionally) smoked	53.8	53.5	-0.1	0.1	-0.3
Total					
Current cigarette smokers	26.1	26.9	0.8	0.8	0.8
Ex-regular cigarette smokers	24.2	23.6	-0.9	-1.0	-0.6
Never or (only occasionally) smoked	49.7	49.5	0.1	0.3	-0.2
Weekly alcohol consumption by sex					
Men					
non-drinker	8.9	8.9	-0.1	0.3	0.0
under 1 unit	11.3	11.2	-0.2	-0.2	-0.1
1-10 units	31.4	31.0	-0.6	-0.6	-0.4
11-20 units	21.9	21.9	0.1	-0.1	0.0
21-35 units	14.2	14.2	0.1	0.2	0.0
36-50 units	6.3	6.5	0.2	0.1	0.2
51 + units	6.0	6.4	0.5	0.3	0.4
Women					
non-drinker	14.8	14.9	0.0	0.4	0.1
under 1 unit	22.1	22.0	0.0	-0.1	-0.1
1-7 units	32.5	32.5	-0.1	-0.3	0.0
8-14 units	15.4	15.3	0.0	-0.1	-0.1
15-25 units	9.3	9.3	0.1	0.1	0.0
26 -35 units	2.9	2.9	0.0	0.0	0.0
36+ units	3.0	3.0	0.1	0.0	0.0

Appendix E

Changes to classifications in the 2001 data set

In line with National Statistics guidelines and to maintain a harmonised approach to data collection and outputs, some of the classification systems used previously on the GHS have been amended or replaced for 2001. These include:

- the replacement of Socio-economic Group (SEG) and Social Class (SC) with the National Statistics Socio-economic Classification (NS-SEC);
- changes to the ethnic classification system;
- the introduction of a new national identity classification system.

The outputs for the these classifications have been developed from the new harmonised questions in the 2001 survey. This has had major implications for the presentation in the report of data using any of these classification systems or variables based on them.

The introduction of NS-SEC

NS-SEC is an occupational based classification which can be extended to cover the whole adult population. To create NS-SEC information is required on the following:

- Occupation- using the Standard Occupation Classification 2000 (SOC 2000).
- Employment status - whether an individual is an employer, self-employed or employee; whether a supervisor and the number of employees at the workplace.

NS-SEC consists of 14 operational categories and 3 residual categories (See Figure E.A). The three residual categories: L15 (full time students); L16 (occupation not stated or inadequately described) and L17 (not classifiable for other reasons) are excluded when the classification is collapsed into its analytical classes.

Figure E.A

Analytical classes

Within the conceptual model, it is possible to have eight, five and three class versions of NS-SEC. The nested relationship between the 8, 5 and 3-class version is given in Figure E.B, whilst examples of occupations in the NS-SEC categories can be found in figure E.C The number of classes used depends on the purpose of the analysis and the quality of available data. Note should be taken that none of the class versions should be considered as ordinal (i.e. the class numbers do not necessarily indicate a 'progression' of classes).

Figures E.B, E.C

Figure E.A **Analytic classes and operational categories and sub categories of NS-SEC**

Analytic Classes	Operational Categories and Sub-Categories
1.1	L1 Employers in large organisations
	L2 Higher managerial occupations
1.2	L3 Higher professional occupations
	L3.1 'Traditional' employees
	L3.2 'New' employees
	L3.3 'Traditional' self-employed
	L3.4 'New' self-employed
2	L4 Lower professional and higher technical occupations
	L4.1 'Traditional' employees
	L4.2 'New' employees
	L4.3 'Traditional' self-employed
	L4.4 'New' self-employed
	L5 Lower managerial occupations
	L6 Higher supervisory occupations
3	L7 Intermediate occupations
	L7.1 Intermediate clerical and administrative
	L7.2 Intermediate sales and service
	L7.3 Intermediate technical and auxiliary
	L7.4 Intermediate engineering
4	L8 Employers in small organisations
	L8.1 Employers in small organisations (non-professional)
	L8.2 Employers in small organisations (agriculture)
	L9 Own account workers
	L9.1 Own account workers (non-professional)
	L9.2 Own account workers (agriculture)
5	L10 Lower supervisory occupations
	L11 Lower technical occupations
	L11.1 Lower technical craft
	L11.2 Lower technical process operative
6	L12 Semi-routine occupations
	L12.1 Semi-routine sales
	L12.2 Semi-routine service
	L12.3 Semi-routine technical
	L12.4 Semi-routine operative
	L12.5 Semi-routine agricultural
	L12.6 Semi-routine clerical
	L12.7 Semi-routine childcare
7	L13 Routine occupations
	L13.1 Routine sales and service
	L13.2 Routine production
	L13.3 Routine technical
	L13.4 Routine operative
	L13.5 Routine agricultural
8	L14 Never worked and long-term unemployed
	L14.1 Never worked
	L14.2 Long-term unemployed
*	L15 Full-time students
*	L16 Occupations not stated or inadequately described
*	L17 Not classifiable for other reasons

Continuity issues relating to Socio-economic Group (SEG)

The operational categories of NS-SEC can be aggregated to produce an approximated version of the previous Socio-economic Group (Figure E.D). These approximations have been shown to achieve an overall continuity level of 87%. Full details regarding the NS-SEC classification and continuity issues relating to SEG and Social Class (SC) can be found at:
http://www.statistics.gov.uk/methods_quality/ns_sec

The main differences users need to be aware of are:

- the introduction of SOC2000 which includes various new occupations not previously defined in SOC90;
- definitional variations in employment status in particular with reference to the term 'supervisor';
- the inclusion of armed forces personnel in the appropriate occupation group;
- the separate classification of full-time students, whether or not they have been or are presently in paid employment;
- the separate classification of long term unemployed who previously were classified by their most recent occupation.

Figure E.D

Comparison of GHS NS-SEC outputs with the Labour Force Survey (LFS)

Table E.1 compares GHS outputs for the eight analytical classes of NS-SEC with those obtained from the Labour Force Survey for the working age population of Great Britain. The combinations are broadly similar with the exception that the LFS was slightly more likely to classify people into the lower managerial occupational group. This anomaly is probably the result of different methodologies in data collection and slight operational differences between the GHS and LFS in the derivation of NS-SEC.

Table E.1

Figure E.B **NS-SEC classes and collapses**

8 Classes		5 Classes		3 classes	
1	Higher managerial and professional occupations	1	Managerial and professional occupations	1	Managerial and professional occupations
1.1	Large employers and higher managerial occupations				
1.2	Higher professional occupations				
2	Lower managerial and professional occupations				
3	Intermediate occupations	2	Intermediate occupations	2	Intermediate occupations
4	Small employers and own account workers	3	Small employers and own account workers		
5	Lower supervisory and technical occupations	4	Lower supervisory and technical occupations	3	Routine + manual occupations
6	Semi-routine occupations	5	Semi-routine and routine occupations		
7	Routine occupations				
8	Never worked and long-term unemployed		Never worked and long-term unemployed		Never worked and long-term unemployed

Figure E.C **Examples of occupations in each of the main NS-SEC categories**

Managerial & professional occupations	Accountant, artist, civil/mechanical engineer, medical practitioner, musician, nurse, police officer (sergeant or above), physiotherapist. Scientist, social worker, software designer, solicitor, teacher, welfare officer. Those usually responsible for planning, organising and co-ordinating work and for finance - e.g. finance manager, chief executive
Intermediate occupations	Call centre agent, clerical worker, nursery auxillary, office clerk, secretary
Small employers & own account workers	
Lower supervisory technical occupations	Electrician, fitter, gardener, inspector, plumber, printer, train driver, tool maker
Semi-routine & routine occupations	Bar staff, caretaker, catering assistant, cleaner, farm worker, HGV driver, labourer, machine operative, messenger, packer, porter, postal worker, receptionist, sales assistant, security guard, sewing machinist, van driver, waiter/waitress

Figure E.D **Operational categories of the NS-SEC linked to socio-economic group (SEG)**

Socio-economic group		NS-SEC Operational Categories
1	Employers and managers in central and local government, industry, commerce, etc. - large establishments	1, 2
2	Employers and managers in industry, commerce, etc. - small establishments	5, 8.1
3	Professional workers - self-employed	3.3
4	Professional workers - employees	3.1
5	Intermediate non-manual workers	3.2, 3.4, 4.1, 4.3, 7.3, 6
6	Junior non-manual workers	4.2, 7.1, 7.2, 12.1, 12.6
7	Personal service workers	12.7, 13.1
8	Foremen and supervisors - manual	10
9	Skilled manual workers	7.4, 11.1, 12.3, 13.3
10	Semi-skilled manual workers	11.2, 12.2, 12.4, 13.2
11	Unskilled manual workers	13.4
12	Own account workers (other than professional)	4.4, 9.1
13	Farmers - employers and managers	8.2
14	Farmers - own account	9.2
15	Agricultural workers	12.5, 13.5
16	Members of armed forces	-
17	Inadequately described and not stated occupations	16

Figure E.E **National Statistics ethnic group classifications**

Level 1	Level 2
WHITE	British Other White background
MIXED BACKGROUND	White and Black Caribbean White and Black African White and Asian Other Mixed background
ASIAN or ASIAN BRITISH	Indian Pakistani Bangladeshi Other Asian background
BLACK or BLACK BRITISH	Caribbean African Other Black background All Black groups
CHINESE or OTHER ETHNIC GROUP	Chinese Other ethnic group All Chinese or Other groups
NOT STATED	NOT STATED

The change in ethnic classification

The harmonised ethnic classification was changed in preparation for the 2001 census. The new classification (see Figure E.E) has a separate category for people from mixed ethnic backgrounds, in order to improve its relevance of the ethnic classification to the changing nature of the ethnic composition of the population. In the previous system, people with these backgrounds had to select a specific ethnic group or categorise themselves as 'other'.

A large scale trial was conducted using the LFS to investigate the effects of the change to the new classification. Respondents to the LFS were asked to classify their ethnic background based on the old system when they were first interviewed and then asked again using the new system when they were re-interviewed 3 months later. The results are shown in Table E.2 It can be seen that among those who classified themselves as having a mixed ethnic background using the new system, 13% had selected one of the minority ethnic groups under the old system, 18% had selected White and 69% had selected Other. This means it is not possible to recreate the categories previously used in the GHS and all major Government surveys.

This has affected the data presentation in two ways. It is no longer possible to continue the time series table nor to add years together to increase the sample size. Full details about this change can be found at:

http://www.statistics.gov.uk/about/classifications/downloads/ns_ethnicity_statement.doc

The GHS 2001/2 used Level 2 for collection of the data (see Figure E.E) and has used Level 1 for the table in the report. Both levels of classification are available for future data users.

Table E.2 Figure E.E

Comparison of GHS ethnic classification data with the LFS

Table E.3 compares the new ethnic classification based on GHS data with that from the LFS and indicates that the two data sets show the same distribution by broad ethnic group.

Table E.3

National identity

In addition to ethnic classification, interest has been shown in UK national identities to inform service and policy needs. In recognition of these requirements, and after testing and consultation with experts, the Office for National Statistics recommended a second dimension of national group information. The national categories tested and proposed were English; Scottish; Welsh; Irish; British and Other. The GHS adopted this proposal and included this question in the 2001/2 questionnaire. The question allowed respondents to choose more than one category. Three different prompt cards were produced with categories ordered to give priority to 'English, Scottish or Welsh' depending upon the area in which the interview was taking place.

Comparison of GHS national identity with the LFS

Table E.4 compares data from the GHS on national identity with that from the LFS. The table reveals close comparison with LFS data for people reporting 'English', 'Welsh', 'Scottish', 'Irish' and 'Other' in terms of their national identity. However GHS and LFS data differed in terms of people defining themselves as British (GHS 47%, LFS 37%) and the number of categories selected. This can be explained in terms of methodological differences since the GHS uses a show-card for this question and the LFS does not. As a result GHS respondents were more likely to select 'British' as a second response using the show card, whilst LFS responders were more likely to select a single option.

Table E.4

Table E.1 NS-SEC: Comparison of the General Household Survey and Labour Force Survey

Males 16-64, females 16-59 *Great Britain: 2001*

NS-SEC8	GHS	LFS
	%	%
1.1 Large employers and higher managerial occupations	4	5
1.2 Higher professional occupations	7	7
2.0 Lower managerial occupations	22	25
3.0 Intermediate occupations	13	12
4.0 Small employers and own account workers	8	8
5.0 Lower supervisory and technical occupations	10	11
6.0 Semi-routine occupations	17	16
7.0 Routine occupations	13	12
8.0 Never worked and long-term unemployed	5	4
Weighted base (000's)= 100%	*32,777*	*31,043*
Unweighted sample	*11792*	

Table E.2 Comparison of old and new ethnic classification using data from the Labour Force Survey

All persons *Labour Force Survey: 2001*

Old ethnic classification	New ethnic classification 2001						
	White	Mixed	Indian	Asian	Black	Other	All
	%	%	%	%	%	%	%
White	100	18	2	2	2	7	93
Black	0	12	0	1	89	0	2
Indian	0	1	95	3	0	1	2
Asian	0	0	0	77	0	0	1
Other	0	69	3	17	9	91	2
% in each of the new classification	93	1	2	2	2	1	100
Weighted base (000's) = 100%	*40,074*	*356*	*677*	*776*	*827*	*297*	*43,006*

Table E.3 Ethnic group: GHS and LFS compared

All persons *Great Britain: 2001*

Ethnic group	GHS		LFS	
	%		%	
White British	89	92	89	92
Other White	3		3	
Mixed background	1		1	
Indian	2	4	2	4
Other Asian background	3		2	
Black Caribbean	1	2	1	2*
Black African	1		1	
Other ethnic origin	1		1	
Weighted base (000's)= 100%	*57,034*		*57,483*	
Unweighted sample	*21102*			

* Including other Black groups not shown separately.

Table E.4 National identity: Comparison of the General Household Survey and Labour Force Survey

All persons *Great Britain: 2001*

National identity	GHS	LFS
	%	%
British	47	37
English	50	51
Welsh	4	4
Scottish	9	8
Irish	1	1
Other	5	5
Weighted base (000's) = 100%	*57,034*	*57,483*
Unweighted sample	*21102*	

* Percentages sum to more than 100% because some respondents give more than one answer.

Appendix F
General Household Survey 2001/02
Household Questionnaire

Areacode Information already entered

Address Information already entered

1..30

HHold Information already entered

1..4

StartDat ENTER DATE INTERVIEW WITH THIS HOUSEHOLD WAS STARTED

DateChk IS THIS...

The first time you've opened this questionnaire 1
or the second or later time? 2
EMERGENCY CODE IF COMPUTER'S DATE IS WRONG AT LATER CHECK 5

IntEdit CODE WHETHER THIS IS THE INTERVIEW STAGE, A PROXY CONVERSION OR THE EDIT STAGE

Interview 1
Proxy Conversion by telephone (TELEPHONE INTERVIEW UNIT ONLY) 2
OFFICE ONLY - EDIT 7

HOUSEHOLD INFORMATION

Information to be collected for all persons in all households

1. Name Who normally lives at this address?

RECORD THE NAME (OR A UNIQUE IDENTIFIER) FOR HOH, THEN A NAME / IDENTIFIER FOR EACH MEMBER OF THE HOUSEHOLD ....

ENTER TEXT OF AT MOST 12 CHARACTERS

2. Sex Male 1
Female 2

3. Birth What is your date of birth?

FOR DAY NOT GIVEN...........ENTER 15 FOR DAY.
FOR MONTH NOT GIVEN.....ENTER 6 FOR MONTH

4. AgeIf **Ask those who did not know, or refused to give their date of birth *(Birth = DK OR REFUSAL)***

What was your age last birthday?

98 or more = CODE 97

0..97

5. MarStat **Ask if respondent is aged 16 or over *(DVAge > 15)***

ASK OR RECORD CODE FIRST THAT APPLIES

Are you

single, that is, never married? 1
married and living with your husband/wife? 2
married and separated from your husband/wife? 3
divorced? 4
or widowed? 5

6. LiveWith **Ask if there is more than one person in the household AND respondent is aged 16 or over AND is single, separated, divorced or widowed *(Household size > 1 & DVAge > 15& Marstat = 1, 3, 4 or 5)***

ASK OR RECORD

May I just check, are you living with someone in the household as a couple?

Yes 1
No 2
SPONTANEOUS ONLY - same sex couple 3

7. Hhldr **Ask if there is more than one person in the household, AND the respondent is aged 16 or over *(Household size > 1 & DVAge > 15)***

In whose name is the accommodation owned or rented?
ASK OR RECORD

This person alone 1
This person jointly 3
NOT owner/renter 5

8. HiHNum **Ask if there is more than one person in the household, AND the accommodation is jointly owned *(Household size > 1 & Hhldr = 3)***

You have told me that...jointly own or rent the accommodation. Which of you/ who has the highest income (from earnings, benefits, pensions and any other sources)?

INTERVIEWER: THESE ARE THE JOINT HOUSEHOLDERS

ENTER PERSON NUMBER - IF TWO OR MORE HAVE SAME INCOME, ENTER 15
1..14

9. JntEldA **Ask if there is more than one person in the household, AND the joint householders have the same income *(Household size > 1 & HiHNum = 15)***

ENTER PERSON NUMBER OF THE ELDEST JOINT HOUSEHOLDER FROM THOSE WITH THE SAME HIGHEST INCOME

ASK OR RECORD

1..14

10. JntEldB **Ask if household size is greater than one, AND the joint householders do not know, or refuse to say who has the greatest income *(Household size > 1 & HiHNum = Don't know or Refusal)***

ENTER PERSON NUMBER OF THE ELDEST JOINT HOUSEHOLDER

ASK OR RECORD

1..14

11. HRPnum **Ask all households**

PERSON NUMBER OF HRP. (Computed in Blaise)

12. HRPprtnr **Ask if the HRP is married or cohabiting *(HRPnum = 1..14 & Marstat = 2 or LiveWith = 1)***

THE HRP IS (HRP's NAME)

ENTER THE PERSON NUMBER OF THE HRP's SPOUSE/PARTNER
NO SPOUSE/PARTNER = 15

1..15

13. R **Ask all households**

I would now like to ask how the people in your household are related to each other

CODE RELATIONSHIP - ... IS ...'S ....

Spouse	1
Cohabitee	2
Son/daughter (inc. adopted)	3
Step-son/daughter	4
Foster child	5
Son- in -law/daughter - in -law	6
Parent/Guardian	7
Step-parent	8
Foster parent	9
Parent- In - law	10
Brother/sister (inc. adopted)	11
Step-brother/sister	12
Foster brother/sister	13
Brother/sister-in-law	14
Grand-child	15
Grand-parent	16
Other relative	17
Other non-relative	18

14. IntroAcc **ACCOMMODATION TYPE**

The next section looks at the standard of people's housing.

15. Accom **All households**

IS THE HOUSEHOLD'S ACCOMMODATION:

N.B. MUST BE SPACE USED BY HOUSEHOLD

a house or bungalow	1	→ Q16
a flat or maisonette	2	→ Q17
a room/rooms	3	→ Q19
or something else?	4	→ Q18

16. HseType **Ask if respondents live in a house or bungalow *(Accom = 1)***

IS THE HOUSE/BUNGALOW:

detached	1	→ Q21
semi-detached	2	
or terraced/end of terrace?	3	

17. FltTyp **Ask if respondents live in a flat or maisonette *(Accom = 2)***

IS THE FLAT/MAISONETTE:

a purpose-built block	1	→ Q19
a converted house/some other kind of building?	2	

18. AccOth **Ask if respondents said their accommodation was 'something else'*(Accom = 4)***

IS THE ACCOMMODATION A:

caravan, mobile home or houseboat	1	→ Q22
or some other kind of accommodation?	2	→ Q21

19. Storey **Ask if respondents live in a flat, maisonette, OR a room or rooms *(Accom = 2 or 3)***

What is the floor level of the main living part of the accommodation?

ASK OR RECORD.

Basement/semi-basement	1	→ Q20
Ground floor/street level	2	
1st floor	3	
2nd floor	4	
3rd floor	5	
4th to 9th floor	6	
10th floor or higher	7	

20. HasLift **Ask if respondents live in a flat, maisonette, OR a room or rooms *(Accom = 2 or 3)***

INTERVIEWER CODE: IS THERE A LIFT?

Yes	1	→ Q21
No	2	

21. DateBlt **Ask all households, EXCEPT those living in a caravan, mobile house or houseboat *(AccOth ≠ 1)***

When was this building first built?

PROMPT IF NECESSARY - IF DK CODE YOUR ESTIMATE

before 1919	1	→See Q22
between 1919 and 1944	2	
between 1945 and 1964	3	
between 1965 and 1984	4	
1985 or later	5	
DK but after 1944	6	

22. ShareH **Ask if living in a house, bungalow OR a converted flat/maisonette OR 'something else' *(Accom = 1, 4 or FltTyp = 2)***

INTERVIEWER ASK OR RECORD

May I just check, does anyone else live in this building apart from the people in your household?

(I.E. IS THERE ANYONE ELSE IN THE BUILDING WITH WHOM THE HOUSEHOLD COULD SHARE ROOMS OR FACILITIES?)

Yes .... 1]→ Q23
No .... 2]

23. ShareE INTERVIEWER ASK OR RECORD

Is there any empty living accommodation in this building outside your household's accommodation?

Yes .... 1]→See Q24
No .... 2]

24. Share2 **Ask if other people live in the building, apart from the household, OR respondents live in a flat, maisonette or room(s) *(ShareH = 1 orAccom = 2 or 3)***

Does your household (do you) have the whole accommodation to yourselves (yourself) or do you share any of it with someone outside your household?

Have the whole accommodation .... 1]→See Q25
Share with someone else outside ....
the household .... 2]

25. Share3 **Ask if there is empty living accommodation in the building outside the household's accommodation, AND the accommodation is not shared with someone outside the household *(ShareE = 1 & Share2 (2)***

If all the empty accommodation in this building were occupied, would your household (you) have to share any part of your accommodation with anyone who had moved in?

Yes .... 1]→See Q26
No .... 2]

26. Rooms1 **Ask if household shares part of its accommodation with someone else outside the household OR would have to share part of the accommodation if someone moved in to an empty part of the accommodation *(Share2 = 2 orShare3 = 1)***

I want to ask you about all the rooms you have in your household's accommodation. Please include any rooms you sublet to other people and any rooms you share with people who are not in your household (or would share if someone moved into the empty accommodation). →See Q27

27. Rooms2 **Ask if household does not share part of the accommodation *(Share2 (2 ORShare3 ≠ 1)***

I want to ask you about all the rooms you have in your household's accommodation (including any rooms you sublet to other people). (How many of the following rooms do you have in this house/flat ...) →See Q28

28. Bedrooms **Ask all households**

How many bedrooms do you have?

INCLUDE BEDSITTERS, BOXROOMS, ATTIC BEDROOMS

0..20 →See Q29

29. BedCoook **Ask those who have at least one bedroom *(Bedrooms > 0)***

Are any of them used by your household for cooking in - like a bedsitter for example?

Yes .... 1]→See Q30
No .... 2]

30. KitOver **Ask all households**

How many Kitchens over 6.5 feet wide do you have?

NARROWEST SIDE MUST BE AT LEAST 6.5 FEET FROM WALL TO WALL

0..20 → Q31

31. KitUnder How many kitchens under 6.5 feet do you have?

0..20 → See Q32

32. ShareKit **Ask those who have a kitchen AND share accommodation *(KitOver > 0 orKitUnder > 0) AND (Share2 =2 or Share3=1)***

Do you share the kitchen with any other household?

Yes .... 1]→ Q33
No .... 2]

33. Living **Ask all households**

How many LIVING ROOMS do you have?

INCLUDE DINING ROOMS, SUNLOUNGE OR CONSERVATORY USED ALL YEAR ROUND.

0..20 → Q34

34. Bathrooms How many BATHROOMS do you have with PLUMBED IN BATH/SHOWER?

0..20 → Q35

35. Utility How many UTILITY and other rooms do you have?

0..20 → Q36

36. GHSCentH ASK OR RECORD

Do you have any form of central heating, including electric storage heaters, in your (part of the) accommodation

Yes .... 1 → Q37
No .... 2 → Q38

37. GHSCHFuel **Ask if the household has some form of central heating *(GHSCentH = 1)***

Which type of fuel does it use?

CODE MAIN METHOD ONLYPROBE 'Hot Air' FOR FUEL

Solid fuel: incl. coal, coke, wood, peat ... 1
Electricity: storage heaters 2
Electricity: other (incl. oil filled radiators) .... 3 → Q38
Gas/Calor gas 4
Oil 5
Other 6

CONSUMER DURABLES

38. IntroDur **Ask all households**

Now I'd like to ask you about various household items you may have - this gives us an indication of how living standards are changing.

39. HasDur Does your household have any of the following items in your (part of the) accommodation?

INCLUDE ITEMS STORED OR UNDER REPAIR

40. TVcol ...Colour TV set?

PROMPT AS NECESSARY TO PROBE FOR NUMBER OF TVS

0..7 →See Q41

41. UseColTV **Ask if has colour TV *(TVcol > 0)***

ASK OR RECORD

Is this/are any of these colour TV set(s) currently in use?

Yes .... 1 → Q43
No .... 2 → Q42

42. BrkColTV **Ask if no colour TV sets currently in use *(UseColTV = 2)***

Is this/are any of these colour TV set(s) broken but due to be repaired within 7 days?

Yes 1
No .... 2 → Q43

43. TVbw **Ask all households**

Black and white TV set?

PROMPT AS NECESSARY TO PROBE FOR NUMBER OF TVS

0..7 →See Q44

44. UseBwTV **Ask if NO colour TV set in use and none intended for repair AND has black and white TV *(Tvcol = 0 or BrkColTV = 2) & (TvBw > 0)***

ASK OR RECORD

Is this/are any of these black and white TV set(s) currently in use?

Yes .... 1 → Q46
No .... 2 → Q45

45. BrkBwTV **If no black and white TV sets currently in use *(UseBwTV = 2)***

Is this/are any of these black and white TV set(s) broken but due to be repaired within 7 days?

Yes 1
No .... 2 → Q46

46. SatCab **Ask all households**

Satellite, Cable or Digital TV receiver?

CODE ALL THAT APPLY

Satellite 1
Cable 2
Digital: terrestrial, cable or satellite .... 3 → Q47
None of these 4

47. Video Video recorder?

Yes 1
No .... 2 → Q48

48. Freezer Deep freezer or fridge freezer?

EXCLUDE FRIDGE ONLY

Yes 1
No .... 2 → Q49

49. WashMach Washing machine?

Yes 1
No .... 2 → Q50

50. Drier Tumble drier?

IF COMBINED WASHING MACHINE AND TUMBLE DRIER, CODE 1 FOR BOTH

Yes 1
No .... 2 → Q51

51. DishWash Dish washer?

Yes 1
No .... 2 → Q52

52. MicroWve Microwave oven?

Yes 1
No .... 2 → Q53

53. Telephon Telephone?

SHARED TELEPHONES LOCATED IN PUBLIC HALLWAYS TO BE INCLUDED ONLY IF THIS HOUSEHOLD IS RESPONSIBLE FOR PAYING THE ACCOUNT.

	Yes, fixed telephone	1	→ Q54
	Yes, mobile telephone	2	
	Yes, fixed and mobile telephone	3	
	No	4	

54. CDplay Compact disc (CD) player?

Yes	1	→ Q55
No	2	

55. Computer Home computer?

EXCLUDE: VIDEO GAMES

Yes	1	→ Q56
No	2	

56. Internet Does your household have access to the internet at home?

Yes	1	→ Q57
No	2	→ Q60

57. Access **Ask if has home access to the internet *(Internet = 1)***

How does your household access the internet from home?

CODE ALL THAT APPLY

Home computer	1	→ Q59
Digital television	2	
Mobile phone	3	
Games console	4	
Other	5	→ Q58

58. Xaccess **Ask if has access to the internet through 'other' means *(Access = 5)***

Please specify other access to the internet → Q59

59. WWWeb **Ask if has home access to the internet *(Internet = 1)***

May I just check, are you able to access the World Wide Web via your home internet connection?

Yes	1	→ Q60
No	2	

60. UseVcl **Ask all households**

Do you, or any members of your household, at present own or have continuous use of any motor vehicles?

INCLUDE COMPANY CARS (IF AVAILABLE FOR PRIVATE USE)

Yes	1	→ Q61
No	2	→ Q64

61. TypeVcl **Ask if the household has use of any motor vehicles *(If UseVcl =1)***

FOR EACH VEHICLE IN TURN:
I would now like to ask about the (Nth) vehicle. Is it...

CAR INCLUDES MINIBUSES, MOTOR CARAVANS, 'PEOPLE CARRIERS' AND 4- WHEEL DRIVE PASSENGER VEHICLES.

LIGHT VAN INCLUDES PICKUPS AND THOSE 4-WHEEL DRIVE VEHICLES, LAND ROVERS AND JEEPS THAT DO NOT HAVE SIDE WINDOWS BEHIND THE DRIVER

a car	1	→ Q62
a light van	2	→ Q63
a motor cycle	3	
or some other motor vehicle?	4	

62. PrivVcl FOR EACH VEHICLE IN TURN:
Is the [vehicle]

privately owned	1	→ Q63
or is it a company vehicle?	2	

63. AnyMore Do (any of) you at present own or have continuous use of any more motor vehicles?

INCLUDE COMPANY CARS - UNLESS NO PRIVATE USE ALLOWED

Yes	1	→ Q64
No	2	

TENURE

64. Ten1 **Ask all households**

In which of these ways do you occupy this accommodation?

SHOW CARD A
MAKE SURE ANSWER APPLIES TO HRP

Own outright	1	→ See ELD-A
Buying it with the help of a mortgage or loan	2	
Pay part rent and part mortgage (shared ownership)	3	→ Q69
Rent it	4	→ Q65
Live here rent-free (including rent-free in relative's/friend's property; excluding squatting)	5	
Squatting	6	→ See ELD-A

65. Tied **Ask if household rents the accommodation, or lives there rent-free *(Ten1 = 4 or 5)***

Does the accommodation go with the job of anyone in the household?

Yes	1	→ Q66
No	2	

66. LLord Who is your landlord?...

CODE FIRST THAT APPLIES

the local authority/council/New Town Development/Scottish Homes	1	→ Q67
a housing association or co-operative or charitable trust	2	
employer (organisation) of a household member	3	
another organisation	4	

relative/friend (before you lived here) of a household member 5
employer (individual) of a household .... 6 → Q67
member another individual private landlord? 7

67. Furn

Is the accommodation provided: ...

furnished 1
partly furnished (e.g. carpets and curtains only) .... 2 →See Q68
or unfurnished? 3

68. LandLive

Ask if rented from an individual *(Llord = 5, 6 or 7)*

Does the landlord live in this building?

Yes 1
No .... 2 →See Q69

69. HB

Ask if 'shared ownership' or 'rents' or 'rents free' *(Ten1 = 3, 4 or 5)*

Some people qualify for Housing Benefit, that is a rent rebate or allowance.

Are you (or HRP) receiving Housing Benefit from your local authority or local Social Security office?

Yes .... 1 →See Q72
No .... 2 → Q70

70. HbWait

Ask if not receiving Housing Benefit *(HB = 2)*

Are you (or HRP) waiting to receive Housing Benefit or to hear the outcome of a claim?

Yes .... 1 →See Q72
No .... 2 → Q71

71. HbChk

Ask if not waiting to receive Housing Benefit or to hear the outcome of a claim *(HBWait = 2)*

May I just check, does the local authority or local Social Security office pay any part of your rent?

Yes 1
No .... 2 →See Q72

72. HbOthr

Ask if there is someone aged 16 and over, apart from HRP and partner, in the household

Is anyone (else) in the household receiving a rent rebate, a rent allowance or Housing Benefit?

Yes 1
No .... 2 → See ELD-A

ELD - A. CTband

Ask if any household member aged 65 or more *(Any member of household - DVAge>64)*

Could you please tell me which Council Tax band this accommodation is in? (Council Tax is banded A to H)

THIS MUST BE THE BAND SET BY THE COUNCIL - DO NOT ACCEPT RESPONDENT'S OWN ESTIMATE OF THE VALUE OF THE PROPERTY.

IF THIS HOUSEHOLD'S ACCOMMODATION IS NOT VALUED SEPARATELY THEN USE CODE 9.

Band A 1
Band B 2
Band C 3
Band D 4
Band E .... 5 → ELD-B
Band F 6
Band G 7
Band H 8
Household accommodation not valued separately .... 9 → Q73

ELD - B. Ctdisab

Ask if a council tax band is given *(CTband = 1 - 8)*

Was your council tax bill reduced to a lower band because there is a disabled person in your household?

Yes .... 1 → See ELD-C
No .... 2 → Q73

ELD - C. CTLVchk

Ask if the council tax band was lowered, and the council tax band is B to H *(CTdisab = 1 AND CTband = 2 - 8)*

You said that you were in band {x}; is that the band after this lower valuation, or before?

After lower valuation 1
Before .... 2 → Q73

MIGRATION

73. Reslen

Ask All

How many years have you /has(...) lived at this address?

IF UNDER 1, CODE AS 0

0..97 →See Q74

74. Hmnths

Ask if respondent has lived at the address for less than a year *(Reslen = 0)*

How many months have you/has (...) lived here?

1..12 →See Q75

75. Nmoves

Ask if respondent has lived at the address for less than five years *(Reslen < 5 years)*

How many moves have you /has (...) made in the last 5 years, not counting moves between places outside Great Britain?

0..97 → Q76

76. Cry1

All persons

In what country were you/was (...) born? ...

UK, British .... 1 → Q80
Irish Republic 6
Jamaica 26
Bangladesh .... 33 → Q79
India 34
Pakistan 56
Other .... 59 → Q77

77. CrySpec **Ask if country of birth was 'other'** ***(Cry1 = 59)***

TYPE IN COUNTRY

ENTER TEXT OF AT MOST 40 CHARACTERS →Q78

78. CryCode **Ask if country of birth was 'other'** ***(Cry1 = 59)***

CHOOSE COUNTRY FROM CODING FRAME

1..116 → Q79

79. Arruk **Ask if not born in the UK** ***(Cry1 ≠ 1)***

In what year did you (...) first arrive in the United Kingdom? ...

ENTER IN 4 DIGIT FORMAT E.G.: 2000

1900..2005 → Q80

80. FathCob **All persons**

ASK OR RECORD

In what country was your / (...'s) father born?

UK, British	1	→ Q83
Irish Republic	6	
Jamaica	26	
Bangladesh	33	
India	34	
Pakistan	56	
Other	59	→ Q81

81. CrySpec1 **Ask if father's country of birth was 'other'** ***(FathCob = 59)***

TYPE IN COUNTRY

ENTER TEXT OF AT MOST 40 CHARACTERS → Q82

82. CryCode1 **Ask if father's country of birth was 'other'** ***(FathCob = 59)***

CHOOSE COUNTRY FROM CODING FRAME

1..116 → Q83

83. MothCob **Ask all persons**

ASK OR RECORD

In what country was your/ (...'s) mother born?

UK, British	1	→ Q86
Irish Republic	6	
Jamaica	26	
Bangladesh	33	
India	34	
Pakistan	56	
Other	59	→ Q84

84. CrySpec2 **Ask if mother's country of birth was 'other'** ***(MothCob = 59)***

TYPE IN COUNTRY

ENTER TEXT OF AT MOST 40 CHARACTERS → Q85

85. CryCode2 **Ask if mother's country of birth was 'other'** ***(MothCob = 59)***

CHOOSE COUNTRY FROM CODING FRAME

1..116 → Q86

86. Nation [*] **All persons**

SHOWCARD NAT(E) in England, NAT(S) in Scotland, NAT(W) in Wales

What do you consider your national identity to be? Please choose your answer from this card, choose as many or as few as apply.

English	1	→ Q88
Scottish	2	
Welsh	3	
Irish	4	
British	5	
Other answer	6	→ Q87

87. NatSpec [*] **If answered other** ***(Nation = 6)***

How would you describe your national identity?

ENTER DESCRIPTION OF NATIONAL IDENTITY → Q88

88. Ethnic [*] **All persons**

SHOW CARD B

To which of these ethnic groups do you consider you belong?

White - British	1	→See Q89
White - Any other White background	2	
Mixed - White and Black Caribbean	3	
Mixed - White and Black African	4	
Mixed - White and Asian	5	
Mixed - Any other Mixed background	6	
Asian or Asian British - Indian	7	
Asian or Asian British - Pakistani	8	
Asian or Asian British - Bangladeshi	9	
Asian or Asian British - Any other Asian background	10	
Black or Black British - Caribbean	11	
Black or Black British - African	12	
Black or Black British - Any other Black background	13	
Chinese	14	
Any other ethnic group	15	

89. Ethdes **Ask those who describe themselves as:**
Any other White background.
Any other Mixed background
Any other Asian background
Any other Black background
Any other ethnic group
(Ethnic = 2, 6, 10, 13 or 15)

Please can you describe your ethnic group.
ENTER DESCRIPTION OF ETHNIC GROUP

END OF HOUSEHOLD QUESTIONNAIRE

General Houshold Survey 2001/02
Individual Questionnaire

1. Iswitch **Ask this section of all adults**

THIS IS WHERE YOU START RECORDING ANSWERS FOR INDIVIDUALS
DO YOU WANT TO RECORD ANSWERS FOR (name) NOW OR LATER?

Yes, now 1
Later 2
or is there no interview with this person? 3

2. PersProx **Ask if answers are to be recorded now *(Iswitch = 1)***

INTERVIEWER: IS THE INTERVIEW ABOUT (name) BEING GIVEN:

In person 1
or by someone else? 2

3.ProxyNum **Ask if answers are to be recorded now, but are being answered by someone else *(Iswitch = 1 & PersProx = 2)***

ENTER PERSON NUMBER OF PERSON GIVING THE INFORMATION

1..14

EMPLOYMENT

1. Wrking **Ask this section of all adults**

Did you do any paid work in the 7 days ending Sunday the (n), either as an employee or as self-employed?

Yes .... 1 → Q14
No .... 2 → See Q2

2. Scheme **Ask if respondent is not in paid work and is a man aged 16-64, or a woman aged 16-62 *(Wrking = 2 & man aged 16-64 or woman aged 16-62)***

Were you on a government scheme for employment training?

Yes .... 1 → Q3
No .... 2 → See Q4

3. Trn **Ask those on a government scheme for employment training *(SchemeET = Yes)***

Last week were you ...

CODE FIRST THAT APPLIES

with an employer, or on a project providing work experience
or practical training? .... 1 ⎤
or at a college or training centre? .... 2 ⎦ → Q14

4. JbAway **Ask if not in paid work AND not on a government scheme for employment training *(Wrking = 2 & (SchemeET = 2 or not asked SchemeET because not in the age bracket asked))***

Did you have a job or business that you were away from?

Yes .... 1 → Q14
No .... 2 ⎤
Waiting to take up a new job/business already obtained .... 3 ⎦ → Q15

5. OwnBus **Ask if not in paid work AND not on a government scheme for employment training AND not away from a job *(JbAway = 2 or 3)***

Did you do any unpaid work in that week for any business that you own?

Yes .... 1 → See Q8
No .... 2 → Q6

6. RelBus **Ask if the respondent did not do any unpaid work for a business that they own *(OwnBus = 2)***

..or that a relative owns?

Yes .... 1 → See Q8
No .... 2 → See Q7

7. Looked **Ask if not in paid work AND not on a government scheme for employment training AND not doing unpaid work *(Wrking = 2 & (SchemeET = 2 or not asked SchemeET because not in the age bracket asked) & (RelBus = 2 OR JbAway = 2))***

Thinking of the 4 weeks ending Sunday the (date last Sunday), were you looking for any kind of paid work or government training scheme at any time in those 4 weeks?

Yes .... 1 → See Q8
No .... 2 → Q9
Waiting to take up a new job or business already obtained .... 3 → See Q8

8. StartJ **Ask if looking for paid work OR waiting to take up a new job or business already obtained *(Looked = 1 or 3 OR JbAway = 3)***

If a job or a place on a government scheme had been available in the week ending Sunday the (n), would you have been able to start within 2 weeks?

Yes .... 1 → See Q10
No .... 2 → Q9

9. Yinact **Ask if not looking for paid work, and would not be able to start work or training within 2 weeks (*Looked = 2 or StartJ = 2*)**

What was the main reason you did not seek any work in the last 4 weeks/would not be able to start in the next 2 weeks?

Student .... 1 ⎤
Looking after the family/home .... 2 ⎥
Temporarily sick or injured .... 3 ⎥
Long-term sick or disabled .... 4 ⎥ → See Q10
Retired from paid work .... 5 ⎥
None of these .... 6 ⎦

10. Everwk **Ask if not in paid work**

Have you ever had a paid job, apart from casual or holiday work?

Yes .... 1 → Q11
No .... 2 →See Q12

11. Dtbl **Ask if not in paid work, but has worked before *(Everwk = 1)***

When did you leave your last PAID job?

FOR DAY NOT GIVEN.......ENTER 15 FOR DAY
FOR MONTH NOT GIVEN......ENTER 6 FOR MONTH

DATE

12. WantaJob **Ask if respondent is aged 16-68 and male, or 16-64 and female, and is not working because is a student, is looking after the family/home, is retired, or is at a college or training centre*((DVAge = 16-68 & Sex =1) or (DVAge = 16-64 & Sex = 2) & YInAct = 1, 2, 5 or 6 or Trn = 2)***

Even though you were not looking for work (last week) would you like tohave a regular paid job at the moment - either a full or part-time job?

Yes .... 1 → Q13
No .... 2 →See Q14

13. NablStrt **Ask if respondent would like a job *(WantaJob = 1)***

If a job or a place on a government scheme had been available last week, would you have been able to start within 2 weeks?

Yes .... 1 ⎤ →See Q14
No .... 2 ⎦

14. IndD **Ask those who are in current employment or have had a job in the past**

CURRENT OR LAST JOB

What did the firm/organisation you worked for mainly make or do (at the place where you worked)?

DESCRIBE FULLY - PROBE MANUFACTURING or PROCESSING or DISTRIBUTING ETC. AND MAIN GOODS PRODUCED, MATERIALS USED WHOLESALE or RETAIL ETC.

ENTER TEXT AT MOST 80 CHARACTERS → Q15

15. OccT JOBTITLE CURRENT OR LAST JOB

What was your (main) job (in the week ending Sunday the (n))?

ENTER TEXT AT MOST 30 CHARACTERS → Q16

16. OccD CURRENT OR LAST JOB

What did you mainly do in your job?
CHECK SPECIAL QUALIFICATIONS/TRAINING NEEDED TO DO THE JOB

ENTER TEXT AT MOST 80 CHARACTERS → Q17

17. Stat Were you working as an employee or were you self-employed?

Employee .... 1 → Q18
Self-employed .... 2 → Q20

18. Svise **Ask if employee *(Stat = 1)***

In your job, did you have formal responsibility for supervising the work of other employees?
DO NOT INCLUDE PEOPLE WHO ONLY SUPERVISE:
- children, e.g. teachers, nannies, childminders
- animals
- security of buildings, e.g. caretakers, security guards

Yes .... 1 ⎤ → Q19
No .... 2 ⎦

19. Manage ASK OR RECORD

Did you have any managerial duties?

Manager .... 1 ⎤
Foreman/supervisor .... 2 ⎥ → Q20
Not manager/supervisor .... 3 ⎦

20. NEmplee How many people worked for your employer at the place where you worked?

1-2 .... 1 ⎤
3-24 .... 2 ⎥
25-99 .... 3 ⎥
100-499 .... 4 ⎥
500-999 .... 5 ⎥ → Q23
1000 or more .... 6 ⎥
DK, but less than 25 .... 7 ⎥
DK, but between 25 and 499 .... 8 ⎥
DK, but 500 or more .... 9 ⎦

21. Solo **Ask if self-employed *(Stat = 2)***

Were you working on your own or did you have employees?

on own/with partner(s) but no employees 1 → Q23
with employees .... 2 → Q22

22. SNEemplee **Ask if self-employed with employees *(Solo = 2)***

How many people did you employ at the place where you worked?

1-5 .... 1 ⎤
6-24 .... 2 ⎥
25-499 .... 3 ⎥ → Q23
500 or more .... 4 ⎥
DK but has/had employees .... 5 ⎦

23. FtPtWk **Ask those who are in current employment or have had a job in the past**

In your (main) job were you working:

full time .... 1 ⎤ → See Qs 24 & 25
or part time? .... 2 ⎦

24. EmpStY **Ask if employee *(Stat = 1)***

In which year did you start working continuously for your current employer?

1900..2005 →See Q26

25. SempStY **Ask if self-employed *(Stat = 2)***

In which year did you start working continuously as a self-employed person?

1900..2005 →See Q26

26. JobstM **If less than or equal to 8 years since started working continuously for current employer/ as a self-employed person? *(EmpStY (≤ less than the present date or SEmpStY ≤ 8 less than the present date)***

and which month in (YEAR) was that?

0..12 →See Q27

27. Tothrs **Ask all working *(Working = 1 or JbAway = 1 or SchemeET = 1)***

How many hours a week do you usually work in your (main) job/business? Please exclude mealbreaks but include any paid or unpaid overtime that you usually work.

HOURS IN MAIN JOB ONLY

97 OR MORE = 97

0.00..99.00 →See Q28

28. UnpaidHr **Ask if did unpaid work for a business *(OwnBus = 1 or RelBus = 1)***

Thinking of the business that you did unpaid work for how many hours unpaid work did you do for that business in the 7 days ending lastSunday?

1..97 →See Q29

29. UnPaidHm Did you do this work mainly...

somewhere quite separate from home, . 1
in different places using home as a base, ... 2
or in your own home or in the same grounds or buildings as your home?, ... 3
SPONTANEOUSLY ONLY: some days at home, other days somewhere quite separate from home 4
→Pensions

PENSIONS

The whole section on pensions (apart from the last question) is only asked of those in paid work, (including those temporarily away from job or on a government scheme), but excluding unpaid family workers. *((Wrking = 1 OR JbAway = 1 OR SchemeET = 1) & (OwnBus = 2 & RelBus = 2))* The routing instructions above each question apply only to those who meet the above criteria.

1. PenSchm **If employee or on a government scheme *(Stat = 1 or SchemeET = 1)***

(Thinking now of your present job,) some people (will) receive a pensionfrom their employer when they retire, as well as the state pension.

Does your present employer run an occupational pension scheme or superannuation scheme for any employees?
INCLUDE CONTRIBUTORY AND NON-CONTRIBUTORY SCHEMES
EXCLUDE EMPLOYER SPONSORED GROUP PERSONAL PENSION AND STAKEHOLDER PENSIONS

Yes .... 1 → Q2
No .... 2 → Q5

2. Eligible **Ask if employer runs an occupational pension scheme *(PenSchm = 1)***

Are you eligible to belong to your employer's occupational pension scheme?

Yes .... 1 → Q3
No .... 2 → Q5

3. EmPenShm **Ask if eligible for employer's pension scheme *(Eligible = 1)***

Do you belong to your employer's occupational pension scheme?

Yes 1
No 2
→ Q5

4. PschPoss **Ask if did not know or refused to say whether the employer offered an occupational pension scheme, or whether they were eligible, or whether they belonged to one *(PenSchm or Eligible or EmPenShm = DK / refusal)***

So do you think it's possible that you belong to an occupational pension scheme run by your employer, or do you definitely not belong to one?

Possibly belongs 1
Definitely not 2
→ Q5

5. PersPnt1 **Ask if employee OR (under pensionable age and not self-employed) - this is to select those who may have answered don't know, or refused to answer Stat *(Stat = 1 OR (under pensionable age & Stat ≠ 2))***

INTERVIEWER - INTRODUCE IF NECESSARY.
Now I would like to ask you about personal pensions and stakeholder pensions (rather than employers' occupational pension schemes).

6. PersPens People can now save for retirement by contracting out of the State Earnings Related Pension Scheme (SERPS) and arranging their own personal pension or stakeholder pension. Part of your National Insurance contributions are then repaid into your chosen pension plan by the Inland Revenue (or formerly by the DSS).

Do you at present have any such arrangements?

Yes .... 1 → Q7
No .... 2 →See Q10

7. OutSERPS **If contracted out of SERPS *(PersPens = 1)***

Is the arrangement you use to contract out of SERPS...

CODE ONE ONLY (most recent arrangement)

a personal pension .... 1 → Q8
or a stakeholder pension? .... 2 → Q8

8. PersCont Do you make any extra contributions over and above any rebated National Insurance contributions made by the Inland Revenue (or formerly by the DSS) on your behalf?

Yes .... 1 → See Q9
No .... 2 → See Q9

9. EmpCont **Ask if employee and has arranged own contracted out pension scheme *(Stat = 1 &Pers Pens = 1)***

Does your employer contribute to the scheme?

Yes .... 1 →See Q11
No .... 2 →See Q11

10. EverPers **Ask if employee and has not, or does not know if they have arranged own pension scheme *(Stat =1 & PersPens = 2 or DK)***

Have you ever had any such arrangements?

Yes .... 1 →See Q11
No .... 2 →See Q11

11. OthPers **Ask if employee OR(under pensionable age and not self-employed) - this is to select those who may have answered don't know, or refused to answer Stat *(Stat = 1 OR (under pensionable age & Stat ≠ 2)***

SHOW CARD PEN1

Please look at card PEN1. (Apart from the contributions you've already told me about,) do you have any other pension arrangements, such as those listed on the card, on which you receive income tax relief?

Yes .... 1 → Q12
No .... 2 →See Q13

12. OtDetail **Ask if respondent has other arrangements *(OthPers = 1)***

What arrangements do you have?

SHOW CARD PEN1

CODE ALL THAT APPLY

Personal pension 1
Stakeholder pension 2
Additional Voluntary Contribution 3
Free-Standing Additional Voluntary Contribution 4
Retirement annuities 5
→See Q13

13. EmpConOt **Ask if employee, and does not belong to employer's occupational scheme, and has other pension arrangements (*Stat = 1 & EmPenShm = 2 & OthPers = 1*)**

Does your employer contribute to (any of) the arrangement(s)?

Yes .... 1 →See Q14
No .... 2 →See Q14

14. PersPnt2 **Ask if self-employed *(Stat = 2)***

INTERVIEWER - INTRODUCE IF NECESSARY. Now I would like to ask you about personal pension schemes.

15. SePrsPen Self-employed people may arrange pensions for themselves and get tax relief on their contributions. These schemes include personal pensions, stakeholder pensions and 'self-employed pensions' (sometimes called 'Section 226 Retirement Annuities').

Do you at present contribute to one of these schemes?

Yes .... 1 → Q16
No .... 2 → Q17

16. SePrsShp **Ask if contributes to one of the schemes *(SePrsPen = 1)***

Which types of scheme are you contributing to - personal pension, stakeholder pension, or some other scheme?

CODE ALL THAT APPLY

Personal pension 1
Stakeholder pension 2
Other.. 3
→See Q18

17. SeEvPers **Ask if does not, or does not know if they contribute to one of the above schemes *(SePrsPen = 2 or DK)***

Have you ever contributed to one of these schemes?

Yes .... 1 →See Q18
No .... 2 →See Q18

18. NewShp **This question is asked of anyone under pensionable age who is not currently in paid work (*Under pensionable age AND (Wrking ≠ 1 OR JbAway ≠ 1 OR SchemeET ≠ 1)*)**

Since April 2001, anyone can arrange a stakeholder pension for themselves and get tax relief on the contribution.

Do you at present have a stakeholder pension?

Yes .... 1 Education
No .... 2 Education

EDUCATION

1. QualCh **Ask this section of those aged 16-69 (it is not asked of proxies) *(DVAge = 16-69)***

I would now like to ask you about education and work-related training. Do you have any qualifications from school, college or university, connected with work or from government schemes?

- Yes .... 1 → Q2
- No .... 2 → Q20
- Don't know .... 3 → Q2

2. Quals **Ask if respondent has a qualification, or answers don't know (*QualCh = 1 or 3*)**

Which qualifications do (you think) you have, starting with the highest qualifications?

SHOW CARD C

CODE ALL THAT APPLY - PROMPT AS NECESSARY

- Degree level qualifications including graduate membership of a professional institute or PGCE or higher .... 1 → Q3
- Diploma in higher education 2
- HNC/HND 3
- ONC/OND 4
- BTEC, BEC OR TEC 5
- SCOTVEC, SCOTEC OR SCOTBEC .. 6
- Teaching qualification (excluding PGCE) 7
- Nursing or other medical qualification not yet mentioned 8
- Other higher education qualification below degree level 9
- A level or equivalent 10
- SCE highers 11
- NVQ/SVQ 12
- GNVQ/GSVQ 13
- AS level 14
- Certificate of sixth year studies (CSYS) or equivalent 15
- O level or equivalent 16
- SCE STANDARD/ORDINARY (O) GRADE 17
- GCSE 18
- CSE 19
- RSA 20
- City and Guilds 21
- YT Certificate/YTP 22
- Any other professional/vocational qualifications/ foreign qualifications 23
- Don't know 24

(2-24) → See Qs 5-19

3. Degree **Ask if highest qualification is a degree level qualification *(Quals = 1 AND does NOT have a higher qualification)***

Is your degree...

- a higher degree (including PGCE)? ...... 1 → Q4
- a first degree? 2
- other (eg graduate member of a professional institute or chartered accountant)? 3
- Don't know 4

(2-4) →See Q10

4. HighO **Ask if has a higher degree *(Degree = 1)***

ASK OR RECORD

Was your higher degree...

CODE FIRST THAT APPLIES

- a Doctorate? 1
- a Masters? 2
- a Postgraduate Certificate in Education? 3
- or some other postgraduate degree or professional qualification? 4
- Don't know 5

→See Q10

5. BTEC **Ask if highest qualification is BTEC, BEC or TEC *(Quals = 5 AND does NOT have a higher qualification)***

Is your highest BTEC qualification...

CODE FIRST THAT APPLIES

- at higher level? 1
- at National Certificate or National Diploma level? 2
- a first diploma or general diploma? 3
- a first certificate or general certificate? . 4
- Don't know 5

→See Q10

6. SCTVEC **Ask if highest qualification is SCOTVEC *(Quals = 6 AND does NOT have a higher qualification)***

Is your highest SCOTVEC qualification...

CODE FIRST THAT APPLIES

- higher level? 1
- full National Certificate? 2
- a first diploma or general diploma? 3
- a first certificate or general certificate? .. 4
- modules towards a National Certificate? . 5
- Don't know 6

→See Q10

7. Teach **Ask if highest qualification is a teaching qualification excluding PGCE *(Quals = 7AND does NOT have a higher qualification)***

Was your teaching qualification for...

- Further education 1
- Secondary education 2
- or primary education? 3
- Don't know 4

→See Q10

8. NumAL **Ask if highest qualification is A levels *(Quals = 10 AND does NOT have a higher qualification)***

Do you have...

- one A level or equivalent 1
- or more than one? 2
- Don't know 3

→See Q10

9. NumSCE **Ask if highest qualification is Scottish highers *(Quals = 11 AND does NOT have a higher qualification)***

Do you have...

1 or 2 SCE highers 1
3 or more highers .... 2 →See Q10
Don't know 3

10. NVQlev **Ask if has NVQ/SVQ *(Quals = 12)***

What is your highest level of full NVQ/SVQ?

Level 1 1
Level 2 2
Level 3 3
Level 4 .... 4 →See Q11
Level 5 5
Don't know 6

11. GNVQ **Ask if highest qualification is GNVQ/GSVQ *(Quals = 13 AND does NOT have a higher qualification)***

Is your highest GNVQ/GSVQ at...

CODE FIRST THAT APPLIES

advanced level? 1
intermediate level? 2
foundation level? .... 3 →See Q17
Don't know 4

12. NumAS **Ask if highest qualification is AS levels *(Quals = 14 AND does NOT have a higher qualification)***

Do you have...

one AS level 1
2 or 3 AS levels 2
or 4 or more passes at this level? .... 3 →See Q17
Don't know 4

13. RSA **Ask if highest qualification is RSA *(Quals = 20 AND does NOT have a higher qualification)***

Is your highest RSA...

CODE FIRST THAT APPLIES

a higher diploma? 1
an advanced diploma or advanced certificate? 2
a diploma? .... 3 →See Q17
or some other RSA (including Stage I, II & III)? 4
Don't know 5

14. CandG **Ask if highest qualification is City and Guilds *(Quals = 21 AND does NOT have a higher qualification)***

Is your highest City and Guilds qualification....

CODE FIRST THAT APPLIES

advanced craft/part 3? 1
craft/part 2? 2
foundation/part 1? .... 3 →See Q17
Don't know 4

15. GCSE **Ask if highest qualification is SCE Standard/ Ordinary Grade or GCSE *(Quals = 17 OR Quals = 18 AND does NOT have a higher qualification)***

Do you have any (GCSEs at grade C or above) (SCE Standard grades 1-3/ O grades at grade C or above)?

Yes 1
No .... 2 →See Q17
Don't know 3

16. CSE **Ask if highest qualification is CSE *(Quals = 19 AND does NOT have a higher qualification)***

Do you have any CSEs at grade 1?

Yes 1
No .... 2 →See Q17
Don't know 3

17. NumOL **Ask if passes at GCSE at Grade C or above OR CSE Grade 1 or O level or equivalent OR SCE level or equivalent) *(CSE = 1 or GCSE = 1 or Quals = 16 or Quals = 17)***

ASK OR RECORD

You mentioned that you have passes at (GCSE at Grade C or above) (CSE Grade 1) (O level or equivalent) (SCE level or equivalent). Do you have...

fewer than 5 passes, ... 1
or 5 or more passes at this level? .... 2 →See Q18
Don't know 3

18. EngMath **Ask if has O levels, SCE Standard/Ordinary (O) Grade or GCSEs or CSEs *(Quals = 16 or GCSE = 1 or CSE = 1 or Quals = 19)***

Do you have (GCSEs at Grade C or above) (CSE Grade 1) (O levels or equivalent) in English or Mathematics?

EXCLUDE ENGLISH LITERATURE

English 1
Maths 2
Both .... 3 →See Q19
Neither 4

19. Appren **Ask if highest qualification is 'any other professional/vocational qualifications/foreign qualifications', or the respondent answered 'don't know' *(Quals = 23 or 24 or Qualch = 3 AND does NOT have a higher qualification)***

Are you doing or have you completed, a recognised trade apprenticeship?

Yes, (completed) 1
Yes, (still doing) .... 2 →See Q20
No (including apprenticeships begun but discontinued) 3

20. Enroll Are you at present (at school or sixth form college or) enrolled on any full-time or part-time education course excluding leisure classes? (Include correspondence courses and open learning as well as other forms of full-time or part-time education course.)

Yes .... 1 →See Q21
No 2
Don't know .... 3 → Q23

21. Attend **Ask if enrolled on a education course *(Enroll = 1)***

And are you ...

Still attending .... 1 → Q22
Waiting for term to (re)start .... 2 → Q22
Or have you stopped going? .... 3 → Q23

22. Course **Ask if respondent is still attending school or college, or waiting for term to [re]start *(Attend = 1 or 2)***

Are you (at school or 6th form college), on a full or part-time course, a medical or nursing course, a sandwich course, or some other kind of course?

CODE FIRST THAT APPLIES

School/full-time (age < 20 years only) .. 1
School/part-time (age < 20 years only) .. 2
sandwich course 3
studying at a university or college including sixth form college FULL-TIME 4
training for a qualification in nursing, physiotherapy, or a similar medical subject 5
on a part-time course at university or college INCLUDING day release and block release 6
on an Open College Course 7
on an Open University Course 8
any other correspondence course 9
any other self/open learning course 10
(all → Q23)

23. EdAge **Asked of all aged 16-69 *(DVAge = 16-69)***

How old were you when you finished your continuous full-time education?

CODE AS 97 IF NO EDUCATION;
CODE AS 96 IF STILL IN EDUCATION

1..97 → Q24

24. EducPres Are you at present attending any sort of leisure or recreation classes during the day, in the evenings or at weekends?

Yes .... 1 → Q25
No .... 2 → Adult Health

25. EdTyp **Ask if respondent is attending a leisure or recreation class *(EducPres = 1)***

What type of college or organisation runs these classes?

CODE ALL THAT APPLY
(Enter at most 4 codes)

Evening institute/Local Education Authority/College or Centre of Adult Education 1
College of Further Education/Technical College 2
University Extra-Mural Department 3
Other 4
(all → Adult Health)

ADULT HEALTH

Ask this section of all adults (except GenHlth which excludes proxy informants)

1. Genhlth [*] **Ask all (except proxy informants)**

Over the last twelve months would you say your health has on the whole been good, fairly good, or not good?

Good 1
Fairly Good 2
Not Good 3
(all → Q2)

2. Illness [*] **Ask all**

Do you have any long-standing illness, disability or infirmity? Bylong-standing, I mean anything that has troubled you over a period of time or that is likely to affect you over a period of time?

Yes .... 1 → Q3
No .... 2 → Q8

3. Lmatter [*] **Ask if has a long-standing illness *(Illness = 1)***

What is the matter with you?

RECORD ONLY WHAT RESPONDENT SAYS.

ENTER TEXT OF AT MOST 100 CHARACTERS → Q4

4. LMatNum HOW MANY LONGSTANDING ILLNESSES OR INFIRMITIES DOES RESPONDENT HAVE?

ENTER NUMBER OF LONGSTANDING COMPLAINTS MENTIONEDIF MORE THAN 6 - TAKE THE SIX THAT THE RESPONDENT CONSIDERS THE MOST IMPORTANT

1..6 → Q5

For each illness mentioned above

5. LMat WHAT IS THE MATTER WITH RESPONDENT?

ENTER THE (FIRST/SECOND/etc.) CONDITION/ SYMPTOM RESPONDENT MENTIONED

ENTER TEXT OF AT MOST 40 CHARACTERS → Q6

6. ICD CODE FOR COMPLAINT AT LMAT

ENTER TEXT OF AT MOST 12 CHARACTERS → Q7

7. LimitAct Does this illness or disability (Do any of these illnesses or disabilities) limit your activities in any way?

Yes 1
No 2
(all → Q8)

8. CutDown **Ask all**

Now I'd like you to think about the 2 weeks ending yesterday. During those 2 weeks, did you have to cut down on any of the things you usually do (about the house/at work or in your free time) because of (answers atLMatter) or some other illness or injury?

Yes .... 1 → Q9
No .... 2 → Q11

9. NdysCutD **Ask if had to cut down on normal activities because of illness or injury *(CutDown = 1)***

How many days was this in all during these 2 weeks, including Saturdays and Sundays?

1..14 → Q10

10. Cmatter [*] What was the matter with you?

ENTER TEXT OF AT MOST 40 CHARACTERS → Q11

11. DocTalk **Ask all**

During the 2 weeks ending yesterday, apart from any visit to a hospital, did you talk to a doctor for any reason at all, either in person or by telephone?

EXCLUDE: CONSULTATIONS MADE ON BEHALF OF CHILDREN UNDER 16 AND PERSONS OUTSIDE THE HOUSEHOLD.

Yes .... 1 → Q12
No .... 2 → Q19

12. NChats **Ask if contact with doctor during the last 2 weeks *(DocTalk = 1)***

How many times did you talk to a doctor in these 2 weeks?

1..9 → Q13

For each consultation

13. WhsBhlf On whose behalf was this consultation made?

Informant .... 1 → Q15
Other member of household 16 or over . 2 → Q14

14. ForPerNo **Ask if consultation was on the behalf of another member of the household *(WhsBhlf = 2)***

CODE WHO CONSULTATION WAS MADE FOR

(PERSON NUMBER) → Q15

15. NHS **For each consultation**

Was this consultation...

Under the National Health Service .... 1 ⎤
or paid for privately? .... 2 ⎦ → Q16

16. GP Was the doctor...

RUNNING PROMPT

A GP (ie a family doctor) .... 1 ⎤
or a specialist .... 2 ⎥ → Q17
or some other kind of doctor? .... 3 ⎦

17. DocWhere Did you talk to the doctor...

RUNNING PROMPT

By telephone .... 1 ⎤
at your home .... 2 ⎥
in the doctor's surgery .... 3 ⎥ → Q18
at a health centre .... 4 ⎥
or elsewhere? .... 5 ⎦

18. Presc Did the doctor give (send) you a prescription?

Yes .... 1 ⎤
No .... 2 ⎦ → Q19

19. SeeNurse **Ask all**

During the last 2 weeks ending yesterday, did you see a practice nurse at the GP surgery on your own behalf?

EXCLUDE CONSULTATIONS WITH COMMUNITY NURSES

Yes .... 1 → Q20
No .... 2 → Q21

20. Nnurse **Ask if the respondent saw a nurse *(SeeNurse = 1)***

How many times did you see a practice nurse at the GP surgery in these 2 weeks?

RECORD NUMBER OF TIMES

1..9 → Q21

21.OutPatnt **Ask all**

During the months of (LAST 3 COMPLETE CALENDAR MONTHS) did you attend as a patient the casualty or outpatient department of a hospital (apart from straightforward ante- or post-natal visits)?

Yes .... 1 → Q22
No .... 2 → Q29

22. Ntimes1 **Ask if respondent attended outpatients *(OutPatnt = 1)***

How many times did you attend in (EARLIEST MONTH IN REFERENCE PERIOD)?

0..97 → Q23

23. NTimes2 How many times did you attend in (SECOND MONTH IN REFERENCE PERIOD)?

0..97 → Q24

24. NTimes3 How many times did you attend in (THIRD MONTH IN REFERENCE PERIOD)?

0..97 → Q25

25. Casualty Was this visit (were any of these visits) to the Casualty department or was it (were they all) to some other part of the hospital?

At least one visit to Casualty .... 1 → Q26
No Casualty visits .... 2 → Q27

26. NcasVis **Ask if respondent visited casualty *(Casualty = 1)***

(May I just check) How many times did you go to Casualty altogether?

1..31 → Q27

27. PrVists **Ask if respondent attended outpatients *(OutPatnt = 1)***

Was your outpatient visit (were any of your outpatient visits) during(REFERENCE PERIOD) made under the NHS, or was it (were any of them) paid for privately?

All under NHS .... 1 → Q29
At least one paid for privately .... 2 → Q28

28. NprVists **Ask if some private visits *(PrVists = 2)***

ASK OR RECORD

(May I just check), How many of the visits were paid for privately?

1..31 → Q29

29. DayPatnt **Ask all**

During the last year, that is, since (DATE ONE YEAR AGO), have you been in hospital for treatment as a day patient, ie admitted to a hospital bed or day ward, but not required to remain overnight?

Yes .... 1 →See Q30
No .... 2 → Q37

30. MatDPat **Ask if has been a day patient AND is a women aged between 16-49 *(DayPatnt = 1 & Sex = 2 & DVAge = 16-49)***

May I just check, was that/were any of those day patient admissions for you to have a baby?

Yes .... 1 → Q31
No .... 2 → Q34

31. NumMatDP **Ask if respondent was a day patient because she was having a baby (*MatDPat = Yes*)**

How many separate days have you had as a day patient for having a baby since (DATE ONE YEAR AGO)?

97 DAYS OR MORE - CODE 97

1..97 → Q32

32. PrMatDP Was this day-patient stay (were any of these day-patient stays) for having a baby under the NHS, or was it (were any of them) paid for privately?

All under NHS .... 1 → Q34
At least one paid for privately .... 2 →See Q33

33. NprMatDP **Ask if day patient stay for having a baby was paid for privately AND respondent was in hospital for more than one day *(PrMatDP = 2 & NumMatDP > 1)***

ASK OR RECORD

How many of the visits were paid for privately?

1..31 → Q34

34. NHSPDays **Ask if the respondent was a day patient *(DayPatnt = 1)***

(Apart from those maternity stays) how many separate days in hospitalhave you had as a day patient since (DATE ONE YEAR AGO)?

97 DAYS OR MORE - CODE 97

0..97 →See Q35

35. PrDptnt **Ask if had one or more days in hospital *(NHSPDays > 0)***

Was this day-patient treatment (were any of these day-patient treatments) under the NHS, or was it (were any of them) paid for privately?

All under NHS .... 1 → Q37
At least one paid for privately .... 2 →See Q36

36. NPrDpTnt **Ask if day patient stay was paid for privately AND they were in hospital for more than one day *(PrDptnt = 2 & NHSPDays > 1)***

ASK OR RECORD

How many of the visits were paid for privately?

1..31 → Q37

37. InPatnt **Ask all**

During the last year, that is, since (DATE 1 YEAR AGO), have you been in hospital as an inpatient, overnight or longer?

Yes .... 1 →See Q38
No .... 2 → Child Health

38. MatInPat **Ask if respondent has been an inpatient AND she is a women aged 16-49 *(InPatnt = 1 & Sex = 2 & DVAge = 16-49)***

May I just check, was that/were any of those inpatient admissions for you to have a baby?

Yes .... 1 → Q39
No .... 2 → Q43

39. NmtStay **Ask if inpatient admission was to have a baby *(MatInPat = 1)***

How many separate stays in hospital as an inpatient in order to have a baby have you had since (DATE 1 YEAR AGO)?

1..6 → Q40

40. MtNights **Ask for each maternity stay**

How many nights altogether were you in hospital on your (no.) stay to have a baby?

1..97 → Q41

41. MatNHSTr Were you treated under the NHS or were you a private patient on that occasion?

NHS .... 1 → Q43
Private Patient .... 2 → Q42

42. MtPrvSty **If private patient *(MatNHSTr = 2)***

Were you treated in an NHS hospital or in a private one?

NHS hospital .... 1 → Q43
Private hospital .... 2 → Q43

43. Nstays **Ask if respondent has been an inpatient *(InPatnt = 1)***

(Apart from those maternity stays) how many separate stays in hospital as an inpatient have you had since (DATE 1 YEAR AGO)?

0..6 → Q44

44. Nights **Ask for each stay**

How many nights altogether were you in hospital on your (first/second/...sixth) stay?

1..97 → Q45

45. NHSTreat Were you treated under the NHS or were you a private patient on that occasion?

NHS .... 1 → Child Health
Private Patient .... 2 → Q46

46. PrvStay **Ask if a private patient *(NHSTreat = 2)***

Were you treated in an NHS hospital or in a private one?

NHS hospital .... 1 → Child Health
Private hospital .... 2 → Child Health

CHILD HEALTH

1. AskHlth **Ask if there is a child / there are children under 16 in household (not asked of proxy informants)**

THE NEXT SECTION IS ABOUT CHILD HEALTH. WE ONLY NEEDTO COLLECT THIS INFORMATION ONCE FOR EACH CHILD IN THE HOUSEHOLD. WHO WILL ANSWER THE CHILD HEALTH SECTION FOR (CHILD'S NAME)?

INTERVIEWER ENTER PERSON NUMBER.

1..14 → Q2

2. AskNowCH INTERVIEWER: DO YOU WANT TO ASK THIS SECTION FOR..... (CHILD'S NAME) NOW OR LATER?

IF YOU HAVE ALREADY ASKED THIS SECTION FOR (CHILD'SNAME), DO NOT CHANGE FROM CODE 1.

Yes, now/Already asked .... 1 → Q4
Later .... 2 → Q3

3. Cstill **If the section is to be asked later *(AskNowCH = 2)***

REMINDER
THE FOLLOWING ADULTS STILL NEED TO ANSWER THE CHILD HEALTH SECTION ON BEHALF OF SOME OF THE CHILDREN.

4. Genhlth [*] **For each child**

Over the last twelve months would you say (NAME's) health has on the whole been good, fairly good, or not good?

Good .... 1 → Q5
Fairly Good .... 2 → Q5
Not Good .... 3 → Q5

5. Illness [*] Does (NAME) have any long-standing illness, disability orinfirmity? By long-standing, I mean anything that has troubled them over a period of time or that is likely to affect them over a period of time?

Yes .... 1 → Q6
No .... 2 → Q11

6. Lmatter [*] **Ask if child has a longstanding illness, disability or infirmity *(Illness =1)***

What is the matter with (NAME)?

THIS IS TO ENSURE THAT THE RESPONDENT MENTIONS ALL LONGSTANDING ILLNESSES. YOU DO NOT HAVE TO RECORD VERBATIM HERE - A SUMMARY WILL DO.

ENTER TEXT OF AT MOST 40 CHARACTERS → Q7

7. LMatNum HOW MANY LONGSTANDING ILLNESSES OR INFIRMITIES DOES (NAME) HAVE?

ENTER NUMBER OF LONGSTANDING COMPLAINTS MENTIONED
IF MORE THAN 6 - TAKE THE SIX THAT THE RESPONDENT CONSIDERS THE MOST IMPORTANT.

1..6 → Q8

8. LmatCH **For each illness mentioned at LMatNum**

WHAT IS THE MATTER WITH (NAME)?

ENTER THE (FIRST/SECOND/etc.) CONDITION/ SYMPTOM RESPONDENT MENTIONED

ENTER TEXT OF AT MOST 40 CHARACTERS → Q9

9. ICDCH CODE FOR EACH COMPLAINT AT LMatCH → Q10

10. LimitAct [*] **If child has a longstanding illness, disability or infirmity *(Illness =1)***

Does this illness or disability (Do any of these illnesses or disabilities) limit (NAME)'s activities in any way?

Yes .... 1 → Q11
No .... 2 → Q11

11. CutDown [*] For each child

Now I'd like you to think about the 2 weeks ending yesterday. During those 2 weeks, did (NAME) have to cut down on any of the things he/she usually does (at school or in his/her free time) because of (answer at LMatter or some other) illness or injury?

Yes .... 1 → Q12
No .... 2 → Q14

12. NdysCutD **Ask if child has had to cut down *(CutDown = 1)***

How many days did (NAME) have to cut down in all during these 2 weeks, including Saturdays and Sundays?

1..14 → Q13

13. Matter [*] **What was the matter with (NAME)?**

ENTER TEXT OF AT MOST 80 CHARACTERS → Q14

14. DocTalk **For each child**

During the 2 weeks ending yesterday, apart from visits to a hospital, did (NAME) talk to a doctor for any reason at all, or did you or any other member of the household talk to a doctor on his/her behalf?

Include being seen by a doctor at a school clinic, but exclude visits to a child welfare clinic run by a local authority.

INCLUDE TELEPHONE CONSULTATIONS AND CONSULTATIONSMADE ON BEHALF OF CHILDREN.

Yes .... 1 → Q15
No .... 2 → Q20

15. Nchats **If child consulted a doctor *(DocTalk = 1)***

How many times did (NAME) talk to the doctor (or you or any other member of the household consult the doctor on NAME's behalf) in those 2 weeks?

1..9 → Q16

16. NHS **For each consultation**

Was this consultation...

Under the National Health Service .... 1 → Q17
or paid for privately? .... 2 → Q17

17. GP **Was the doctor...**

RUNNING PROMPT

A GP (ie a family doctor) .... 1 → Q18
or a specialist .... 2 → Q18
or some other kind of doctor? .... 3 → Q18

18. DocWhere Did you or any other member of the household (or NAME) talk to the doctor...

By telephone .... 1 → Q19
at your home .... 2 → Q19
in the doctor's surgery .... 3 → Q19
at a health centre .... 4 → Q19
or elsewhere? .... 5 → Q19

19. Presc Did the doctor give (send) (NAME) a prescription?

Yes .... 1 → Q20
No .... 2 → Q20

20. Seenurse **For each child**

During the last 2 weeks ending yesterday, did (NAME)

RUNNING PROMPT
CODE ALL THAT APPLY

EXCLUDE CONSULTATIONS WITH COMMUNITY NURSES

see a practice nurse at the GP surgery, .. 1 → Q21
see a health visitor at the GP surgery, . 2 → Q22
go to child health clinic, ... 3 → Q22
go to child welfare clinic, ... 4 → Q22
did not go to any of these. .... 5 → Q22

21. Nnurse **Ask if child saw a practice nurse *(Seenurse = 1)***

How many times did (NAME) see a practice nurse at the GP surgery in these 2 weeks?

RECORD NUMBER OF TIMES

1..9 → Q22

22. OutPatnt **For each child**

During the months of (LAST 3 COMPLETE CALENDAR MONTHS), did (NAME) attend as a patient the casualty or outpatient department of a hospital (apart from straightforward post-natal visits)?

Yes .... 1 → Q23
No .... 2 → Q28

23. Ntimes1 **Ask if child has been an outpatient *(OutPatnt = 1)***

How many times did (NAME) attend in (EARLIEST MONTH IN REFERENCE PERIOD)?

0..97 → Q24

24. NTimes2 How many times did (NAME) attend in (SECOND MONTH IN REFERENCE PERIOD)?

0..97 → Q25

25. NTimes3 How many times did (NAME) attend in (THIRD MONTH IN REFERENCE PERIOD)?

0..97 → Q26

26. Casualty Was the visit (were any of the visits) to the Casualty department or was it (were they) to some other part of the hospital?

At least one visit to Casualty .... 1 → Q27
No Casualty visits .... 2 → Q28

27. NcasVis **Ask if child went to casualty *(Casualty = 1)***

(May I just check) How many times did (NAME) go to Casualty altogether?

1..31 → Q28

28. DayPatnt **For each child**

During the last year, that is since (DATE 1 YEAR AGO) has (NAME) been in hospital for treatment as a day patient, ie admitted to a hospital bed or day ward, but not required to remain in hospital overnight?

Yes .... 1 → Q29
No .... 2 → Q30

29. NHSPDays **Ask if child has been a day patient *(DayPatnt = 1)***

How many separate days in hospital has (NAME) had as a day patient since (DATE 1 YEAR AGO)?

1..97 → Q30

30. InPatnt **For each child**

During the last year, that is, since (DATE 1 YEAR AGO) has (NAME) been in hospital as an inpatient, overnight or longer?

EXCLUDE: Births unless baby stayed in hospital after mother had left.

Yes .... 1 → Q31
No .... 2 → Elderly

31. Nstays **Ask if child has been an inpatient *(InPatnt = 1)***

How many separate stays in hospital as an inpatient has (NAME) had since (DATE 1 YEAR AGO)?

IF 6 OR MORE, CODE 6

1..6 → Q32

32. Nights **For each stay**

How many nights altogether was (NAME) in hospital during stay number (...)?

1..97 → Elderly

ELDERLY

1. SeeDiff [*] **Ask all adults aged 65 and over (not proxy informants)**

Does your sight ever cause you difficulties?

Yes .... 1 ⎤
No .... 2 ⎦ → Q2

2. HearDiff [*] Do you ever have any difficulties with your hearing?

Yes .... 1 → Q3
No .... 2 → See Q4

3. HearAid **If has difficulty with hearing *(HearDiff = 1)***

(Can I just check) do you ever wear a hearing aid?

Yes .... 1 ⎤
No .... 2 ⎦ → See Q4

4. LimStart **If has a limiting longstanding illness *(LimitAct = 1)***

You mentioned earlier that your activities are limited by ill health or disability. How long ago did this start to limit your activities?

Less than one year ago .... 1 ⎤
1-4 years ago .... 2 ⎥ → Q5
5 years or more ago .... 3 ⎦

5. CompHlth [*] **Ask all (except proxy informants)**

Compared with this time last year, that's (month, year) would you say that, on the whole, your health is now...

better .... 1 ⎤
much the same .... 2 ⎥ → Q6
or worse? .... 3 ⎦

6. EldInt1 **Ask all (except proxy informants)**

Now I'd like to ask about a few tasks that some people may be able to do on their own, while others may need help, or not do them at all. For some tasks, I will ask you to look at these cards and tell me whether you usually manage to do it on your own, only with help from someone else, or not at all.

7. Stairs SHOW CARD TEL1
Do you usually manage to get up and down stairs or steps...

on your own .... 1 → Q8
only with help from someone else .... 2 ⎤
or not at all? .... 3 ⎦ → Q9

8. StrsEasy [*] **If manages on own *(Stairs = 1)***

SHOW CARD TEL2

Do you find it ...

very easy .... 1 ⎤
fairly easy .... 2 ⎦ → Q11
fairly difficult .... 3 ⎤
or very difficult to do this on your own? .. 4 ⎦ → Q9

9. StairLoo **If needs help/cannot manage to get up and down steps or stairs, or finds it difficult *(Stairs = 2 or 3 or StrsEasy = 3 or 4)***

ASK OR RECORD
May I just check, do you have to use stairs to get from the rooms you use during the daytime to the toilet?

Yes .... 1 → Q10
No .... 2 → Q10

10. StairBed ASK OR RECORD
And do you have to use stairs to get from the rooms you use during the daytime to your bedroom?

Yes .... 1 → Q11
No .... 2 → Q11

11. House SHOW CARD TEL1
Do you usually manage to get around the house (except for any stairs) ...

on your own .... 1 → Q12
only with help from someone else .... 2 →See Q13
or not at all? .... 3 →See Q13

12. HousEasy **If manages on own *(House = 1)***

[*] SHOW CARD TEL2
Do you find it ...

very easy 1
fairly easy 2
fairly difficult 3
or very difficult to do this on your own? .. 4
→See Q13

13. Toilet **If needs help/cannot manage to get up and down steps or stairs, or finds it difficult *(Stairs = 2 or 3 or StrsEasy = 3 or 4)***

SHOW CARD TEL1
Do you usually manage to get to the toilet ...

on your own .... 1 → Q14
only with help from someone else .... 2 →See Q15
or not at all? .... 3 →See Q15

14. ToilEasy **If manages on own *(Toilet = 1)***

[*] SHOW CARD TEL2
Do you find it ...

very easy 1
fairly easy 2
fairly difficult 3
or very difficult to do this on your own? .. 4
→See Q15

15. CanHlp1 **If finds it difficult to use stairs, get to the toilet or get around the house AND has not already stated that they need help with stairs, getting to the toilet or getting around the house *(StrsEasy = 3 or 4 OR HouseEasy = 3 or 4 OR ToilEasy = 3 or 4 AND StairLoo ≠ 1 OR StairBed ≠ 1 OR House ≠ 2 OR Toilet ≠ 2)***

Although you said you usually manage on your own, does anyone help you to get around the house/to the toilet/up and down stairs?

Yes .... 1 →See Q16
No .... 2 →See Q16

16.WhoHlp **If needs help with stairs, getting to the toilet or getting around the house *((Stairs = 2 AND StairLoo = 1 OR StairBed = 1) OR House = 2 OR Toilet = 2) OR CanHlp1 = 1)***

Who usually helps you to get around the house/to the toilet/up and down stairs? Is it someone in the household, or someone from outside the household?

Someone in the household .... 1 → Q17
Someone from outside the household .. 2 → Q18

17. WhoHlpA **If usually gets help from someone in the household *(WhoHlp = 1)***

Who is the person in the household?

INTERVIEWER: ENTER PERSON NUMBER 1..14 →See Q19

18. WhoHlpB **If usually gets help from someone outside the household *(WhoHlp = 2)***

Who is the person from outside the household?

Son 2
Daughter 3
Brother 4
Sister 5
Other relation 6
Friend / Neighbour 7
Social Services 8
District Nurse / Health Visitor 9
Paid Help 10
Other 15
→See Q19

19. Bed **If needs help/cannot manage to get up and down step or stairs, or finds it difficult *(Stairs = 2 or 3 or StrsEasy = 3 or 4)***

SHOW CARD TEL1
Do you usually manage to get in and out of bed...

on your own .... 1 → Q20
only with help from someone else .... 2 →See Q21
or not at all? .... 3 →See Q21

20. BedEasy [*] **If manages on own (*Bed = 1*)**

SHOW CARD TEL2
Do you find it ...

very easy 1
fairly easy 2
fairly difficult 3
or very difficult to do this on your own? .. 4
→See Q21

21. Dress **If needs help to get up and down step or stairs, or finds it difficult *(Stairs = 2 or 3 or StrsEasy = 3 or 4)***

SHOW CARD TEL1
Do you usually manage to dress and undress yourself ...

on your own .... 1 → Q22
only with help from someone else .... 2 →See Q23
or not at all? .... 3 →See Q23

22. DresEasy [*] **If manages on own *(Dress = 1)***

SHOW CARD TEL2
Do you find it ...

very easy .... 1 →See Q23
fairly easy .... 2 →See Q23
fairly difficult .... 3 →See Q23
or very difficult to do this on your own? .. 4 →See Q23

23. CanHlp2 **If finds it difficult to get in and out of bed or to dress and undress AND has not already stated they need help to get in and out of bed or to dress and undress *(Bed ≠ 2 OR Dress ≠ 2 AND BedEasy = 3 or 4 OR DresEasy = 3 or 4)***

Although you said you usually manage on your own, does anyone help you get in and out of bed/dress and undress?

Yes .... 1 →See Q24
No .... 2 →See Q24

24. BedHlp **If needs help to get in and out of bed or to dress and undress *(Bed = 2 OR Dress = 2 OR CanHlp2 = 1)***

Who usually helps you to get in and out of bed/dress? Is it someone in the household, or someone from outside the household?

Someone in the household .... 1 → Q25
Someone from outside the household .. 2 → Q26

25. BedHlpA **If usually gets help from someone in the household *(BedHlp = 1)***

Who is the person in the household?

INTERVIEWER: ENTER PERSON NUMBER 1..14 →See Q27

26. BedHlpB **If usually gets help from someone outside the household *(BedHlp = 2)***

Who is the person from outside the household?

Son .... 2 →See Q27
Daughter .... 3 →See Q27
Brother .... 4 →See Q27
Sister .... 5 →See Q27
Other relation .... 6 →See Q27
Friend / Neighbour .... 7 →See Q27
Social Services .... 8 →See Q27
District Nurse / Health Visitor .... 9 →See Q27
Paid Help .... 10 →See Q27
Other 15

27. Feed **If needs help to get up and down step or stairs, or finds it difficult *(Stairs = 2 or 3 or StrsEasy = 3 or 4)***

SHOW CARD TEL1
Do you usually manage to feed yourself...

on your own .... 1 → Q28
only with help from someone else .... 2 →See Q30
or not at all? .... 3 →See Q30

28. FeedEasy [*] **If manages on own *(Feed = 1)***

SHOW CARD TEL2

Do you find it...

very easy .... 1 → Q33
fairly easy .... 2 → Q33
fairly difficult .... 3 → Q29
or very difficult to do this on your own? .. 4 → Q29

29. CanHlp3 **If finds if difficult to feed themselves *(FeedEasy = 3 or 4)***

Although you said you usually manage on your own, does anyone help you to feed yourself?

Yes .... 1 → Q30
No .... 2 → Q33

30. FeedHlp **If needs help to feed *(Feed = 2 OR CanHlp3 = 1)***

Who usually helps you to feed yourself? Is it someone in the household, or someone from outside the household?

Someone in the household .... 1 → Q31
Someone from outside the household .. 2 → Q32

31. FeedHlpA **If usually gets help from someone in the household *(FeedHlp = 1)***

Who is the person in the household?

INTERVIEWER: ENTER PERSON NUMBER 1..14 → Q33

32. FeedHlpB **If usually gets help from someone outside the household *(FeedHlp = 2)***

Who is the person from outside the household?

Son .... 2 → Q33
Daughter .... 3 → Q33
Brother .... 4 → Q33
Sister .... 5 → Q33
Other relation .... 6 → Q33
Friend / Neighbour .... 7 → Q33
Social Services .... 8 → Q33
District Nurse / Health Visitor .... 9 → Q33
Paid Help .... 10 → Q33
Other .... 15 → Q33

33. Toenails **Ask all (except proxy informants)**

Do you usually manage to cut your toenails yourself, or does someone else do it for you?

Self .... 1 → Q34
Someone else .... 2 → Q35

34. TnailEas [*] **If cuts own toenails *(Toenails = 1)***

SHOW CARD TEL2
(Still looking at the card) do you find it...

very easy 1
fairly easy 2
fairly difficult 3
or very difficult to do this on your own? .. 4 → Q38

35. TnHlp **If someone else does it *(Toenails = 2)***

Who usually helps you? Is it someone in the household, or someone from outside the household?

Someone in the household .... 1 → Q36
Someone from outside the household .. 2 → Q37

36. TnlHlpA **If usually gets help from someone in the household *(TnlHlp = 1)***

Who is the person in the household?

INTERVIEWER: ENTER PERSON NUMBER 1..14 → Q38

37. TnlHlpB **If usually gets help from someone outside the household *(TnlHlp = 2)***

Who is the person from outside the household?

Son 2
Daughter 3
Brother 4
Sister 5
Other relation 6
Friend / Neighbour 7
Social Services 8
District Nurse / Health Visitor 9
Paid Help 10
Chiropodist 11
Other .... 15 → Q38

38. Bath **Ask all (except proxy informants)**

SHOW CARD TEL1
Do you usually manage to bath, shower or wash all over...

on your own .... 1 → Q39
only with help from someone else .... 2 → Q41
or not at all? .... 3 →See Q44

39. BathEasy [*] **If manages on own *(Bath = 1)***

SHOW CARD TEL2
Do you find it...

very easy 1
fairly easy .... 2 →See Q44
fairly difficult 3
or very difficult to do this on your own? .. 4 → Q40

40. CanHlp4 **If finds if difficult to bath, shower or wash all over *(BathEasy = 3 or 4)***

Although you said you usually manage on your own , does anyone help you bath, shower or wash all over?

Yes .... 1 → Q41
No .... 2 →See Q44

41. BthHlp **If needs help to bath, shower or wash all over *(Bath = 2 OR CanHlp4 =1)***

Who usually helps you? Is it someone in the household, or someone from outside the household?

Someone in the household .... 1 → Q42
Someone from outside the household ... 2 → Q43

42. BthHlpA **If usually gets help from someone in the household *(BthHlp = 1)***

Who is the person in the household?

INTERVIEWER: ENTER PERSON NUMBER 1..14 →See Q44

43. BthHlpB **If usually gets help from someone outside the household *(BthHlp = 2)***

Who is the person from outside the household?

Son 2
Daughter 3
Brother 4
Sister 5
Other relation 6
Friend / Neighbour 7
Social Services 8
District Nurse / Health Visitor 9
Paid Help 10
Other .... 15 →See Q44

44. Wash **If does not manage to bath, or can only bath with help from someone else OR finds it difficult to bath *(Bath = 2 or 3 OR BathEasy = 3 or 4)***

Do you usually manage to wash your face and hands...

on your own .... 1 → Q45
or only with help from someone else? .. 2 → Q47

45. WashEasy [*] **If manages on own *(Wash = 1)***

SHOW CARD TEL2
Do you find it...

very easy 1
fairly easy .... 2 → Q50
fairly difficult 3
or very difficult to do this on your own? 4 → Q46

46. CanHlp5 **If finds if difficult to wash face and hands *(WashEasy = 3 or 4)***

Although you said you usually manage on your own, does anyone help you wash your face and hands?

Yes .... 1 → Q47
No .... 2 → Q50

47. WshHlp **If needs help to wash face and hands *(Wash = 2 OR CanHlp5 = 1)***

Who usually helps you? Is it someone in the household, or someone from outside the household?

Someone in the household .... 1 → Q48
Someone from outside the household .. 2 → Q49

48. WshHlpA **If usually gets help from someone in the household *(WshHlp = 1)***

Who is the person in the household?

INTERVIEWER: ENTER PERSON NUMBER 1..14 → Q50

49. WshHlpB **If usually gets help from someone outside the household *(WshHlp = 2)***

Who is the person from outside the household?

Son 2
Daughter 3
Brother 4
Sister 5
Other relation 6
Friend / Neighbour 7
Social Services 8
District Nurse / Health Visitor 9
Paid Help 10
Other 15
→ Q50

50. Medicine **Ask all (except proxy informants)**

Do you need medical care such as taking medicines or pills, having injections or changes of dressing?

Yes .... 1 → Q51
No .... 2 → Q57

51. MediYou **If needs medical care *(Medicine = 1)***

Do you usually do this yourself, or does someone else help you?

Self .... 1 → Q52
Someone else .... 2 → Q54

52. MediEasy [*] **If self *(MediYou = 1)***

SHOW CARD TEL2
Do you find it ...

very easy 1
fairly easy 2
→ Q57
fairly difficult 3
or very difficult to do this on your own? .. 4
→ Q53

53. CanHlp6 **If finds it difficult to manage own medical care *(MediEasy = 3 or 4)***

Although you said you usually manage on your own, does anyone help you with your medical care?

Yes .... 1 → Q54
No .... 2 → Q57

54. MediHlp **If needs help with medical care *(MediYou = 2 or CanHlp6 = 1)***

Who usually helps you with your medical care? Is it someone in the household, or someone from outside the household?

Someone in the household .... 1 → Q55
Someone from outside the household .. 2 → Q56

55. MediHlpA **If usually gets help from someone in the household *(MediHlp = 1)***

Who is the person in the household?

INTERVIEWER: ENTER PERSON NUMBER 1..14 → Q57

56. MediHlpB **If usually gets help from someone outside the household *(MediHlp = 2)***

Who is the person from outside the household?

Son 2
Daughter 3
Brother 4
Sister 5
Other relation 6
Friend / Neighbour 7
Social Services 8
District Nurse / Health Visitor 9
Paid Help 10
Other 15
→ Q57

57.Walk **Ask all (except proxy informants)**

SHOW CARD TEL1
Do you usually manage to go out of doors and walk down the road...

on your own .... 1 → Q58
only with help from someone else .... 2 → Q60
or not at all? .... 3 → Q63

58. WalkEasy [*] **If manages on own *(Walk =1)***

SHOW CARD TEL2

Do you find it...

very easy 1
fairly easy 2
→ Q63
fairly difficult 3
or very difficult to do this on your own? .. 4
→ Q59

59. CanHlp7 **If finds if difficult to walk down the road *(WalkEasy = 3 or 4)***

Although you said you usually manage on your own, does anyone help you to go out doors and walk down the road?

Yes .... 1 → Q60
No .... 2 → Q63

60. WlkHlp **If needs help to walk down the road *(Walk = 2 OR CanHlp7 = 1)***

Who usually helps you? Is it someone in the household, or someone from outside the household?

Someone in the household .... 1 → Q61
Someone from outside the household .. 2 → Q62

61. WlkHlpA **If usually gets help from someone in the household *(WlkHlp = 1)***

Who is the person in the household?

INTERVIEWER: ENTER PERSON NUMBER 1..14 → Q63

62. WlkHlpB **If usually gets help from someone outside the household *(WlkHlp = 2)***

Who is the person from outside the household?

Son 2
Daughter 3
Brother 4
Sister 5
Other relation 6
Friend / Neighbour 7
Social Services 8
District Nurse / Health Visitor 9
Paid Help 10
Other 15
→ Q63

63. PubTrans **Ask all (except proxy informants)**

Do you use public transport at all nowadays?

Yes .... 1 → Q64
No .... 2 → Q70

64. PTOwn **If uses public transport *(PubTrans = 1)***

Do you usually manage on your own, or only with help from someone else?

On own .... 1 → Q65
With help .... 2 → Q67

65. PTEasy [*] **If manages on own *(PTOwn = 1)***

SHOW CARD TEL2
Do you find it...

very easy 1
fairly easy 2
→ Q71
fairly difficult 3
or very difficult to do this on your own? .. 4
→ Q66

66. CanHlp8 **If finds if difficult to use public transport *(PTEasy = 3 or 4)***

Although you said you usually manage on your own , does anyone help you to use public transport?

Yes .... 1 → Q67
No .... 2 → Q71

67. PTHlp **If needs help to use public transport *(PTOwn = 2 OR CanHlp8 = 1)***

Who usually helps you? Is it someone in the household, or someone from outside the household?

Someone in the household .... 1 → Q68
Someone from outside the household .. 2 → Q69

68. PTHlpA **If usually gets help from someone in the household *(PTHlp = 1)***

Who is the person in the household?

INTERVIEWER: ENTER PERSON NUMBER 1..14 → Q71

69. PTHlpB **If usually gets help from someone outside the household *(PTHlp = 2)***

Who is the person from outside the household?

Son 2
Daughter 3
Brother 4
Sister 5
Other relation 6
Friend / Neighbour 7
Social Services 8
District Nurse / Health Visitor 9
Paid Help 10
Other 15
→ Q71

70. PTYNot [*] **If does not use public transport *(PubTrans = 2)***

Why is that?
CODE ALL THAT APPLY

Health problem or physical difficulty 1
Uses own or household's car 2
Uses other car/cycles/walks/no need to use public transport 3
Public transport is inconvenient 4
Public transport is too expensive 5
Other 6
→ Q71

71. Prctcal **Ask all (except proxy informants)**

Do you do practical activities, such as gardening, decorating, or doing household repairs, by yourself?

Yes .... 1 → Q76
No .... 2 → Q72

72. PrctOwn **If does not do practical activities themselves *(Prctcal = 2)***

Could you if you had to?

Yes 1
No 2
→ Q73

73. PrctHlp Who usually does this for you? Is it someone in the household, or someone from outside the household?

Someone in the household .... 1 → Q74
Someone from outside the household .. 2 → Q75

74. PrctHlpA **If usually gets help from someone in the household *(PrctHlp = 1)***

Who is the person in the household?

INTERVIEWER: ENTER PERSON NUMBER 1..14 → Q76

75. PrctHlpB **If usually gets help from someone outside the household *(PrctHlp = 2)***

Who is the person from outside the household?

Son 2
Daughter 3
Brother 4
Sister 5
Other relation 6
Friend / Neighbour .... 7 → Q76
Social Services 8
District Nurse / Health Visitor 9
Paid Help 10
Other 15
Nobody does it 16

76. Shopping **Ask all (except proxy informants)**

Do you do the household shopping yourself?

Yes .... 1 → Q81
No .... 2 → Q77

77. ShopOwn **If does not do the household shopping themselves *(Shopping = 2)***

Could you if you had to?

Yes 1
No .... 2 → Q78

78. ShpHlp Who usually does this for you? Is it someone in the household, or someone from outside the household?

Someone in the household .... 1 → Q79
Someone from outside the household .. 2 → Q80

79. ShpHlpA **If usually gets help from someone in the household *(ShpHlp = 1)***

Who is the person in the household?

INTERVIEWER: ENTER PERSON NUMBER 1..14 → Q81

80. ShpHlpB **If usually gets help from someone outside the household *(ShpHlp = 2)***

Who is the person from outside the household?

Son 2
Daughter 3
Brother 4
Sister 5
Other relation 6
Friend / Neighbour .... 7 → Q81
Social Services 8
District Nurse / Health Visitor 9
Paid Help 10
Other 15
Nobody does it 16

81. Business **Ask all (except proxy informants)**

Do you deal with personal affairs - for example, paying bills, writing letters - by yourself?

Yes .... 1 → Q86
No .... 2 → Q82

82. BusOwn **If does not deal with personal affairs themselves *(Business = 2)***

Could you if you had to?

Yes 1
No .... 2 → Q83

83. BusHlp Who usually does this for you? Is it someone in the household, or someone from outside the household?

Someone in the household .... 1 → Q84
Someone from outside the household .. 2 → Q85

84. BusHlpA **If usually gets help from someone in the household *(BusHlp = 1)***

Who is the person in the household?

INTERVIEWER: ENTER PERSON NUMBER 1..14 → Q86

85. BusHlpB **If usually gets help from someone outside the household *(BusHlp = 2)***

Who is the person from outside the household?

Son 2
Daughter 3
Brother 4
Sister 5
Other relation 6
Friend / Neighbour .... 7 → Q86
Social Services 8
District Nurse / Health Visitor 9
Paid Help 10
Other 15
Nobody does it 16

86. Dishes **Ask all (except proxy informants)**

Do you wash up and dry dishes?

Yes .... 1 → Q88
No .... 2 → Q87

87. DishOwn **If does not wash up and dry dishes *(Dishes = 2)***

Could you if you had to?

Yes 1
No .... 2 → Q88

88. Windows **Ask all (except proxy informants)**

Do you clean windows inside yourself?

Yes .... 1 → Q90
No .... 2 → Q89

89. WindwOwn **If does not clean windows themselves *(Windows = 2)***

Could you if you had to?

Yes 1
No .... 2 → Q90

90. Vacuum **Ask all (except proxy informants)**

Do you use a vacuum cleaner?

Yes .... 1 → Q92
No .... 2 → Q91

91. VacOwn **If does not use a vacuum cleaner *(Vacuum = 2)***

Could you if you had to?

Yes .... 1 ⎤
No .... 2 ⎦ → Q92

92. Steps **Ask all (except proxy informants)**

Do you do jobs involving climbing a stepladder, steps or a chair?

Yes .... 1 → Q94
No .... 2 → Q93

93. StpsOwn **If does not do jobs that involve climbing *(Steps = 2)***

Could you if you had to?

Yes .... 1 ⎤
No .... 2 ⎦ → Q94

94. Laundry **Ask all (except proxy informants)**

Do you wash small amounts of clothing by hand?

Yes .... 1 → Q96
No .... 2 → Q95

95. LaundOwn **If does not wash small amounts of clothing by hand *(Laundry = 2)***

Could you if you had to?

Yes .... 1 ⎤
No .... 2 ⎦ → Q96

96. Bottles **Ask all (except proxy informants)**

Do you open screw top bottles and jars?

Yes .... 1 →See Q98
No .... 2 → Q97

97. BottlOwn **If does not open screw top bottles and jars *(Bottles = 2)***

Could you if you had to?

Yes .... 1 ⎤
No .... 2 ⎦ →See Q98

98. DomHlp **If does not wash up and dry dishes OR does not clean windows OR does not use a vacuum cleaner OR does not do jobs that involve climbing OR does not open screw top bottles and jars *(Dishes = 2 OR Windows = 2 OR Vacuum = 2 OR Steps = 2 OR Bottles = 2)***

You've said that there are some things that may need doing around the house which you don't do yourself. Who usually does them for you?

INTERVIEWER ASK OR CODE Is it someone in the household, or someone from outside the household?

Someone in the household .... 1 → Q99
Someone from outside the household .. 2 → Q100

99. DomHlpA **If usually gets help from someone in the household *(DomHlp = 1)***

Who is the person in the household?

INTERVIEWER : ENTER PERSON NUMBER 1..14 → Q101

100. DomHlpB **If usually gets help from someone outside the household *(DomHlp = 2)***

Who is the person from outside the household?

Son 2
Daughter 3
Brother 4
Sister 5
Other relation 6
Friend / Neighbour 7
Social Services 8
District Nurse / Health Visitor 9
Paid Help 10
Other 15
Nobody does it .... 16 → Q101

101. Cook Ask all (except proxy informants)

Do you prepare hot meals for yourself?

Yes .... 1 →See Q110
No .... 2 → Q102

102. CookOwn **If does not prepare hot meals *(Cook = 2)***

Could you if you had to?

Yes .... 1 ⎤
No .... 2 ⎦ → Q103

103. CookHlp Who usually prepares hot meals for you .

ASK OR CODE Is it someone in the household, or someone from outside the household?

Someone in the household .... 1 → Q104
Someone from outside the household .. 2 → Q105

104. CookHpA **If usually gets help from someone in the household *(CookHlp = 1)***

Who is the person in the household?

INTERVIEWER : ENTER PERSON NUMBER 1..14 → Q106

105. CookHpB **If usually gets help from someone outside the household *(CookHlp = 2)***

Who is the person from outside the household?

Son 2
Daughter 3
Brother 4
Sister 5
Other relation 6
Friend / Neighbour .... 7 → Q106

Social Services 8
District Nurse / Health Visitor 9
Paid Help .... 10 → Q106
Other 15
Nobody does it 16

106. Snack **If does not prepare hot meals *(Cook = 2)***

Do you prepare snacks for yourself?

Yes .... 1 →See Q110
No .... 2 → Q107

107. SnackOwn **If does not prepare Snacks (*Snack = 2*)**

Could you if you had to?

Yes 1
No .... 2 → Q108

108. CupTea Do you make cups of tea?

Yes .... 1 →See Q110
No .... 2 → Q109

109. TeaOwn **If does not make cups of tea *(CupTea = 2)***

Could you if you had to?

Yes 1
No .... 2 →See Q110

110. RegCare **If needs help with stairs, getting around the house, getting to the toilet, getting in and out of bed, getting dressed and undressed, feeding, bathing or washing *(StairLoo = 1 OR StairBed = 1 OR House = 2 OR Toilet = 2 OR Bed = 2 OR Dress =2 OR Feed = 2 OR Bath =2 OR Wash = 2 OR CanHlp1 = 1 OR CanHlp2 = 1 OR CanHlp3 = 1 OR CanHlp4 = 1 OR CanHlp5 = 1)***

Thinking of all the things we've been talking about, may I just check, do you need REGULAR DAILY HELP with things that fit and healthy people would normally do for themselves?

Yes .... 1 → Q111
No .... 2 → Q115

111. Ncarers **If needs regular daily help *(RegCare = 1)***

How many REGULAR carers do you have to help you?

1..8 → Q112

112. CreHlpB ASK OR CODE: Is the carer someone in the household, or someone from outside the household?

Someone in the household .... 1 → Q113
Someone from outside the household .. 2 → Q114

113. CreHlpC **If usually gets help from someone in the household *(CreHlpB = 1)***

Who is the person number of the person in the household?
INTERVIEWER: ENTER PERSON NUMBER

1..14 → Q115

114. CreHlpD **If usually gets help from someone outside the household *(CreHlpB = 2)***

Who is the person from outside the household?

Son 2
Daughter 3
Brother 4
Sister 5
Other relation 6
Friend / Neighbour .... 7 → Q115
Social Services 8
District Nurse / Health Visitor 9
Paid Help 10
Other 15

115 GoVisit **Ask all (except proxy informants)**

Do you ever go to see, or call in on, relatives or friends nowadays?

Yes .... 1 → Q116
No .... 2 → Q118

116. GvisFreq **If goes to see, or calls in on, relatives or friends *(GoVisit = 1)***

SHOW CARD TEL3
About how often do you go to see relatives or friends?

Every day or nearly 1
Two or three times a week .... 2 → Q118
Once a week 3
Once or twice a month 4
Less than once a month .... 5 → Q117

117. GvisLMth **If goes to see, or calls in on, relatives or friends once or twice a month or less *(GVisFreq = 4 or 5)***

(May I just check) did you go to see any relatives or friends last month,that is during (LAST COMPLETE CALENDAR MONTH)?

Yes 1
No .... 2 → Q118

118. ComVisit **Ask all (except proxy informants)**

Do any relatives or friends come to see you or call in on you here
nowadays?

Yes .... 1 → Q119
No .... 2 → Q121

119. CvisFreq **If relatives or friends come or call in *(ComVisit = 1)***

SHOW CARD TEL3
About how often do relatives and friends come to see you here?

Every day or nearly 1
Two or three times a week .... 2 → Q121
Once a week 3
Once or twice a month 4
Less than once a month .... 5 → Q120

120. CvisLMth **If relatives or friends come or call in once or twice a month or less *(CVisFreq = 4 or 5)***

(May I just check) did any friends or relatives come to see you last month, that is during (LAST COMPLETE CALENDAR MONTH)?

Yes .... 1]→ Q121
No .... 2]

121 Neighbrs **Ask all (except proxy informants)**

Apart from relatives or friends, do you see any of your neighbours to chat to?

Yes .... 1 → Q122
No .... 2 → Q123

122. NbrsFreq **If they see neighbours to chat to *(Neighbrs = 1)***

SHOW CARD TEL3
About how often do you see any of your neighbours to chat to?

Every day or nearly .... 1]
Two or three times a week .... 2]
Once a week .... 3]→ Q123
Once or twice a month .... 4]
Less than once a month .... 5]

123. EldInt3 **Ask all (except proxy informants)**

I'm going to ask you about services that people can make use of. Some of them won't apply to you, but others may. Which of these services did you make use of last month that is during (LAST COMPLETE CALENDAR MONTH)

124. HomeHelp Local Authority home help or home care worker?

Used last month .... 1]→ Q125
Not used last month .... 2]

125. PrivHelp Private domestic help?

Used last month .... 1]→ Q126
Not used last month .... 2]

126. DistNrse District nurse, health visitor, or other kind of nurse visiting you at
home?

Used last month .... 1]→ Q127
Not used last month .... 2]

127. MlsnWhls Meals on Wheels?

Used last month .... 1]→ Q128
Not used last month .... 2]

128. LnchClub Lunch club run by the council or a voluntary body?

Used last month .... 1]→ Q129
Not used last month .... 2]

129. DayCen Day Centre for the elderly?

Used last month .... 1]→ Q130
Not used last month .... 2]

130. VolHelpr Helper from a voluntary organisation?

Used last month .... 1]→See Q131
Not used last month .... 2]

131. HHTimes **If used a home help or home care worker last month *(HomeHelp = 1)***

SHOW CARD TEL4
About how often did you have your Local Authority home help last month?

Every day or nearly .... 1]
Two or three times a week .... 2]→ Q132
Once a week .... 3]
Less often .... 4]

132. HHHours About how many hours each week do you have the home help for?

1..97 →See Q133

133. PHTimes **If used private domestic help last month *(PrivHelp = 1)***

SHOW CARD TEL4
About how often did you have private domestic help last month?

Every day or nearly .... 1]
Two or three times a week .... 2]→See Q134
Once a week .... 3]
Less often .... 4]

134. DNTimes **If visited by a nurse or health visitor last month *(DistNrse = 1)***

SHOW CARD TEL4
About how often did you have visits from a nurse last month?

Every day or nearly .... 1]
Two or three times a week .... 2]→See Q135
Once a week .... 3]
Less often .... 4]

135. MWTimes **If used 'Meals on Wheels' last month *(MlsnWhls = 1)***

SHOW CARD TEL4
About how often did you have Meals on Wheels last month?

Every day or nearly .... 1]
Two or three times a week .... 2]→See Q136
Once a week .... 3]
Less often .... 4]

136. LCTimes **If used a 'lunch club' last month *(LnchClub = 1)***

SHOW CARD TEL4
About how often did you have lunch at a lunch club last month?

Every day or nearly .... 1]
Two or three times a week .... 2]→See Q137
Once a week .... 3]
Less often .... 4]

137. CenTimes **If used a day centre last month *(DayCen = 1)***

SHOW CARD TEL4
About how often did you go to the Day Centre last month?

Every day or nearly 1
Two or three times a week 2
Once a week 3
Less often 4
→See Q138

138. VHTimes **If visited by a helper from a voluntary organisation last month *(VolHlpr = 1)***

SHOW CARD TEL4
About how often were you visited by a voluntary worker last month?

Every day or nearly 1
Two or three times a week 2
Once a week 3
Less often 4
→ Q139

139. EldInt4 **Ask all (except proxy informants)**

Now here is another list. Which of these health and social services did you make use of during the months of (LAST 3 COMPLETE CALENDAR MONTHS)?

140. DsLst3M Doctor/GP at his/her surgery? INCLUDE BOTH NHS AND PRIVATE

Yes 1
No 2
→ Q141

141. DaLst3M Doctor attending you at home? INCLUDE BOTH NHS AND PRIVATE

Yes 1
No 2
→ Q142

142. HdLst3M Hospital doctor? INCLUDE BOTH NHS AND PRIVATE

Yes 1
No 2
→ Q143

143. NsLst3M Nurse at a surgery or health centre? INCLUDE BOTH NHS AND PRIVATE

Yes 1
No 2
→ Q144

144. SwLst3M Local Authority social worker or care manager?

Yes 1
No 2
→ Q145

145. DtLst3M Dentist? INCLUDE NHS AND PRIVATE

Yes 1
No 2
→ Q146

146. ChLst3M Chiropodist at home, clinic or hospital? . INCLUDE BOTH NHS AND PRIVATE

Yes 1
No 2
→ Q147

147. OpLst3M Optician? INCLUDE BOTH NHS AND PRIVATE

Yes 1
No 2
→See Q148

148. DsLstMth **If visited doctor or GP at the surgery *(DsLst3M = 1)***

Did you see the doctor at the surgery last month, that is, in(LAST COMPLETE CALENDAR MONTH)?

Yes 1
No 2
→See Q149

149. DaLstMth **If doctor attended them at home *(DaLst3M = 2)***

Did the doctor come and see you at home last month, that is, in(LAST COMPLETE CALENDAR MONTH)?

Yes 1
No 2
→See Q150

150. HdLstMth **If visited a hospital doctor *(HdLst3M = 1)***

Did you see the doctor at the hospital last month, that is, in (LAST COMPLETE CALENDAR MONTH)?

Yes 1
No 2
→See Q151

151. NsLstMth **If visited nurse at the surgery or health centre *(NsLst3M = 1)***

Did you see the nurse at the surgery last month, that is, in(LAST COMPLETE CALENDAR MONTH)?

Yes 1
No 2
→See Q152

152. SwLstMth **If saw a local Authority social worker or care manager *(SwLst3M = 1)***

Did you see the social worker or care manager last month, that is, in *(LAST COMPLETE CALENDAR MONTH)?*

Yes 1
No 2
→See Q153

153. DtLstMth **If saw a dentist *(DtLst3M = 1)***

Did you see the dentist last month, that is, in *(LAST COMPLETE CALENDAR MONTH)?*

Yes 1
No 2
→See Q154

154. ChLstMth **If saw a chiropodist *(ChLst3M = 1)***

Did you see the chiropodist last month, that is, in (LAST COMPLETE CALENDAR MONTH)?

Yes 1
No 2
→See Q155

155. OpLstMth **If saw an optician *(OpLst3M = 1)***

Did you see the optician last month, that is, in (LAST COMPLETE CALENDAR MONTH)?

Yes .... 1 → Q156
No .... 2 → Q156

156. Shelter **Ask all (except proxy informants)**

IS THE RESPONDENT LIVING IN SHELTERED ACCOMMODATION?

Sheltered: warden on premises 1
Sheltered: no warden on premises, but premises have a central alarm system 2
Not sheltered 3
Not sure 4
→ Mobility Aids

MOBILITY AIDS

1. IntrMob **Ask all**

(We have already talked a bit about mobility.) In this section we are interested in whether people have anything to help them get around, either inside or outside the home → Q2

2. MobDiff [*] ASK OR RECORD

Do you have any difficulty getting about the house/flat without assistance of any kind?

Yes .... 1 → Q3
No .... 2 → Q4

3. MobAid **If they have difficulty getting about the house/flat without assistance *(MobDiff = 1)***

What type of assistance do you require?

SHOW CARD TMO1

CODE ALL THAT APPLY
ENTER AT MOST 4 CODES

Walking aid 1
Wheelchair 2
Assistance from another person 3
Other 4
Can't get about house 5
→ Q4

4. MobOut [*] **Ask all**

ASK OR RECORD

Do you have any difficulty going out of doors and walking down the road without assistance of any kind?

Yes .... 1 → Q5
No .... 2 → Q7

5. Mobbed **If has difficulty walking down the road without assistance *(MobOut = 1)***

What type of assistance do you require?

SHOW CARD TMO2

CODE ALL THAT APPLY
ENTER AT MOST 4 CODES

Walking aid 1
Wheelchair 2
Assistance from another person 3
Other 4
Can't get outside house 5
→ Q6

6. MobTemp [*] **If needs assistance getting about *(MobDiff =1 or MobOut =1)***

CODE 1 IF INFORMANT WILL RECOVER AND NO LONGER NEED ASSISTANCE OF ANY KIND

Is this...

A temporary difficulty due to an accident or illness 1
Or is this likely to be a permanent difficulty? 2
→ Q7

7. MobCard **Ask all**

SHOW CARD TMO3

(Can I just check) Do you have any aids to walking or getting about, either inside or outside your home, such as those shown on this card, including any that you no longer use?

Yes .... 1 → Q8
No .... 2 → Smoking

8. MobNum **If has any aids *(MobCard = 1)***

How many aids to walking do you have?

1..6 → Q9

9. MobType **For each aid**

What is the (first/second etc) type of aid that you have?

RECORD EACH AID MENTIONED AT MOBNUM

SHOW CARD TMO3

Walking stick 1
Crutches 2
Walking frame, tripod, zimmer 3
Trolley (not shopping) 4
Wheelchair - manual 5
Wheelchair - electric 6
Buggy/scooter 7
Other 8
→ Q10

10. MobWhere **Ask for each aid coded at MobType**

Where did you get the (type of mobility aid) from?

Health/social services 1
Bought yourself or by spouse partner 2
Provided by friend/relative 3
Voluntary organisation 4
Other 5
→ Q11

11. MobPlace **For each aid**

Do you use this (type of mobility aid) for...

RUNNING PROMPT

Indoor use only .... 1 →See Q13
Outdoor use only .... 2 → Q12
Indoor and outdoor use? .... 3 → Q12
Aid not in use .... 4 →See Q13

12. MobWhen **If used for outdoor use *(MobPlace = 2 or 3)***

When going out do you use (type of mobility aid) ...

All the time .... 1 →See Q13
Regularly .... 2 →See Q13
Occasionally? .... 3 →See Q13

13. ChairMan **If uses a manual or electric wheelchair *(MobType = 5 or 6 AND MobPlace = 1,2 or 3)***

Can you manage this wheelchair on your own or do you need someone to help push/control it?

Manage yourself .... 1 →Smoking
Always need help .... 2 →Smoking
Sometimes need help .... 3 →Smoking

SMOKING

1. SmkIntro **Ask this section of all adults, except proxy informants**

The next section consists of a series of questions about SMOKING (Not asked of proxy respondents)

2. SelfCom1 **Ask all 16 and 17 year olds *(DVAge = 16-17)***

INFORMANT IS AGED 16 OR 17 - OFFER SELF-COMPLETION FORMAND ENTER CODE.

Informant accepted self-completion ...... 1 → Q3
Informant refused self-completion .... 2 → Drinking
Data now to be keyed by interviewer .... 3 → Q3

3. SmokEver **Ask if aged 18 or over (except proxy informants) *(DVAge (≥18)***

Have you ever smoked a cigarette, a cigar, or a pipe?

Yes .... 1 → Q4
No .... 2 → Drinking

4. CigNow **Ask if respondent has ever smoked *(SmokEver = 1)***

Do you smoke cigarettes at all nowadays?

Yes .... 1 → Q5
No .... 2 → Q13

5. QtyWkEnd **Ask if respondent smokes cigarettes now *(CigNow = 1)***

About how many cigarettes A DAY do you usually smoke at weekends?

IF LESS THAN 1, ENTER 0.

0..97 → Q6

6. QtyWkDay About how many cigarettes A DAY do you usually smoke on weekdays?

IF LESS THAN 1, ENTER 0.

0..97 → Q7

7. CigType Do you mainly smoke.....

RUNNING PROMPT

filter-tipped cigarettes .... 1 → Q8
or plain or untipped cigarettes .... 2 → Q8
or hand-rolled cigarettes? .... 3 → Q10

8. CiglDesc **Ask if cigarette types include plain or filter cigarettes *(CigType = 1 or 2)***

Which brand of cigarette do you usually smoke?

GIVE 1) FULL BRAND NAME 2) SIZE, eg King, luxury, regular.IF NO REGULAR BRAND THEN TYPE 'no reg' HERE.
IF INFORMANT SMOKES TWO BRANDS EQUALLY TYPE 'two' HERE.
IF INFORMANT SMOKES SUPERKINGS (WITH NO OTHER BRAND NAME ON THE PACKET) CODE AS JOHN PLAYERS SUPERKINGS.

ENTER TEXT OF AT MOST 60 CHARACTERS → Q9

9. CigCODE Code for brand at CiglDesc → Q10

10. NoSmoke [*] **Ask if respondent smokes cigarettes now *(CigNow = 1)***

How easy or difficult would you find it to go without smoking for a whole day? Would you find it...

RUNNING PROMPT

Very easy .... 1 → Q11
Fairly easy .... 2 → Q11
Fairly difficult or .... 3 → Q11
Very difficult? .... 4 → Q11

11. GiveUp [*] Would you like to give up smoking altogether?

Yes .... 1 → Q12
No .... 2 → Q12

12. FirstCig How soon after waking do you USUALLY smoke your first cigarette of the day?

PROMPT AS NECESSARY

Less than 5 minutes .... 1 → Q16
5-14 minutes .... 2 → Q16
15-29 minutes .... 3 → Q16
30 minutes but less than 1 hour .... 4 → Q16
1 hour but less than 2 hours .... 5 → Q16
2 hours or more .... 6 → Q16

13. CigEver **Ask if respondent does not smoke cigarettes now but has smoked a cigarette or cigar or pipe *(SmokEver = 1 & CigNow = 2)***

Have you ever smoked cigarettes regularly?

Yes .... 1 → Q14
No .... 2 → Q17

14. CigUsed **Ask if respondent has ever smoked cigarettes regularly *(CigEver = 1)***

About how many cigarettes did you smoke IN A DAY when you smoked them regularly?

IF LESS THAN 1, ENTER 0.

0..97 → Q15

15. CigStop How long ago did you stop smoking cigarettes regularly?

PROMPT AS NECESSARY

Less than 6 months ago 1
6 months but less than a year ago 2
1 year but less than 2 years ago 3
2 years but less than 5 years ago 4
5 years but less than 10 years ago 5
10 years or more ago 6
(1–6) → Q16

16. CigAge **Ask of all respondents who have ever smoked cigarettes *(CigNow = 1 or CigEver = 1)***

How old were you when you started to smoke cigarettes regularly?

SPONTANEOUS: NEVER SMOKED CIGARETTES REGULARLY - CODE 0

0..97 → Q17

17. CigarReg **Ask respondents who have ever smoked *(SmokEver = 1)***

Do you smoke at least one cigar of any kind per month nowadays?

Yes .... 1 → Q18
No .... 2 → Q19

18. CigarsWk **Ask if respondent smokes at least one cigar per month *(CigarReg = 1)***

About how many cigars do you usually smoke in a week?

IF LESS THAN 1, ENTER 0.

0..97 →See Q20

19. CigarEvr **Ask if respondent does not smoke at least one cigar per month *(CigarReg = 2)***

Have you ever regularly smoked at least one cigar of any kind per month?

Yes 1
No 2
(1–2) →See Q20

20. PipeNow **Ask men who have ever smoked *(CigNow = 1 AND Sex = 1)***

Do you smoke a pipe at all nowadays?

Yes .... 1 → Drinking
No .... 2 → Q21

21. PipEver **Ask if respondent doesn't currently smoke a pipe *(PipeNow = 2)***

Have you ever smoked a pipe regularly?

Yes 1
No 2
(1–2) → Drinking

DRINKING

Ask this section of all adults except proxy informants

1. Selfcom2 **Ask all 16 and 17 year olds *(DVAge = 16-17)***

(INFORMANT IS AGED 16 OR 17) - OFFER SELF-COMPLETIONFORM AND ENTER CODE.

Interviewer asked section 1
Informant accepted self-completion 2
Data now keyed by interviewer 3
(1–3) → Q2

2. DrinkNow **Ask all (except proxy informants) *(DVAge (≥18 or Selfcom2 = 1)***

I'm now going to ask you a few questions about what you drink - that is if you do drink.

Do you ever drink alcohol nowadays, including drinks you brew or make at home?

Yes .... 1 → Q7
No .... 2 → Q3

3. DrinkAny **Ask if does not drink nowadays *(DrinkNow = 2)***

Could I just check, does that mean you never have an alcoholic drink nowadays, or do you have an alcoholic drink very occasionally, perhaps for medicinal purposes or on special occasions like Christmas or New Year?

Very occasionally .... 1 → Q7
Never .... 2 → Q4

4. TeeTotal **Ask if never drinks *(DrinkAny = 2)***

Have you always been a non-drinker, or did you stop drinking for some reason?

Always a non-drinker .... 1 → Q5
Used to drink but stopped .... 2 → Q6

5. NonDrink [*] **Ask if respondent has always been a non-drinker *(TeeTotal = 1)***

What would you say is the MAIN reason you have always been a non-drinker?

Religious reasons	1
Don't like it	2
Parent's advice/influence	3
Health reasons	4
Can't afford it	5
Other	6

→ Family Information

6. StopDrin [*] **Ask if respondent used to drink but stopped** ***(TeeTotal = 2)***

What would you say was the MAIN reason you stopped drinking?

Religious reasons	1
Don't like it	2
Parent's advice/influence	3
Health reasons	4
Can't afford it	5
Other	6

→ Family Information

7. DrinkAmt [*] **Ask if respondent drinks at all nowadays** **(*Drinknow = 1 or DrinkAny = 1*)**

I'm going to read out a few descriptions about the amounts of alcoholpeople drink, and I'd like you to say which one fits you best. Would you say you:

hardly drink at all	1
drink a little	2
drink a moderate amount	3
drink quite a lot	4
or drink heavily?	5

→ Q8

8. Intro INTERVIEWER - READ OUT:

I'd like to ask you whether you have drunk different types of alcoholic drink in the last 12 months. I'd like to hear about ALL types of alcoholic drinks you have had. If you are not sure whether a drink you have had goes into a category, please let me know. I do not need to know about non-alcoholic or low alcohol drinks. → Q9

9. Nbeer SHOW CARD D

I'd like to ask you first about NORMAL STRENGTH beer or cider which has less than 6% alcohol.

How often have you had a drink of NORMAL STRENGTH BEER, LAGER, STOUT, CIDER or SHANDY (excluding cans and bottles of shandy) during the last 12 months?

INTERVIEWER: (NORMAL = LESS THAN 6% ALCOHOL BY VOLUME)

IF RESPONDENT DOES NOT KNOW WHETHER BEER ETC DRUNK IS STRONG OR NORMAL, INCLUDE HERE AS NORMAL

Almost every day	1	→ Q10
5 or 6 days a week	2	
3 or 4 days a week	3	
once or twice a week	4	
once or twice a month	5	
once every couple of months	6	
once or twice a year	7	
not at all in last 12 months	8	→ Q14

10. NBeerM **Ask if respondent drank normal strength beer (lager/stout/cider/shandy) at all this year** ***(Nbeer = 1-7)***

How much NORMAL STRENGTH BEER, LAGER, STOUT, CIDER or SHANDY (excluding cans and bottles of shandy) have you usually drunk on any one day during the last 12 months?

CODE MEASURES THAT YOU ARE GOING TO USE.
CODE ALL THAT APPLY.
PROBE IF NECESSARY.

Half pints	1
Small cans	2
Large cans	3
Bottles	4

→ Q11

11. NBeerQ **For each measure mentioned at NbeerM**

ASK OR RECORD:

How many (Answer AT NBeerM) of NORMAL STRENGTH BEER, LAGER, STOUT, CIDER OR SHANDY (EXCLUDING CANS AND BOTTLES OF SHANDY) have you usually drunk on any one day during the last 12 months?

1..97 →See Q12

12. NBrlDesc **Ask if respondent described measures in 'Bottles'** ***(NBeerM = 4)***

What make of NORMAL STRENGTH BEER, LAGER, STOUT or CIDER do you usually drink from bottles?

IF RESPONDENT DOES NOT KNOW WHAT MAKE, OR RESPONDENT DRINKS DIFFERENT MAKES OF NORMAL STRENGTH BEER, LAGER, STOUT OR CIDER, PROBE:
'What make have you drunk most frequently or most recently?'

ENTER TEXT OF AT MOST 21 CHARACTERS → Q13

13. NBrCODE Code for brand at NBrlDesc → Q14

14. SBeer **Ask if respondent drinks at all nowadays** ***(Drinknow = 1 or DrinkAny = 1)***

SHOW CARD D

Now I'd like to ask you about STRONG BEER OR CIDER which has 6% or more alcohol (eg Tennants Extra, Special Brew, Diamond White).
How often have you had a drink of strong BEER, LAGER, STOUT or CIDER during the last 12 months?

(STRONG=6% and over Alcohol by volume)

IF RESPONDENT DOES NOT KNOW WHETHER BEER ETC DRUNK IS STRONG OR NORMAL, INCLUDE AS NORMAL STRENGTH AT NBeer ABOVE.

Almost every day	1
5 or 6 days a week	2

→ Q15

3 or 4 days a week 3
once or twice a week 4
once or twice a month .... 5 → Q15
once every couple of months 6
once or twice a year 7
not at all in last 12 months .... 8 → Q19

15. SBeerM **Ask if respondent drank strong beer (lager/stout/ cider) at all this year *(SBeer = 1-7)***

How much STRONG BEER, LAGER, STOUT or CIDER have you usually drunk on any one day during the last 12 months?

CODE MEASURES THAT YOU ARE GOING TO USE
CODE ALL THAT APPLY.
PROBE IF NECESSARY.

Half pints 1
Small cans 2
Large cans .... 3 → Q16
Bottles 4

16. SBeerQ **For each measure mentioned at SBeerM**

ASK OR RECORD

How many (ANSWER AT SBeerM) of STRONG BEER, LAGER, STOUT or CIDER have you usually drunk on any one day during the last 12 months?

1..97 →See Q17

17. SBrlDesc **Ask if respondent described measures in 'Bottles' *(SBeerM = 4)***

What make of STRONG BEER, LAGER, STOUT or CIDER do you usually drink from bottles?

IF RESPONDENT DOES NOT KNOW WHAT MAKE, OR RESPONDENT DRINKS DIFFERENT MAKES OF STRONG BEER, LAGER, STOUT OR CIDER, PROBE:
'What make have you drunk most frequently or most recently?'

ENTER TEXT OF AT MOST 21 CHARACTERS → Q18

18. SBrCODE Code for brand at SBrlDesc → Q19

19. Spirits **Ask if respondent drinks at all nowadays *(Drinknow = 1 or DrinkAny = 1)***

SHOW CARD D

How often have you had a drink of SPIRITS or LIQUEURS, such as gin, whisky, brandy, rum, vodka, advocaat or cocktails during the last 12 months?

Almost every day 1
5 or 6 days a week 2
3 or 4 days a week 3
once or twice a week .... 4 → Q20
once or twice a month 5
once every couple of months 6
once or twice a year 7
not at all in last 12 months .... 8 → Q21

20. SpiritsQ **Ask if respondent drank spirits or liqueurs at all this year *(Spirits = 1-7)***

How much SPIRITS or LIQUEURS (such as gin, whisky, brandy, rum, vodka, advocaat or cocktails) have you usually drunk on any one day during the last 12 months?

CODE THE NUMBER OF SINGLES - COUNT DOUBLES AS TWO SINGLES.

1..97 → Q21

21. Sherry **Ask if respondent drinks at all nowadays *(Drinknow = 1 or DrinkAny = 1)***

SHOW CARD D

How often have you had a drink of SHERRY or MARTINI including port, vermouth, Cinzano and Dubonnet, during the last 12 months?

Almost every day 1
5 or 6 days a week 2
3 or 4 days a week 3
once or twice a week .... 4 → Q22
once or twice a month 5
once every couple of months 6
once or twice a year 7
not at all in last 12 months .... 8 → Q23

22. SherryQ **Ask if respondent drank sherry or martini at all this year *(Sherry = 1-7)***

How much SHERRY or MARTINI, including port, vermouth, Cinzano and Dubonnet have you usually drunk on any one day during the last 12 months?

CODE THE NUMBER OF GLASSES.

1..97 → Q23

23. Wine **Ask if respondent drinks at all nowadays *(Drinknow = 1 or DrinkAny = 1)***

SHOW CARD D

How often have you had a drink of WINE, including Babycham and champagne, during the last 12 months?

Almost every day 1
5 or 6 days a week 2
3 or 4 days a week 3
once or twice a week .... 4 → Q24
once or twice a month 5
once every couple of months 6
once or twice a year 7
not at all in last 12 months .... 8 → Q25

24. WineQ **Ask if respondent drank wine at all this year *(Wine = 1-7)***

How much WINE, including Babycham and champagne, have you usually drunk on any one day during the last 12 months?

CODE THE NUMBER OF GLASSES.
1 BOTTLE = 6 GLASSES, 1 LITRE = 8 GLASSES

1..97 → Q25

25. Pops **Ask if respondent drinks at all nowadays *(Drinknow = 1 or DrinkAny = 1)***

SHOW CARD D

How often have you had a drink of ALCOPOPS (ie alcoholic lemonade, alcoholic colas or other alcoholic fruit- or herb-flavoured drinks(eg. Hooch, Two Dogs, Alcola etc), during the last 12 months?

Almost every day	1	→	Q26
5 or 6 days a week	2		
3 or 4 days a week	3		
once or twice a week	4		
once or twice a month	5		
once every couple of months	6		
once or twice a year	7		
not at all in last 12 months	8	→	Q27

26. PopsQ **As if respondent drank alcopops at all this year *(Pops = 1-7)***

How much alcopops (ie alcoholic lemonade, alcoholic colas or other alcoholic fruit- or herb-flavoured drinks) have you usually drunk on any one day during the last 12 months?

CODE THE NUMBER OF BOTTLES

1..97 → Q27

27. DrinkOft [*] **Ask if respondent drinks at all nowadays *(Drinknow = 1 or DrinkAny = 1)***

SHOW CARD D

Thinking now about all kinds of drinks, how often have you had an alcoholic drink of any kind during the last 12 months?

Almost every day	1	→	Q28
5 or 6 days a week	2		
3 or 4 days a week	3		
once or twice a week	4		
once or twice a month	5		
once every couple of months	6		
once or twice a year	7		
not at all in last 12 months	8		

28. DrinkL7 You have told me what you have drunk over the last 12 months, but we know that what people drink can vary a lot from week to week, so I'd like to ask you a few questions about last week. Did you have an alcoholic drink in the seven days ending yesterday?

Yes	1	→	Q29
No	2	→	Q45

29. DrnkDay **Ask if respondent has had an alcoholic drink in the last week *(DrinkL7 = 1)***

On how many days out of the last seven did you have an alcoholic drink?

1..7 →See Q30

30. DrnkSame **Ask if respondent had an alcoholic drink on two or more days last week *(DrnkDay = 2-7)***

Did you drink more on some days than others/one of the days, or did you drink about the same on each of these/both days?

Drank more on one/some day(s) than other(s)	1	→	Q31
Same each day	2		

31. WhichDay **Ask if respondent had an alcoholic drink last week *(DrinkL7 = 1)***

Which day (last week) did you last have an alcoholic drink/have the most to drink?

Sunday	1	→	Q32
Monday	2		
Tuesday	3		
Wednesday	4		
Thursday	5		
Friday	6		
Saturday	7		

32. DrnkType **Ask if respondent has had an alcoholic drink in the last week *(DrinkL7 = 1)***

SHOW CARD E

Thinking about last (DAY AT WHICHDAY) what types of drink did you have that day?

CODE ALL THAT APPLY

Normal strength beer/lager/cider/shandy	1	→	Q33
Strong beer/lager/cider	2	→	Q37
Spirits or liqueurs	3	→	Q41
Sherry or martini	4	→	Q42
Wine	5	→	Q43
Alcoholic lemonades/colas	6	→	Q44

33. NBrL7 **Ask if respondent drank 'normal strength beer/ lager/cider/shandy' on that day *(DrnkType = 1)***

Still thinking about last (DAY AT WHICHDAY), how much NORMALSTRENGTH BEER, LAGER, STOUT, CIDER or SHANDY (excluding cans and bottles of shandy) did you drink that day?

CODE MEASURES THAT YOU ARE GOING TO USE,
CODE ALL THAT APPLY.
PROBE IF NECESSARY.

Half pints	1	→	Q34
Small cans	2		
Large cans	3		
Bottles	4		

34. NBrL7Q **For each measure mentioned at NBrL7**

ASK OR RECORD

How many (Answer AT NBrL7) of NORMAL STRENGTH BEER, LAGER, STOUT OR CIDER/ CIDER OR SHANDY (EXCLUDING CANS AND BOTTLES OF SHANDY) did you drink that day?

1..97 →See Q35

35. NB7IDesc **Ask if respondent described measures in 'Bottles' *(NBrL7 = 4)***

ASK OR RECORD

What make of NORMAL STRENGTH BEER, LAGER, STOUT or CIDER do you usually drink from bottles?

IF RESPONDENT DRANK DIFFERENT MAKES CODE WHICH THEY DRANK MOST.

ENTER TEXT OF AT MOST 21 CHARACTERS → Q36

36. NB7CODE Code for brand at NB7IDesc →See Q37

37. SBrL7 **Ask if respondent drank 'strong beer/lager/cider' on that day *(DrnkType = 2)***

Still thinking about last (DAY AT WHICHDAY), how much STRONG BEER, LAGER, STOUT, CIDER did you drink that day?

CODE MEASURES THAT YOU ARE GOING TO USE CODE ALL THAT APPLY. PROBE IF NECESSARY.

Half pints	1	→ Q38
Small cans	2	
Large cans	3	
Bottles	4	

38. SBrL7Q **For each measure mentioned at SBrL7**

ASK OR RECORD

How many (Answer AT SBrL7) of STRONG BEER,LAGER, STOUT or CIDER did you drink that day?

1..97 →See Q39

39. SB7IDesc **Ask if respondent described measures in 'Bottles' *(SBrL7 = 4)***

ASK OR RECORD

What make of STRONG BEER, LAGER, STOUT or CIDER do you usually drink from bottles?

IF RESPONDENT DRANK DIFFERENT MAKES CODE WHICH THEY DRANK MOST.

ENTER TEXT OF AT MOST 21 CHARACTERS → Q40

40. SB7CODE Code for brand at SB7IDesc →See Q41

41. SpirL7 **Ask if respondent drank spirits or liqueurs on that day *(DrnkType = 3)***

Still thinking about last (DAY AT WHICHDAY), how much spirits or liqueurs (such as gin, whisky, brandy, rum, vodka, advocaat or cocktails) did you drink on that day?

CODE THE NUMBER OF SINGLES - COUNT DOUBLES AS TWO SINGLES

1..97 →See Q42

42. ShryL7 **Ask if respondent drank sherry or martini on that day *(DrnkType = 4)***

Still thinking about last (DAY AT WHICHDAY), how much sherry or martini, including port, vermouth, Cinzano and Dubonnet did you drink on that day?

CODE THE NUMBER OF GLASSES

1..97 →See Q43

43. WineL7 **Ask if respondent drank wine on that day *(DrnkType = 5)***

Still thinking about last (DAY AT WHICHDAY), how much wine,including Babycham and champagne, did you drink on that day?

CODE THE NUMBER OF GLASSES
1 BOTTLE = 6 GLASSES. 1 LITRE = 8 GLASSES.

1..97 →See Q44

44. PopsL7 **Ask if respondent drank alcopops on that day *(DrnkType = 6)***

Still thinking about last (DAY AT WHICHDAY), how much alcopops(ie alcoholic lemonade, alcoholic colas or other alcoholic fruit- or herb-flavoured drinks) did you drink on that day?

CODE THE NUMBER OF BOTTLES →See Q45

45. DrAmount [*] **Ask if respondent drinks at all nowadays *(Drinknow = 1 or DrinkAny = 1)***

Compared to five years ago, would you say that on the whole you drink more, about the same or less nowadays?

More nowadays	1	→ Family Information
About the same	2	
Less nowadays	3	

FAMILY INFORMATION

1. FamIntro **Ask this section of all aged 16-59 (except proxy informants)**

THE NEXT SECTION CONSISTS OF A SERIES OF QUESTIONS ABOUT FAMILY INFORMATION
(Not asked of proxy respondents)
Others go to View of your local area

2. ChkFIA **To all aged 16-59, if not single or same sex cohabiting, except proxy informants**

INTERVIEWER CODE

Informant is married or cohabiting but their partner is NOT a household member	1	→ Q3
Everyone else	2	→ Q4

3. HusbAway **Ask if married/cohabiting, but partner not a household member**

INTRODUCE AS NECESSARY

Is your husband, wife or partner absent because he/she usually works away from home, or for some other reason?

Usually works away (include Armed Forces, Merchant Navy) .... 1 → Q4
Marriage/partnership broken down .... 2 → Q4

4. SelfCom3 **To all**

OFFER (COLOUR) SELF-COMPLETION FORM TO RESPONDENT AND ENTER CODE.

Interviewer asked section .... 1 →See Q5
Informant accepted self-completion...... 2 →See Q5
Data now being keyed by interviewer ... 3 →See Q5
Interpreter aged under 16- section not asked .... 4 →View of your local area
Respondent refused whole section ...... 5 →View of your local area

5. WhereWed **Ask people who have been married *(Marstat = 2, 3, 4 or 5)***

Thinking of your present / most recent marriage, did you get married with a religious ceremony of some kind, or at a register office or approved premises, or are you simply living together as a couple?

Religious ceremony of some kind......... 1 → Q6
Civil marriage in register office or approved premises .... 2 → Q6
Religious ceremony and register office/approved premises .... 3 → Q6
Living together as a couple .... 4 → Q7

6. NumMar **Ask if respondent has been legally married *(WhereWed = 1-3)***

How many times have you been legally married?

(NUMBER INCLUDING PRESENT MARRIAGE)

1..7 → Q11

7. CLMon **Ask all cohabiting couples, including single sex couples (exc. couples now separated) *(Livewith = 1 or 3 or WhereWed = 4)***

When did you and your partner start living together as a couple?

ENTER MONTH

1..12 → Q8

8. ClYr ENTER YEAR IN 4 DIGIT FORMAT E.G. 2000

1900..2005 → Q9

9. ClMar Have you yourself ever been legally married?

Yes .... 1 → Q10
No .... 2 → Q25

10. ClNumMar **Ask if respondent has been legally married *(ClMar = 1)***

How many times have you been legally married altogether?

1..7

11. Intro **Ask of all who are, or have been, legally married *(NumMar (≥1 or ClNumMar (≥1)***

THE NEXT SCREEN CONSISTS OF A TABLE OF MARRIAGES FOR (NAME). PLEASE ENTER DETAILS OF MARRIAGES STARTING WITH THE EARLIEST AND ENDING WITH THE CURRENT OR MOST RECENT. → Q12

12. MonMar For each marriage

What month and year were you married?

ENTER MONTH 1..12 → Q13

13. YrMar ENTER YEAR IN 4 DIGIT FORMAT E.G. 2000

1900..2005 → Q14

14. LvTgthr Before getting married did you and your husband/wife live together as a couple?

Yes .... 1 → Q15
No .... 2 → Q17

15. MonLvTg **Ask if lived as a couple before getting married *(LvTgthr = 1)***

What month and year did you start living together?

ENTER MONTH 1..12 → Q16

16. YrLvTg ENTER YEAR IN 4 DIGIT FORM E.G.2000

1900..2005 → Q17

17. Current **Ask all who are or have been legally married *(NumMar (≥1 or ClNumMar (≥1)***

For last marriage entered

INTERVIEWER - IS THIS MARRIAGE CURRENT OR HAS IT ENDED?

Current .... 1 → Q25
Ended .... 2 → Q18

18. HowEnded **Ask if marriage ended *(Current = 2 or marriage number less than total marriages)***

Did your marriage end in ...

death .... 1 → Q19
divorce .... 2 → Q21
or separation?. .... 3 → Q21

19. MonDie **Ask if marriage ended in death *(HowEnded = 1)***

What month and year did your husband/wife die?

ENTER MONTH 1..12 → Q20

20. YrDie ENTER YEAR IN 4 DIGIT FORMAT E.G. 2000

1900-2005 → Q25

21. MonSep **Ask if marriage ended in divorce or separation *(HowEnded = 2 or 3)***

What month and year did you stop living together?

ENTER MONTH 1..12 → Q22

22. YrSep ENTER YEAR IN 4 DIGIT FORMAT E.G. 2000

1900-2005 →See Q23

23. MonDiv **Ask if marriage ended in divorce *(HowEnded =2)***

What month and year was your decree absolute granted?

ENTER MONTH 1..12 → Q24

24. YrDiv ENTER YEAR IN 4 DIGIT FORMAT E.G. 2000

1900-2005 → Q25

25. Cohab **Ask if respondent is aged 16-59 *(DVAge = 16-59)***

Have you had any previous relationships in which you lived together with someone as a couple but did not get married?

Yes. .... 1 → Q26
No .... 2 → Q41

26. Numcohab **Ask if respondent is aged 16-59, and has had previous cohabiting relationships *(DVAge = 16-59 & Cohab = 1)***

How many relationships have you had altogether in which you lived together with someone as a couple but did not get married?
(Please exclude your present relationship)

1..7 → Q27

27. Intro Now I would like to ask you some questions about the first three of these relationships.

RECORD DETAILS OF THE FIRST THREE RELATIONSHIPS, STARTING WITH THE FIRST → Q28

28. TimeCoy **Ask each question for the first, second and third relationship**

Thinking about the first/second/third relationships where you lived as a couple but did not get married, how long did you live together?

INTERVIEWER - ENTER NUMBER OF YEARS

0..99 → Q29

29. Timecom INTERVIEWER - ENTER NUMBER OF MONTHS

0..11 → Q30

30. WhencoM Can you tell me the month and year in which you started or stopped living together as a couple with your partner?

INTERVIEWER ENTER THE MONTH

1..12 → Q31

31. WhencoY ENTER THE YEAR

1950..2005 → Q32

32. Starten INTERVIEWER: IS THIS WHEN THE RESPONDENT AND HIS/HER PARTNER STARTED OR STOPPED LIVING TOGETHER AS A COUPLE?

ASK RESPONDENT IF YOU ARE UNSURE

Start date .... 1 ⎤ → Q33
End date .... 2 ⎦

33. Othdate If that was the date you started/stopped living together, then you stopped/started living together in ...(month) ...(year)
Does that seem about right?

Yes .... 1 → Q36
No .... 2 → Q34

34. RghtdtM **Ask if computed start/end date not correct *(Othdate1 = 2)***

What is the correct date?

INTERVIEWER ENTER THE MONTH

1..12 → Q35

35. RghtdtY ENTER THE YEAR

1950..2005 → Q36

36. EndCoh **Ask if respondent is aged 16-59, and has had previous cohabiting relationships (*DVAge = 16-59 & Cohab = 1*)**

Ask each question for the first, second and third relationship

You said you stopped living together in ...(month) ...(year). May I just check, was this when you stopped living in the same accommodation or when the relationship ended?

Stopped living in the same accommodation .... 1 → Q37
End of the relationship .... 2 → Q39
Both .... 3 ⎤ next
Partner died .... 4 ⎥ relationship
Stopped living in same accommodation, ⎥ (Q28)
but still having a relationship .... 5 ⎦ or Q41

37. EndrelM **Ask if date given is when they stopped living together *(EndCoh = 1)***

When did the relationship end?

INTERVIEWER ENTER THE MONTH

1..12 → Q38

38. EndrelY ENTER THE YEAR

1950..2005 → next relationship (Q28) or Q41

39. EndlivM **Ask if the date given is when relationship ended *(EndCoh = 2)***

When did you stop living in the same accommodation?

INTERVIEWER ENTER THE MONTH

1..12 → Q40

40. EndlivY ENTER THE YEAR

1950..2005 → next relationship (Q28) or Q41

Children

41. Children **Ask respondents aged 16-59 *(DVAge = 16-59)***

INTERVIEWER: DOES THIS PERSON HAVE ANY CHILDREN IN THE HOUSEHOLD (INCLUDES ADULT CHILDREN AND/OR STEP OR FOSTER CHILDREN)

Yes .... 1 → See Qs42&43
No .... 2 →See Q52

42. StpChldF **Ask women who have a child in the household *(Sex = 2 & Children =1)***

(The next questions are about the family.) Have you any step, foster, or adopted children living with you, (including any children from your partner's previous relationship)?

Yes .... 1 → Q44
No .... 2 →See Q52

43. StpChldM **Ask men who have a child in the household *(Sex = 1 & Children =1)***

Have you any stepchildren of any age living with you, (including any children from your partner's previous relationship)?

Yes .... 1 → Q44
No .... 2 → View of your local area

44. NumStep **Ask women with a step, foster or adopted child, or a man with a stepchild living with them *(StpChldF = 1 or StpChldM=1)***

How many step children have you living with you altogether?

1..7 →See Q45

45. NumFost **Ask women with a step, foster or adopted child living with them *(StpChldF = 1), others see Q47***

How many foster children have you living with you altogether?

0..7 → Q46

46. NumAdop How many adopted children have you living with you altogether?

0..7 → Q47

47. StepInt **Ask women with a step, foster or adopted child, or a man with a stepchild living with them *(StpChldF = 1 or StpChldM=1)***

THE NEXT SCREEN CONSISTS OF A TABLE FOR THE STEP-CHILDREN (AND ADOPTED AND FOSTER- CHILDREN) OF (NAME)PLEASE ENTER DETAILS FOR EACH CHILD. → Q48

48. ChildNo **Ask for each step/foster/adopted child**

ENTER PERSON NUMBER(S) OF THE STEP/ FOSTER/ADOPTED CHILD (INCLUDES ADULT CHILDREN)

1..20 → Q49

49. ChldType ENTER CODE AS FOLLOWS

Step 1
Foster .... 2 → Q50
Adopted 3

50. ChLivMon DATE CHILD STARTED LIVING WITH INFORMANT

ENTER MONTH

1..12 → Q51

51. ChLivYr YEAR (IN 4 DIGIT FORMAT, E.G. 2000)

1900..2005 →See Q52

52. Baby **Ask all women *(Sex = 2)*, others go to View of your local area**

ASK OR RECORD
EXCLUDE: ANY STILLBORN.
INCLUDE ANY WHO ONLY LIVED FOR A SHORT TIME.

Have you ever had a baby - even one who only lived for a short time?

Yes .... 1 → Q53
No .... 2 →See Q58

53. NumBaby **Ask women who have had a baby(Baby = 1)**

EXCLUDE: ANY STILLBORN

How many children have you given birth to, including any who are not living here and any who may have died since birth?

1..20 → Q54

54. BirthInt THE NEXT SCREEN CONSISTS OF A TABLE OF CHILDREN TO WHOM (...) HAS GIVEN BIRTH. PLEASE ENTER DETAILS FOR EACH CHILD. .... → Q55

55. BirthDte **For each child**

Date of birth

PLEASE ENTER IN DATE OF BIRTH ORDER - ELDEST FIRST, YOUNGEST LAST.

AS A GUIDE, THE D.O.B. OF EACH HOUSEHOLD MEMBER IS LISTED BELOW .... → Q56

56. BirthSex Sex of child

Male 1
Female .... 2 → Q57

57. ChldLive Is child living with informant?

Yes 1
No, lives elsewhere 2
No, deceased .... 3 → See Q58

58. Pregnant **Ask all women aged 16-49 *(Sex = 2 & DVAge = 16-49)*, others go to View of your local area**

(May I just check), are you pregnant now?

Yes 1
No/unsure .... 2 → Q59

59. MoreChld [*] Do you think that you will have any (more) children (after the one you are expecting)? Could you choose your answers from this card.

SHOW CARD F

Yes 1
Probably yes .... 2 → Q61
Probably not 3
No .... 4 → View of your local area

60. ProbMore [*] **Ask if respondent answered don't know above *(MoreChld = DK)***

On the whole do you think...

You will probably have any/more children .... 1 → Q61
Or you will probably not have any/more children? .... 2 → View of your local area

61. TotChld [*] **Ask if respondent is likely to have more children (*MoreChld = 1 or 2 or ProbMore = 1*)**

(Can I just check, you have ... children still alive). How many children do you think you will have born to you in all including those you already have had already(who are still alive)(and the one you are expecting)?

1..14 → Q62

62. NextAge [*] How old do you think you will be when you have your first/next baby (after the one you are expecting)?

1..97 → View of your local area

VIEW OF YOUR LOCAL AREA
(taken from the social capital question set)

1. AskNow **Ask selected adult**

(NAME) HAS BEEN PICKED TO ANSWER THE SECTION ON VIEW OF YOUR LOCAL AREA. DO YOU WANT TO ASK THIS SECTION FOR (NAME) NOW OR LATER?

IF YOU HAVE ALREADY ASKED THIS SECTION FOR (NAME), DO NOT CHANGE FROM CODE 1.

Yes, now/already asked 1
Later .... 2 → Q2

2. Areaint Now I would like to ask you some questions about your local area. (By area I mean within about a 15-20 minute walk or 5-10 minute drive from your home). → Q3

3. Arealive **Ask selected adult**

How long have you lived in this area?

CODE YEARS
IF LESS THAN 1 CODE AS 0

0..97 → See Q4

4. Areamth **Ask if they have lived in the area for less than a year *(Arealive = 0)***

How many months have you lived in this area?

0..11 → Q5

5. Enjyliv [*] **Ask selected adult**

Would you say this is an area you enjoy living in?

Yes 1
No 2
Don't know .... 3 → Q6

6. Locserv [*] Thinking generally about what you expect of local services, how would you rate the following; → Q7

7. Leisyou [*] Social & leisure facilities for people like yourself

SHOW CARD TSC1

Very good 1
Good 2
Average 3
Poor 4
Very poor 5
Don't know or have had no experience . 6 → Q8

8. Leiskids [*] Facilities for young children up to the age of 12

SHOW CARD TSC1

Very good 1
Good 2
Average 3
Poor 4
Very poor 5
Don't know or have had no experience . 6 → Q9

9. Leisteen [*] Facilities for teenagers (those aged 13 to 17)

SHOW CARD TSC1

Very good ... 1
Good ... 2
Average ... 3
Poor ... 4
Very poor ... 5
Don't know or have had no experience . 6
→ Q10

10. Bins [*] Rubbish collection

SHOW CARD TSC1

Very good ... 1
Good ... 2
Average ... 3
Poor ... 4
Very poor ... 5
Don't know or have had no experience . 6
→ Q11

11. Lochlth [*] Local health services (e.g. your GP or the local hospital)

SHOW CARD TSC1

Very good ... 1
Good ... 2
Average ... 3
Poor ... 4
Very poor ... 5
Don't know or have had no experience . 6
→ Q12

12. Schools [*] Local schools, colleges and adult education

SHOW CARD TSC1

Very good ... 1
Good ... 2
Average ... 3
Poor ... 4
Very poor ... 5
Don't know or have had no experience 6
→ Q13

13. Police [*] Local police service

SHOW CARD TSC1

Very good ... 1
Good ... 2
Average ... 3
Poor ... 4
Very poor ... 5
Don't know or have had no experience . 6
→ Q14

14. Transprt What is your main form of transport?

Car/Motorcycle/moped ... 1
Public transport (ie buses and trains) ... 2
Cycling ... 3
Walking ... 4
Other ... 5
Never goes out ... 6
→ Q15

15. Loctrans [*] Would you say this area has good local transport for where you want to get to?

Yes ... 1
No ... 2
Don't know ... 3
→ Q16

16. Walkday [*] How safe do you feel walking alone in this area during daytime? Do you feel ...

RUNNING PROMPT

very safe ... 1
fairly safe ... 2
a bit unsafe ... 3
very unsafe ... 4
or do you never go out alone during daytime? ... 5
→ Q17

17. Walkdark [*] How safe do you feel walking alone in this area after dark? Do you feel ...

RUNNING PROMPT

very safe ... 1
fairly safe ... 2
a bit unsafe ... 3
very unsafe ... 4
or do you never go out alone after dark? .. 5
→ Q18

18. Traffic [*] Still thinking about the same area, can you tell me how much of a problem these things are.

The speed or volume of road traffic

SHOW CARD TSC2

Very big problem ... 1
Fairly big problem ... 2
Minor problem ... 3
Not at all a problem ... 4
It happens but is not a problem ... 5
Don't know ... 6
→ Q19

19. Parking [*] Parking in residential streets

SHOW CARD TSC2

Very big problem ... 1
Fairly big problem ... 2
Minor problem ... 3
Not at all a problem ... 4
It happens but is not a problem ... 5
Don't know ... 6
→ Q20

20. Carcrime [*] Car crime (e.g. damage, theft and joyriding)

SHOW CARD TSC2

Very big problem ... 1
Fairly big problem ... 2
Minor problem ... 3
Not at all a problem ... 4
It happens but is not a problem ... 5
Don't know ... 6
→ Q21

21. Rubbish [*] Rubbish and litter lying around

SHOW CARD TSC2

Very big problem ... 1
Fairly big problem ... 2
Minor problem ... 3
Not at all a problem ... 4
It happens but is not a problem ... 5
Don't know ... 6
→ Q22

22. DogMess [*] Dog mess

SHOW CARD TSC2

Very big problem 1
Fairly big problem 2
Minor problem 3
Not at all a problem 4
It happens but is not a problem 5
Don't know 6
→ Q23

23. Graffiti [*] Graffiti or vandalism

SHOW CARD TSC2

Very big problem 1
Fairly big problem 2
Minor problem 3
Not at all a problem 4
It happens but is not a problem 5
Don't know 6
→ Q24

24. NoiseNbr [*] Level of noise

SHOW CARD TSC2

Very big problem 1
Fairly big problem 2
Minor problem 3
Not at all a problem 4
It happens but is not a problem 5
Don't know 6
→ Q25

25. Teenager [*] Teenagers hanging around on the streets

SHOW CARD TSC2

Very big problem 1
Fairly big problem 2
Minor problem 3
Not at all a problem 4
It happens but is not a problem 5
Don't know 6
→ Q26

26. Alcdrug [*] Alcohol or drug use

SHOW CARD TSC2

Very big problem 1
Fairly big problem 2
Minor problem 3
Not at all a problem 4
It happens but is not a problem 5
Don't know 6
→ Q27

27. Victim Have you personally been a victim of any of the following crimes in the past 12 months?

CODE ALL THAT APPLY

SHOW CARD TSC3

Theft or break-in to house or flat 1
Theft or break-in to car parked in the area 2
Personal experience of theft or mugging in the area 3
Physical attack in the area (i.e. hit or kicked in a way that hurt you) 4
Racist attack in the area (either verbal or physical) 5
None of these 6
→ Income

INCOME

1. Intro **Ask all adults (except proxy informants), proxy informants go to Q49**

THE NEXT SECTION IS ABOUT BENEFITS AND OTHER SOURCES OF INCOME.

2. Ben1YN SHOW CARD G

Looking at this card, are you at present receiving any of these state benefits in your own right: that is, where you are the named recipient?

Yes .... 1 → Q3
No .... 2 →See Q11
Refused whole income section .... 7 → Q49

3. Ben1Q **Ask if receiving a state benefit *(Ben1YN = 1)***

SHOW CARD G

RECORD BENEFITS RECEIVED
CODE ALL THAT APPLY (NONE OF THESE = CODE 8)
ENTER AT MOST 6 CODES

Child Benefit 1
Guardian's Allowance 2
Invalid Care Allowance 3
Retirement pension (National Insurance), or Old Person's pension 4
Widow's pension, Bereavement Allowance or Widowed Parents (formerly Widowed Mother's) Allowance 5
War Disablement Pension or War Widow's Pension (and related allowances) 6
Severe Disablement Allowance 7
None of these 8
→ Q4

4. Ben2Q SHOW CARD H

And looking at this card, are you at present receiving any of the state benefits shown on this card - either in your own name, or on behalf of someone else in the household?

CODE ALL THAT APPLY

CARE COMPONENT of Disability Living Allowance .... 1 → Q5
MOBILITY COMPONENT of Disability Living Allowance .... 2 → Q6
Attendance Allowance .... 3 → Q7
None of these .... 4 → Q9

5. WhoReCar **Ask if receiving CARE component of Disability Living Allowance *(Ben2Q = 1)***

Whom do you receive it for?
IF CURRENT HOUSEHOLD MEMBER, ENTER PERSON NUMBER OTHERWISE ENTER 97 .... → See Q6

6. WhoReMob **Ask if receiving MOBILITY component of Disability Living Allowance *(Ben2Q = 2)***

Whom do you receive it for?
IF CURRENT HOUSEHOLD MEMBER, ENTER PERSON NUMBER.
OTHERWISE ENTER 97 .... → See Q7

7. WhoReAtt **Ask if receiving Attendance Allowance *(Ben2Q = 3)***

Whom do you receive it for?
IF CURRENT HOUSEHOLD MEMBER, ENTER PERSON NUMBER.
OTHERWISE ENTER 97 .... → Q8

8. AttAllFU Is this paid as part of your retirement pension or do you receive a separate payment?

Together with pension .... 1 → Q9
Separate payment .... 2 → Q9

9. BEN3Q **Ask all except proxy informants**

CODE ALL THAT APPLY
ENTER AT MOST 5 CODES

SHOW CARD I

Now looking at this card, are you at present receiving any of these benefits in your own right: that is, where you are the named recipient?

Job Seekers' Allowance .... 1 → Q10
Income Support .... 2 → See Q11
Incapacity Benefit .... 3 → See Q11
Statutory Sick Pay .... 4 → See Q11
Industrial Injury Disablement Benefit .... 5 → See Q11
None of these .... 6 → See Q11

10. JSAType **Ask if respondent is receiving Job Seekers' Allowance *(Ben3Q = 1)***

There are two types of Job Seekers' Allowance. Is your allowance...

RUNNING PROMPT

'contributory' that is, based on your National Insurance contributions .... 1 → See Q11
or is it 'income-based' Job Seekers' Allowance, which is based on an assessment of your income? .... 2 → See Q11

11. Ben4Q **Ask women under 55 years *(Sex = 2 & DVAge <55 years)*, others Q12**

SHOW CARD J
Are you currently getting either of the things shown on this card, in your own right?

Maternity Allowance .... 1 → Q12
Statutory maternity pay from your employer or a former employer .... 2 → Q12
Neither of these .... 3 → Q12

12. Ben4AQ **Ask all except proxy informants**

SHOW CARD K

Now looking at this card, are you at present receiving any of these Tax Credits, in your own right? Please include any lump sum payments received in the last six months.

Working Families' Tax Credit .... 1 → Q13
Disabled Person's Tax Credit .... 2 → Q13
Children's Tax Credit .... 3 → Q13
None of these .... 4 → Q13

13. Ben5Q **All except proxy informants**

SHOW CARD L

In the last 6 months, have you received any of the things shown on this card, in your own right?

CODE ALL THAT APPLY

A grant from the Social Fund for funeral expenses .... 1 → See Q14
A grant from Social Fund for maternity expenses/Sure Start Maternity Grant .. 2 → See Q14
A Social Fund loan or Community Care grant .... 3 → See Q14
A Back to Work bonus .... 4 → See Q14
'Extended payment' of Housing Benefit/ rent rebate, or Council Tax Benefit .... 5 → See Q14
Widow's payment or Bereavement payment- lump sum .... 6 → See Q14
Child Maintenance Bonus .... 7 → See Q14
Lone Parent's Benefit Run-On .... 8 → See Q14
Any National Insurance or State Benefit not mentioned earlier .... 9 → See Q14
None of these .... 10 → See Q14

14. Ben1Amt **Code for each benefit mentioned *(Ben1Q, Ben2Q (except Attendance Allowance combined with pension), Ben3Q, Ben4Q, Ben4AQ (except for Children's Tax Credit), Ben5Q)***

How much did you get last time?

(IF COMBINED WITH ANOTHER BENEFIT AND UNABLE TO GIVE SEPARATE AMOUNT, ENTER 'Don't know')

0.00..997.00 .... → See Q15

15. Ben1AmtDK **If don't know or refusal at the amount of benefit received *(Ben1Amt = DK or Refusal)***

INTERVIEWER: IS THIS 'DON'T KNOW' BECAUSE IT'S PAID IN COMBINATION WITH ANOTHER BENEFIT, AND YOU CANNOT ESTABLISH A SEPARATE AMOUNT?

Yes (Please give full details in a Note) . 1 → See Q16
No .... 2 → See Q16

16. Ben1Pd **Ask if amount of benefit received was greater than zero *(Ben1Amt > 0.00)*, others Q17**

How long did this cover?

one week .... 1 → Q17
two weeks .... 2 → Q17
three weeks .... 3 → Q17
four weeks .... 4 → Q17

calendar month	5	→	Q17
two calendar months	7		
eight times a year	8		
nine times a year	9		
ten times a year	10		
three months/13 weeks	13		
six months/26 weeks	26		
one year/12 months/52 weeks	52		
less than one week	90		
one off lump sum	95		
none of these	97		

17. OthSourc **Ask all (except proxy informants)**

SHOW CARD M

Please look at this card and tell me whether you are receiving any regular payment of the kinds listed on it?

Yes receiving benefits - code at next question	1	→	Q18
No, not receiving any	2	→	Q21

18. OthSrcM **Ask if receiving any of the benefits mentioned above *(OthSourc = 1)***

SHOW CARD M

RECORD PAYMENTS RECEIVED
CODE ALL THAT APPLY
(ENTER AT MOST 4 CODES)

Occupational pensions from former employer(s)	1	→	Q19
Occupational pensions from a spouse's former employer(s)	2		
Private pensions or annuities	3		
Regular redundancy payments from former employer(s)	4		
Government Training Schemes, such as YT allowance	5		

19. OthNetAm In total how much do you receive each month from (...../all these sources) AFTER tax is deducted? (ie net)

DO NOT PROBE MONTH. ACCEPT CALENDAR MONTH OR 4 WEEKLY.

0.01..99999.97 → Q20

20. OthGrsAm In total how much do you receive each month from ..... (all these sources) BEFORE tax is deducted? (ie GROSS)?

DO NOT PROBE MONTH. ACCEPT CALENDAR MONTH OR 4 WEEKLY.

0.01..99999.97 → Q21

21. ReglrPay **Ask all (except proxy informants)**

SHOW CARD N

Now please look at this card and tell me whether you are receiving any regular payments of the kind listed on it?

Yes receiving benefits - code at next question	1	→	Q22
No, not receiving any	2	→	Q24

22. ReglrPM **If receiving one of the benefits mentioned above *(ReglrPay = 1)***

SHOW CARD N

RECORD TYPES OF PAYMENT RECEIVED.

CODE ALL THAT APPLY

Educational grant	1	→	Q23
Regular payments from friends or relatives outside the household	2		
Maintenance, alimony or separation allowance	3		

23. ReglrpAm In total how much do you receive from these each month?

0.01..99999.97 → Q24

24. Rentpay **Ask all (except proxy informants)**

Are you currently receiving any rent from property or subletting?

Yes	1	→	Q25
No	2	→	See Q26

25. Rentamt **Ask if they are receiving rent *(Rentpay = 1)***

In total how much do you receive each month?

0.01..99999.97 →See Q26

The next group of questions (Q26-Q44) are only asked of those in paid work, (including those temporarily away from job or on a government scheme), but excluding unpaid family workers. *((Wrking = 1 OR JbAway = 1 OR SchemeET = 1) & (OwnBus = 2 & RelBus = 2))*

The routing instructions above each question apply only to those who meet the above criteria.

26. PyPeriod **Ask if an employee *(Stat = 1)*, others see Q36**

THE NEXT QUESTIONS ARE ABOUT EARNINGS

How long a period does your wage/salary usually cover?

one week	1	→	Q27
two weeks	2		
three weeks	3		
four weeks	4		
calendar month	5		
two calendar months	7		
eight times a year	8		
nine times a year	9		
ten times a year	10		
three months/13 weeks	13		
six months/26 weeks	26		
one year/12 months/52 weeks	52		

less than one week .... 90 ⎤
one off lump sum .... 95 ⎬ → Q28
none of these .... 97 ⎦

27. TakeHome Ask all, except those who are paid less than once a week, or in a one off sum, or answered none of these *(PyPeriod <= 52)*

How much is your usual take home pay per (period at PyPeriod) after all deductions? (Please do not include any Working Families' Tax Credit / Disabled Person's Tax Credit payment that you received)

0.00..99999.97 →See Q28

28. TakHmEst Ask if paid less than once a week, or in a one off sum, or in none of these ways, or did not know how much money they usually took home *(PyPeriod = 90, 95 or 97 orTakeHome = DK)*

SHOW CARD O

Please look at this card and estimate your usual take home pay per(period at PyPeriod) after all deductions? (Please do not include any Working Families Tax Credit / Disabled Person's Tax Credit payment that you received)

0..30 →See Q29

29. GrossAm Ask if an employee *(Stat = 1)*

How much are your usual gross earnings per (period at PyPeriod) before any deductions?

0.01..99999.97 →See Q30

30. GrossEst Ask if respondent does not know how much their usual gross earnings are (*GrossAm = DK*)

SHOW CARD O

Please look at this card and estimate your usual gross earnings per(period at PyPeriod) before any deductions?

0..30 → Q31

31. PaySlip Ask if an employee *(Stat = 1)*

INTERVIEWER - CODE WHETHER PAYSLIP WAS CONSULTED

Pay slip consulted by respondent, but not by interviewer .... 1 ⎤
Pay slip consulted by interviewer .... 2 ⎬ →See Q32
Pay slip not consulted .... 3 ⎦

32. PayBonus Ask if answered PyPeriod

In your present job, have you ever received an occasional addition to pay in the last 12 months (that is since DATE 1 YEAR AGO) such as a Christmas bonus or a quarterly bonus?

EXCLUDE SHARES AND VOUCHERS.

Yes .... 1 → Q33
No .... 2 →See Q40

33. HowBonus Ask if respondent received a pay bonus *(PayBonus = 1)*

Was the bonus or commission paid.....

after tax was deducted (net) .... 1 → Q34
or before tax was deducted (gross) ...... 2 → Q35
or some before and some after? .... 3 → Q34

34. NetBonus If some or all tax was deducted, or they did not know if tax was deducted from pay bonus *(HowBonus = 1 or 3 or DK)*

What was the total amount you received in the last 12 months (that issince DATE 1 YEAR AGO) AFTER tax was deducted (ie net)?

0.01..99999.97 →See Q35

35. GrsBonus Ask if some or all tax was deducted from the pay bonus *(HowBonus = 2 or 3)*

What was the total amount you received in the last 12 months (that is since DATE A YEAR AGO) before tax was deducted (ie gross)?

0.01..99999.97 →See Q40

36. GrsPrLTY If self-employed less than 12 months, others see Q38

How much did you earn before tax but after deductions of any expenses and wages since becoming self-employed?

IF NOTHING OR MADE A LOSS, ENTER ZERO.

0.00..999999.97 → Q37

37. PrLTYEst SHOW CARD O

Please look at this card and estimate the amount that you expect to earn before tax but after deductions of any expenses and wages in thefirst full 12 months that you will have been self-employed, that is up to the end of (month) next?

0..30 →See Q40

38. GrsPrft If self-employed more than 12 months, others see Q40

How much did you earn in the last tax year, before tax but after deduction of any expenses and wages.

IF NOTHING OR MADE A LOSS, ENTER ZERO.

0.00..999999.97 →See Q39

39. PrftEst If respondent does not know how much they earned last year *(GrsPrft = DK)*

SHOW CARD O

Please look at this card and estimate the amount that you earned inthe last tax year before tax but after the deduction of any expenses or wages?

0..30 →See Q40

40. SecJob2 **Ask all (see criteria for this section on page 121)**

(Apart from your main job) do you earn any money from other jobs, from odd jobs or from work that you do from time to time?

PROMPT AS NECESSARY & INCLUDE BABYSITTING, MAIL ORDER AGENT, POOLS AGENT ETC.

Yes .... 1 → Q41
No .... 2 → Q45

41. SjEmplee **Ask if respondent has other jobs *(SecJob2 = 1)***

In that (those) job(s) do you work as an employee or are you self-employed?

employee .... 1 → Q42
self-employed .... 2 → Q44

42. SjNetAm **Ask if doing other jobs as employee *(SjEmplee = 1)***

In the last month, how much did you earn from your other/occasional job(s) after deductions for tax and National Insurance (ie net)?

0.01..99999.97 → Q43

43. SjGrsAm In the last month, how much did you earn from your other/occasional job(s) before deductions for tax and National Insurance (ie gross)?

0.01..99999.97 → Q45

44. SjPrfGrs **Ask if doing other jobs as self-employed *(SjEmplee = 2)***

In the last 12 months (that is since DATE 1 YEAR AGO) how much have you earned from this work, before deducting income tax, and National Insurance contributions, and money drawn for your own use, but after deducting all business expenses?

IF MADE NO PROFIT ENTER 0.

0.00..99999.97 → Q45

45. OthRgPay **Ask all (except proxy informants) - NOTE: End of the section of questions which are only asked of those in paid work**

And finally, apart from anything you have already mentioned, have you received any regular payment from any of the following sources in the last 12 months (that is since DATE 1 YEAR AGO)?

ENTER AT MOST 3 CODES

EXCLUDE BENEFITS NO LONGER RECEIVED.

Interest from savings, Bank or Building Society accounts .... 1 → See Qs 46 to 48
Income from shares, bonds, unit trusts or gilt-edged stock .... 2 → See Qs 46 to 48
Other .... 3 → See Qs 46 to 48
None of these .... 4 → End of interview

46. Investpy **Ask if respondent is receiving interest from savings *(OthRgPay = 1)***

(Apart from interest and income from shares) how much have you received in total from interest on savings, Bank or Building Society accounts in the last 12 months?

0.01..99999.97 → See Qs 47 & 48

47. Sharepy **Ask if respondent is receiving income from shares, bonds, unit trusts or gilt-edged stock *(OthRgPay = 2)***

(Apart from interest and income from shares) how much have you received in total from shares, bonds, unit trusts or gilt-edged stock in the last 12 months?

0.01..99999.97 →See Q48

48. OthRgPAm **Ask if respondent is receiving income from another source *(OthRgPay = 3)***

How much have you received from other sources in the last 12 months?

0.01..99999.97 → End of interview

49. NtIncEst **If proxy informant or refused whole income section *(proxy informant or Ben1YN = 7)***

SHOW CARD O

I would now like to ask you about the income of (NAME).Please could you look at this card and estimate the total net income, that is after deduction of tax, National Insurance and any expenses (NAME) brings into the household in a year from all sources (benefits, employment, investments etc)?

0....30 → End of interview

Appendix G
Summary of main topics included in the GHS questionnaires 1971 to 2001

Topic	Years
ACTIVITIES ON SCHOOL PREMISES	**1984**
Whether attended any event/activity on school premises in last 12 months	
Whether activities organised by school or parent teacher's association	
Type of activity attended (if not organised by school/parent teacher's association), number of times attended and whether attended a day or evening class	
BURGLARIES AND THEFTS FROM PRIVATE HOUSEHOLDS	
Incidence of burglaries in the 12 months before interview; Value of stolen goods and whether insured; Whether incident was reported to the police	**1972-73, 1979-80, 1985-86, 1991, 1993, 1996**
Reasons for not reporting to the police	**1972-73, 1979-80, 1985-86**
Incidence of attempted burglary in the 12 months before interview	**1985-86**
BUS TRAVEL	**1982**
Frequency of use of buses in the six months before interview	
Physical and other difficulties using buses	
Reasons for not using buses	
CAREER OPPORTUNITIES	**1972**
Attitudes towards careers in the Armed Forces and the Police Force	
Whether ever been in one of the Armed Forces	
CAR OWNERSHIP	
Number of cars or vans, if any, available to the household for private use	**1971-96, 1998, 2000-01**
Type of vehicle and whether privately/company owned	**1998, 2000-01**
In whose name (person or firm) each car/van was registered	**1980, 1992-93**
Driving licences and private motoring	**1980**
Whether held current licence for driving a car or van, and for how long full licence held	
Whether non-licence holders (aged 17-70) intended to apply for a licence (again), and reasons for not having done so or for not intending to do so	
Frequency of use, for private motoring, of car/van available to the household	
If household car/van not available, or not used for private motoring in the year before interview:	
- whether used any car/van for private motoring in that year	
- whether drove a car, van, lorry, or bus in the course of work in that year	
COLOUR AND COUNTRY OF BIRTH	
Colour, assessment of persons seen*	**1971-92**
Country of birth	
of adults and their parents	**1971-96, 1998, 2000-01**
of children	**1979-96, 1998, 2000-01**
Year of entry to UK	
adults	**1971-96, 1998, 2000-01**
children	**1979-96, 1998, 2000-01**
Ethnic origin	**1983-96, 1998, 2000-01**
National identity	**2001**
DRINKING	
Rating of drinking behaviour according to quantity - frequency (QF) index based on reported alcohol consumption in the 12 months before interview	**1978, 1980, 1982, 1984**
Rating of drinking behaviour according to average weekly alcohol consumption (AC) rating	**1986-2000 (alternate years), 2001**
Alcohol consumption on the heaviest drinking day in the 7 days before interview	**1998, 2000-01**
Personal rating of own drinking behaviour	**1978-2000 (alternate years), 2001**
Whether think drinking/smoking can damage health	**1978, 1980, 1982, 1984, 1986, 1988, 1990**
Whether non-drinkers have always been non-drinkers or used to drink but stopped, and reasons; Whether drink more or less than the recommended sensible amount	**1992-2000 (alternate years), 2001**
EDUCATION	
Current education	
Current education status	**1971-96, 1998, 2000-01**
Type of educational establishment currently attended	
- by adults aged under 50	**1971-81, 1984-90**
- by adults aged under 70	**1991-96, 1998, 2000-01**
- by children aged 5-15	**1971-77**

* *Including children*

Qualification/examination aimed at **1971, 1974-76**

Expected date of completion of full-time education **1971-76**

Whether intend to do any paid work while still in full-time education, and if so when **1971-76**

Whether currently attending any leisure or recreation classes **1973-78, 1981, 1983, 1993-96, 2000-01**

Past education

Age on leaving school **1972-96, 1998**

Age on leaving last place of full-time education **1971-96, 1998, 2000-01**

Type of educational establishment last attended full time **1971-96, 1998**

Qualifications obtained **1971-96, 1998, 2000-01**

Pre-school children (aged under 5)

Whether currently attending nursery/primary school, day nursery, playgroup, creche etc **1971-79, 1986**

Frequency of attendance **1979, 1986**

Whether received regular day care from person other than parents, and for how many hours per week **1979**

Whether working mothers would have to stop work if existing arrangements for the care of their children were no longer available, or whether they could make other care arrangements **1979**

Child care (for children aged 0-11) **1991**

Whether uses any child care arrangements

Frequency of use and cost

Whether employer contributes towards cost, and if so, the amount

Child care (for children under 14) **1998**

Whether uses any child care arrangements, and if so, type and frequency of use

Job training

Whether currently doing a trade apprenticeship **1971-84**

Identification of persons seriously thinking of taking a course of training or education for a particular type of job, with some details of the course and the source of any financial support **1973-74**

Students in institutional accommodation **1981-87**

Estimate of numbers of full-time students at university or college living away from home in institutional accommodation, and therefore excluded from the GHS sample

EMPLOYMENT

Those currently working

Main job - occupation and industry; - employee/self-employed **1971-96, 1998, 2000-01**

Subsidiary job - occupation and industry; - employee/self-employed **1971-78, 1980-84, 1987-91**

Last job - occupation and industry; - employee/self-employed **1986**

Whether has a second job **1992-96, 1998, 2000-01**

Whether present job was obtained through a government scheme **1989-92**

Youth Opportunities Programme Schemes **1982-84**

- identification of young persons aged 16-18 receiving training or work experience through the Youth Opportunities Programme or Youth Training Scheme

Youth Training Scheme **1985-95**

- identification of young persons aged 16-19 who were on the YTS and whether they were working with an employer or at college or training school

Journey time to work **1971-76, 1978**

Usual number of hours worked per week (excluding overtime) **1971-96, 1998, 2000-01**

Hours of paid/unpaid overtime usually worked per week **1973-83, 1998**

Usual number of days worked per week **1973, 1979-84**

Number of days worked in reference week **1977-78**

Length of time with present employer/present spell of self-employment **1971-96, 1998, 2000-01**

Whether self-employed during the previous 12 months **1986-91**

Number of changes of employer in 12 months before interview **1971-76, 1979-91**

Number of new employee jobs started in 12 months before interview **1977-78, 1983-91**

Source of hearing about present job started in 12 months before interview **1971-77, 1980-84**

Source of hearing about all jobs started in 12 months before interview **1974-77, 1980-84**

Whether paid by employer when sick **1971-76, 1979-81**

Whether employer is in the public/private sector **1983, 1985, 1987**

Trade Union and Staff Association membership **1983**

Whether people work all or part of the time at home, reasons for doing so, whether employer makes any financial contribution to expenses of working at home, equipment provided by employer **1993**

Whether does any unpaid work for members of the family and if so, for whom, number of hours a week, type of work and where **1993-95**

Whether has ever been a company director **1987**

Type of National Insurance contribution paid by:
- married and widowed women
  - aged 16 or over **1972-79**
  - aged 16-59 **1980**
- married, widowed, and separated women
  - aged 16-59 **1981-82**
  - aged 20-59 **1983**

Level of satisfaction with present job as a whole **1971-83**
Level of satisfaction with specific aspects of present job **1974-83**
Whether thinking of leaving present employer, and if so why **1971-76**

Whether signed on at an Unemployment Benefit Office in the reference week, either to claim benefit or to receive National Insurance credits **1984-90, 1994-96**

Absence from work in the reference week
- reasons for absence **1971-72, 1974-84**
- length of period of absence **1971-72, 1974-80, 1984**
- number of working days off last week **1981-84**
- whether absent because of illness or accident, and length of absence **1973**
- whether in receipt of National Insurance sickness benefit (and supplementary allowance) for the absence **1971-76**

Sickness absence in the four weeks before interview **1981-84**
Sickness absence in the 3 months before interview **1992**
Whether registered as unemployed in the reference week (if had worked less than full week) **1977-82**
Unemployment experience in 12 months before interview **1975-77, 1983-84**

Economic activity status 12 months before interview and, if economically inactive then, reasons for (re-)entering the labour force **1979-81**

Economic activity status 12 months before interview, including whether a full-time student and working **1982-91**

Whether in employment prior to present job, and if so **1986**
- whether that job was full/part time
- reasons for leaving

Whether on any government schemes **1985-96**

Usual job of father
- of all persons aged 16 or over **1971-76**
- of persons aged 16-49 in full-time or part-time education **1977-78**
- of all persons aged 16-49 **1979-89**
- of all persons aged 16-59 **1989-91**

Those currently unemployed

Most recent job - occupation and industry; - employee/self-employed **1971-96, 1998, 2000-01**

Whether most recent job was obtained through a government scheme **1989-92**
Whether has ever had a paid job **1986-96, 1998, 2000-01**
Whether has ever worked for an employer as part of a government scheme **1989-91**
Whether registered as unemployed in the reference week; Methods of seeking work in the reference week **1971-83**

Whether signed on at an Unemployment Benefit Office in the reference week, either to claim benefit or to receive National Insurance credits **1984-90, 1994-96**

Whether looking for full or part-time work **1983**

Whether taking part in either the Youth Training Scheme or the Youth Opportunities Programme last week **1984**

Whether last job was organised through the Youth Opportunities Programme (persons aged 16-19) **1982**

For those who in the reference week were looking for work
- would they have been able to start within 2 weeks if a job had been available **1991-96, 1998, 2000-01**

For those who in the reference week were waiting to take up a new job already obtained:
- would they have started that job in the reference week if it had been available then, or would they have chosen to wait **1977-82**
- when was the new job obtained and when did they expect to start it **1979**

Whether paid unemployment benefit (and supplementary allowance) for reference week **1971-74**

When last worked and reasons for stopping work **1971-73, 1974-79, 1986**
Reasons for leaving last job **1981-82, 1986**
Whether last job was full/part time **1986**
Length of current spell of unemployment **1974-96, 1998**
Unemployment experience in 12 months before interview **1975-77, 1983-84**

Economic activity status 12 months before interview and, if economically inactive then, reasons for (re-)entering the labour force **1979-81**

Economic activity status 12 months before interview, including whether a full-time student and working **1982-91**

Number of new employee jobs started in 12 months before interview **1977, 1982-91**
Source of hearing about all jobs started in 12 months before interview **1982-84**

Whether on any government schemes **1985-96, 1998, 2000-01**

Whether does any unpaid work for members of the family and if so: **1993-96,**
number of hours a week and where **1998, 2000-01**
for whom and type of work **1993-96**

Whether has ever been a company director **1987**

Type of National Insurance contribution paid in the preceding two completed tax years by:
- married, widowed, and separated women aged 20-59, who were not working in the week before interview **1982-83**

Usual job of father
- of all persons aged 16 or over **1971-76**
- of persons aged 16-49 in full-time or part-time education **1977-78**
- of all persons aged 16-49 **1979-88**
- of all persons aged 16-59 **1989-92**

The economically inactive

Major activity in the reference week
Last job - occupation and industry
 - employee/self-employed
} **1971-96, 1998, 2000-01**

Usual job (of retired persons)
- occupation and industry
- employee/self-employed
} **1973-76, 1979-88**

When finished last job **1971-73, 1977-78, 1986**
Reasons for stopping work **1971-73, 1978-82, 1986**

Whether registered as unemployed in the reference week **1972-83**
Whether signed on at an Unemployment Benefit Office in the reference week, either to claim benefit or to receive National Insurance credits **1984-90, 1994-96**
Whether paid unemployment benefit (and supplementary allowance) for reference week **1972-74**

Whether would like a regular paid job, whether looking for work, and if a job had been available would they have been able to start within 2 weeks **1991-96, 1998, 2000-01**
Length of time currently out of employment **1993-96, 1998, 2000-01**

Main reason for not looking for work **1986-87**
Whether would like regular paid job **1986-87**
Whether has ever had a paid job **1986-96, 1998, 2000-01**
Whether has had a paid job in last 12 months **1987-91**
Whether has ever worked for an employer as part of a government scheme **1989-91**
Whether has had a paid job in previous 3 years **1986**
Whether last job was full/part time **1986**

Unemployment experience in 12 months before interview **1975-77, 1983-84**

Economic activity status 12 months before interview (persons aged 16-69) **1980-81**

Economic activity status 12 months before interview including whether a full-time student and working **1982-91**

Number of new employee jobs started in 12 months before interview **1977, 1984-91**
Source of hearing about all jobs started in 12 months before interview **1977**

Whether on any government schemes **1985-96, 1998, 2000-01**

Whether does any unpaid work for members of the family and if so, for whom, number of hours a week, type of work and where **1993-96, 1998, 2000-01**

Whether has ever been a company director **1987**

Type of National Insurance contribution paid in the preceding two completed tax years by:
- married, widowed, and separated women aged 20-59, who were not working in the week before interview **1982**

Future work intentions, including whether would seek work earlier if satisfactory arrangements could be made for looking after children **1971-76**

Usual job of father
- of all persons aged 16 or over **1971-76**
- of persons aged 16-49 in full-time or part-time education **1977-78**
- of all persons aged 16-49 **1979-88**
- of all persons aged 16-59 **1989-92**

FAMILY INFORMATION/FERTILITY

Marriage, cohabitation and childbirth

Marital history **1979-96, 1998, 2000-01**
Date of present marriage **1971-78**
Whether first marriage **1974-78**
Expected family size:
at time of present marriage
at time of interview
Whether woman thinks she has completed her family
Age when most recent baby was born
Age when expects to have last baby
Date of birth and sex of each child born in present marriage **1971-78**
Date of birth and sex of all liveborn children and whether they live with mother **1979-96, 1998, 2000-01**
Where children under 16, not living with mother, are currently living **1979**
Where children under 19, not living with mother, are currently living **1982**
Date of birth of step, foster, and adopted children living in the household, and how long they have lived there **1979-87, 1989-96, 1998, 2000-01**
Whether women think they will have any (more) children, how many in all, and age at which they think will have their first/next baby **1979-96, 1998, 2000-01**

* *Including children*

Current cohabitation **1979-96, 1998, 2000-01**
Cohabitation before current or most recent marriage **1979, 1981-88**
Cohabitation before all marriages **1989-96, 1998, 2000-01**
Number of cohabiting relationships that did not lead to marriage **1998, 2000-01**

Contraception and sterilisation

Whether woman/partner has been sterilised for contraceptive reason
Details of sterilisation operations
Whether woman/partner has had other sterilising operation **1983-84, 1986-87, 1989,1991,1993, 1995, 1998**

Details of any reversal of sterilisation operations **1983-84, 1986-87**
Current use of contraception/reason for not using contraception **1983, 1986, 1989, 1991, 1993, 1995, 1998**

Previous usual method of contraception **1989, 1991, 1993, 1995, 1998**
Use of contraception in the previous 12 months **1989**
Use of contraception in previous 2 years **1991, 1993, 1995, 1998**

Use of emergency contraception in previous 2 years **1993, 1995, 1998**
Whether woman/partner would have difficulties in having (more) children
Reasons for difficulties and whether consulted a doctor about difficulties in getting pregnant **1983-84, 1986-87, 1989, 1991,1993, 1995, 1998**

FORESTS

Whether ever visits forests or woodland areas, facilities visitors would like to see there **1987**

HEALTH

Chronic sickness (longstanding illness or disability)

Prevalence of longstanding illness or disability* **1971-76, 1979-96, 1998, 2000-01**

Causes of the illness or disability* **1971-75**
When the illness or disability started* **1971**

Type of illness or disability **1988-89, 1994-96, 1998, 2000-01**

Prevalence of limiting longstanding illness or disability* **1972-76, 1979-96, 1998, 2000-01**

When it started to limit activities and whether housebound or bedfast because of it* **1972-76**

Acute sickness (restricted activity in a two-week reference period)
Prevalence and duration of restricted activity* **1971-76, 1979-96, 1998, 2000-01**

Causes of restricted activity* **1971-75**
Number of days in bed and number of days of (certificated) absence from work/school* **1971-76**
Help from people outside household with housework or shopping **1971-74**

Health in general in the 12 months before interview **1977-96, 1998, 2000-01**

Chronic health problems **1977-78**
Prevalence of chronic health problems
Constant effects of chronic health problems (eg taking things easy, using prescribed/non-prescribed medication, watching diet, taking account of weather)

Contact with health services in 12 months before interview because of chronic health problems

Effect of chronic health problems in the 14 days before interview (eg resting more than usual, using prescribed/non-prescribed medication, changing eating or drinking habits, cutting down on activities, consulting GP, seeking advice from other persons)

Short-term health problems (in the 14 days before interview) **1977-78**
Prevalence of short-term health problems
Effects of short-term health problems in the 14 days before interview

GP consultations
Consultations in the two weeks before interview:
number of consultations*
NHS or private*
type of doctor*
site of consultation*
} **1971-96, 1998, 2000-01**

cause of consultation* **1971-75**

whether consulted because something was the matter, or for some other reason* **1981**

whether consultation about reported long-standing illness or restricted activity* **1983-84, 1986-87**

whether was given a prescription* **1981-96, 1998, 2000-01**
whether was referred to hospital* **1981-85, 1988-90**
whether was given National Insurance medical certificate **1981-85**
whether saw a practice nurse and, if so, the number of times* **2000-01**

Access to GPs: **1977**
whether own doctor worked alone or with other doctors
whether could usually see doctor of own choice at surgery
most recent consultation at surgery:
- when it took place
- NHS or private
- by appointment or not
- how far ahead appointment made
- time spent waiting at surgery
- attitudes towards waiting time for appointment, waiting time at surgery, and length of consultation

Outpatient (OP) attendances
Attendances at hospital OP departments in a three-month reference period:
number of attendances* **1971-96, 1998, 2000-01**
NHS or private **1973-76, 1982-83, 1985-87, 1995-96, 1998, 2000-01**
nature of complaint causing attendance* **1974-76**
whether claimed for under private medical insurance **1982-83, 1987, 1995**
number of casualty visits* **1995-96, 1998, 2000-01**

Appointments with OP departments: **1973-76**
whether had (or was waiting for) an appointment* how long ago since told appointment would be made*

Day patient visits
Number of separate days in hospital as a day patient in the last year* **1992-96, 1998, 2000-01**
whether NHS or private **1995-96, 1998, 2000-01**

Inpatient spells
Spells in hospital as an inpatient in a three-month reference period:
number and length of spells* **1971-76**
NHS or private patient* **1973-75**

Stays in hospital as an inpatient in a 12-month reference period:
number of stays* **1982-96, 1998, 2000-01**
number of nights on each stay* **1992-96, 1998, 2000-01**

* *Including children*

NHS or private patient **1982-83, 1985-87, 1995-96, 1998, 2000-01**

whether private patients were treated in an NHS/private hospital **1998, 2000-01**

whether claimed for under private medical insurance **1982-83, 1987**

Whether on waiting list for admission to hospital and length of time on list* **1973-76**

Mobility aids **1993, 1996, 2001**

Whether has any difficulty getting about without assistance, and if so, what help is needed, whether the problem is temporary or permanent, the number and types of walking aids, and who supplied them

Accidents **1987-89**

Accidents in the three-month reference period that resulted in seeing a GP or going to a hospital:

whether saw GP or went to hospital or did both and in the last case, which first*
type of accident and where occurred*
whether occurred during sport*
whether occurred during working hours*
time off work as a result of accident
whether went to hospital A & E Department (Casualty) or other part of hospital*
whether stayed in hospital overnight as a result of accident, and if so how many nights*

Accidents at home **1981, 1984**

Accidents at home, in a three-month reference period, that resulted in seeing a GP or going to hospital:

whether saw GP or went to hospital or did both and, in the last case, which first*
whether went to hospital A & E Department (Casualty) or other part of hospital*

Health and personal social services

Use of various services:

- by adults and children **1971-76**
- by persons aged 60 or over **1979**
- by persons aged 65 or over **1980-85, 1991, 1994, 1998, 2001**

Elderly persons

Whether any relatives living nearby:

- persons aged 60 or over **1979-80**
- persons aged 65 or over **1994**

Persons aged 65 or over:

- whether need help in getting about inside the house and outside, and with a range of personal and household tasks **1980, 1985, 1991, 1994, 1996, 1998, 2001**
- if help is needed, who usually helps
- frequency of social contacts with relatives and friends
- use of public transport

  1980, 1985 1991, 1994, 1998, 2001
- whether needs a regular daily carer
- whether lives in sheltered accommodation

  1998, 2001

Informal carers

Whether looks after a sick, handicapped or elderlyperson in same or other household, nature of careprovided and time spent, whether help receivedfrom other people or statutory services **1985, 1990, 1995,2000**

Reasons for not receiving help from statutory services **1995**

Whether dependent receives respite care **1995, 2000**

Whether carer's health has been affected **2000**

Informal carers aged 8-17 **1996**

- whether looks after a sick, handicapped or elderly person in the same household, nature of care provided and time spent, whether help received from other people or statutory services

Sight and hearing

Difficulty with sight and whether wears glasses or contact lenses:

- persons aged 16 or over **1977-79, 1981-82, 1987, 1994**
- persons aged 65 or over **1980, 1985, 1987, 1991, 1994, 1998, 2001**

Whether wears glasses or contact lenses*
Whether obtained new glasses in previous 12 months and number of pairs*
Whether had a sight test in previous 12 months*
1987, 1990-1994

Whether sight test was NHS or private **1990-94**

Whether sight test was paid for by informant or employer, provided free by optician, or covered by insurance **1991-94**

Whether obtained any ready made reading glasses in the previous 12 months **1992-94**

Types of contact lens worn, and whether obtained through NHS or privately
Reasons for trying contact lenses
Reasons stopped wearing contact lenses
Care of contact lenses
1982

* *Including children*

Difficulty with hearing and whether wears an aid:
- persons aged 16 or over **1977-79, 1981, 1992, 1995, 1998**
- persons aged 65 or over **1980, 1985, 1991, 1994, 1998, 2001**

Types of hearing aid worn, and whether obtained through NHS or privately **1979**
Reasons for not wearing an aid **1979, 1992, 1995, 1998**
Whether hearing aid was obtained through NHS or bought privately, and if bought privately, the reason(s) **1992, 1995, 1998**

Tinnitus (sensation of noise in the ears or head)
Prevalence of tinnitus, frequency and duration of symptoms, whether ever consulted a doctor about it **1981**

Dental health
Whether has any natural teeth **1983, 1985, 1987, 1989, 1991, 1993, 1995**
To those aged under 18, how long since last visit to the dentist, and whether registered with a dentist* **1993, 1995**
How long since last visit to the dentist*
Treatment received* } **1983**

Whether goes to the dentist for check-ups, or only when having trouble with teeth* **1983, 1985, 1987, 1989, 1991, 1993, 1995**

Medicine-taking **4th qtr 1972, 1973**
Medicines taken in the seven days before interview:
- categories of medicine
- patterns of consumption of analgesics

Private medical insurance **1982-83, 1986-87, 1995**
Whether covered by private medical insurance and, if so:
- whether policy holder or dependant on someone else's policy*
- whether subscription paid by employer

Whether covered by private medical insurance in the last 12 months **1987**
Whether company director's private medical insurance subscription is paid for by the company of which he is a director **1987, 1995**

HOUSEHOLD COMPOSITION
Age*, sex*, marital status of household members
Relationship to head of household*
Family unit(s) } **1971-96, 1998, 2000-01**
Housewife **1971-80**

* *Including children*

HOUSING (see also MIGRATION)
Present accommodation: amenities
Length of residence at present address*
Age of building
Type of accommodation
Number of rooms and number of bedrooms
Whether have separate kitchen } **1971-96, 1998, 2000-01**
Bath/WC: sole use, shared, none
WC: inside or outside the accommodation } **1971-90**

Installation/replacement of bath or WC
Cost of improvements made to the accommodation } **1971-76**

Floor level of main accommodation
Whether there is a lift } **1973-96, 1998, 2000-01**

Tenure
Whether present home is owned or rented **1971-96, 1998, 2000-01**
Whether in co-ownership housing association scheme **1981-95**

Change of tenure on divorce or remarriage **1991-93**
Change of tenure on marriage or cohabitation **1998**

Housing history of local authority tenants and owner occupiers who had become owners in the previous five years **1985-86**

Whether ever rented from a local authority, and if so, whether bought that accommodation, source of finance, whether have since moved and distance moved **1991-93**

Owner occupiers:
- in whose name the property is owned **1978-96, 1998, 2000-01**
- whether property is owned outright or being bought with a mortgage or loan **1971-96, 1998, 2000-01**
- how outright owners originally acquired their home **1978-80, 1982-83, 1985-86**
- source of mortgage or loan **1978-80, 1982-86, 1992-93**
- whether currently using present home as security for a (second) mortgage or loan of any kind, and if so, details **1980-82, 1992-93**
- whether owner occupiers with a mortgage have taken out a remortgage on their present home, and if so, details **1985-87, 1992-93**
- whether recent owner occupiers had previously rented this accommodation and, if so, from whom and for how long **1981-82, 1985-86**
- whether had rented present accommodation before deciding to buy **1992-93**

- whether previous accommodation was owned and if so, details of the sale **1992-93**

Renters:
- in whose name the property is rented **1985-96, 1998, 2000-01**
- from whom the accommodation is rented **1971-96, 1998, 2000-01**
- whether landlord lives in the same building **1971-72, 1975-76, 1979-96, 1998, 2000-01**
- whether have considered buying present home and, if not why not **1980-89**
- tenure preference **1985-88**
- whether previously owned/buying accommodation and reasons for leaving **1995-96**

Local authority renters: **1990-91**
- whether expect to move soon, and if so whether expect to rent or buy
- whether expect to buy present home
- landlord preference
- awareness of Tenants' Choice Scheme

Housing costs

Gross value **1971-86**
Net rateable value (Scotland only) **1971-86**
Yearly rate poundage (Scotland only) **1972-86**

Type of mortgage **1972-77, 1979, 1981, 1984-86**
Current mortgage payments **1972-77, 1979, 1981, 1984**
Purchase price of present home, amount of mortgage or loan and date mortgage started **1985-86, 1992-93**
Current rent; Amount of any rent rebate/allowance and/or rate rebate received **1972-77, 1979, 1981**
Whether in receipt of housing benefit **1985-95, 1998, 2000-01**
Whether rent paid by DSS or local authority **1998, 2000-01**

Method of obtaining mortgage tax relief **1984**
Council Tax band for households containing person(s) aged 65 or more **2001**

Central heating and fuel use

Whether have central heating **1971-96, 1998, 2000-01**
Type of fuel used for central heating **1978-92**
Type of fuel mainly used for central heating **1993-96, 1998, 2000-01**
Type of fuel mainly used for room heating in winter **1978-81, 1983, 1985**

Consumer durables

Possession of various consumer durables **1972-76, 1978-96, 1998, 2000-01**
Possession of a telephone **1972-76, 1979-96, 1998, 2000-01**
Possession of a mobile telephone: **1992, 2000-01**
- number available for use
- in whose name each is owned or rented
- whether fitted in a car or van

(these three: **1992**)

Access to the Internet **2000-01**

Deep frying **1986**

Whether does any deep frying, frequency and methods used

HOUSING SATISFACTION

Overall level of satisfaction with present accommodation **1978, 1988, 1990**
Reasons for dissatisfaction; Satisfaction with specified aspects of accommodation; Troublesome features **1978**
Housing preferences **1978, 1987, 1988**
Satisfaction with landlord **1990**

INCOME

Income over 12 months before interview **1971-78**
Gross earnings as employee, from self-employment
Income from state benefits, investments, and other sources
Number of weeks for which income received from each source

Whether currently receiving income from each source **1974-78**

Current income **1979-96, 1998, 2000-01**
Current earnings (gross, take-home, usual) as employee, from self-employment, and from second or occasional jobs
Current income from state benefits, occupational pensions (own or husband's), rents, savings and investments, and any other regular sources

Current income from maintenance, alimony or separation allowance **1981-96, 1998, 2000-01**

Financial help received from former husband towards household bills **1982-83**

INHERITANCE	**1995**
Number, type, value and dates of inheritances received	
Details of property inheritance	

LEISURE	
Holidays away from home in the four weeks before interview:	**1973, 1977, 1980, 1983, 1986**
length of holiday	
countries visited (in UK)	
Leisure activities in the four weeks before interview:	**1973, 1977, 1980, 1983, 1986**
types of activity	
number of days on which engaged in each activity	
whether activity done while away on holiday	
Sports activities in the four weeks and year before interview:	**1987, 1990, 1993, 1996**
- number of days on which engaged in each sport	
- where activities took place	**1996**
- whether member of a sports club	**1996**
Arts and entertainments, museums, galleries, historic buildings:	**1987**
- whether visited in the 4 weeks before interview	
- number of days on which visited	
Social activities and hobbies in the four weeks before interview	**1973, 1977, 1980, 1983, 1986, 1987, 1990, 1993, 1996**

LIBRARIES	**1987**
Whether visited a public library in the 4 weeks before interview:	
- number of visits	
- library services used	

LONG-DISTANCE TRAVEL	**1971-72**
Number of long-distance journeys made in the 14 days before interview	
Starting and finishing points of journeys	
Type of transport used for longest part of journeys	
Main purpose of journeys	
Number of people travelled with	

MIGRATION

Past movement

Length of residence at previous address*	**1971-77**
Previous accommodation:	
- tenure	**1971-73, 1978-80**
- household composition	**1971**
- number of rooms	**1971**
- bath/WC: sole use, shared, none	**1971**
- WC: inside or outside accommodation	**1971**
Reasons for moving from previous address	**1971-77**
Number of moves in last five years*	**1971-77, 1979-96, 1998, 2000-01**

Potential movement

Identification of households containing persons who are currently thinking of moving*	**1971-78, 1980-81, 1983**
Whether will be moving as whole household or splitting up*	**1971-78, 1980-81, 1983**
Reasons for moving	**1971-76,1978, 1980-81**
Proposed future tenure	**1980-81, 1983**
Actions taken to find somewhere to live	**1971-76, 1980-81**
Whether had experienced difficulties	**1980-81**
- in finding somewhere else to live	**1980-81**
- in raising a mortgage/loan or in finding a deposit	**1980-81**

Frustrated potential movement

Identification of households containing persons who, though not currently thinking of moving, had seriously thought of doing so in the two years before interview*	**1974-76, 1980, 1983**
Whether would have moved as whole household or would have split up*	**1974-76, 1980, 1983**
Proposed tenure	**1974-76, 1980**
Reasons for deciding not to move	**1974-76, 1980, 1983**
Whether decision not to move was connected with rise in house prices	**1974-76, 1980**
Whether reasons for thinking about moving were work-related	**1983**
Whether had experienced difficulties in raising a mortgage/loan or in finding a deposit	**1980**

PENSIONS	
Whether covered by employer's pension scheme	**1971-76, 1979, 1982-83, 1985, 1987-96, 1998, 2000-01**
Whether the scheme is contributory, reasons for not belonging to the scheme	**1971-76, 1979, 1982-83, 1985, 1987**

* *Including children*

Item	Years
Whether ever belonged to present employer's pension scheme	**1985, 1987**
Length of time in present employer's pension scheme Whether transferred any previous pension rights to present employer's pension scheme Whether in receipt of a pension from a previous employer, and if so, at what age they first drew it Whether ever belonged to a previous employer's pension scheme	**1983, 1985, 1987**
Length of time in last employer's pension scheme and in last job	**1985**
Whether retained any pension rights from any previous employer	**1971-76, 1979, 1982-83, 1985, 1987**
Whether pays Additional Voluntary Contributions into employer's pension scheme	**1987**
Whether has a stakeholder pension	**2001**
Whether currently belongs to a personal pension scheme and whether employer contributes	**1991-96, 1998, 2000-01**
Whether has ever contributed towards a personal pension	**1987-96, 1998, 2000-01**
Date the personal pension was taken out	**1989-90**
Whether belonged to an employer's pension scheme during the 6 months prior to taking out a personal pension	**1989-90**
Whether makes any other income tax deductible pension contributions	**1993-96, 1998, 2000-01**
- whether free standing additional voluntary contributions	**2000-01**
Whether receiving an occupational pension, and if so, how many Age first drew occupational pension and whether this was earlier or later than the usual age Reasons for drawing the pension early or late, and whether the amount of pension was affected	**1990**

SHARE OWNERSHIP

Item	Years
Whether owns any shares	**1987-88**
Whether shares are owned solely or jointly with spouse	**1987**
Whether shares owned are in employer's company	**1987-88**
Whether has a Personal Equity Plan	**1988, 1992-96, 1998**

SMOKING

Cigarette smoking

Item	Years
Prevalence of cigarette smoking	**1972-76, 1978-2000 (alternate years), 2001**
Current cigarette smokers:	
number of cigarettes smoked per day type of cigarette smoked mainly	**1972-76, 1978-2000 (alternate years), 2001**
usual brand of cigarette smoked	**1984-2000 (alternate years), 2001**
age when started to smoke cigarettes regularly	**1988-2000 (alternate years), 2001**
whether would find it difficult to not smoke for a day whether would like to give up smoking altogether when is the first cigarette of the day smoked	**1992-2000 (alternate years), 2001**
Regular cigarette smokers:	
- age when started smoking cigarettes regularly	**1972-73**
Occasional cigarette smokers: - whether ever smoked cigarettes regularly - age when started to smoke cigarettes regularly - number smoked per day when smoking regularly - how long ago stopped smoking cigarettes regularly	**1972-73**
Current non-smokers:	
whether ever smoked cigarettes regularly	**1972-76, 1978-2000 (alternate years), 2001**
age when started to smoke cigarettes regularly number smoked per day when smoking regularly how long ago stopped smoking cigarettes regularly	**1972-73, 1980-2000 (alternate years), 2001**

Cigar smoking

Item	Years
Prevalence of cigar smoking	**1972-76, 1978-2000 (alternate years), 2001**
Current cigar smokers:	
number of cigars smoked per week	**1988-2000 (alternate years), 2001**
number of cigars smoked per month type of cigar smoked	**1972-73**
age when started to smoke cigars regularly	**1972**

Current non-smokers:
- whether ever smoked cigars regularly — **1972-76, 1978-2000 (alternate years), 2001**
- age when started to smoke cigars regularly / how long ago stopped smoking cigars regularly — **1972**

Pipe smoking

Prevalence of pipe smoking among males — **1972, 1978, 1986-2000 (alternate years), 2001**

Current pipe smokers:
- amount of tobacco smoked per week — **1972-75**
- age when started to smoke a pipe regularly — **1972**

Current non-smokers:
- whether ever smoked a pipe regularly — **1972-76, 1978, 1986-2000 (alternate years), 2001**
- age when started to smoke a pipe regularly / how long ago stopped smoking a pipe regularly — **1972**

SOCIAL CAPITAL

Opinion of local services, amenities, organisations, safety in the area, local problems — **2000-01**

TRAINING

Whether received any job training in the previous 4 weeks, and if so:
- the type of training / hours spent in last 4 weeks — **1987-89**
- whether paid by employer while training / whether compulsory / reasons for doing training — **1987**

VOLUNTARY WORK

Whether did any voluntary work in the 12 months before interview and, if so:
- what kind of work, whether also done in the last 4 weeks, and amount of time spent — **1981, 1987, 1992**
- whether done regularly or from time to time — **1981**
- on how many days — **1987, 1992**
- number of hours spent — **1992**
- whether any organisation was involved — **1981**
- which organisations were involved — **1987, 1992**
- whether the organisation was a trade union or political party — **1987**
- who mainly benefited from the work — **1981**

Appendix H
List of tables

Table number		Most recent equivalent Report table (*=modified)	
3 Households, families and people			
3.1	Household size: 1971 to 2001	2000	**3.1**
3.2	Household type: 1971 to 2001	2000	**3.2**
3.3	Percentage living alone by age: 1973 to 2001	2000	**3.3**
3.4	Percentage living alone by age and sex	2000	**3.4**
3.5	Type of household: 1979 to 2001	2000	**3.5**
3.6	Family type and marital status of lone mothers: 1971 to 2001	2000	**3.6**
3.7	Family type and number of dependent children: 1972 to 2001	2000	**3.7**
3.8	Average (mean) number of dependent children by family type: 1971 to 2001	2000	**3.8**
3.9	Age of youngest dependent child by family type	2000	**3.9**
3.10	Stepfamilies by family type	2000	**3.10**
3.11	Usual gross weekly household income by family type	2000	**3.11**
3.12	Age by sex: 1971 to 2001	2000	**3.12**
3.13	Sex by age	2000	**3.13**
3.14	Socio-economic classification based on own current or last job by age and sex	2000	**3.14***
3.15	Ethnic group	2000	**3.15***
3.16	National identity and age	-	-
3.17	Combined national identities and age	-	-
3.18	National identity and Government Office Region	-	-
3.19	National identity and ethnic origin	-	-
3.20	Combined national identities and ethnic origin	-	-
3.21	Weighted bases for Tables 3.3 and 3.8	2000	**3.21**
4 Housing and consumer durables			
4.1	Tenure: 1971 to 2001	2000	**4.1**
4.2	Type of accommodation: 1971 to 2001	2000	**4.2**
4.3	Type of accommodation occupied by households renting from a council compared with other households: 1981 to 2001	2000	**4.3**
4.4	(a) Type of accommodation by tenure (b) Tenure by type of accommodation	2000	**4.4**
4.5	Age of building by tenure	2000	**4.5**
4.6	(a) Household type by tenure (b) Tenure by household type	2000	**4.6**
4.7	Housing profile by family type: lone parent families compared with other families	2000	**4.7**
4.8	Type of accommodation by household type	2000	**4.8**
4.9	Usual gross weekly income by tenure	2000	**4.9**
4.10	(a) Age of household reference person by tenure (b) Tenure by age of household reference person	2000	**4.10**
4.11	Tenure by sex and marital status of household reference person	2000	**4.11**
4.12	(a) Socio-economic classification and economic activity status of household reference person by tenure (b) Tenure by socio-economic classification and economic activity status of household reference person	2000	**4.13***
4.13	(a) Length of residence of household reference person by tenure (b) Tenure by length of residence of household reference person	2000	**4.14**
4.14	Persons per room: 1971 to 2001	2000	**4.15**
4.15	Persons per room and mean household size by tenure	2000	**4.16**
4.16	Closeness of fit relative to the bedroom standard by tenure	2000	**4.17**
4.17	Cars or vans: 1972 to 2001	2000	**4.18**
4.18	Availability of a car or van by socio-economic classification of household reference person	2000	**4.19***

Table number		Most recent equivalent Report table (*=modified)	
4.19	Consumer durables, central heating and cars: 1972 to 2001	2000	**4.20**
4.20	Consumer durables, central heating and cars by socio-economic classification of household reference person	2000	**4.21***
4.21	Consumer durables, central heating and cars by usual gross weekly household income	2000	**4.22**
4.22	Consumer durables, central heating and cars by household type	2000	**4.23**
4.23	Consumer durables, central heating and cars by family type: lone-parent families compared with other families	2000	**4.24**
5 Marriage and cohabitation			
5.1	Sex by marital status	2000	**5.1**
5.2	(a) Age by sex and marital status (b) Marital status by sex and age	2000	**5.2**
5.3	Percentage currently cohabiting by sex and age	2000	**5.3**
5.4	Percentage currently cohabiting by legal marital status and age	2000	**5.4**
5.5	Cohabiters: age by legal marital status	-	-
5.6	Cohabiters: age by sex	2000	**5.5**
5.7	Legal marital status of women aged 18-49: 1979 to 2001	2000	**5.6**
5.8	Percentage of women aged 18-49 cohabiting by legal marital status: 1979 to 2001	2000	**5.7**
5.9	(a) Whether had dependent children in the household by marital status (b) Marital status by whether had dependent children in the household	-	-
5.10	Women aged 16-59: percentage cohabiting by legal marital status and whether has dependent children in the household	2000	**5.8**
5.11	Cohabiting women aged 16-59: whether has dependent children in the household by legal marital status	-	-
5.12	Number of past cohabitations not ending in marriage by sex and age	2000	**5.9**
5.13	Number of past cohabitations not ending in marriage by current marital status and sex	2000	**5.10**
5.14	Age at first cohabitation which did not end in marriage by year cohabitation began and sex	2000	**5.12**
5.15	Duration of past cohabitations which did not end in marriage by number of past cohabitations and sex	2000	**5.13**
5.16	How people chose to date the end of 'living together', by the date given	2000	**5.14**
6 Occupational and personal pension schemes			
6.1	Current pension scheme membership by age and sex	2000	**6.1**
6.2	Membership of current employer's pension scheme by sex and whether working full time or part time	2000	**6.2***
6.3	Membership of current employer's pension scheme by sex: 1983 to 2001	2000	**6.4**
6.4	Current pension scheme membership by socio-economic classification	2000	**6.5***
6.5	Membership of current employer's pension scheme by sex and socio-economic classification	-	-
6.6	Current pension scheme membership by sex and usual gross weekly earnings: employees	2000	**6.6**
6.7	Current pension scheme membership by sex and length of time with current employer	2000	**6.7**
6.8	Membership of current employer's pension scheme by sex and length of time with current employer	-	-
6.9	Current pension scheme membership by sex and number of employees in the establishment	2000	**6.8**
6.10	Membership of current employer's pension scheme by sex and number of employees in the establishment	-	-

Table number		Most recent equivalent Report table (*=modified)	
6.11	Current pension scheme membership by sex and industry group	2000	**6.9**
6.12	Membership of personal pension scheme by sex and whether working full time or part time: self-employed persons	2000	**6.10**
6.13	Membership of personal pension scheme for self-employed men working full time: 1991 to 2001	-	-
6.14	Membership of personal pension scheme by sex and length of time in self-employment	2000	**6.11**
7 General health and use of health services			
7.1	Trends in self-reported sickness by sex and age, 1972 to 2001: percentage of persons who reported (a) longstanding illness (b) limiting longstanding illness (c) restricted activity in the 14 days before interview	2000	**7.1**
7.2	Self perception of general health during the last 12 months: 1977 to 2001	2000	**7.2**
7.3	Acute sickness: average number of restricted activity days per person per year, by sex and age	2000	**7.3**
7.4	Chronic sickness: prevalence of reported longstanding illness by sex, age and socio-economic classification of household reference person	2000	**7.4***
7.5	Chronic sickness: prevalence of reported limiting longstanding illness by sex, age and socio-economic classification of household reference person	2000	**7.5***
7.6	Acute sickness: (a) Prevalence of reported restricted activity in the 14 days before interview, by sex, age and socio-economic classification of household reference person (b) Average number of restricted activity days per person per year, by sex, age and socio-economic classification of household reference person	2000	**7.6***
7.7	Chronic sickness: prevalence of reported longstanding illness by sex, age and economic activity status	2000	**7.7**
7.8	Chronic sickness: prevalence of reported limiting longstanding illness by sex, age and economic activity status	2000	**7.8**
7.9	Acute sickness (a) Prevalence of reported restricted activity in the 14 days before interview, by sex, age and economic activity status (b) Average number of restricted activity days per person per year, by sex, age and economic activity status	2000	**7.9**
7.10	Self-reported sickness by sex and Government Office Region: percentage of persons who reported (a) longstanding illness (b) limiting longstanding illness (c) restricted activity in the 14 days before interview	2000	**7.10**
7.11	Prevalence of: (a) longstanding illness by sex and NHS Regional Office area (b) limiting longstanding illness by sex and NHS Regional Office area (c) reported restricted activity in the 14 days before interview, by sex and NHS Regional Office area	2000	**7.11**
7.12	Chronic sickness: rate per 1000 reporting longstanding conditions groups by sex	2000	**7.12**
7.13	Chronic sickness: rate per 1000 reporting longstanding conditions groups by age	2000	**7.13**
7.14	Chronic sickness: rate per 1000 reporting longstanding conditions groups by age and sex	2000	**7.14**
7.15	Chronic sickness: rate per 1000 reporting longstanding conditions groups by age and sex	2000	**7.15**

Table number		Most recent equivalent Report table (*=modified)	
7.16	Chronic sickness: rate per 1000 reporting longstanding conditions groups by socio-economic classification of household reference person	2000	**7.16***
7.17	Chronic sickness: rate per 1000 reporting longstanding conditions groups by age, sex and socio-economic classification of household reference person	2000	**7.17***
7.18	Trends in consultations with an NHS GP in the 14 days before interview: 1972 to 2001	2000	**7.18**
7.19	Average number of NHS GP consultations per person per year: 1972 to 2001	2000	**7.19**
7.20	(NHS) GP consultations: trends in site of consultations; 1971 to 2001	2000	**7.20**
7.21	(NHS) GP consultations: consultations with doctors in the 14 days before interview, by sex and age of person consulting, and by site of consultation	2000	**7.21**
7.22	(NHS) GP consultations: percentage of persons consulting a doctor in the 14 days before interview, by sex and by site of consultation, and by age and by site of consultation	2000	**7.22**
7.23	(NHS) GP consultations (a) Percentage of persons who consulted a doctor in the 14 days before interview, by sex, age and socio-economic classification of household reference person (b) Average number of consultations per person per year, by sex, age and socio-economic classification of household reference person	2000	**7.23***
7.24	(NHS) GP consultations (a) Percentage of persons who consulted a doctor in the 14 days before interview, by sex, age and economic activity status (b) Average number of consultations per person per year, by sex, age and economic activity status	2000	**7.24**
7.25	(NHS) GP consultations: percentage of persons consulting a doctor in the 14 days before interview who obtained a prescription from the doctor, by sex, age and socio-economic classification of household reference person	2000	**7.25***
7.26	GP consultations: consultations with doctors in the 14 days before interview by whether consultation was NHS or private	2000	**7.26**
7.27	Trends in reported consultations with a practice nurse by age and sex: 2000 and 2001 (a) percentage consulting a practice nurse in the 14 days before interview (b) average number of consultations with a practice nurse per person per year	2000	**7.27**
7.28	Percentage of children using health services in the 14 days before interview	2000	**7.28**
7.29	Trends in percentages of persons who reported attending an outpatient or casualty department in the 3 months before interview: 1972 to 2001	2000	**7.29**
7.30	Trends in day-patient treatment in the 12 months before interview, 1992 to 2001	2000	**7.30**
7.31	Average number of separate days spent in hospital as a day patient during the 12 months before interview	2000	**7.32**
7.32	Trends in inpatient stays in the 12 months before interview: 1982 to 2001	2000	**7.31**
7.33	Average number of nights spent in hospital as an inpatient during the 12 months before interview	2000	**7.34**
7.34	Inpatient stays and outpatient attendances (a) Average number of inpatient stays per 100 persons in a 12-month reference period, by sex and age (b) Average number of outpatient attendances per 100 persons per year, by sex and age	2000	**7.33**

8 Smoking

8.1	Prevalence of cigarette smoking by sex and age: 1974 to 2001	2000	**8.1**
8.2	Ex-regular cigarette smokers by sex and age: 1974 to 2001	2000	**8.2**
8.3	Percentage who have never smoked cigarettes regularly by sex and age: 1974 to 2001	2000	**8.3**

Table number		Most recent equivalent Report table (*=modified)	
8.4	Cigarette-smoking status by sex and marital status	2000	**8.4**
8.5	Cigarette-smoking status by age and marital status	-	-
8.6	Prevalence of cigarette smoking by sex and country of Great Britain: 1978 to 2001	2000	**8.6***
8.7	Prevalence of cigarette smoking by sex and Government Office Region: 1998 to 2001	-	-
8.8	Cigarette-smoking status by sex and age: England	2000	**8.5**
8.9	Prevalence of cigarette smoking by sex and whether household reference person is in a non-manual or manual socio-economic group: England, 1992 to 2001	2000	**8.10**
8.10	Prevalence of cigarette smoking by sex and socio-economic classification based on the current or last job of the household reference person	2000	**8.9***
8.11	Prevalence of cigarette smoking by sex and socio-economic classification based on own current or last job, whether economically active or inactive, and, for economically inactive persons, age	2000	**8.12***
8.12	Cigarette-smoking status by sex: 1974 to 2001	2000	**8.14**
8.13	Cigarette-smoking status by sex and age	2000	**8.15**
8.14	Average daily cigarette consumption per smoker by sex and age: 1974 to 2001	2000	**8.13***
8.15	Average daily cigarette consumption per smoker by sex and socio-economic classification based on the current or last job of the household reference person	2000	**8.18***
8.16	Type of cigarette smoked by sex: 1974 to 2001	2000	**8.19**
8.17	Type of cigarette smoked by sex and age	2000	**8.20**
8.18	Tar yield per cigarette: 1986 to 2001	2000	**8.21**
8.19	Tar yields by sex and age	2000	**8.22**
8.20	Tar yields by sex and socio-economic classification based on the current or last job of the household reference person	2000	**8.23***
8.21	Prevalence of smoking by sex and type of product smoked: 1974 to 2001	2000	**8.24**
8.22	Prevalence of smoking by sex and age and type of product smoked	2000	**8.25**
8.23	Proportion of smokers who would like to give up smoking altogether, by sex and number of cigarettes smoked per day: 1992 to 2001	2000	**8.29**
8.24	Proportion of smokers who would find it difficult to go without smoking for a day, by sex and number of cigarettes smoked per day: 1992 to 2001	2000	**8.27**
8.25	Proportion of smokers who have their first cigarette within five minutes of waking, by sex and number of cigarettes smoked per day: 1992 to 2001	2000	**8.32**
9 Drinking			
9.1	Whether drank last week and number of drinking days by sex and age	2000	**9.1**
9.2	Drinking last week by sex and age: 1998 to 2001	2000	**9.4**
9.3	Maximum daily amount drunk last week by sex and age	2000	**9.3**
9.4	Drinking last week by sex, age and marital status	-	-
9.5	Whether drank last week by sex and socio-economic classification based on the current or last job of the household reference person	2000	**9.9***
9.6	Percentage who drank on 5 or more days last week, by sex and socio-economic classification based on the current or last job of the household reference person	-	-
9.7	Percentage who drank more than 4 units (men) and 3 units (women) on at least one day last week, by sex and socio-economic classification based on the current or last job of the household reference person	-	-
9.8	Percentage who drank more than 8 units (men) and 6 units (women) on at least one day last week, by sex and socio-economic classification based on the current or last job of the household reference person	2000	**9.10***
9.9	Drinking last week by sex and usual gross weekly household income	-	-
9.10	Drinking last week by sex and economic activity status	-	-
9.11	Drinking last week by sex and usual gross weekly earnings	-	-

Table number		Most recent equivalent Report table (*=modified)	
9.12	Drinking last week by sex and Government Office Region	2000	**9.15***
9.13	Weekly alcohol consumption level: percentage exceeding specified amounts by sex and age: 1988 to 2001	2000	**9.17**
9.14	Average weekly alcohol consumption by sex and age: 1992 to 2001	2000	**9.18**
9.15	Average weekly alcohol consumption by sex and socio-economic classification based on the current or last job of the household reference person	2000	**9.20***
9.16	Average weekly alcohol consumption by sex and usual gross weekly household income	-	-
9.17	Average weekly alcohol consumption by sex and economic activity status	-	-
9.18	Average weekly alcohol consumption by sex and usual gross weekly earnings	-	-
9.19	Average weekly alcohol consumption by sex and Government Office Region	-	-
10 Mobility aids			
10.1	Percentage of persons reporting mobility difficulties, by sex and by age	1996	**9.1**
10.2	Percentage of people with mobility aid(s), by sex and by age	-	-
10.3	Percentage of people with mobility aid(s) by type of mobility difficulties	1996	**9.4**
10.4	Percentage of people with mobility aid(s) by age and whether has mobility difficulties	1996	**9.3**
10.5	Where mobility difficulties were experienced by age	1996	**9.2**
10.6	Percentage of people with mobility aid(s) by where mobility difficulties were experienced	1996	**9.5**
10.7	Percentage of people with the type of equipment they required ('met need')	1996	**9.6**
10.8	Source of mobility aids and percentage in use by source	1996	**9.7**
10.9	Type of mobility aid as a percentage of all mobility aids and percentage in use according to type of aid	1996	**9.8**
10.10	Regularity of use outdoors of mobility aids by type	1996	**9.9**
10.11	Where mobility aids were used by type	1996	**9.10**
10.12	Percentage of people who use wheelchairs by whether they require assistance	-	-

Previous Volumes in the GHS Series

General Household Survey: Introductory report HMSO 1973
Origin and development of the survey - Population - Housing - Employment - Education - Health

General Household Survey 1972 HMSO 1975
Population - Household theft - Housing - Employment - Education - Health - Medicine-taking - Smoking - Sampling error

General Household Survey 1973 HMSO 1976
Population - Housing - Employment - Leisure - Education - Health - Medicine-taking - Smoking

General Household Survey 1974 HMSO 1977
Population - Housing and migration - Employment - Education - Health - Smoking

General Household Survey 1975 HMSO 1978
Population - Housing and migration - Employment - Education - Health - Smoking

General Household Survey 1976 HMSO 1978
Trends 1971 to 1976 - Population - Housing and migration - Employment - Education - Health - Smoking - Sampling error

General Household Survey 1977 HMSO 1979
Population - Housing and migration - Employment - Education - Health - Leisure

General Household Survey 1978 HMSO 1980
Population - Housing and migration - Housing satisfaction - Employment - Education - Health - Smoking, drinking, and health

General Household Survey 1979 HMSO 1981
Population - Housing - Burglaries and thefts from private households - Employment - Education - Health - Family information - Income

General Household Survey 1980 HMSO 1982
Population - Housing and household mobility - Burglaries and thefts from private households - Employment - Education - Health - Smoking - Drinking - Elderly people in private households

General Household Survey 1981 HMSO 1983
Population - Housing - Employment - Education - Health - The prevalence of tinnitus - Voluntary work

General Household Survey 1982 HMSO 1984
Population - Marriage and fertility - Housing - Employment - Education - Health - Smoking - Drinking - Cigarette smoking, drinking and health - Bus travel - Non-government users of the GHS

General Household Survey 1983 HMSO 1985
Population - Marriage and fertility - Contraception, sterilisation and infertility - Housing - Employment - Education - Health - Leisure

General Household Survey 1984 HMSO 1986
Population - Marital history, fertility and sterilisation - Housing - Employment - Education - Health - GP consultations in relation to need for health care - Cigarette smoking: 1972 to 1984 - Drinking

General Household Survey 1985 HMSO 1987
Population - Marital status and cohabitation - Housing - Employment - Education - Health

General Household Survey 1985 HMSO 1988
Supplement A: Informal carers
by Hazel Green

General Household Survey 1986 HMSO 1989
Population - Marriage and fertility - Contraception, sterilisation and infertility - Housing - Burglary - Employment - Education - Health - Smoking - Elderly people in private households 1985 - Leisure

General Household Survey 1986 HMSO 1989
Supplement A: Drinking
by Hazel Green

General Household Survey HMSO 1990
Report on sampling error
Based on 1985 and 1986 data
by Elizabeth Breeze

General Household Survey 1987 HMSO 1989
People, households and families - Housing - Health - Sterilisation and infertility - Entertainments, libraries, forests - Occupational pension scheme coverage - Share ownership - Employment - Education - Family information and fertility

General Household Survey 1987 HMSO 1990
Supplement A: Voluntary work
by Jil Matheson

General Household Survey 1987 HMSO 1991
Supplement B: Participation in sport
by Jil Matheson

General Household Survey 1988 HMSO 1990
by Kate Foster, Amanda Wilmot and Joy Dobbs
People, households and families - Family information and fertility - Health - Smoking - Drinking - Education - Share-ownership - Employment - Occupational and personal pensions - Housing

General Household Survey 1989 HMSO 1991
by Elizabeth Breeze, Gill Trevor and Amanda Wilmot
People, households and families - Employment and pension schemes - Health - Accidents - Marriages and cohabitation - Fertility and contraception - Housing

General Household Survey 1990 HMSO 1992
by Malcolm Smyth and Fiona Browne
People, households and families - Housing - Occupational pension scheme coverage and receipt of occupational pensions - Health - Smoking - Drinking - Sport, physical activities and entertainment

General Household Survey: OPCS 1992
Carers in 1990
OPCS Monitor SS 92/2

General Household Survey 1991 HMSO 1993
by Ann Bridgwood and David Savage
People, households and families - Housing - Burglaries in private households - Employment - Occupational and personal pension scheme coverage - Childcare - Health - Contraception - Education - Family information

General Household Survey 1991 HMSO 1994
Supplement A: People aged 65 and over
by Eileen Goddard and David Savage

General Household Survey 1992 HMSO 1994
by Margaret Thomas, Eileen Goddard, Mary Hickman and Paul Hunter
People, families and households - Health - Smoking - Drinking - Occupational and personal pension scheme coverage - Employment - Education - Family Information - Housing

General Household Survey 1992 HMSO 1994
Supplement A: Voluntary work
by Eileen Goddard

General Household Survey 1993 HMSO 1995
by Kate Foster, Beverley Jackson, Margaret Thomas, Paul Hunter, Nikki Bennett
People, families and households - Housing - Burglaries in private households - Employment - Health - Contraception - Sport and leisure activities - Family Information - Education - Pensions

Living in Britain HMSO 1995
Preliminary results from the 1994 General Household Survey

Living in Britain HMSO 1996
Results from the 1994 General Household Survey
by Nikki Bennett, Lindsey Jarvis, Olwen Rowlands, Nicola Singleton, Lucy Haselden
Households, families and people- Health - Smoking - Drinking - Elderly people in private households - Employment - Pensions - Family information - Education - Housing

1994 General Household Survey: follow-up survey of the health of people aged 65 and over ONS 1998
by Eileen Goddard

Living in Britain The Stationery Office 1996
Preliminary results from the 1995 General Household Survey

Living in Britain The Stationery Office 1997
Results from the 1995 General Household Survey
by Olwen Rowlands, Nicola Singleton, Joanne Maher, Vanessa Higgins
Households, families and people - Housing and consumer durables - Employment - Pensions - Education - Health - Private medical insurance - Dental health - Hearing - Contraception - Family information

General Household Survey 1995 Supplement A: Informal carers The Stationery Office 1998
by Olwen Rowlands

Living in Britain The Stationery Office 1997
Preliminary results from the 1996 General Household Survey

Living in Britain The Stationery Office 1998
Results from the 1996 General Household Survey
by Margaret Thomas, Alison Walker, Amanda Wilmot, Nikki Bennett
Households, families and people - Housing and consumer durables - Burglaries in private households - Employment - Pensions - Education - Health - Mobility and mobility aids - Smoking - Drinking - Marriage and cohabitation - Sports and leisure activities

First release of results from the 1998 General Household Survey ONS 1999

Living in Britain The Stationery Office 2000
Results from the 1998 General Household Survey
by Ann Bridgwood, Robert Lilly, Margaret Thomas, Jo Bacon, Wendy Sykes, Stephen Morris
Households, families and people - Housing and consumer durables - Marriage and cohabitation - Pensions - Health - Smoking - Drinking - Contraception - Day care - Cross-topic analysis

People aged 65 and over - results from the 1998 General Household Survey ONS 2000
by Ann Bridgwood

Living in Britain The Stationery Office 2001
Results from the 2000 General Household Survey
by Alison Walker, Joanne Maher, Melissa Coulthard, Eileen Goddard, Margaret Thomas
Changes over time - Households, families and people - Housing and consumer durables - Marriage and cohabitation - Pensions - Health - Smoking - Drinking

People's perceptions of their neighbourhood and community involvement - results from the social capital module of the General Household Survey 2000 The Stationery Office 2002
by Melissa Coulthard, Alison Walker, Antony Morgan

Carers 2000 The Stationery Office 2002
by Joanne Maher, Hazel Green

Disadvantaged households: results from the 2000 General Household Survey Supplement A ONS 2002
by Wendy Sykes, Alison Walker